Garden Bulbs for the South

Garden
Bulbs
for the
South

Second Edition

Scott Ogden

TIMBER PRESS

Published in 2007 by
Timber Press, Inc.
The Haseltine Building
133 S.W. Second Avenue, Suite 450
Portland, Oregon 97204-3527, U.S.A.
www.timberpress.com
For contact information regarding editorial, marketing, sales, and
distribution in the United Kingdom, see www.timberpress.co.uk.

Printed in China

Library of Congress Cataloging-in-Publication Data

Ogden, Scott.
   Garden bulbs for the South / Scott Ogden. — 2nd ed.
      p. cm.
   Includes bibliographical references and index.
   ISBN 978-0-88192-813-6
 1. Bulbs—Southern States. I. Title.
   SB425.O44 2007
   635.9'40975—dc22

                                        2006013496

A catalog record for this book is also available from the British Library.

Contents

 Preface

THE BULB-GROWING WORLD and my own experiences with bulbs have changed greatly since I wrote the first edition of *Garden Bulbs for the South* in 1993. The Internet has allowed a community of gardeners to readily exchange information and plants. It has also made many unusual bulb varieties available and made it easier for specialty nurseries to market them. The advent of tissue culture in commercial plant propagation now permits new bulbs to be almost instantly produced at modest prices. Nurseries in countries previously closed to plant export, such as China, can regularly distribute bulbs and other novel plants to the United States, sometimes directly to gardeners. New cultivars, species, and even genera appear on nursery lists at a steady pace.

In the last decade I have been privileged to visit gardens in many areas of the South and to help design gardens in Florida, Georgia, and Texas. I've also visited the wilds of Mexico, Argentina, and South Africa to see bulbs flowering in their native habitats. In July 2004 I married Lauren Springer, and I now enjoy gardening with her at our homes in Austin, Texas, and Fort Collins, Colorado. Both gardens brim with all the bulbs that space and climate allow.

In this second edition of *Garden Bulbs for the South* I've updated information on bulb varieties, especially the sections devoted to gingers and aroids, to reflect the many new types now available to Southern gardeners. I have also added a chapter on designing with Southern bulbs to suggest practical ways to make the most of these spectacular plants in gardens. Photographs for the book have been chosen to show the bulbs in beautiful garden settings. For those with a botanical inclination, modern taxonomic treatments of Southern bulbs are given throughout. Botanical names, as always, remain subject to change; taxonomists are presently revising concepts of many bulb genera through the use of molecular DNA.

Acknowledgments

Thanks to Tom Peace, Steve Lowe, Carl Schoenfeld, Tony Avent, Greg Grant, Joe Tocquigny, Russell Adams, Mike McCaffery, Russell Studebaker, and Brent and Becky Heath for cheerfully sharing bulbs and their own excitement about plants. Appreciation also goes to Linda Gay for her efforts to promote interest and share information about gingers, crinums, and rain lilies through Mercer Arboretum, and to Alan Shapiro for furthering interest in Southern bulbs through the annual Perennial Field Day in Gainesville, Florida. Thanks to my wife, Lauren, for her thoughtful advice. Special thanks to Tom Fischer for inviting me to create this new edition for Timber Press.

The flowers come forth like the belles of the day,
have their short reign of beauty and splendor,
and retire like them to the more interesting office
of reproducing their like. The hyacinths and tulips
are off the stage, the Irises are giving place to the
Belladonnas, as they will to the Tuberoses.

THOMAS JEFFERSON, in a letter to
Anne Randolph Bankhead, 26 May 1811

Introduction

BULBS HAVE a bewitching quality that sets them apart from ordinary flowers. They resurrect gardens from drab dormancy and appear suddenly, heralding the season of growth and bloom. Some exude the exotic glamour of orchids; others radiate the freshness of fields and meadows. Through their succulent, crystalline textures they convey the charm and intimacy of woodland, or the brilliant iridescence of mountain heights.

Nearly all bulbs share in the miraculous habit of reawakening to growth and bloom. Many are so precocious they seem to appear overnight, as if by magic. The lively blossoms emerge from hiding to selflessly spend their substance on the air. After a few vigorous weeks of growth the plants disappear below ground to sleep, leaving gardeners to await their return.

Because of their hardy, easy growth, bulbs are among the most democratic flowers. They present their glories within reach of casual gardeners, and can be shared easily over the garden fence. The entire routine of growth, bloom, and dormancy pursued by tuberous plants ensures survival in the most difficult circumstances. With only modest encouragement, these flowers succeed famously. They travel readily, multiply swiftly, and endure in almost any garden.

All this is well known in cold climates, where springs have long been enlivened by bulbs from Holland. These imports are ideal for the gardens of the North, but have limited application in warmer climates. Southern gardeners participate in the tradition of bedding spring bulbs, but only through contrivance. A few dedicated flower lovers purchase fresh bulbs each autumn to deposit in their refrigerators. After a few weeks of chilling, they exhume their prizes and inter them in the cold winter ground, along with a sprinkling of bone meal.

These ministrations are intended to trick the bulbs into thinking they are back in the Netherlands. The technique works surprisingly well, and in March or April the dutiful bulb gardener will usually be rewarded with a handful of lovely, fleeting blossoms. However, this imported glory soon yields to the grim task of yanking out spent plants and sending them on to the compost pile. The same destination awaits the gruesome remains lying in the refrigerators of the forgetful.

This is not to suggest that Southerners should not enjoy growing the hardy bulbs of the trade. These can be showy and successful in warm climates, if properly treated. Modest plantings of tulips or narcissi tucked here and there among other border flowers are certainly worthwhile. Even in the North such bulbs are more often used as seasonal bedding than as honest perennials.

For public gardens this kind of contrived display can be justified, but for the average home dirt dauber there are more rewarding activities. The effort and expense invested in temporary bulb displays might as readily be employed on something new, exotic, or extraordinary—even on flowers that like the South. There really are bulbs that blossom in warm climates without spending the fall in the icebox. Quite a few return on their own and increase in beauty from season to season.

Numerous references describe the needs and wants of the common hardy flowers of the Dutch trade, and there is little reason to repeat such information here. Our concerns are the historic, neglected, and little-known bulbs whose beauties belong rightly and traditionally to the South. Warm-climate bulbs are part of an ancient horticultural legacy, and connect Southern gardens with predecessors dating back to the beginnings of settled life.

Naturalizing

Bulbs that establish themselves as perennials are said to naturalize. Like living plants everywhere, naturalizing bulbs must successfully grow, flower, and multiply (either through seed or through vegetative division). All of these must occur together if the bulbs can truly be said to naturalize.

Some failures take several seasons to reveal themselves. A planting of daffodils may return faithfully, yet remain hatefully barren of bloom. A patch of crocuses might diminish gradually over years, rather than collapse in a sudden catastrophe. As a rule, if flowers don't show clear signs of increase, they are wasting away toward a certain end.

Bulbs and Other Devices

At what must have been a very early moment in the natural development of plants, the storage of food and water became an important convenience. This permitted survival during periods of cold or drought and hastened growth and reproduction when favorable conditions returned. Even such primitive examples of greenery as the cycads (order Cycadales) display swollen stems and leaf bases that serve to store starch and moisture. Gardeners refer to any such devices as bulbs.

The proper botanical names for these reservoirs vary, depending on which components of plant tissue have been enlarged to serve the storage function. True bulbs develop from the swollen bases of leaves, as may be seen at an early stage in the barely developed bulb of a leek. The primitive bulbs of lilies (*Lilium* spp.), wood sorrels (*Oxalis* spp.), and magic flowers (*Achimenes* spp.) retain the separate scales formed from the leaves. These types of bulbs resemble artichokes.

More advanced tunicated bulbs like onions, daffodils, and amaryllises have scales that completely encircle the growing axis. Stems of these plants frequently are reduced to mere disks known as basal plates, from which roots may sprout and offsets may bud.

Quite a few of the flowers that gardeners categorize as bulbs depend on storage organs developed from the bases of stems. These stem tubers are known as corms and are common to members of the iris family such as *Crocus* and *Gladiolus*. While true bulbs may grow and increase in dimension over several years, corms completely replace themselves each season, often forming new tubers atop the shrivelled remains of the old.

Rhizomes are swollen stems that creep along horizontally. Unspecialized, yet effective, storage structures, they belong to some of the most common bulbs: irises, cannas, gingers, aroids, and other favorites possess these easily divided rootstocks.

Tuberous roots are also widespread. A range of plants such as those in the genera *Anemone*, *Ranunculus*, and *Cyclamen* depend on miscellaneous storage organs developed from the roots. Clear-cut distinctions between root tubers and rhizomes often are wanting, so these classes tend to blur.

These storage strategies, all enabling their possessors to compete in cold or semi-arid climates, appear to have evolved many times in the history of growing things. The single genus *Iris* includes within its ranks species with true bulbs, corms, rhizomes, and fleshy roots. The onions (*Allium* spp.) are also varied in their choice of storage mechanisms. The unique rootstocks of tuberoses (*Polianthes* spp.) combine swollen roots, fleshy rhizomes, and true bulbs together.

Many bulbs form a natural group centered around the lilies. The three best-known bulb families, Liliaceae, Iridaceae, and Amaryllidaceae, are all monocots and share a common ancestry. However, many flowers gardeners know as bulbs are only distantly related to these.

What unites all of them from the gardening standpoint is ease of handling. Unlike most of the world's flora, bulbs may rest contentedly in a paper bag on a shelf for as much as three-quarters of the year, or be shipped thousands of miles packed only in dry sacking. As long as they can be replanted in time to complete annual growth and flowering, they seem none the worse for their journeys. This fantastic portability opens wide possibilities for the gardener to acquire rare blooms from distant lands and permits fully mature flowering effects the first season after planting.

Botany

Surprising as it may seem, many bulbs are meagerly known to botanists. Fleshy bulb flowers preserve poorly and leave little to study in herbaria. Few professionals receive an opportunity to learn about these plants in a living condition, so gardeners may often observe characteristics unrecorded by scientists. Several bulbs popular in Southern gardens have never been adequately studied or designated with a Latin name.

Latin names often tell useful information about a plant's character, habit, or history. Many of the botanical names of bulbs allude to classical or mythological figures, while others are charmingly descriptive. The rain lilies, which are the subject of the first chapter, have an especially lovely name, *Zephyranthes*, which translates as "flower of the west wind."

Chapter 1
🌀 Rain Lily Day

As AUGUST FADES the worn-out fields in the Southern countryside come to life with late-season wildflowers. Thistle-leafed eryngo (*Eryngium leavenworthii*) blushes steel-purple, while snow-on-the-prairie (*Euphorbia marginata*) casts a milky bloom over the landscape. The summer sky responds in kind, as the relentless blue of the heavens softens to hazy amethyst. It's still hot as the devil, but gardeners may begin to hope for the cooling rains of fall.

Sometimes it's a short wait, and a hurricane in the Gulf of Mexico or some lesser cloudburst intercedes to make things tolerably moist and pleasant. In most years, though, the meadows parch to tawny brown, and gaping cracks appear in the hardened clay. It's often mid-September before relief arrives.

As the first norther of the season approaches, a great wall of thunderstorms moves in and drenches the earth. The soaking rains initiate a floral miracle peculiar to this region. Northerners search longingly for the first crocus in the melting snow. Here it's rain lilies thrusting from crusted earth which bring special joy.

Plants that have sulked through summer heat veritably jump into growth with the autumn drenchings. The electrical storms bring nitrogen from the atmosphere in the spattering drops of rain. Rain lilies know the difference between this thunderstorm water and the bland effluent from the hose. They have patiently reserved their blooms for the real thing.

These miniatures have sputtered in flower all summer, but nothing like what is to be. Five days after the deluge comes a miracle of the floral year: rain lily day. On this prodigal morning every unspent zephyranthes and habranthus in the garden explodes in blossom.

The rains restore freshness to the air, and the coolness of the passing front lingers. The mushroomlike growth of the little amaryllids slows, and their warm colors deepen. It has been five days since the autumn soaking stirred the bulbs from dormancy. With patient progress the tiny scapes have steadily risen from the ground.

Now starry bouquets of pink, gold, copper, and cream dance along the edges of paths and borders. In meadows and fields beyond, the wild rain lilies are in flower and the air is filled with their musky perfume. You need to shrink down and stroll among the grassy leaves to find the true measure of the brightly colored trumpets and goblets proffered by these little bulbs.

It seems certain that every Southerner who knows them holds the rain lilies dear, yet most meet only a handful of these beauties. Few realize the vastness of the rain lily clan or how many jewels and treasures it holds.

Rain lilies, fairy lilies, zephyr lilies, or atamascos are tiny kin of the tropical amaryllises. Botanists have assigned these bulbs to *Zephyranthes* and to related genera such as *Habranthus*, *Haylockia*, and *Pyrolirion*. Most are native to the American tropics, but a dozen species range into the southern United States. Wherever rain lilies grow, they count on thunderstorms to stir them into bloom.

Old Favorites

The most familiar rain lily in cultivation, *Zephyranthes candida*, is a true autumnal. It just begins to blossom with late summer rains. Instead of the flattened grassy foliage typical of its clan, this species produces tapered, rushlike leaves. This dark green foliage stands through winter frost and offers a foil for the starry white autumn blooms.

Handsome winter-growing foliage and cheerful clusters of white fall blooms make *Zephyranthes candida* popular for edging borders.

In much of the South, *Zephyranthes candida* is a naturalized roadside wildflower. It is common to see the immaculate blossoms fluttering over pools of coffee-colored water. In their native South America these little amaryllids line delta shores along the Rio de La Plata. Spying these white blossoms in the marshes, a romantic Spanish explorer gave the name "river of silver" to the vast estuary, and this later inspired the title Argentina for the silver republic beyond its shores.

In the garden *Zephyranthes candida* is not at all particular. It flowers happily on gumbo clay or flour sand and luxuriates as an aquatic in the bog garden. It's a favorite for borders, where its stiff, upright foliage shows smartly. *Zephyranthes candida* benefits from a little extra water to help carry it through summer and some vigilance to exclude moisture-thieving roots of trees from the plantings. Otherwise, it's absurdly easy and prolific. Every storm from September through November stirs the clumps to flower.

The tiny bulbs of this rain lily suffer from drying, and it's always best to obtain *Zephyranthes candida* in a growing condition. In most parts of the South, nurseries offer this species in pots swollen with bulbs ready to divide. If by some misfortune all you succeed in finding are dried bulbs, be prepared to wait a year for flowers.

After this prolific variety the rain lily most often met in Southern gardens is the lavish pink *Zephyranthes grandiflora*. Succulent, rosy blooms over three inches across rise above its grassy foliage following summer downpours. The six or eight, gracefully expanded petals are complemented by yellow anthers and an opulently long, white stigma.

Mystery surrounds the origin of *Zephyranthes grandiflora*. It's certainly a native of tropical America, but nobody seems sure exactly where. The cultivated strain of this flower is sterile and refuses to seed, yet may be found naturalized in many warm countries, including our Gulf Coast. Generations of affectionate gardeners are to blame. They have spread this species far and wide, for it is among the best-loved subtropical flowers.

If rain lilies ever become popular entries for flower shows, this variety could certainly set standards for judging. In size, proportion, texture, and depth of coloring *Zephyranthes grandiflora* reigns supreme. Only a half-hardy constitution limits its popularity. In the middle and upper South, a good mulch of hay or pine straw will help carry the freeze-tender bulbs through winter.

Like most subtropicals, *Zephyranthes grandiflora* covets rich ground and gives its best when fed generously. This requires continuous effort from Southerners, for organic matter swiftly decays in our warm climate. On very chalky or limy ground, a pocket of acid sand mixed with compost affords a practical home. Gardeners with heavy clay will receive gratifying results from annual dressings of compost or manure.

A third rain lily common to Southern gardens is the startlingly golden

Zephyranthes grandiflora flowering among evergreen sedges (*Carex retroflexa*), author's garden, Austin.

Zephyranthes citrina. It's one of the easiest varieties in the drier gardens of Texas, as it accepts impoverished soils and droughty summers. It's also remarkably hardy considering a native range in the Yucatan; zero-degree weather is no threat.

If the rains are willing, *Zephyranthes citrina* begins flowering in early summer, but its best shows wait for fall. Then the bright golden goblets rise in masses above its narrow, dull green foliage. The collective impact of several hundred of these glowing blossoms on a sunny September day is truly heartwarming.

This rain lily makes a lot of seed, which may be gathered and planted straight away or left to fall and naturalize. As with most amaryllids, the flat black seeds of *Zephyranthes citrina* lose viability when not sown immediately. They grow easily in pots if scattered thickly and barely covered with sandy compost, however. When well fertilized, they can grow to flowering size in eighteen months or less.

The abundant seed of *Zephyranthes citrina* invariably comes true to its golden mother, even if the blossoms have been dusted with pollen from another species. This is due to what botanists call parthenogenesis, an ability among certain plants to clone themselves. This reproductive strategy enables species to aggressively multiply and colonize disturbed habitats. Such common garden weeds as dandelions and familiar trees as mayhaws (*Crataegus* spp.) and citrus have this capacity. Even if bees fail to bring pollen to the blossoms, the seeds mature and grow into genetically identical copies of the mother plants.

Zephyranthes citrina produces its yellow flowers following rains from June through October.

The parents of the old, pale yellow rain lily 'Ajax' seem to have been *Zephyranthes citrina* and *Z. candida*. It's likely that *Z. candida* was the seed parent, or "mother" of this hybrid. *Zephyranthes citrina* must have been the pollen parent of 'Ajax', for parthenogenesis would otherwise have blocked the cross.

For reasons that defy explanation, the bulb trade commonly markets both *Zephyranthes citrina* and *Z. grandiflora* under patently erroneous names. *Zephyranthes citrina* usually reaches shelves as *Z. sulphurea*. This seems simple enough to decipher, since both citron and sulfur indicate yellow. The confusion comes with *Z. grandiflora*, which often arrives as *Z. rosea* or *Z. robusta*.

The true *Zephyranthes rosea* is a

charming, deep rose rain lily from Cuba. Its rounded, often eight-petaled, blooms are only a third the size of *Z. grandiflora*'s. Wide, green foliage and low stature also set it apart. *Zephyranthes rosea* is popular in Florida gardens as an edging plant, where its colorful, chocolate-scented blooms brighten the hurricane season. Unfortunately for gardeners north of the Gulf, the shallow, clustered bulbs of this species have poor resistance to hard frost.

The same tenderness afflicts *Zephyranthes rosea*'s white-flowered cousin, *Z. insularum*. This is another Caribbean species that often appears in Florida gardens. The original plants came from an old home in Key West, hence their specific epithet, which means "of the island." *Zephyranthes insularum* makes a thrifty clump for foregrounds of tropical borders. It thrives on almost any soil, including barren chalk. Where frosts visit regularly, these tender bulbs may be kept in pots plunged in the ground for summer. Dazzling white blossoms appear above their dark, strappy foliage from August through October.

Often what is called *Zephyranthes robusta* in the nursery trade is actually *Habranthus robustus*, a lavender-pink amaryllid from Argentina. This species matches *Z. grandiflora* in size and stature, but its blooms nod and face outward from the stems like a little amaryllis. It's this character which leads botanists to place this rain lily in the genus *Habranthus*.

Zephyranthes 'Ajax' flowering among sedges in Austin.

Zephyranthes rosea flowering near a silvery clump of little bluestem (*Schizachyrium scoparium*).

Massed blooms of *Habranthus robustus* create lavish displays following summer showers.

The wild Easter lily of the South, *Zephyranthes atamasca*.

Established clumps of *Habranthus robustus* make fine shows in gardens of the lower South. At regular intervals through summer, the gray-toned foliage disappears behind masses of lilac blossom. Although comparable in hardiness to *Zephyranthes grandiflora*, the fast-multiplying bulbs of this habranthus grow shallowly and need winter protection, except in the lower South.

Atamascos

The common rain lilies of Southeastern wilds are atamasco lilies (*Zephyranthes atamasca*). Their curious traditional name (which means "stained with red") comes from the indigenous peoples who formerly lived near Jamestown, Virginia; Cherokees, another tribe, called them *culowhee*. To many Southerners these showy spring blooms are familiar as "wild Easter lilies." Atamascos inhabit swampy forests and coastal prairies from Florida west to Alabama, and northward to Virginia and Pennsylvania.

For woodland gardens, atamasco lilies afford ideal early-season accents. In the South their white funnels appear in March or April. The trumpet-shaped blooms emit a sweet fragrance and make pleasant companions for the azaleas and Louisiana phlox blooming at the same season.

The broad, grassy foliage of atamasco lilies comes up in early winter. The bulbs prosper under deciduous trees, whose bare branches allow sun to reach the ground. The rich leaf mold and acid soils found under hardwoods favor these flowers, and damp or boggy conditions are accepted eagerly.

Where soils are alkaline or drought-prone, atamascos may be grown in pots. On a sheltered patio or a cool greenhouse, they often sputter in flower through the entire winter. In the summer the bulbs go dormant, but should not be allowed to dry out entirely.

In addition to the typical broad-leafed atamascos, there are two specialized variants native to Florida that some botanists accord species status, as *Zephyranthes treatiae* and *Z. simpsonii*. Both have narrow foliage and favor sandy pine flatwoods or roadside meadows, rather than the swampy woodlands enjoyed by *Z. atamasca*. Typical *Z. treatiae* blossoms are smaller than those of *Z. atamasca*, with slender petals that recurve like little tiger lilies. *Zephyranthes simpsonii* produces funnel-shaped blooms flushed pink on the exterior, and populations seem to occur in the sandy soils of coastal North Carolina as well as in Florida. All three types grow readily in gardens and may often be found around old homesteads in the South.

Arnold Puetz, a Jacksonville, Florida, nurseryman, advertised them this way:

A New Lily of Great Promise.

The Easter Lily of The South.

Zepheranthus Treatae.

One of the most charming spring and summer flowering bulbs, whose slender stems bear a large, pure white sweet, lily shaped flower.

To introduce these Fairy Lilies everywhere, and to give every lover of flowers a chance to try them with very little outlay, I will forward during the year 1881 by mail postpaid one dozen for 25 cents or five dozen for $1. After January 1st, 1882, 5 cents each or 50 cents per dozen will be charged. It is worth double the money.

Zephyr Gardens

Many years ago I received a copy of a catalog belonging to an enterprise run under the delightful name of Zephyr Gardens. By the time I got the list the proprietor, Thaddeus Monroe Howard, D.V.M., had long retired from the bulb business. Yet the plants described were so extraordinary and full of promise that gardeners had continued to pass along his catalog years afterwards. When I came to live in San Antonio, I introduced myself to Dr. Howard, and we began a long discussion concerning the bulbs he had collected and the hybrids he had created. Over several seasons he related his work with bulbs of many kinds. What follows is a tale about rain lilies and the marvelous discoveries of Dr. Howard and others.

When Thad Howard began collecting rain lilies in San Antonio during the early 1950s, the *Zephyranthes* world was still rather small. His garden included the "old" species just described and several of the wild rain lilies of South Texas. The only hybridizing that had been done with the group had taken place in far-away India.

Early in the century Sydney Percy Lancaster, secretary of the Agricultural and Horticultural Society of India, crossed several rain lilies into a strain known as ×*Cooperanthes*. These were hybrids of *Zephyranthes grandiflora*, *Z. citrina*, and a species obtained from a German plant collector in Austin, Texas. In deference to this source, a Mr. Peter Henry Oberwetter, Lancaster referred to these bulbs in his notes as "*Cooperia Oberwetterii.*"

Oberwetter's activities will be discussed further in the next chapter. For now, what merits attention is the essential direction of Lancaster's hybridizing. He had united the colorful tropical species of *Zephyranthes* with a fragrant, hardy rain lily from central Texas. The resulting offspring grew robustly and displayed a range of warm pastel colors.

Howard tried importing Lancaster's crosses from India to Texas. The bulbs were shipped but never arrived, and Howard resolved to make his own hybrids from scratch. Along with breeding, dedicated collecting in Texas and Mexico soon expanded his rain lily garden to undreamed-of proportions.

Cooperia

A number of the bulbs Howard listed in his catalog fall into a group long known as *Cooperia*. These are essentially night-blooming zephyranthes with white, ivory, or sulfur-colored blooms and sweet, primrose fragrances. Their long-tubed blossoms attract visits from night-flying moths, who pollinate them with equally long tongues. Flowering from early summer to fall, the most widespread of these is *Zephyranthes chlorosolen* (*Cooperia drummondii*). This hardy flower ranges through Texas and into adjacent Louisiana, Oklahoma, Mexico, and New Mexico, with outposts scattered from Brazil to Kansas.

Through most of this territory, *Zephyranthes chlorosolen* presents a homely aspect. Typical strains bear small-cupped blossoms rising above bunches of wiry, olive-drab leaves. The occasional fine specimen offers wider blooms that open to flat stars. The best shimmer with a satiny sparkle. In cool weather the blooms assume a pink tinge.

Even modest strains of this zephyranthes have the capacity to transform barren fields and vacant lots into floral wonderlands. It's impressive to see the multitudes of tiny blossoms magically emerge from hiding. They rise over the dormant summer grass, expand their waxy petals as the sun sets, and fill the night air with heady fragrance.

In gardens *Zephyranthes chlorosolen* thrives in varied situations, from flower borders and rockeries to rough turf. The thick-textured blooms show well among overplantings of sweet alyssum (*Lobularia maritima*) or moss rose (*Portulaca grandiflora*), and groundhugging evergreens such as stonecrop (*Sedum* spp.) or caric sedge (*Carex* spp.) make good drought-tolerant companions. The robust bulbs propagate readily from capsules of flat, black seed and self-sow where offered mulches of grit or pea gravel. They soon offset into large clumps.

Very similar to *Zephyranthes chlorosolen*, but with elegant, floppy-petaled blooms, is *Z. traubii*. *Zephyranthes traubii* luxuriates in the moist ground of coastal prairies between Houston and Victoria, Texas, where it flowers in bar ditches and roadside swales each autumn. Tiny, clustering bulbs and narrow foliage give this species a delicate character.

Farther south, in eastern Mexico, *Zephyranthes traubii* shows up again in a summer-blooming race that favors savannahs or rough woodland. These Mexican traubiis (if that's what they are) are easier growing and more drought-tolerant than their Texas cousins but lack some of their size and grace.

Zephyranthes chlorosolen flowering in October along a roadside in central Texas. Photo by Lauren S. Ogden.

The blunt-tipped stigma of *Zephyranthes traubii* projects slightly above the long tubes of the flowers.

Within the city limits of Brownsville, Texas, and up the coast near Corpus Christi, grow two curious rain lilies with pale sulfur blooms. The first is *Zephyranthes smallii*, an apparently natural hybrid of *Z. chlorosolen* and the bright yellow, day-blooming *Z. pulchella*. It looks like a lemony version of *Z. chlorosolen* and seems even more amenable to cultivation. Its charmingly fragrant flowers appear continuously through summer and fall, opening in early afternoon.

It is fortunate that *Zephyranthes smallii* makes such a congenial garden plant, for it seems destined to oblivion in the wild. Nearly all the natural habitat of these small flowers has disappeared in suburban development. The bulbs persist mainly in yards, vacant fields, and baseball diamonds in the city of Brownsville, Texas. Gardeners can do this plant a favor by sharing bulbs and seed and maintaining it in cultivation.

The other yellow cooperia is *Zephyranthes jonesii*. It has round, solitary bulbs and straw-colored flowers, tinged russet in bud. *Zephyranthes jonesii* also seems to be of hybrid origin but is less prolific in gardens than its Brownsville cousin. It flowers from September to November, in company with *Z. traubii*, *Z. chlorosolen*, and three yellow, day-flowering rain lilies. One of these, perhaps the coppery *Habranthus tubispathus*, is the probable parent of *Z. jonesii*, along with one of the night-flowering species.

Drummond's Legacy

The common white cooperia (*Zephyranthes chlorosolen*) makes a useful garden plant, but it has never attracted the following of a similar rain lily that grows alongside it in central Texas. This other cooperia casually resembles *Z. chlorosolen*, but it is really very distinctive. One nineteenth-century botanist actually proposed a separate genus, *Sceptranthes*, for this unique amaryllid, which is now known botanically as *Zephyranthes drummondii* (or sometimes as *Cooperia pedunculata*) and horticulturally as the giant prairie lily.

Before this discussion goes further and readers tire of tripping past names like *Cooperia* and *Sceptranthes*, it's appropriate to review the origin of a bit of taxonomic chaos. *Zephyranthes drummondii* and *Z. chlorosolen* first found their way to scientific attention through the efforts of Scottish plant collector Thomas Drummond. Drummond collected widely in Louisiana and south-central Texas during the early nineteenth century, and the botanical names of many Southern wildflowers commemorate his work. Unfortunately for students of rain lilies, both these night-blooming zephyranthes have been honored with Mr. Drummond's name, one as *Cooperia drummondii*, the other as *Zephyranthes drummondii*.

If botanists decide to class these flowers together as *Cooperia*, then *Z. drummondii* becomes *Cooperia pedunculata*. If both are regarded as *Zephyranthes* (the route chosen here), then *Cooperia drummondii* becomes *Zephyranthes chlorosolen*. Either interpretation generates a measure of confusion, for *Cooperia drummondii* (*Zephyranthes chlorosolen*) and *Zephyranthes drummondii* are distinct plants.

Giant Prairie Lilies

One may only hope these entanglements will not dissuade gardeners from enjoying these fine flowers. *Zephyranthes drummondii* produces its good-sized, milky blooms as early as March and then on through midsummer. If rains are sparse, flowering continues into the fall. The broad, grayish leaves remain active

Giant prairie lily (*Zephyranthes drummondii*) produces its long-tubed flowers atop short pedicels largely hidden by the clasping, pinkish spathe valves. Photo by Lauren S. Ogden.

and lush most of the year, but may die away briefly in late summer. The globular, brownish black bulbs approach the size of tennis balls when grown in rich soil.

With lush, swirling, sage-green foliage to set off its sweet-scented blooms, the giant prairie lily makes a good border citizen, ideal for edging a bed, filling a planter, or nestling among rocks on a slope. It accepts most types of soil and any watering regime from drought to deluge. The bulbs are hardy throughout the South. Few summer blossoms offer a more pleasing fragrance than these waxy, white blooms.

Giant prairie lilies differ from other cooperias in several curious ways. They prefer an earlier blooming season and generally seek higher ground than the other night-blooming rain lilies. Small stems (pedicels) appear beneath the ovaries at the base of the blooms. The three longest of the six stamens may just be seen protruding from the mouth of the floral tube. The other three stamens and the very short stigma are completely hidden from view. This arrangement gives the flowers a ghostly appearance reminiscent of moonflowers.

In most of its range, *Zephyranthes drummondii* produces blooms with blunt, rounded petals. These look like coarse white crocuses and are common from central Texas west into eastern New Mexico. Some large south Texas strains of the species have more star-shaped flowers with pointed petals, which may spread

Zephyranthes drummondii carpets prairies in central Texas following late spring and early summer rains. Photo by Lauren S. Ogden.

over three inches across. They make an impressive sight dotting rugged hillsides among craggy mesquites and silvery bushes of Texas sage (*Leucophyllum frutescens*).

In northern Mexico *Zephyranthes drummondii* inhabits rough and little-known deserts and brushlands. Thad Howard visited these regions in the summer of 1964 and discovered a curious new rain lily blooming near the town of Iturbide, Nuevo Leon. The coarse, pale pink flowers of this zephyranthes opened in midafternoon and seemed intermediate between the night-flowering *Z. drummondii* and a pink, day-blooming rain lily native to adjacent mountains. Howard named the unusual find *Z. morrisclintii* (for fellow plant collector Morris Clint) and noted its relationship to the giant prairie lily.

Zephyranthes morrisclintii usually has frosty pink blossoms, but occasional white forms may also be found in the rugged sierras of northern Mexico. With a little effort, these may be distinguished from true *Z. drummondii* by their more upright, dull blue foliage and funnel-shaped blooms. Both the white and pink strains of *Z. morrisclintii* make hardy, successful bulbs for Southern gardens.

The Laredo Yellow

Nature is remarkably complex at times, and sleuthing among old gardens occasionally turns up a puzzle that takes years to unravel. In April of 1949, Texas plantsman Fred Jones happened upon an odd rain lily growing in a garden in Laredo. The plants had large, turnip-shaped, black-skinned bulbs, strappy gray leaves like *Zephyranthes drummondii*, and funnel-shaped greenish yellow blooms.

Jones wondered if these Laredo plants might be hybrids between *Zephyranthes drummondii* and the golden *Z. pulchella*, which grew in marshes nearby. He set about crossing these two species to test his hypothesis—no mean task, since the long-tubed blooms of *Z. drummondii* had to be sliced open and de-anthered to prevent self-fertilization. After several seasons a few seedlings flowered. Most were maternal (parthenogenic) and resembled one or the other parent, but two were a beautiful primrose. Jones' hybrids were lovely and showed that *Z. drummondii* and *Z. pulchella* could cross. Nevertheless, they weren't quite the same as the curious Laredo plants.

Several years passed before Thad Howard encountered what appeared to be 'Laredo Yellow' growing in the wild, brush-covered mountains of northern Mexico. This region is home for many unusual flowers, among them a yellow-flowered species of *Habranthus*. These grow along with *Zephyranthes drummondii* near Cuesta de Mamulique, a rugged ridge.

Howard sent specimens of the yellow rain lilies to Dr. Hamilton Traub, who named the new species *Zephyranthes howardii* in Howard's honor. Botanists have since transferred this species to *Habranthus*, so its proper name is now *H. howardii*. This rain lily is similar to the cultivated plant from Laredo but makes smaller, solitary bulbs and flowers less freely. The blooms also differ on technical points such as tube length and anther placement.

After years of puzzling over these curious plants Howard realized that 'Laredo Yellow' had probably originated as a natural hybrid between *Zephyranthes drummondii* and the yellow *Habranthus howardii*. Someone must have brought it down from the mountains years ago. Since then, its large, black-skinned bulbs have passed into many gardens. Through the 1960s Howard distributed these bulbs as Fred Jones' 'Laredo Yellow'. In 1990 he described them botanically as ×*Coobranthus coryi*.

This chartreuse hybrid of the giant prairie lily thrives in both arid and humid regions of the South, multipling steadily with offsets and seed. Although the strangely colored blossoms are more curious than beautiful, 'Laredo Yellow' adds intriguing variation to the nocturnal cooperia group. It's also considerably easier to grow in gardens than the yellow habranthus presumed to be its parent. Rain lily enthusiast Alex Korsakoff of Florida successfully crossed 'Laredo Yellow' with *Zephyranthes grandiflora* to create the lovely hybrid 'Hjalmar Sandre'.

Golden blooms of *Zephyranthes pulchella*.

True Yellow

The richest gold among rain lilies belongs to a relative of *Zephyranthes citrina* from the western Gulf Coast. This species, aptly named *Z. pulchella* ("pretty" in Latin), is a fall bloomer with slender leaves and long-necked, black-coated bulbs. The golden blossoms, further gilded by fat anthers dusted in orange pollen, glow like jewels set among the green grass.

Zephyranthes pulchella grows in scattered groups over the coastal prairies and fills swales and bar ditches with sprightly colonies. After fall rains, blooms appear over standing water under the guard of swarming black mosquitoes. The brilliant flowers and bright green, rushlike leaves illuminate grasslands in Texas and eastern Mexico from August till November. Although commonly small and crocuslike in appearance, good forms of *Z. pulchella* have nice-sized blooms with well-formed, wide-spreading, waxy petals.

Zephyranthes refugiensis is a unique localized relation of *Z. pulchella* with greenish gold blooms and a neat, clumping habit. This species grows in a small area where the ranges of *Z. pulchella* and *Z. jonesii* overlap. Theorists have suggested that the lemon-tinted *Z. refugiensis* originated as a hybrid between these species.

Zephyranthes pulchella and *Z. refugiensis* both need damp conditions to flower successfully in gardens, but otherwise are easily accommodated. Their half-hardy foliage grows through the winter months and dries off in early summer. They enjoy rich, heavy soils but get along on sandy ground if well watered.

A Rain Lily Safari

A favorite autumn adventure is a rain lily safari to the soggy Texas coastal prairies where these yellow varieties abound. If you visit about five days after a drenching shower, you may see six or seven different rain lily species at once. This makes quite an exotic bouquet.

Proceeding east from the old presidio at Goliad, the land flattens out in a

Author examining a native colony of *Zephyranthes pulchella* near Sutherland Springs, Texas. Photo by Lauren S. Ogden.

broad plain dotted with stunted live oaks. Along the roadsides the common white cooperias (*Zephyranthes chlorosolen*) show among the tall grasses. Soon these are joined by large-flowered *Z. traubii* and sulfury *Z. jonesii*. An occasional giant prairie lily or Texas copper lily (*Habranthus tubispathus* var. *texensis*) may join these. By the time the road reaches the town of Refugio *Z. pulchella* and *Z. refugiensis* dot the fields with their golden chalices.

Mexican Yellows

In eastern Mexico Howard discovered a number of colorful rain lilies with good drought tolerance and everblooming habits. One of the best is the queen's rain lily, *Zephyranthes reginae*. Howard found this light apricot species on one of his early collecting expeditions near Valles, San Luis Potosí, and he distributed it for many years as 'Valles Yellow'.

Like *Zephyranthes citrina*, this species happily self-sows and multiplies into thrifty patches. A handful of seed is all that's necessary to start a thriving population. It's one of the most rewarding rain lilies for Southern gardens and flowers steadily from early summer till frost. *Zephyranthes reginae* seems quite hardy to cold.

Near the town of El Naranjo, S.L.P., grow two more yellowish zephyranthes, one with bright lemony blooms and another with pale, ivory-colored petals. These occur together on prairies thick with black clay. The yellow-green species is *Zephyranthes nymphaea*, a Mexican ally of *Z. pulchella*. Its long-necked bulbs root deeply in the muddy soil. Slender leaves and stems raise cup-shaped flowers above the meadows. Its cream-colored companion, *Z. subflava*, expands starry, two-inch blossoms. Both species succeed in the lower South, but need protective mulching where winter temperatures drop below 20°F.

In 1996 Howard described two additional peach-colored rain lilies from this region of eastern Mexico, *Zephyranthes dichromantha* and *Z. moctezumae*. The first is a copper-flushed ally of *Z. nymphaea*. The second seems similar to a plant introduced by Yucca Do Nursery as 'Tenexico Apricot'. This is a charming rain lily with blooms opening rich peach, fading to light pink on their second day. The vigorous plants multiply readily, blooming sporadically through much of the summer.

In the provincial town of Tamazunchale ("Thomas and Charlie") on the old Pan-American Highway, some of the windowboxes overlooking the main street house an elegant long-tubed rain lily with wide, channeled, dark green foliage. This is *Zephyranthes primulina*, a beautiful species whose light primrose blooms carry a pronounced pink tinge on the backs of the petals. As it comes from a subtropical section of Mexico, *Z. primulina* appreciates protection from hard freezes, but otherwise makes an easy, floriferous garden plant.

Mayitos

In the same region where *Zephyranthes primulina* grows are rain lilies with large, pink blossoms and lush green, keeled foliage. These beauties rival *Z. grandiflora* in size, and they surpass it in precision and symmetry of design. J. G. Baker christened this species *Z. macrosiphon* in reference to the long tubes of the flowers.

In the wild these showy blooms are most often a rich rose, but light pink forms also occur. Whites have never been reported, yet other Mexican rain lilies have pale forms. There is probably a pristine white *Zephyranthes macrosiphon* awaiting discovery on some remote mountainside. *Zephyranthes primulina* may be thought of as a yellow phase of this species.

Zephyranthes macrosiphon responds to good culture and enjoys rich soil. It declines rapidly, however, when subjected to drought, extreme heat, or serious cold. Although less reliable in gardens than *Z. grandiflora*, *Z. macrosiphon* grows quickly and easily from seed. It makes a fine subject for a pot on a terrace or windowsill. Its tidy clumps of foliage bear a succession of rose blooms through the growing season.

In mountains to the north, in the state of Tamaulipas, Carl Schoenfeld of Yucca Do Nursery and John Fairey have done a great deal of plant exploring; here they discovered a similar rain lily with slender, spoon-shaped, light pink petals. This cloud forest species has been introduced by Yucca Do as *Zephyranthes* sp. 'El Cielo' and seems to grow well in the South if offered a shaded position. Its handsome blooms appear in April, several weeks earlier than those of the June-flowering *Z. macrosiphon*.

Other pink rain lilies in Mexico come mostly from regions seasonally beset with drought. The most common ones tolerate a range of growing conditions and adapt to gardens where frost does not penetrate the soil deeply. In

Zephyranthes macrosiphon flowering along the Pan-American Highway south of Tamazunchale.

colder regions they may be potted or dug and stored over winter like gladioli. They bloom promptly when replanted in early summer.

Botanists assign most of the variable zephyranthes of central and western Mexico among three roughly defined species. In the valley of Mexico and nearby central plateau, the common pink-to-white variety is *Zephyranthes verecunda*. It's a modest little flower, on average about six inches or less in height; occasional individuals may reach twice this size. Some of the most beautiful are white with delicate streaks and pencilings of pink.

An ally of *Zephyranthes verecunda* from near Morelia, Guanajuato, has been tongue-twistingly described as *Z. latissimafolia* ("very wide-leafed"), for this species has broad, green foliage that spreads across the ground. Katherine Clint, its discoverer, nicknamed this little bulb the lady-in-green. This seems appropriate when the blushing blooms nestle among the leaves in early summer.

Florida bromeliad collector Mulford Foster discovered *Zephyranthes fosteri* on a trip through the old Mexican territory of Nuevo Galicia, or Tepic. This rain lily grows near Guadalajara and through much of west-central Mexico. Although the original plants Foster collected were a deep rose, shades from pink to blush-white may be found as well. *Zephyranthes fosteri* is a short rain lily with spoon-shaped petals and tufts of narrow, grassy leaves. Its colonies look like emerging crocuses as they flower among brown grass in late June.

On the plateau near the city of San Luis Potosí and through much of the eastern Sierra Madre, the local rain lilies are known as *mayitos* ("May flowers")

Zephyranthes fosteri flowering among volcanic boulders, July, near Lake Chapala.

for their early summer blooms. One of the most common is *Zephyranthes lindleyana*. It has a short pedicel like *Z. drummondii* and comes in a variety of sizes and colors from pink to white. Dark rose selections have been called *Z. clintiae* by some authors.

Carl Schoenfeld collected a beautiful and floriferous white rain lily near Ciudad Maize and introduced it as 'Cookie Cutter Moon'. This seems to be a special form of *Zephyranthes lindleyana* or perhaps a hybrid of it with *Z. traubii*, which grows in the same area.

In the neighboring state of Tamaulipas, John Fairey and Carl Schoenfeld discovered another interesting rain lily. This undescribed species occurs in both pink and white editions and has a long blooming season beginning in midsummer and extending till frost. Topped with glossy, green leaves like those of *Liriope*, its small, brown-skinned bulbs rapidly multiply into thick clumps in the garden. In the wild they are often seen clinging to crevices of volcanic rocks along with clusters of succulent hen-and-chicks (*Echeveria runyonii*). The discoverers of this lovely plant have nicknamed their find *Zephyranthes* sp. 'Labuffarosa', the pink rain lily of La Buffa.

In their native Sierra Chiquita these rain lilies make a stunning show in varied shades from white and blush to pink and rose, blooming anytime rains

Zephyranthes lindleyana with lipferns (*Cheilanthes* spp.) among limestone boulders, Valle de los Fantasmas, San Luis Potosí, Mexico.

Zephyranthes sp. 'Labuffarosa' flowering in late summer after its foliage has gone dormant.

A richly colored *Zephyranthes* sp. 'Labuf-farosa' clone selected by Carl Schoenfeld, growing at Yucca Do Nursery in Hempstead, Texas.

strike from July to November. Especially fine flowers, such as those of 'Lily Pies', another Yucca Do introduction, display snowy blossoms marked with cerise flashes on the petal tips. Another Yucca Do introduction, 'Itsy Bitsy', offers spidery white blossoms. Selections of 'Labuffarosa' made by Tony Avent, 'Big Dude' and 'Pink Panther', provide oversized white flowers and rounded, rose-pink blooms, respectively.

These Mexican wildflowers seem to be intermediate between night- and day-flowering sections of *Zephyranthes*. They may be natural hybrids between *Z. traubii* and a dark-rose-flowered species similar to *Z. lindleyana* that occurs in the mountains with them. Whatever their origin, they offer fine material for gardens and seem entirely hardy in the South, with excellent foliage through the winter months and good tolerance for shade. Their large, colorful blooms and robust growth are sure to win many followers.

Near Monterrey another species close to *Zephyranthes lindleyana* appears in a robust strain approaching *Z. drummondii* in the size of its bulb and width of its foliage. These light pink rain lilies bloom early in the year, often around the first of March, and then sporadically into May and June. Thad Howard distributed this hardy bulb for many years as 'Horsetail Falls' and later described it as a new species, *Z. huastecana*.

This rain lily makes an excellent garden plant for the South and seems hardy to cold. It develops large, solitary bulbs crowned with wide, pale green leaves and good-sized, light pink blooms. In the South it flowers along with atamasco lilies and thrives in sun or part shade. *Zephyranthes huastecana* grows readily from seed and makes a valuable early show when planted in groups.

Desert Denizens

A desert seems like an odd place to find something as delicately beautiful and fragile as a rain lily blossom, but the arid parts of Mexico are endowed with a variety of *Zephyranthes*. Beyond truly dry regions such as the Southwest of the

United States, these species are unlikely prospects for garden cultivation except in raised rockeries.

Within the booming industrial city of Saltillo, Coahuila, one may find occasional clumps of rain lilies with distinctive, goblet-shaped blossoms. These are white with a pink flush and appear in clumps scattered through desert scrub. Their name, *Zephyranthes crociflora*, is suggested by their crocuslike form.

On first discovery *Zephyranthes crociflora* looks much like another desert species, *Z. erubescens*, which grows farther south in the states of San Luis Potosí and Queretaro. Despite the superficial resemblances, a quick look down into the center of its blossoms reveals distinct arrangements of anthers and stigma. *Zephyranthes erubescens* usually grows as a solitary bulb or with only a few offsets, in contrast to the clumps typical for *Z. crociflora*. In addition to a pink-on-white color scheme, *Z. erubescens* also appears in a lovely deep rose. The desert-dwelling introduction 'Palmillas' appears to be a typical *Z. erubescens* form.

After rain showers in early summer, the barren creosote flats in southern Nuevo Leon brighten with tufts of a tiny, pink rain lily. The blossoms seem to sparkle like ice crystals in the high desert air, for they have enlarged water storage cells in their succulent petals. This gives them special radiance, so that they resemble orchids or Guernsey lilies (*Nerine* spp.). Their name, *Zephyranthes chichimeca*, recalls the Chichimec people who once roamed the dry central plateau of northern Mexico.

The tiniest and most charming of these desert species is *Zephyranthes bella*, a tiny, refined ally of *Z. fosteri*. This elfin amaryllid grows in barren country southwest of the city of San Luis Potosí, dotting the earth with blooms hardly larger than a quarter. Its colonies look like fields of pale, pink-etched crocuses.

Throughout the deserts of northern Mexico, and through most of Arizona, New Mexico, and west Texas, summer visitors may encounter tiny greenish gold rain lilies with wispy blue-green foliage. These have been aptly named *Zephyranthes longifolia* for their long, narrow leaves. The small, cup-shaped blossoms appear within days following the erratic summer rains and offer a welcome bonus to bleak desert gardens. Unlike other dryland species, *Z. longifolia* is rather hardy to cold.

Mañanitas

Following late spring rains that awaken the *mayitos*, heavy June thunderstorms arrive to bring forth the *mañanitas* ("tomorrow flowers"). These larger rain lilies belong to *Habranthus* and have the graceful, inclined blossoms that give this genus its character.

Habranthus concolor, the best-known *mañanita,* is found in cactus-filled deserts surrounding the city of San Luis Potosí. Its large blossoms are accompanied by broad, gray foliage. As with the slightly smaller *H. howardii* from brushlands south of Laredo, flowers of *H. concolor* come in a peculiar shade of desert green, a chartreuse-yellow common to a number of flowers native to arid regions.

Habranthus concolor is certainly worthy of cultivation for its showy blossoms. To assure proper flowering, the bulbs should be given a dry winter rest. This may be accomplished by annual lifting and storing or by planting in raised beds of gritty soil. The large, black-coated bulbs should be protected from penetrating frost and not allowed to remain overly damp during cool weather.

On a trip through Guanajuato in July 1954, Morris and Katherine Clint found rain lilies in leaf which they presumed to be robust specimens of *Habranthus concolor.* They took the big bulbs home and grew them on in their Brownsville, Texas, garden. The next spring they received a delightful surprise when their plantings produced several huge, snow-white blossoms with rich yellow throats. They had discovered a new species, *H. immaculatus.*

Habranthus immaculatus is a good grower in gardens and soon offsets to form large clumps. When the Clints discovered it, they were especially impressed, for it looked for all the world like a pure white amaryllis. *Habranthus immaculatus* grows and flowers in ordinary garden loam and adapts wherever it receives protection from penetrating frost. The Clints once succeeded in crossing this species with a beautiful salmon zephyranthes from the Caribbean, but the delicate hybrids proved difficult to maintain. *Habranthus immaculatus* would be well worth crossing again.

Habranthus concolor.

In addition to these large white and yellow *mañanitas,* Mexico has several smaller *Habranthus* species in shades of pink or white, and one in Oaxaca, *H. vittatus,* has peppermint stripes. Although lovely, most lack the vigor needed to recommend them for garden use.

Along the roadsides of central Texas, the common yellow rain lilies of summer and autumn are a small, hardy *Habranthus* formerly called *Zephyranthes andersonii.* These Texas copper lilies (*H. tubispathus* var. *texensis*) range over dry fields and prairies. Flattened, grassy foliage appears through the cool season, and diminutive glowing blooms follow after summer thunderstorms. The thimble-sized flowers have streaks and stains of bronze, which make them look orange when sun shines through their translucent petals.

This little rain lily seeds and naturalizes in neglected areas and rough turfs. It seems to accept any amount of drought or abuse but seldom tarries in well-tended or -irrigated gardens. This wildling apparently resents such attempts to settle it down.

Habranthus tubispathus ranges widely through central Texas and also turns up in northern Argentina and Uruguay. This is a curious natural distribution shared by several bulbs and implies past floral connections between the American continents. In addition to forms resembling the Texas bulbs, South American populations of *H. tubispathus* occur in a lovely pink strain, var. *roseus*.

South America seems to be the headquarters for *Habranthus*, and many beautiful sorts grow there on red clays like those of Georgia or Oklahoma. Most of the species thrive in the southern United States if offered rich, acid soil and winter mulches to retard frost. As a group, these South American species are some of the most valuable garden rain lilies. Many multiply into substantial clumps with good gray-green foliage, disappearing several times during summer and fall under thick crops of blossoms.

'Russell Manning' is a select variety often listed as a form of *Habranthus robustus*. Enormous, funnel-shaped blossoms top its twelve-inch stems, suggesting a light pink amaryllis. 'Russell Manning' makes a striking accent for subtropic borders, flowering freely through summer.

Texas copper lilies, *Habranthus tubispathus* var. *texensis*.

The orchid trumpets of *Habranthus brachyandrus* darken romantically to deep burgundy throats like blooms of old-fashioned rose of Sharon (*Hibiscus syriacus*). These natives of Argentina and Brazil are happily floriferous from late spring through autumn. Their medium-sized blossoms complement similar tones of soft pink tropical sage (*Salvia coccinea* 'Coral Nymph'), shrub morning glory (*Ipomoea fistulosa*), Virginia saltmarsh mallow (*Kosteletzkya virginica*), or the old, pale pink crapemyrtle, *Lagerstroemia indica* 'Near East'. The light-colored blooms of *H. brachyandrus* resonate against the strong foliage of purple heart (*Setcreasea pallida*), purple Chinese witch-hazel (*Loropetalum chinense* var. *rubrum* 'Zhuzhou Fuchsia') or purple wood sorrel (*Oxalis regnellii* 'Triangularis').

Another rain lily with blossoms shaded toward lavender or lilac, *Habranthus caeruleus* is a smaller species than *H. brachyandrus*. This so-called blue habranthus remains uncommon in cultivation. Since it is a native of northeastern Argentina, it should do well in the South.

With a spotty distribution from near Salta in the northwest, through central and northeastern Argentina, *Habranthus martinezii* accents creamy-petaled flowers with dark olive throats. Small stature, slender foliage, and a graceful aspect give it considerable charm. It looks like a paler version of *H. tubispathus* top-heavy with blossoms, and makes an easy-growing garden plant.

Habranthus pedunculosus is a species from northeastern Argentina that includes plants formerly known as *H. teretifolius*, *H. juncifolius*, and *H. concordiae*. Its gracefully deported, slender blooms, suffused with rosy pink, appear in small clusters on ten-inch stems after autumn rains. *Habranthus pedunculosus* bears distinctively round, stiff foliage, recalled in one of its former epithets, *juncifolius* ("rush-leafed"). *Habranthus gracilifolius* and *H. estensis* are similar species native to Uruguay with more flattened foliage. All keep their leaves through the winter. Their bulbs remain mostly dormant during summer heat, with blooms appearing in autumn.

Habranthus martinezii.

Dark-throated *Habranthus brachyandrus.*   *Habranthus pedunculosus.*

South American Zephyranthes

With the exception of *Zephyranthes candida* and the several habranthus just discussed, South American rain lilies have been slow to enter cultivation. Jose Alberto Castillo of Buenos Aires, Argentina, has introduced a few choice varieties that seem admirably suited to the reddish, acid clays of the South.

Zephyranthes minima is a tiny curiosity with white blossoms no larger than an onion floret. Its threadlike foliage reveals a kinship to *Z. candida*, but the scale of the plant is entirely unique. This little Argentine bulb would be a wonderful choice for a pot or trough planting, where its charms could be appreciated close up. *Zephyranthes minima* is vigorous and multiplies rapidly from seed. A related white-flowering species, *Z. mesochloa*, is intermediate in size and character between *Z. minima* and *Z. candida*.

Zephyranthes flavissima, a golden beauty from Argentina and Brazil, displays one-inch blooms with tongue-shaped petals spread into small stars. It lacks the drought resistance of the North American yellows, but seems easy to grow on damp, acid soils. Like *Z. pulchella*, this bulb makes winter foliage that tolerates light frosts. *Zephyranthes flavissima* is entirely at home in the Southeast and naturalizes readily in Carolina gardens, blooming from early summer through fall. These moisture-tolerant bulbs may also be potted for immersion in a garden pond.

Another rain lily from Argentina and Uruguay is so original and odd in its design that botanists place it in a separate genus, *Haylockia*, distinguished by a subterranean ovary. This gives these nocturnal blossoms something of the character of a crocus. The most widespread species, and the one most likely to do well in the South, is *H. americana*, now included by some botanists in *Habranthus*. Its starry, cream, or primrose-yellow blooms appear in late summer. Three or four weeks later the underground capsules emerge and shed papery black seeds. These may be planted immediately for increase.

The bulbs of *Haylockia americana* are large, with thick, black coats like rain lilies of the cooperia group. They send up several narrow, sprawling, green leaves over winter. These rain lilies come from hot, subtropical regions, so they should be offered a good baking in summer.

Pyrolirion flammeum (fire lily, flame lily) of Peru is another exotic relation of *Habranthus*. Its shocking tangerine blossoms appear in early summer with the first warm rains. The similar golden flame lily, *P. aureum*, produces orange-yellow blooms that rival daffodils. Both of these bulbs are rare and entirely tender. Except in frost-free regions, they should be dug and stored for winter.

Hybrids

When Thad Howard began to hybridize rain lilies in the 1950s, he started by crossing *Zephyranthes rosea* and *Z. citrina*. He envisioned creating a vibrant orange blossom from the mix, but the child of this union was 'Ruth Page', a rich pink, star-shaped flower with a white throat.

'Ruth Page' grew vigorously and proved a good parent. By mixing in turn with *Zephyranthes smallii*, *Z. traubii*, *Z. pulchella*, *Z. reginae*, and *Z. lindleyana*, Howard was able to generate a series of beautiful miniature amaryllids in a rainbow of colors, including, eventually, the orange tone he had hoped for. He grew

Zephyranthes 'Ruth Page'. Photo by Lauren S. Ogden.

A pastel *Zephyranthes* hybrid derived from 'Ruth Page'.

and distributed his best crosses, as well as a number of fine hybrids from other breeders. These and hybrids from several other rain lily enthusiasts may be found in the gardens of fortunate Southerners. All are treasures.

'Starfrost' is a lovely soft lilac-rose with a contrasting white central star. This is overlaid by a silvery sheen, as if frosted. Since it descends from *Zephyranthes smallii*, 'Starfrost' inherits some of the sweet fragrance of that parent, as well as its free-blooming habit.

'Big Shot' is a remarkable hybrid that produces flowers up to five inches across. These are pale cream, lightly tinged rose, and, despite their size, quite graceful. This one descends from the Mexican strain of *Zephyranthes traubii*.

'Apricot Queen' reserves her warm-colored blossoms for late summer, just as does her parent, *Zephyranthes pulchella*. The medium-sized flowers open widely to rich apricot with a yellow throat. The dark green foliage grows vigorously through fall and winter. Seedlings usually come true, so 'Apricot Queen' may be multiplied readily.

'Libra' is a robust child of 'Ruth Page' crossed with *Zephyranthes huaste-cana*. It answers the need for a vigorous garden rain lily with good rose-pink flowers. These are goblet-shaped and appear from mid-spring through early fall.

Zephyranthes 'Grandjax'.

The wide foliage is an attractive asset. The big, black bulbs multiply swiftly, and this is another hybrid that comes true from seed. 'Libra' seems thoroughly hardy in the South.

'Grandjax' descends from a Ray Flagg cross of *Zephyranthes grandiflora* and an old, creamy yellow rain lily, 'Ajax', which is itself presumed to be a hybrid between *Z. candida* and *Z. citrina*. The light pink blossoms of 'Grandjax' resemble *Z. candida* in form, with white throats and a green central star. They bloom furiously through summer and fall, and quickly multiply into thrifty patches.

'Aquarius' is a parallel hybrid produced by E. L. Brasol from 'Ajax' and *Zephyranthes candida*. When fall rains arrive, its grassy leaves are smothered by masses of creamy yellow funnels. Like 'Grandjax' this one is a rapid multiplier.

A creation named for the wife of Florida breeder Alex Korsakoff, 'Ellen Korsakoff' derives from the same parentage as 'Ruth Page', but instead of a pink flower produces a lovely pineapple blend. Although rather tender, 'Ellen Korsakoff' responds to good culture and rich soil.

'Teddy Buhler' is a unique Korsakoff offspring of *Zephyranthes albiella*, a tender rain lily from Colombia with white, funnel-shaped blooms, and *Habranthus martinezii*. 'Teddy Buhler' looks much like a little, white habranthus with wide, grass-green foliage. It offsets quickly and provides gorgeous masses of white bloom all summer.

Another valuable *Habranthus* hybrid, *H. ×floryi*, is a cross between *H. robustus* and *H. brachyandrus*, with a lovely mixture of characteristics from each parent. Several different clones of this cross are common in the South, and all make fine garden plants. The fast-multiplying 'Cherry Pink' and large-flowered 'Purple Base' both display large rose-pink, dark-throated blooms like those of *H. brachyandrus*. These soon form robust clumps of flat, gray-green foliage. The bulbs carry crops of two- to three-inch blooms periodically through summer and fall. 'Green Base' offers large, funnel-shaped blossoms with green throats in the style of *H. robustus*.

'Pink Flamingos', another *Habranthus* hybrid introduced by Carl Schoenfeld, makes thick clumps of bulbs, periodically disappearing in clouds of rose-pink blossoms on eight-inch stems. These blooms resemble *H. robustus*, but are more abundant, so that 'Pink Flamingos' makes a showy subject for summer borders.

Korsakoff's hybrid of *Habranthus martinezii* and *H. robustus* is also worthwhile. Flowering shyly when first planted, it soon multiplies into thick patches covered several times each summer with carpets of medium pink blossoms. A plant introduced from Thai nurseries as *Habranthus* 'Mini Cherry' seems similar.

On a trip through Panama, Louisiana plantsman Ira Nelson discovered another hybrid of *Zephyranthes albiella*. He introduced these tender, pink-flowered rain lilies through the Louisiana Society for Horticultural Research. They have since spread widely through Gulf Coast gardens under the name 'Panama Pink'. The tiny bulbs of this tender variety multiply and flower prolifically. The other parent of 'Panama Pink' is presumed to be *Z. rosea*.

Cream-flowered *Zephyranthes* 'Aquarius' with pink *Z.* 'Libra', moss rose (*Portulaca grandiflora*), little gray sedum (*Sedum diffusum* 'Potosinum'), and *Manfreda undulata*.

Habranthus cardinalis (Zephyranthes bifolia). Photo by Marcia Wilson.

On the island of Dominica, Padre Julio Cicero hybridized the native scarlet-flowered rain lily. This unique species, now *Habranthus cardinalis* (formerly *Zephyranthes bifolia*), occupies an anomalous position somewhere between *Habranthus* and *Zephyranthes*. Padre Cicero's crosses involved *Z. rosea* and the white-flowered *Z. puertoricensis*. His hybrids, known as *Z.* ×*bipuertorosea*, come in delectable shades of scarlet, salmon, and apricot-pink. Woefully tender, these beautiful Caribbean rain lilies must be restricted to pots north of south Florida.

Although not yet well tested in gardens, the brilliant multicolored 'Paul Niemi' descends from a cross of *Zephyranthes citrina* and *Z. grandiflora*, so it ought to succeed in much of the South. Bred by Indonesian rain lily enthusiast Fadjar Marta, this spectacularly colorful hybrid has rounded, peach-pink petals that shade to yellow, and finally to green at the throat.

The Jacala Rainbow

Not long after Howard began hybridizing, his collecting trips to Mexico took him along the Pan-American Highway south through the state of Hidalgo. Near the town of Jacala, he stumbled upon a rain lily bonanza he could scarcely have anticipated.

The region is mountainous and lies about six thousand feet above sea level. The hillsides are filled with pock-marked outcroppings of limestone. The lush jungle of lower elevations gives way to open meadows with scattered pines, junipers, and oaks and herds of wandering cattle. This beautiful upland countryside projects a fresh and pleasant aspect.

When early summer rains freshen the moss-covered slopes, the rain lilies appear from each nook and cranny. On some slopes they are golden, on others pink. In many places the blooms are peach-colored, or yellow with red flashes on the petals. In the dry valley south of Jacala, most of the rain lilies are porcelain-white. In a few places the flowers are deep blood-red, a true carmine undiluted by rose or burgundy, set off by green throats and flaming golden anthers.

Katherine Clint collected in this region about the same time that Howard made his discoveries, and she sent some of these red and yellow rain lilies to botanists for determination. Eventually, the bicolored form was described in her honor as a new species, *Zephyranthes katherinae*.

It seems likely that these flowers are hybrids between the various reds and yellows that grow nearby. All the different color forms share certain characters: their foliage is narrow, their bulbs small and globular, and their petals rounded or spoon-shaped. Most of the flowers have long tubes. It would take

The Jacala crimson rain lily, a dark red form of *Zephyranthes katherinae*.

years of research to determine the true relationship of these complex forms, but it takes only a glimpse to appreciate the tremendous beauty of their warmly mingled colors. The hand of nature has gardened as well here as anywhere on earth.

Cooperanthes at Last

As sometimes happens with avid plantsmen, a few rain lilies appeared by surprise among Dr. Howard's collection. These had probably come from a mislabeled assortment received years earlier and had taken several seasons to come to flower. When they finally revealed themselves, Howard realized he had acquired at least two clones of Lancaster's ×*Cooperanthes* hybrids.

One was a large, snowy white, like an all-white *Zephyranthes grandiflora* with an icy sparkle. This he nicknamed 'Bombay'. It seemed to be a slow grower and set no seed, but was hardy and long-lived. The other clone looked to be one of Lancaster's pastel-colored hybrids. Howard christened it 'Prairie Sunset' for its yellow, pink-stained blooms. Unlike 'Bombay', this variety bloomed prolifically all season and ripened large pods of seed. It turned out to be one of the hardiest and most dependable *Zephyranthes* hybrids in Dr. Howard's collection, and it became one of Zephyr Garden's favorites for its warm blend of colors.

On the long journey from Texas to India, and back again, this lily had indeed been gilded. Like a precious gem, 'Prairie Sunset' continues to grace Southern gardens. It's a true treasure, as are all the rain lilies you may meet.

Chapter 2
📖 *Petite Afrique*

I**N THE SOUTH,** fall comes like a second spring, but with decidedly tropical overtones. Long-blooming salvias seem reinvigorated by the shortening days, their flowers enlarging and deepening in color. Marigolds, both annual and perennial, ripen aromatic, golden blossoms. Clear blue Cape plumbagos sag under the weight of phloxlike trusses. Cigar flower (*Cuphea* spp.), shrimp plant (*Justicia brandegeana*), and candle bush (*Senna alata*) swell in exotic late-season bloom.

The freshened air and moderating temperatures invite an array of plants into renewed activity. It's as if a gentle breeze from Africa had blown into the garden to awaken the inhabitants. This rich and rewarding season includes a surprising number of bulbs. Their exceptional flowers grace gardens at a time when they can be specially savored.

Guernsey Lilies

The best known of the late bloomers belong to a group of amaryllids that Southerners have long called Guernsey lilies. In standard horticultural references, this common name refers to the South African *Nerine sarniensis*. In the South, however, the same name is often applied to the oriental *Lycoris radiata*, and Southerners are often chided for their ignorance in these matters. The origin of this confusion lies properly in early botanical history.

Guernsey is one of the Channel Islands, lying between France and England in the straits of the English Channel. Bathed in the mild waters of the Gulf Stream, the island has long been a haven for plants. Since Elizabethan times, flowers raised on Guernsey have been taken to the markets of London.

One of the popular cut flowers produced on the island is *Nerine sarniensis*, a crystalline-textured, orange-red amaryllid originally from the Cape of Good Hope. Known as Guernsey lilies in the flower trade, they became an important export early in the 1700s. According to tradition, these unusual plants arrived on the island as storm-tossed wreckage from a broken ship. The bulbs washed ashore, took root, and naturalized among the dunes.

In 1753 the Swedish naturalist Carl von Linné (Carolus Linnaeus) published descriptions of plants in the collection of his patron George Clifford. The sumptuous *Hortus Cliffortianus* included many of Linnaeus' first attempts at plant classification (he is remembered as the founder of the binomial system of nomenclature for plants and animals). His entry for the Guernsey lily is especially curious. Linnaeus relates an account of the fabled shipwreck: *"Radixes ex Japonia allatae & ex nave naufraga ejectae in littus arenosum insulae Sarniae"* ("The bulbs were brought out of Japan and thrown from the broken ship onto the sandy shore of Guernsey island"). Linnaeus goes on to list *Lilio-narcissus japonicus* and *Lilium sarniense* as synonyms. Clearly, he thinks that the Japanese *Lycoris radiata* is the same plant as the Guernsey lily, *Nerine sarniensis*.

It's easy to see how Linnaeus erred with these two similar bulbs. Both *Nerine* and *Lycoris* share the habit of autumn bloom, and plants of both genera flower on top of slender, naked stems. Strap-shaped leaves follow and grow through the winter. Both have spidery umbels of warm orange-red, narrow-petaled blossoms. The most obvious differences come from the long, projecting stamens of the lycoris. Linnaeus expressly mentions *"genitalibus longissimis"* ("very long stamens") in his entry for the Guernsey lily, which leaves little doubt that it is *L. radiata* he is describing.

Certainly, the bulbs grown on Guernsey for so many years are *Nerine*. Their lasting qualities as cut flowers far surpass *Lycoris*. Linnaeus must have assumed that the spidery flowers in George Clifford's garden were the same as the cut blooms he knew from stalls in the flower markets. The confused identity of *L. radiata* perpetuated in the American South appears to be a genuine inheritance from Linnaeus. The bulbs, along with their mistaken appellation, probably came to the New World with early colonists from Europe.

As for the true *Nerine sarniensis*, its success in America has been limited, so far, to California and Oregon. In Florida and the Gulf states, its bulbs safely winter, but the sweltering Southern summer seems to do a poor job of preparing them to flower. It is rare to get a bloom from *N. sarniensis* in the South and fortunate that we have several lovely lycoris to take their place.

Lycoris has a fascinating denomination of its own. The name commemorates a famous and intriguing mistress of the Roman general Marcus Antonius. Since this is a true Latin name, *Lycoris* follows the rule of receiving the accent on the antepenultimate (third to last) syllable. You may refer to this genus correctly (*LY-cor-is*) when you are alone or among botanists, but if you wish to be understood by most other gardeners, you will probably need to mispronounce it, with the accent in the middle (*ly-COR-is*), as with such genera as *Curcuma* and *Oxalis*.

For a common name distinct from Guernsey lily, *Lycoris* species are often called spiderlilies. This risks confusion with amaryllids such as *Hymenocallis* and *Crinum*, so careful gardeners usually amend the name to fall spiderlily or red spiderlily. The summer-flowering *L. squamigera* is sometimes called surprise lily or hardy amaryllis, and the golden-flowered *L. aurea* appears frequently as hurricane lily. Since lycoris come into bloom without accompanying foliage, they are also known fancifully as naked ladies.

Lycoris radiata probably came to North America before the beginning of the nineteenth century, although early records of its cultivation are few. The heirloom strain found in gardens is, in any case, distinct from the imported types currently available from Japan.

Studies performed by geneticists make clear that this old Southern variety has an extra dose of chromosomes. Such plants are triploid: they have three sets of chromosomes, rather than the diploid, or double, set of typical species. It's

Red *Lycoris radiata* var. *radiata* and golden *L. aurea*, with foliage of *Hippeastrum*, Caribbean coontie cycad (*Zamia pumila*), and *Stahlianthus involucratus*, author's garden, Austin. Photo by Lauren S. Ogden.

a state of affairs that frustrates would-be hybridizers, since the extra genes make the bulbs sterile. For gardeners, however, it's a windfall. Triploid bulbs have tremendous vigor and hardiness, and many types make especially reliable perennials. Such plants grow and flower under conditions ill-suited to ordinary forms.

Through the first half of the twentieth century, most *Lycoris radiata* sold in the United States were this old triploid clone, known as *L. radiata* var. *radiata*, but after World War II commercial growers in Japan began supplying American dealers with a smaller form of their native lycoris, *L. radiata* var. *pumila*. The oriental nurseries introduced many fine bulbs at inexpensive prices, while domestic supplies simultaneously dwindled. The old triploid strain now has become difficult to obtain, although each autumn it flowers by the thousands in gardens throughout the South.

If you are offered offset lycoris bulbs from someone's garden, chances are they will be progeny of this prolific triploid variant. These bulbs may become nearly as large as those of daffodils. On heavy clays they bloom more readily than the diploid types.

Where soils are well drained and on the acid side, the commercial strains of *Lycoris radiata* var. *pumila* succeed nearly as well as the old garden variety, but their smaller bulbs produce flowers a couple of weeks earlier. If both kinds are planted strategically through a garden, the *L. radiata* flowering season may be stretched over a month.

Lycoris rate among the choice bulbs for woodland, and nearly all the species associate well among trees or in borders of shrubs. Their early-ripening foliage matures as growth commences in spring, so they may be planted under leafless hardwoods and even under briefly deciduous live oaks. All lycoris enjoy soils enriched with leaf litter and humus, and the more delicate species require them. Their fragile, spidery flowers are at their best in sheltered groves where wind and sun cannot reach in to cause premature withering.

With their long, feathery stamens, many lycoris recall deciduous azaleas, and their blossoms issue a similar impression of grace and wild woodland beauty. The elegant "bird cages" formed by the clustered flowers attract butterflies, who stop to sip from the quiet blooms as they migrate southward each autumn.

These graceful, slender-stemmed flowers practically arrange themselves in gardens and combine happily in a variety of settings. Dark-leafed green aucuba and cream-variegated pittosporum make good glossy foliage companions. To soften the bareness of the tall, leafless stems, lycoris may be positioned among overplantings of Southern shield fern (*Thelypteris kunthii*), maidenhair fern (*Adiantum capillus-veneris*), Japanese anemone (*Anemone ×hybrida*), or other shade-loving perennials. A simple backdrop of mossy boulders or leaf-littered earth also affords a lovely, dramatic contrast.

Bulbs of *Lycoris radiata* and other lycoris are usually available in late summer. If set immediately in the ground, the larger bulbs may flower the first season, but most lycoris test the planter's patience and take a year of settling in before blooming. These flowers resent frequent disturbances and will punish gardeners by exacting a similar waiting period following division and replanting. These slow starts are one reason for the reputation of the genus for erratic and unreliable flowering. Another is susceptibility to winter cold.

Lycoris may be grouped in two broad hardiness categories: winter-green types, which send up leaves in autumn, and late-leafing varieties, which emerge in early spring. Since the first group keeps foliage through the winter, leaf damage from harsh freezes sometimes prevents bloom the subsequent autumn.

Although tenderness limits a few lycoris to culture in the lower South, several are thoroughly hardy. In their native homelands the species range through

Myanmar, China, Japan, and Korea, where many experience severe cold. In American gardens *Lycoris radiata* regularly endures 5°F without damage, and lower temperatures if protected by leaves or snow cover.

Winter-Green Lycoris

In addition to *Lycoris radiata*, several colorful species and garden hybrids retain leaves through the winter. Their foliage is an attractive feature, helping to give otherwise dormant gardens a lush, lively appearance. The dark green leaves come to blunt tips and have distinctive milky stripes down their centers.

The first lycoris cultivated in American gardens may well have been the golden *Lycoris aurea*, for these bulbs are common about the old Spanish city of St. Augustine and presumably have grown there since colonial times. Although it was at one time known as *L. africana*, *L. aurea*'s homelands are the subtropical provinces of China, Taiwan, and Vietnam. Floridians know these flowers as hurricane lilies, and their spidery clumps of bloom are a September feature of many Gulf Coast gardens.

This golden spiderlily is one of the truly magnificent flowers of the subtropics, in Mandarin called *hu di xiao* ("suddenly the earth smiles"). After autumn rains, its two-foot spikes rise, bearing whorled umbels of cadmium blossoms, each with gracefully recurved and undulating petals. The airy groups of flowers have a jaunty, upright tilt, which gives them special flair.

After blooming, the bulbs throw up lush fountains of dark green, pointed leaves with a bluish cast. These leafy masses resemble giant liriope clumps and persist through winter if protected from frost. The foliage withers in any hard freeze, however, and such disasters inhibit blooming.

October flowers of *Lycoris aurea* with leafy foliage companions, author's garden, Austin. Photo by Lauren S. Ogden.

As with the old garden strain of *Lycoris radiata*, *L. aurea* largely disappeared from the nursery trade following World War II. Its place was taken by an imposter, *L. traubii*, which Japanese nurserymen discovered on Taiwan. These bulbs are invariably sold as *L. aurea*, but reveal their true identity upon blooming. *Lycoris traubii*'s saffron blossoms have wider, more flattened petals than the orange-toned *L. aurea*, and the blooms are disposed symmetrically at 90-degree angles from the stem. The winter foliage of *L. traubii* is dark green and comes up about two weeks later than the leaves of *L. aurea*.

For most gardeners the substitution goes unnoticed, as both species have essentially yellow blossoms. The exchange is welcome in frost-prone regions, for *Lycoris traubii* has greater cold tolerance. It flowers regularly in plantings as far north as Memphis, Tennessee, and may endure temperatures down to 12°F with little damage to the foliage.

Frost-hardiness for both yellow-flowered lycoris improves when they are planted on sand, since such soils hold warmth better than clays. Gardeners in marginal regions may create raised beds of sandy soil to accommodate their bulbs. A small nook near a sheltered south wall offers a suitable home for several of these flamboyant golden blossoms. Where winter cold is not a threat, *Lycoris traubii* and *L. aurea* relish culture on heavy clays and may be treated to plentiful applications of compost and manure.

Lycoris traubii.

At the same time that Japanese importers began shipping *Lycoris traubii* to America they also began distributing bulbs of cream-colored varieties labeled *L. alba*. These resembled *L. radiata*, but had milky blooms tinted various shades of yellow, salmon, or pink. Botanists identified several strains among these "white"-flowered lycoris during the 1950s, and various plants received names such as *L. albiflora*, *L. straminea*, *L. elsiae*, *L. ×houdyshelii*, and *L. caldwellii*.

Lycoris ×houdyshelii, a sterile hybrid of unknown origin introduced to the United States in a shipment of bulbs received from Shanghai, China, in 1948.

Lycoris ×jacksoniana.

These "species" are now regarded as natural hybrids derived from crosses between the scarlet *Lycoris radiata* and the golden *L. aurea*, saffron *L. traubii*, or other oriental species. The hybrids make fine garden subjects and flower usefully along with the red and yellow types in early September. They seem nearly as hardy as *L. radiata* and show excellent vigor. Their pale blossoms offer just the right tones to light up dark places under evergreen oaks, and the bulbs seem not to mind heavy competition from tree roots.

Hybridizers in Japan and the United States have introduced a handful of artificial *Lycoris* crosses bred along lines similar to these wild plants. Most remain rare in the bulb trade, but practically any named lycoris are worth obtaining for trial, if opportunity arises. One fall-foliage type shows special promise. It's a cross of the warm red *L. radiata* and a hardy species with pink-lavender flowers. This *L. ×jacksoniana* grows readily through the South and Southwest, and flowers in September with rich peach-wine blooms touched blue on the petal tips.

Spring-foliage Lycoris

The lavender and pink tones seen in *Lycoris ×jacksoniana* come from *L. sprengeri*, a species in the spring-foliage section of *Lycoris*. These late-leafing types are the most cold-hardy members of the genus, and many thrive in the middle and upper South.

Along the Gulf Coast and in Florida these same lycoris are mysteriously unreliable. They refuse to flower even when their bulbs thrive and increase. High soil temperatures are the apparent culprit, as this seems to thwart blooming. Careful siting in shaded beds of leafy groundcover helps to keep bulbs cooler and may permit blooming in warm regions.

The most popular of the spring growers is *Lycoris squamigera*, an old garden selection known as the magic lily. One rarely finds a more beautiful flower pos-

Lycoris squamigera (surprise lily) flowering in rows in a country garden. Photo by Lauren S. Ogden.

sessed of such an undemanding disposition. It's nearly ideal for gardens in the middle and upper South, and even into the cold climates of the Midwest. On both sandy acid soils and heavy alkaline clays, *L. squamigera* thrives.

This species makes some of the largest bulbs in the genus, and multiplies swiftly into substantial clumps. Its broad, gray leaves look like extraordinarily robust narcissus foliage and appear and disappear in concert with spring daffodils. This tremendous herbage can be something of an embarrassment, as it looks especially untidy while dying away in late spring. Naturalistic treatment in a woodland setting is the usual solution.

Sometime after the Fourth of July, rainfall triggers the thick scapes of surprise lilies to bolt upward from the ground. They rise swiftly, in four or five days expanding to crowns of succulent, lilac-pink buds. The clustered blossoms open to look like small amaryllises, shimmering with lavender highlights on their broad rounded petals.

Like the triploid *Lycoris radiata*, this strong-growing species enjoys an extra set of chromosomes, which fuel unusual vigor. Genetic evidence suggests that these were acquired through hybridization. *Lycoris squamigera* appears to be an unusually lovely garden "mule" descended from a cross between the straw-colored *L. straminea* and the rosy pink *L. incarnata*. Whether this mixing occurred in nature or in the forgotten garden of some oriental flower lover, no one knows.

Lycoris squamigera reportedly came to America with a certain Dr. Hall of Bristol, Rhode Island, who grew the flowers in his garden in Shanghai, China, prior to the American Civil War.

Several other spring-growing lycoris have made their way to North America, but none approach *Lycoris squamigera* in prominence or widespread adaptability. The most commonly available in the trade are *L. sanguinea*, with rather small clusters of orange-red blooms, and *L. sprengeri*, with light pink flowers. *Lycoris incarnata* is occasionally offered as well; its rose blooms are accented by electric-blue petals.

All of these have gray-green spring foliage and produce flowers in late summer along with *Lycoris squamigera*. They perform well in the upper South, but seem to dislike the heat of the Gulf Coast. *Lycoris haywardii*, a natural hybrid imported by Wyndham Hayward of Winter Park, Florida, is exceptional in this regard. Although it produces its foliage in the spring and grows well in cold regions, its orchid-pink blooms appear generously even in the deep South. It remains unfortunately rare in the bulb trade.

Hardy Golden Lycoris

Shortly before the 1949 Communist takeover of China, the U.S. Department of Agriculture received bulbs from the Sun Yat-Sen Memorial Garden in Nanjing. Among them was a lycoris with golden yellow blooms like *Lycoris aurea* and gray spring foliage like *L. squamigera*. These proved hardy at Glenn Dale, Maryland, and Dr. Hamilton Traub described the new plant as *L. chinensis*. Unfortunately, this species proved slow to propagate, and importations from China remained closed for decades.

In the 1950s Nashville garden expert and lycoris fancier Sam Caldwell invited listeners to his radio talk show to share information about the spiderlilies in their gardens. One called in to describe a yellow lycoris she had collected while working as a missionary in the region between Huchow and Hangchow, China. This woman, a Mrs. Henry Sperry, had shared the bulbs among several gardeners in central Tennessee, where they were thriving. Caldwell dubbed the bulbs *Lycoris sperryi* in honor of their collector.

Both of these hardy yellow spiderlilies propagate at a snail's pace from seed or offsets. For many years they remained regretfully rare in gardens. However, the reopening of China to horticultural exchange in the 1990s has once again made these and many other novel lycoris available to gardeners.

One of the exciting new Chinese species worth trying in the middle and upper South is *Lycoris longituba*, a spring-foliage type with beautiful, trumpetlike, creamy white blossoms. These elegant flowers appear along with the surprise lilies in midsummer.

Mediterraneans

Many of the bulbs growing in the countries around the Mediterranean Sea choose to blossom in the fall, for this is the beginning of the growing season in these climes. Several derive from meadows of *terra-rossa*, a peculiar reddish claylike earth similar to many soils found in the South. Bulbs from these regions often perform famously on dry, raised rockeries.

Chief among these autumnal bloomers is *Sternbergia lutea*, a golden flower suggestive of a large, waxen crocus. Its luminous goblet-shaped blossoms appear soon after the arrival of September rains. These living drops of sun brighten gardens for a fortnight. As the brilliant flowers fade, the dark green foliage rises in their place. Narrow and distinctively keeled, it makes short leafy clumps with the somber, pedestrian appearance of mondo grass (*Ophiopogon*). Leaves last through the winter and die down with warm weather.

The generic name of these bulbs commemorates Count Caspar Sternberg (1761–1838), an accomplished German botanist. Early references, such as Parkinson's *Paradisus* and *Hortus Floridus* of Crispin de Pass (1615), identify these bulbs as "autumn daffodils." Gardeners ever since have puzzled over the comparison of this crocuslike flower to a narcissus.

The analogy is actually a sound one from a botanical standpoint, since *Sternbergia* and *Narcissus* both belong to the amaryllis family. Crocuses are members of the iris tribe, growing from corms instead of the true bulbs shared by amaryllids. Still, this hardly satisfies most gardeners.

It may be helpful to understand the origin of the term daffodil, for this name did not always belong to the golden trumpets of spring. The word is a corruption of the Greek *asphodelos*, which in classical times applied to almost any lilylike plant. As a Mediterranean native, *Sternbergia*'s claim on this title seems as valid as that of any narcissus.

Sternbergia lutea.

Nevertheless, those uncomfortable with calling these goblet-shaped blossoms "daffodils" have added several additional sobriquets. Some contend that *Sternbergia* is the biblical "lily of the field." Indeed, this may be, for it is a common wildflower in the Levant. Other names applied to these bulbs are Mt. Etna lily and (of course) yellow autumn crocus.

Modern planters may take their pick of these, for each seems suitable. Unfortunately, none of the monikers applied to these beautiful flowers can really be called a common name, for the bulbs themselves remain relatively obscure. These brilliant flames of autumn ought to be widely planted, yet sternbergias reside primarily in the neglected borders of old homesteads.

These golden blossoms are among those mysterious, sensible flowers that seem to choose the gardeners for whom they will prosper. Invariably, their happiest homes are the humble bungalows of honest folk, rather than the well-tended borders of aristocrats. Leave these flowers benignly to their own devices, and they bloom faithfully for decades. Transplant and pamper them to feature as some conceit of grand design, and they modestly die away.

There is a tradition in the South that Thomas Jefferson was the first to import *Sternbergia* to America, and that the bulbs passed along in gardens descend from his original planting at Monticello. If this is true, then his bulbs must have prospered mightily, for antebellum sternbergia plantings are scattered from Virginia to Texas. In several gardens they spread like fantastic golden carpets beneath the dark, sprawling branches of ancient oaks.

These old bulbs have slightly smaller blooms and narrower leaves than the glossy, wide-leafed *Sternbergia lutea* offered in the Dutch trade. They may represent an old strain or hybrid of the allied species, *S. sicula*, which grows along with *S. lutea* on the stony hills of Sicily and Greece.

The Mediterranean origin of these flowers would seem to imply a love for dry, sunny slopes and fast drainage, but in the middle and upper South *Sternbergia* thrives on heavy clays. In warmer gardens along the Gulf some shade will be appreciated, and the bulbs usually prove more permanent if given raised positions.

In addition to the Dutch and Jeffersonian strains of *Sternbergia*, specialists occasionally import a handful of other types. All are worthy of trial, especially in more temperate sections of the South. *Sternbergia fischeriana* offers its large, light yellow flowers on six-inch stems accompanied by gray-blue, upright foliage. These December blossoms seem none the worse for exposure to 0°F temperatures. *Sternbergia clusiana* is similar, but flowers earlier and holds its blooms close to the ground.

A great rarity discovered in 1978, *Sternbergia candida* has become endangered in its native Turkey, a result of overzealous collecting for the bulb trade. This is no wonder, for the flowers are particularly enticing. The cream-colored blooms break *Sternbergia* tradition not only in their color, but also by blossoming in spring. These bulbs are now in nursery production, although they will remain expensive and hard to come by for some time. They would be well worth trying in Southern gardens.

Autumn Narcissi

Along the Strait of Gibraltar and the adjacent western Mediterranean, the brush-covered hills provide homes for three odd little bulbs that flower in the fall. These aren't sternbergias, but true narcissi. Their tiny blossoms hardly afford the show we envision from daffodils, but these novelties succeed in the South and add diversity to our list of autumn blooms.

The first species, *Narcissus viridiflorus*, makes a slender, little plant with narrow foliage. The clusters of star-shaped, tubular flowers have tiny, practically nonexistent cups, and, as you might expect from the botanical epithet, they are green. You could miss the little blooms altogether, but for their powerfully sweet fragrance.

The others, *Narcissus serotinus* and *N. elegans*, face upward like rain lilies and have rounded, white petals centered around small, yellow cups. The flat-faced flowers are mostly solitary and only an inch or so wide. *Narcissus serotinus* flowers before the appearance of its solitary leaf. This distinguishes it from *N. elegans*, whose bulbs produce several leaves prior to flowering.

Benjamin Yoe Morrison (1891–1966), bulb fancier and principal founder of the American Horticultural Society, reported success with all these species at his Gulf Coast garden in Pass Christian, Mississippi. The biggest challenge faced in growing them seems to have been getting enough of the tiny things to create some garden effect. Such miniatures warrant spots near paths or on raised beds, where their small October blooms can be seen and admired. They also make fine choices for trough plantings.

In the same regions of the Mediterranean where autumn narcissi proliferate, their distant relatives the snowflakes (*Leucojum* spp.) have also experimented with fall flowering. Of the handful of species, the most likely to succeed in Southern gardens is *L. autumnale*, the autumn snowflake. Like *Narcissus viridiflorus*, these are plants of slender build, with narrow, winter-growing foliage that resembles clusters of emerald knitting needles. Tiny, white, bell-shaped blossoms appear before the leaves on top of bright green, threadlike stems.

Autumn snowflakes adapt to beds of sandy soil, but these miniatures are so frail and delicate in appearance that they are customarily reserved for pots. They make fine companions for little narcissi and will continue in bloom over a surprisingly long season if sheltered from hard frost.

Autumn Crocuses

Although there are a number of true autumn crocuses, including several garden varieties to be discussed shortly, the plant most often met under this name is not in the genus *Crocus* at all, but in *Colchicum*. These lilylike perennials form large, fleshy corms, which have the novel ability to flower while still unplanted. Bulb dealers have found them to be a popular item in garden centers.

Colchicum autumnale, the meadow saffron, is the most frequently offered. The stemless, lavender blooms appear in September, often while yet on display at the nursery. Several weeks afterward, the gray, boat-shaped leaves follow. This foliage looks like oversized tulip leaves.

Unfortunately for many Southerners, the commonly available colchicums are as ill-suited to warm climates as most of their tulip cousins. Only in the damper, cooler parts of the South will they remain more than a season. For any hope of success they should be given shady sites in rich woodland where they will never be subjected to drought.

Colchicum has a wide distribution around the eastern Mediterranean, and there are probably several varieties suited to warmer sections. *Colchicum psaridis*, a native of the *terra-rossa* pasturelands of southern Greece, is one that might do. Unfortunately, the varieties in the trade come mostly from the high Alps. For Southern gardeners it seems better to forget these and concentrate on genuine fall-blooming members of *Crocus*.

The most famous autumn crocus is celebrated less for its beauty than for its value as a colorful spice. This need not be, for it is as lovely as any of its tribe. The medium-sized, purple-veined, lavender flowers of *Crocus sativus* have been cultivated since classical times for their long, crimson stigmas, the source of saffron. These are picked and dried to make the flavorful powder used in Spanish paella. Saffron remains among the most costly seasonings, due to the tremendous labor required to process the tiny stigmas. If a gardener enjoys cooking, a homegrown patch of saffron will provide a cost-effective source of culinary flavoring, as well as a warm show of autumn blooms.

Crocus sativus occurs wild in several forms scattered from Italy to Turkey. Present-day commercial production occurs mostly in Spain but also extends through the Middle East to India. The clone in widespread cultivation is a centuries-old selection chosen for its prolific flowering.

Corms of this crocus respond to rich soil by enlarging to the size of gladiolus tubers, each producing several November blossoms. In Spain the saffron growers customarily divide plantings each season and apply a generous manuring. In the humid South, feedings such as this might invite summer attacks from soil fungi. Any fertilizer given should be modestly applied during the cool season of the year.

Under garden cultivation the corms soon break up into a multitude of smaller tubers. These need to be reset every two or three years to keep them flowering, but otherwise persist and multiply indefinitely without additional aid. The large flowers, with their netlike patterns of violet, arrive welcomely just as the garden seems to be giving up for the season. The blooms appear sporadically from the end of October through November, depending on weather.

After flowering, these crocuses send up long grassy foliage. If the garden receives visits from mice or rabbits, these tender leaves will need protection, as they are a favorite winter browse. A few prickly branches taken from a juniper, pine, or other conifer may be laid over the crocus patch to defend the plants from hungry marauders. The foliage will continue to grow through the twigs without ill effect. Thus guarded, the leaves may perform their service of collecting sunlight to feed next year's blossoms.

One of the most valuable fall crocuses in Southern gardens is still making its way around the horticultural world. Now thoroughly established in the bulb trade, *Crocus goulimyi* was described as a new species from southern Greece in 1955. Its excellent vigor and free-flowering nature have won it many friends in warm climates.

The soft lavender blooms of this species hoist themselves above the ground on long, slender perianth tubes. This sets *Crocus goulimyi* apart from other autumn crocuses and gives the plants a particularly elegant appearance. The small corms multiply into large patches and seem to accept many kinds of soil. In their native habitat on the Mani peninsula of the Peloponnese, they grow in *terra-rossa* fields among stones and at the foot of old rock walls.

The delicately tinted blooms of this

The Peloponnesian *Crocus goulimyi* produces goblet-shaped long-stemmed blooms.

crocus combine with groundcovers of prostrate gray sedum, silvery dianthus, or the soft green *Origanum microphyllum*. They also naturalize happily in a sage-toned carpet of unmown buffalograss, along with sternbergias, rain lilies, and other low-growing fall flowers. *Crocus goulimyi* offers an ideal underplanting for a many-stemmed witch hazel (*Hamamelis virginiana*), whose golden froth of autumn blooms lines pliant twigs at the same season. In addition to the common lavender-pink strains of *C. goulimyi*, specialists sometimes offer a beautiful white.

In the cooler portions of the South, the favored crocus of autumn is the showy crocus, *Crocus speciosus*. This Turkish species produces its foliage in spring and needs several weeks to ripen its leaves before hot weather arrives. From the Carolinas northward it can be generous with its large, violet-stained blossoms, and the corms are usually inexpensive and widely available. The big flowers are colored a silvery gray on the exterior and glow inside with yellow throats and large, reddish stigmas like the saffron crocus.

'Cassiope' is a vigorous clone developed by the Dutch firm of Van Tubergen from the old variety 'Aitchisonii'. Its aster-blue flowers appear in late October or November. This seems to be the most heat-tolerant variant, and is more reliable in the South than other cultivars.

Crocus medius bears lilac flowers, with a purple star in the throat made by dark veins in the petals. This species derives from hillsides along the French and Italian Riviera and performs well in much of the South. It looks a great deal like the saffron crocus, but remains smaller. *Crocus laevigatus* is a choice Grecian species with silvery purple blooms, blessed with a honey-lemon scent. These appear in late November and December. Although harder to find and slower growing than some, it's worth seeking out.

Crocus speciosus. Photo by Lauren S. Ogden.

Several other fall crocuses are less easily coaxed into settling down. Leafy woodland soils offer the best opportunities. The white-flowered *Crocus ochroleucus* and the lavender *C. kotschyanus* and its white-throated var. *leucopharynx* bloom successfully almost anywhere for their first season or two. They become finicky after that. If your garden proves not entirely to their liking, beds will need replenishing after three or four years, as the old corms dwindle away.

Cyclamen

In the upper South some of the most beautiful fall flowers come from hardy cyclamen. These are Mediterranean relatives of the tender florist cyclamen (*Cyclamen persicum*). They come from regions where at least some frost can be expected in winter and summers are long and dry. The easiest and most prolific in Southern gardens is the ivy-leafed *C. hederifolium*, still listed in many catalogs as *C. neapolitanum*.

The pale, turned-back petals of these fragile blooms might be overlooked if seen only one or two at a time. Where these tuberous flowers are satisfied, though, they continue to swell and multiply over years until fifty or more rose, white, or carmine blossoms rise from each four-inch corm. The individual blooms are borne on long, corkscrew-like stems that creep briefly under the leaf litter before turning upward toward the autumn sun.

The small, nodding blooms of *Cyclamen hederifolium* glow in soft autumn light.

The places cyclamen like best are shallow, lime-filled soils under oaks or other trees whose roots sop up excess

Self-seeding colonies of *Cyclamen hederifolium* display varied leaf patterns and blossoms ranging from white to rose-pink. Photo by Lauren S. Ogden.

moisture and whose canopy of foliage rains down a gentle manuring each autumn. Here the shallow tubers should remain unmolested, with a natural covering of fallen, brown leaves. In such favorable positions, the plants will seed themselves into large patches. After the flowers appear, the tubers send up masses of succulent, dark green leaves, marked attractively with gray and silver. This winter foliage is a feature lovely enough to warrant cultivation of cyclamen all by itself.

In the lower South, where soils remain warm year-round, the tubers of cyclamen are liable to melt away from rot if not kept absolutely dry over summer. The hardy species are probably best forgotten near the Gulf. However, if the garden includes sheltered positions where frost is rare, the tender *Cyclamen persicum* may be used for winter bedding. The delicate roots of these corms should be disturbed as little as possible, so small cyclamen may be plunged into the ground pot and all, and then removed to dry out over summer. *Cyclamen persicum* is one of the few cool-season flowers that blooms happily in the gloom beneath a live oak.

Oxblood Lilies

Rotting timbers and sagging porches mark the sites of many farms in the South. The old frame houses were once homes of folk who raised cotton. After only a generation of productivity, the greedy crop combined with shortsighted farming techniques to destroy fertility. The worn-out land was abandoned and the populace moved away, leaving homes to molder and decay.

Hard freezes usually kill back the weeds in December, so if you visit the old houses in January or February, it's not unusual to find rows of bright green, strap-shaped leaves shining among the brown grass. Usually, the leaves mark the line of a former path or drive. Sometimes they make circles on the lawn, or edge some old property line or foundation. They are often the only remainder of the garden that once grew around the house.

If you return in early autumn, you may see the flowers of these bulbs. They are not likely to be mistaken for any others, though they bear a strong family resemblance to amaryllises. The deep crimson blossoms appear in small clusters on top of slender stems less than a foot tall, so that the ground seems smothered in red. They are known by several quaint names, but the one most evocative of their singularly brilliant appearance is oxblood lily.

Botanically these little amaryllids have shifted about under several titles and are still the subject of modest debate. In British literature they usually appear under the label *Hippeastrum advenum*. South American floras are more likely

Oxblood lilies (*Rhodophiala bifida*) flowering along a fencerow in an old central Texas garden.
Photo by Lauren S. Ogden.

to name them *Rhodophiala bifida*, and, since the bulbs are natives of Argentina and Uruguay, it seems proper to defer to the Latin American specialists, who presumably know them best.

The waxy, green, two-valved spathe of the oxblood lily is a characteristic it shares with *Hippeastrum*. The narrow foliage and winter growth habit of *Rhodophiala* are more like *Habranthus*. This relationship seems confirmed by the capacity of these two genera to hybridize. The oxblood lily crosses fairly easily with *Habranthus pedunculosus*, although the offspring are sterile.

Several additional *Rhodophiala* species are scattered down the narrow country of Chile, many with lovely blooms in cream, yellow, and vermilion. Few, if any, have successfully entered Southern gardens, for these are denizens of bitterly cold mountains, barren deserts, and windswept Patagonian prairies. They loathe the heat, humidity, and horrendously poor soils on which *R. bifida* thrives.

No other Southern bulb can match the fierce vigor, tenacity, and adaptability of the oxblood lily. Whether planted on worn-out gumbo clay or on impoverished sand, the long-necked, black bulbs make themselves at home. The plants send out thick, white roots that contract and pull them deeply into the soil, sometimes as far as eighteen inches down. Safely hidden in the cool earth, they multiply steadily into healthy clumps. Although probably best divided while dormant, they seem to grow along even when disturbed during their winter growing season.

The brilliant crimson flowers appear along with the first autumn rains. During hot weather, blooms last only a few days, so the bulbs are of most value when shaded from strong sun. Since their foliage grows through the winter, oxblood lilies make good woodland companions for lycoris and sternbergias. If used in a sunny border, these vibrant flowers make a happy contrast to the soft gray and lavender of catmint (*Nepeta* ×*faassenii*), and a dramatic complement to the smoky filigrees of bronze fennel (*Foenic-*

Rhodophiala bifida blooming through a groundcover of gray-green clover fern (*Marsilea macropoda*), author's garden.

ulum vulgare 'Rubrum'). Sage-colored leaves of clover fern (*Marsilea macropoda*) and the silvery rosettes of *Yucca pallida* offer other good foils.

Like the old horticultural stocks of lycoris and sternbergias, the oxblood lilies in Southern gardens constitute a special strain. These heirlooms rarely seed, but they do multiply quickly from offsets. New bulblets form in a curious twisting pattern about the mother bulbs. As the oxblood lilies increase, divisions may be passed from garden to garden. In this way these plants have slowly spread across the South.

A few connoisseurs raise a pink oxblood lily, var. *spathacea*, but this color form is likely to remain rare in gardens. The pinks lack the vigor of the reds and seldom offset. They must be reproduced from seed, which is slow growing and doesn't always come true. Even rarer are orange-red types (*Rhodophiala* 'Granatiflora'). Like the pinks, they must be seed grown.

As beautiful and appealing as the pinks and oranges may seem to our mind's eye, they really have far less to offer gardens than the reds. It's not color that's at issue: it's strength and endurance that makes these bulbs special in the first place. The ability to persist and survive counts a great deal. Our gardens are much richer for plants that happily blossom through adversity, like the old red oxblood lily.

The vigorous heirloom strain of *Rhodophiala* seems to be of true Southern origin, for it is unknown to gardeners in Argentina, where the bulbs are native. Although oxblood lilies are distributed widely through the South, they are especially common in the old Germanic communities of central Texas. Their concentration centers on Austin.

During the 1840s central Texas attracted immigrants from southern and western Germany, who came to the fledgling republic in search of political and intellectual freedom. Many were persons of romantic sensibility, with a love for nature and yearnings for an honest, agricultural life. They were captivated by the rugged, oak-covered hills and clear, flowing springs of the new land.

One among them, Peter Henry Oberwetter, took a special interest in the plants that grew on his farm near Comfort, Texas. Oberwetter began collecting the wild rain lilies he found on the hills, and he sent them through the mail to gardeners around the world. During the Civil War, he moved south into Mexico (many German colonists sided with the Union during this conflict, and left Texas to avoid persecution). While in Mexico Oberwetter continued to collect and export bulbs; when the war ended, he moved to Austin, where he lived until about 1915.

During this period Oberwetter introduced oxblood lilies to America, while he sent the native giant prairie lily, *Zephyranthes drummondii*, around the world.

As he cultivated bulbs in Austin, he must have discovered and selected the vigorous *Rhodophiala* strain we now enjoy. His legacy lives on in the oxblood lilies flowering each autumn in countless dooryard gardens throughout the South.

Coconut Lilies

One of the most intriguing bulbous plants of the fall is a curious native lily. If it were taller, it could pass for a foxtail lily (*Eremurus*), but even at its customary height of eighteen inches, it makes a bold upward thrust in the garden. This audacious plant is the coconut lily, *Schoenocaulon drummondii*. Its leaves look like graceful fountains of green grass, and its flowers resemble skinny bottlebrushes.

The almost unpronounceable generic name comes from the Greek *schoinos kaulos* ("rush stem"), which describes the slender aspect of these flowers. *Schoenocaulon drummondii* has dispensed with petals altogether, so the bottlebrush effect comes from the feathery spikes of creamy stamens. These are tipped with fawn-colored anthers dusted in light yellow pollen, and the whole contraption smells delightfully of fresh coconut. This is a very unusual and pleasant fragrance emanating from a thoroughly hardy, unpretentious flower.

Coconut lilies are wildflowers of prairies in southern Texas and northern Mexico, where they appear during September or October, depending on rainfall. When moisture is sufficient, they keep their bright green foliage year-round.

Coconut lilies (*Schoenocaulon drummondii*) flowering on a chalky bank alongside Monterrey sage (*Leucophyllum langmaniae*), author's garden.

In droughty seasons the leaves die down during midsummer. *Schoenocaulon drummondii* thrives on sunny slopes and seems to accept almost any soil. Plantings quickly increase with offsets and self-sown seedlings. The grassy colonies blend nicely with other prairie perennials in a naturalized meadow.

The bulbs of the coconut lily are papery and thin, and they store poorly if allowed to become completely dry. As long as the roots can be replanted within a week or two after digging, *Schoenocaulon drummondii* transplants readily. The best time for division is in early summer.

Autumnal Onions

One of the most charming of all the late bulbs is another native American, the prairie onion, *Allium stellatum*. Despite its pedestrian common name, these graceful flowers possess an air of sophistication. Globular clusters of starry pink blooms are borne on six- to eight-inch stems, each with the sinuous curve of a swan's neck.

Through several weeks in October and November, orchid-tinted blooms gradually expand from the gently nodding buds into a bomb-burst of crowded star-shaped flowers. The pearly blossoms are clear and bright in the crisp sunlight of Indian summer. They provide the ideal complement to falling drifts of tawny autumn leaves.

After blooming, the green, grassy foliage of the onion follows. The flowers usually ripen hard black seeds, which may be planted straight away. If the capsules are left to open on the stems, the tiny seedlings will sprout below to form a green winter lawn. Their foliage dies away with warm weather. In two or three seasons they will begin to flower with their parent bulbs.

Prairie onions grow in moist grasslands from Texas north to Illinois and Minnesota, flowering in late summer in the northern portions of their range. They perform admirably on heavy clay soils, but also adapt to sandy ones. These lovely wildflowers seem indifferent to the heat and humidity of the South, since fair weather prevails by the time the bulbs begin to grow actively.

Another beautiful fall-flowering onion, *Allium thunbergii*, hails from Korea and Japan. This might be guessed from its specific name, which commemorates famed Swedish botanist Carl Peter Thunberg, known for his numerous plant collections from Japan. These were made in 1776 while that country was still largely closed to westerners.

Forming short tufts of slender, grass-green foliage, this handsome foot-tall species produces its rounded, rose-purple umbels in October and November. The summer-growing, deciduous leaves later change to autumnal tints of orange

Allium thunbergii 'Ozawa'. Photo by Lauren S. Ogden.

as the flowers fade. 'Ozawa', a compact selection of *Allium thunbergii* introduced by George Schenk, makes a choice dwarf bulb for foregrounds of borders or woodland edges. 'Alba' is a lovely white variant. In the South these Asian onions thrive in the high, filtered shade of pines, but they also succeed in full sun if offered dependable summer moisture.

Fall Squills

The Chinese squill, another late-blooming bulb from the Far East, is a common heirloom of gardens in the Carolinas. Long grown as *Scilla chinensis*, this feathery, mauve-pink flower has been recently reclassified as *Barnardia scilloides*. In the spring its small, clustering bulbs send up clumps of bright green, grassy foliage, often sprouting in neglected beds and lawns of older gardens, where this Asian meadow flower happily seeds itself. In late summer fifteen-inch spikes of small, clustered blooms join the leaves, looking like lavender-pink versions of the coconut lily.

Naturally distributed through China, Korea, and Japan, *Barnardia scilloides* may be confused in gardens with a superficially similar fall-blooming squill native to Europe and North Africa, *Prospero autumnale*. Better known under its old name, *Scilla autumnalis*, this species is less commonly grown in the South, but is also something of a garden heirloom. It may be distinguished from *B. scilloides* by its light lavender-toned flowers with anthers that are pink or violet rather than yellow.

Chapter 3
🌀 Winter Blooms

WITH THE ENCOURAGEMENT of September rains and open weather through the first weeks of autumn, December often sees blossoms from the paperwhites, *Narcissus papyraceus.* These are the delicate harbingers of a varied race of polyanthus narcissi to follow. Both the common name and the epithet aptly describe the parchment quality and glistening whiteness of these flowers.

At one time *Narcissus papyraceus* was considered a form of *N. tazetta,* but this name is now reserved for narcissi such as the Chinese sacred lily and its near kin (the epithet *tazetta* originates from the Italian for the "little cups," or coronas, of the blossoms, which are centered like espresso mugs in elfin saucers formed by the surrounding petals). Paperwhites and their hybrids were once popularly known as polyanthus narcissi for their multiple clusters of scented blossoms, which appear in groups of four to twenty, on top of hollow, sharp-edged stems.

Paperwhite narcissi were great favorites of flower growers in England and Holland during the 1500s and 1600s. Large numbers of bulbs were introduced to the south of France and the Channel Islands, where they were cultivated to provide winter blooms. In 1629 Parkinson listed ninety different sorts of *Narcissus,* the greater part of which were forms of *N. tazetta* and its relations.

With the development of hardy hybrid daffodils in the nineteenth century, the old multi-flowered narcissi began to drop from grower's lists. Several cold winters combined with Holland's devastation during World War I to finally end the long reign of *Narcissus tazetta.* Except for the paperwhite and a few other types used for winter forcing, the group largely vanished from commercial trade.

It is in the warm regions of the world, the South, California, New Zealand, and Australia, that the old polyanthus varieties persist. Here they may be found adorning humble country dooryards and neglected cemeteries of previous eras. Some are still passed along with their names intact from the 1600s, but more often these oldsters travel under affectionate bynames like 'White Pearl' or seventeen sisters. Many are superb garden plants. For sheer bounty of color, reliable performance, grace, beauty, and longevity, these old multi-flowered narcissi remain unsurpassed.

Paperwhites

Like the autumn-flowering *Narcissus serotinus* and *N. elegans*, paperwhites are natives of stony *terra-rossa* fields around the Mediterranean. As a gardener might apprehend from this, they thrive in mild, sunny regions but prove finicky in frosty areas. *Narcissus papyraceus* is most common in Spain, southern France, and Italy, where it has been cultivated since gardening began. The paperwhite appears to be an old selection rather than a wild form. It may now be found naturalized throughout the warm regions of the world.

Paperwhites usually begin their season in autumn, initiating new roots with the first rains in September. Between cold blasts from northers, they flower sporadically from late November through February. Temperatures below 20°F occasionally damage these winter blooms, and if the mercury falls below 10°F, their grayish green foliage may be nipped. Nevertheless, they seem to recover from these disasters, annually contributing plentiful flowers to gardens throughout the South.

The blossoms of paperwhites have a translucent quality that makes the most of low-angled winter light, and their small cups issue a distinctive, penetrating fragrance. Maybe so musky and powerful as to be nauseating, it is nevertheless one of the scents whose very essence connotes winter. Even meager stems of paperwhites make fine flowers for cutting or garden adornment.

The major fault of most paperwhites is a tendency to grow shallowly and to

Paperwhites, *Narcissus papyraceus*.

An heirloom tazetta sold as 'White Pearl'.
Photo by Lauren S. Ogden.

split and multiply to excess, thereby reducing bloom. This problem is typical also of several related *Narcissus tazetta* cultivars and of *N. panizzianus*, a miniature species formerly known as 'Paperwhite Minor', with tiny, white blossoms and silvery, channeled foliage. To assure bloom, the matted bulbs of these narcissi should be divided every other year, then reset at depths of four to six inches. This encourages bulbs to enlarge and improves subsequent flowering.

There is a strain of paperwhite in certain gardens in the South that omits this fault, flowering reliably from each bulb, increasing slowly but steadily without undue splitting. It produces lavish clumps of gray-green leaves along with its flowers, coming into bloom first around Christmas and often repeating in a second wave four to six weeks later. The individual flowers of this strain have a more rounded and slightly cupped appearance than in most paperwhites. This heirloom may be seen blooming in older neighborhoods, where the thrifty clumps distinguish themselves by their prolific clusters of alabaster blooms.

Nurseries offer several paperwhite selections developed in the 1970s in Bet Daga, Israel. Under the direction of Herut Yahel, the Volcani Institute introduced 'Ziva', 'Jerusalem', and 'Galilee'. These have superior flower size and substance, but were bred primarily for forcing in pots. In the most popular clone, 'Ziva', the foliage follows, rather than accompanies the blooms, making for a dramatic display, but also shortening the time the bulbs have to replenish themselves in the garden. 'Galilee' seems most like the heirloom types in the South and has been the most successful performer in test gardens established by the Florida Daffodil Society.

Chinese Sacred Lilies

Hurricanes periodically collide with the maze of bays, lagoons, and barrier islands lining the Gulf and Atlantic coasts, their stormy tides inevitably crashing over dunes and levees to tear at homes built foolishly near the waters. They often leave little but rows of wooden pilings projecting through the sand. Early in January the empty fields that once held houses fill with the sweet, exotic perfume of Chinese sacred lilies (*Narcissus tazetta* subsp. *lacticolor*) persisting among the wreckage.

The Chinese sacred lily, or 'Grand Emperor', a first cousin of the paperwhite, is similarly valued for forcing. The fragrance of the blooms is distinctive: a heady aroma suggestive of spiced oranges. Although this narcissus occurs as a waif along the coasts of China and Japan, students of narcissi believe the variety originated in the Mediterranean. Presumably, Middle Eastern traders brought these bulbs to China centuries ago. They are held in high regard in the Orient, where the fragrant flowers are picked as decorations for winter festivals. In Japan fishermen set the large round bulbs with hooks as lures to capture curious octopus.

Everything about this narcissus conveys exuberance. Its sizeable blossoms appear in umbels of five to twelve or more. The broad, white petals are accented by substantial orange cups. Added to these distinctive blossoms are unusually lush, pale green leaves and the vigorous constitution of a true subtropical. Here is a narcissus suitable for underplanting a grove of palms.

The same coastal gardens that house the Chinese sacred lily often include its cousin, *Narcissus tazetta* subsp. *lacticolor* 'Romanus'. This ancient selection is better known by its English name, double Roman. 'Romanus' looks exactly like the Chinese sacred lily in all its characters, save the flowers, which are fully double and extraordinarily scented. In a contest of fragrance the double Roman outclasses all competition, for its many-petaled blooms seem to carry a double dosage of sweet aroma. A slightly different double-flowered tazetta appears occasionally on lists as 'Constantinople'.

These tender narcissi make fine garden subjects, but their January flowering season puts them at risk from cold. Only in regions where winter lows remain faithfully above 20°F will flowers appear dependably. In the South this limits them to gardens south of a line drawn from Austin, Texas, to Charleston, South Carolina. Elsewhere they may be grown in pots for indoor decoration.

As with all bulbs, the verdant foliage of these narcissi feeds flowers for the next season and should be left in place to yellow naturally in late April. Many types of fading bulbs may be hidden under the leaves of later-blooming perennials, but these rampant narcissi are not so easily disguised, and it is sometimes a better course to make a feature of the yellowing foliage. Their fading ochre leaves combine strikingly with vibrant April blooms like Byzantine gladiolus and will mix satisfactorily with the gossamer flowers and straw-toned blades of Mexican feathergrass (*Nassella tenuissima*).

Like their paperwhite allies, the single and double forms of these narcissi incline to overmultiplication. The miniature 'Canaliculatus' of the trade, in effect a tiny version of the Chinese sacred lily, is also notorious in this respect. The simplest solution for gardeners seems to be to divide and reset bulbs every other year. As a dividend, this provides a welcome opportunity to share offsets with other lovers of old flowers.

The Golden Sun

The brilliant yellow, orange-cupped *Narcissus aureus*, best known in its selection 'Soleil d'Or', is another old garden narcissus that contributes glowing blooms and sweet fragrances each winter, just as it has for centuries. As with paperwhites and Chinese sacred lilies, the bulb trade offers this antique for winter forcing. Few bulbous flowers are more bright or cheerful.

'Soleil d'Or' resembles the Chinese sacred lily in its fruity fragrance, its light green foliage, and its deep orangey cups, or coronas. However, its starry petals are clear, lemony yellow. This gives the blossoms a special glow as they appear in early January.

'Soleil d'Or' suffers from the same frost tenderness as its relations but, unfortunately, lacks their vigor. A virus may be the culprit, for a number of the old narcissi show the telltale streaking in their foliage that indicates infection. Such diseases are seldom lethal, but they rob the strength and garden value of any plants infected. Fortunately, the modern technique of tissue culture or plant cloning enables growers to eliminate viruses from infected plants. Nurseries now offer certified virus-free stocks of 'Soleil d'Or'.

Although not as brilliant in color, several yellowish tazettas developed by the Volcani Institute may also help sidestep disease problems. 'Bethlehem' ('Nony') and 'Nazareth' ('Yael') are selections with soft yellow petals and deeper golden cups. 'Israel' ('Omri') opens creamy yellow, but fades to look more like the Chinese sacred lily. All flower in January, and appear to need the same garden treatment as their older relations.

Monarques

Along Mediterranean shorelines paperwhites and Chinese sacred lilies often occur together. Although closely related, they maintain separate populations because their genetic structures isolate them from one another. The paperwhite has a standard diploid (double) set of chromosomes. Its large cousin inherits a tetraploid (quadruple) complement. This accounts for the tremendous vigor of the Chinese sacred lily, and also suggests that hybrids between the two varieties will be sterile mules with a triploid set of genes. As we have already seen, such plants often make fine garden flowers.

Crosses between *Narcissus tazetta* and *N. papyraceus* have, in fact, occurred, and several have been cultivated since the 1600s. These mules possess a number of distinctive characters making them unlike either parent. Instead of gray-green leaves like paperwhites, or fountains of light green foliage like Chinese sacred lilies, these hybrids often produce lush groups of dark green leaves. Their foliage and flowers emerge later and withstand more cold than their parents. In the South they are among the most cherished garden heirlooms.

The first to bloom is a striking plant with slender petals the color of old linen and small citron cups. If the winter is mild, as is often the case, dark green leaves emerge in November and bear flowering stems around the first of February. The effect of the starry blossoms with their cheerful yellow cups is charming, especially when the narcissi are growing around an old homestead nestled under pines.

In early literature this plant is called 'Minor Monarque', but those who prefer Latin refer to it as *Narcissus italicus*. Some botanists regard this as a natural species, rather than a hybrid. It is one of the most distinctive types, and will not likely be confused with other hybrid tazettas.

The confusion comes with a famous seventeenth-century cultivar known as 'Grand Monarque'. As with other horticultural antiques, it is nowadays impossible for anyone to say with certainty to which plant this old name belongs. That hasn't stopped people from trying.

Various plants passing under the name 'Grand Monarque' have become the subjects of discussion among narcissus fanciers. The experts (Californians, of course) are certain the bulbs Southerners know as 'Grand Monarque' are imposters. The "real" 'Grand Monarque', we are told, occurs only in old California gardens. Southern flowers purportedly belong to another ancient selection, 'Grand Primo'. It is probably best here to heed the advice of Hilaire Belloc: "Oh let us never, never doubt / What nobody is sure about."

January flowers of *Narcissus italicus* in an abandoned Gulf Coast garden.

Grand Primo (Grand Monarque)

Certainly no finer flowering bulbs are available for Southerners than the old narcissi now known as 'Grand Primo'. They are by far the most vigorous, persistent, and floriferous members of their genus. Unlike their tender cousins, these oldsters continue flowering indefinitely, never requiring division or resetting. Since they emerge and bloom late in the season (late February or early March), they avoid the usual hazards of winter freezes.

'Grand Primo' is so extraordinarily tough that it thrives even on the heaviest clays. This narcissus also persists and increases in the dry climates of the Southwest. In Texas it is the most common of the old narcissi, and may be seen gracing many nineteenth-century gardens.

Although casual observers dismiss these old plantings as mere paperwhites, the leaves and flowers of 'Grand Primo' have several distinctive characters. The blossoms open with a cream color instead of white, and the bowl-shaped cups are light yellow. These colors are transitory, fading as the flowers age, so that white and yellowish blooms may appear on the same clump. Some plants seem to hold colors better than others, and it's likely that several different strains are lurking in gardens.

French growers once listed a 'Grand Primo Citronière', and a plant matching descriptions of this variety seems to be common in old Southern gardens. Compared to typical 'Grand Primo', this narcissus is one-third shorter, with slender, more tapered foliage and cups distinctively lemon-yellow on opening. The fragrance of this flower is less than ideal, with perhaps too much of the paperwhite's musky overtones. E. A. Bowles said that a prolonged sniff of 'Grand Primo Citronière' would draw out "a scent like that of soot."

In contrast, the fragrance of typical 'Grand Primo' is pleasantly sweet and jasminelike, with none of the over-

Typical strains of *Narcissus tazetta* 'Grand Primo' have light yellow cups that quickly fade to ivory.

Narcissus tazetta 'Grand Primo Citronière' has slender leaves and brighter yellow coronas.

powering qualities of paperwhites. The creamy blooms appear in fat, rounded clusters of eleven to sixteen. These sit atop stiff green stems that display the blossoms to better advantage than in any other garden narcissus. The dark green foliage affords the perfect complement to the abundant groups of pearly flowers.

A narcissus offered in the trade as 'Scilly White' seems very close to 'Grand Primo', but has less precise flowers with more of the thin-textured quality of paperwhites. It is otherwise sturdy and worthwhile as a garden plant and might easily be confused with 'Grand Primo' if used in the same planting. 'White Pearl' and 'Early Pearl' also resemble these but tend to flower earlier. The latter also splits and multiplies excessively, so is less desirable as a garden plant.

Finally, the bulb Californians call 'Grand Monarque' has proven decidedly un-grand in the South, as it often fails to bloom. When it does flower, it may have as many as twenty-two blossoms to a stem. These differ from 'Grand Primo' in having more yellow in the coronas. The cups also have deeper rims and are less spreading than 'Grand Primo'. In any case, this 'Grand Monarque' seldom persists in Southern gardens for more than a few seasons.

Erlicheer

Although 'Grand Primo' is now rather unusual in the bulb trade, the double-flowered 'Erlicheer' has become common. This variety was discovered in New

Zealand, where 'Grand Primo', 'White Pearl', and other old tazettas are still raised as cut flowers. 'Erlicheer' has the same vigor and good green foliage as 'Grand Primo', but bears tightly clustered balls of double blooms. These globular blooms are less versatile in the landscape than 'Grand Primo', but appear to be equally permanent.

'Erlicheer' has become a standard item for Dutch growers, who market it as a novelty narcissus for summer bedding. They do this because Holland lacks sufficient heat to properly ripen these Mediterranean bulbs. The Dutch plant them out in the spring, then dig them in the fall and store them in warm, dry rooms over winter. This effectively simulates a summer baking, reversing the season for these narcissi. When these bulbs, marketed as 'Summer Cheer', are planted in Southern gardens they require several seasons of adjustment before blooming on schedule in early March.

Avalanche (Compressus)

One of the places where tazettas retain some of their former importance is a small group of islands off the southwest coast of England called the Isles of Scilly. Like the Channel Islands, the Isles of Scilly benefit from the warm waters of the Gulf Stream and have a perpetually mild climate. Since Elizabethan times they have been known as a haven for winter flowers.

Tresco is one of these isles, famous for its abbey and gardens. While walking the island one fortunate day, the manager of the estates, T. Dorrien-Smith, discovered an old narcissus growing in a rocky crag along the seashore. The fields above had once been used to raise flowers, and it appeared that the old bulb must have tumbled down the cliff toward the sea. Dorrien-Smith retrieved the bulbs and registered this flower in 1955 as 'Avalanche', a nickname long used for these flowers by local islanders.

This is a fine narcissus with snowy petals and a wide lemony cup. It is probably one of the three hundred historic tazetta narcissi listed by Dutch nurseries during the nineteenth century—which of them, it will never be known for sure. In old Southern gardens, similar yellow-centered narcissi are sometimes called seventeen sisters, and nurseries often use this common name as an alternate for 'Avalanche'. Narcissus fanciers have also suggested that this clone may be the same as 'Compressus', another antique florist variety; it may be met under this name on some nursery lists.

For Southerners 'Avalanche' offers all the gaiety of the true 'Grand Monarque' on a thriftier, more robust plant. The big groups of twenty flowers are borne on strong eighteen-inch stems accompanied by good green foliage. As with 'Grand

Narcissus tazetta 'Avalanche'.

Primo', flowering comes in late February or early March. One could hardly wish for a more pleasant harbinger of winter's demise.

Hoop Petticoats

One of the real garden opportunities available to Southerners comes from an odd group of dwarf narcissi native to the hills and mountains of the western Mediterranean. These curiously designed flowers might be described as all cup and no petals, for that is the impression they give as they rise among their grassy winter foliage. The widely flaring blooms are known as hoop petticoats for their resemblance to nineteenth-century hoop skirts. The petals of the impish flowers form narrow streamers, which fly out to form tiny stars. Their inflated cups reveal a projecting style and six stamens, inclined downward like a little habranthus.

Although these elfin blooms hardly sound like the stuff of garden drama, certain hoop petticoats offer Southerners some of the most likely material for a scene worthy of an exclaiming Wordsworth. These miniatures flower over a tremendously long season and prosper mightily on acid sands or reddish clays. Although this "host of golden daffodils" is a tiny one, few narcissi are so prolific in warm climates.

The varied hoop petticoats, or, as Haworth named them, *Corbularia*, differ widely in shape and size, and in color from white to deep gold. They seem to be a rapidly evolving section of genus *Narcissus*, with headquarters in Spain and across the Mediterranean in North Africa. Modern taxonomies group most of yellow and gold forms under the principal species, *N. bulbocodium*, with a few white or cream-colored types placed under *N. cantabricus*. In the South, the yellowish forms may be expected to bloom from midwinter to spring, the whitish types, in late fall or early winter.

In a normal Southern winter, if there is such a thing, periodic cold waves sweep over the countryside, with intermittent mild weather filling the days between. It takes sustained temperatures below 10°F to damage the hoop petticoat blossoms, which emerge during the mild spells. It takes below 0°F weather to damage their foliage.

The earliest blooming of these miniatures are forms of *Narcissus cantabricus*. This transparent, pearly white blossom is native to both sides of the Strait of Gibraltar, and occurs in several forms. Along with Barbary apes and other bits of regional natural history, this bulbous flower shows that Europe and Africa were once joined together.

The most vigorous form of this species is var. *foliosus*, the leafy Cantabrian narcissus. Along with the pale yellowish *Narcissus romieuxii*, this late fall bloomer has given rise to a series of quaint hybrids introduced around 1950 by Douglas Blanchard, the most famous of which are 'Jessamy', 'Taffeta', and 'Nylon'. In addition to named clones from this cross, nurseries often sell hybrid siblings together as a strain. All have creamy blooms and begin flowering in late November, often continuing until Christmas. Their sweetly fragrant, crepe-textured blooms appear among generous crops of green, threadlike leaves.

The pale yellow *Narcissus bulbocodium* var. *tenuifolius* flowers during the same season as these hybrids. Although attractive and prolific, the small bulbs are less free-flowering than some later varieties. They should be reset periodically in fresh ground to keep them sized up and blooming.

In early January the gossamer yellow *Narcissus romieuxii* comes to flower. This is sometimes placed as a variety of *N. bulbocodium*, but it differs in its sulfury blooms and exerted stamens and style. It comes from the Atlas Mountains in Morocco, where it grows in dry scrub under cedars and oaks. In the South these luminous, waxen blooms appear during the first warm spells of the new year. 'Julia Jane' is an attractive cultivar with a flat, ruffled corona.

With the arrival of spring in late February or March, these miniatures shade more and more toward gold. *Narcissus bulbocodium* var. *citrinus* offers two-inch-long, primrose-yellow blooms, with heavily fluted, flared cups. Some shelter from wind or rain will be appreciated by these oversized blossoms.

Next to flower is the distinctive *Narcissus bulbocodium* var. *obesus*, the portly bulbocodium. Most *N. bulbocodium* variants offer copious tufts of slender foliage, true to their epithet, which means "bulb wool." *Obesus* charts a different course with thick, prostrate rosettes sprawled on the ground like little starfish. The lemony colored and scented blooms appear after the season of northers on fat spears, which rise between the leaves. In this variety there are often a few extra petals beyond the normal six, and each bears a slender green stripe down its backside. Unlike most *N. bulbocodium* varieties, *obesus* enjoys calcareous soils.

The most abundant and vigorous of all the hoop petticoats, *Narcissus bulbocodium* var. *conspicuus*, finishes the flowering season in late March or April. This showy type is a good doer in the South and among the easiest to find on nursery lists. It is truly gold in color and makes a superb bulb for naturalizing in rough grass or, if planted in groups in a raised rockery, a bright complement to spreading blue mounds of Dalmatian bluebells (*Campanula portenschlagiana*) or *Phlox subulata* 'Emerald Blue'.

This one has been in gardens for a long time and is probably the form Jefferson had at Monticello. There are several different stocks blooming at varying seasons, so it's a variety worth acquiring more than once. A clone introduced from Holland in the 1990s, 'Golden Bells' at first seems indistinguishable from ordinary seedlings of var. *conspicuus*, but established plants regularly produce five, and sometimes as many as ten, pleated yellow flowers from each tiny bulb.

Hoop petticoat daffodils (*Narcissus bulbocodium* var. *conspicuus*) naturalized in a rough lawn with spring starflowers (*Ipheion uniflorum*) and white muscari.

These appear later than in most strains, usually not until April. Like all the hoop petticoats, these tiny bulbs are remarkably tough and long-lived on acid red clay or sandy ground.

Lent Lilies

February in the South is a season of false promises. Unsuspecting blossoms are lured out during warm spells, only to be brutally reproached with the blue winds of northers. Strangely enough, there are certain plants whose peculiar demeanor suits them to this chancy weather. None is more welcome in gardens than the wild trumpet daffodil, or Lent lily, *Narcissus pseudonarcissus*.

These wildlings are the earliest flowering of their race, usually appearing at the beginning of February. Perhaps because of the coldness of the season, the stems never reach as high as the daffodils that follow. The entire plant generally stays only six to eight inches tall.

Despite this low stature, the blooms reach a respectable two to three inches in length. These proportions give the plants the charming aspect of alpine miniatures. Pale yellow, dog-eared petals frame the deeper yellow trumpets.

The Lent lily is a wild European daffodil introduced to the South by early settlers. It has since spread far and wide in gardens, and has seeded and naturalized in fields and along roadsides. Although much like modern daffodils in construction, these wildflowers have a more relaxed appearance than their pedigreed descendants.

Daffodils are strangely built flowers, with a unique apparatus for attracting pollinators and protecting pollen and nectar. The value of this becomes immediately apparent with an early flower like the Lent lily. All you need do is stand for a moment in a cold February sleet storm to appreciate the advantage of the trumpet-shaped

Lent lilies (*Narcissus pseudonarcissus*) flowering in February along a Mississippi roadside.

coronas, which provide shelter to pollen and to the brave bees and other insects who venture out to visit the blossoms.

These wild daffodils are a less certain source of garden color than their large brethren, but they offer one of the surest paths to enchantment. If you wish to gaze into their small windblown trumpets, you must kneel down in their presence. If you want to smell their sweet fragrance on the frosty morning air, you must warm a blossom in your hands.

Silver Bells

Some of the old gardens in the South include a beautiful cousin of the Lent lily with nodding milky blooms. By tradition, gardeners who have them call these graceful flowers silver bells. Parkinson knew these bulbs as *Narcissus moschatus*, the "lesser Spanish daffodil." Peter Barre listed them in his 1884 catalog as *N. cernuus*, the "drooping daffodil." They are supposed to have originally come from the Spanish Pyrenees.

These pale daffodils hang their heads the entire time they are in flower, with ghostly twisting petals swirling around the pearly trumpets. They usually flower early in February, in company with several erect, broad, gray leaves.

On poor, sandy soils, these elegant flowers are entirely permanent, but slow of increase. On heavy clays they are apt to vanish, and they dislike heavy feeding. These bulbs are best left to their own devices on a patch of ground where the gardener will not meddle in their affairs.

Although hardly showstopping in size or quantity of bloom, the quietly beautiful flowers are great treasures. Since many of the modern white daffodils fare poorly in the South, heirlooms such as these are doubly valuable for early color. The bulbs of the silver bells are not common in the trade, but they may sometimes be had from generous gardeners, or from dealers in the rarer old narcissi. A nineteenth-century hybrid from this species, 'W. P. Milner' is easier to find and less expensive. It makes a small, early-blooming, pale yellow flower reminiscent of the Lent lily, but with the twisting, nodding grace of *Narcissus moschatus*. Both this and *N. moschatus* perform best in the cooler, more temperate parts of the upper South.

Another winter-flowering trumpet is a standard-sized daffodil with slightly twisted, medium yellow petals and an irregularly ruffled corona shaded gold at its widely flared tip. Introduced in 1943, 'Rijnveld's Early Sensation' recalls the character of the wild Spanish trumpet, *Narcissus hispanicus*, its probable parent. Although these blooms have a coarse appearance in comparison to many modern daffodil cultivars, they appear in January when they can be most appreciated and when generally cool temperatures prolong their bloom for several weeks. 'Rijnveld's Early Sensation' is a better performer in the South than most trumpets and often settles in as a permanent resident on well-drained sandy or loamy soils. The short-statured Tenby daffodil, *N. obvallaris*, is another early trumpet successful in some Southern gardens. It shows much of the wild character of the Lent lily, but on an all-gold flower.

Tommies

Charm is a property of the crocus, and for many of the same reasons as seen in the early daffodils. Miniature stature combines with oversized blossoms to invite us, and the bees, down for inspection. Sadly, it's real a challenge to find early crocuses that persist in the South for more than a season.

Crocus sieberi, *C. biflorus*, and cultivars and hybrids of *C. chrysanthus* can be successful in the middle and upper South, but these do not last near the Gulf. Coming in many shades of yellow, gold, cream, and lavender, these species perform best if given raised positions with fast drainage.

The same range of adaptation applies to the old cloth of gold, *Crocus angustifolius* (*C. susianus*) and the little crocuses called "gold bunch" by the trade (*C. ancyrensis*). These bear thick clusters of brown-feathered, golden blossoms in early February.

The old 'Dutch Yellow' crocus is commonly planted in mixes with large purple and white forms of the Alpine *Crocus vernus*. This most popular of the yellows is an ancient, sterile hybrid between the cloth of gold crocus and the eastern Mediterranean *C. flavus* (*C. aureus*). It frequently persists in Southern gardens long after the purples and whites have failed.

Mediterranean species like *Crocus corsicus* would seem to be good bets, but have not been widely reported in the South. The Italian crocus, *C. imperati*, has been a disappointment for those who have tried it. Despite its southerly pedigree, this species performs well in the northeastern United States, and any such accomplishment generally portends failure in warm climates. Apparently, it naturally grows at high elevations.

The one early crocus that regularly makes itself at home in the South is *Crocus tommasinianus*, a species from the stony limestone hills of Serbia, Bosnia, and Dalmatia. Perhaps in rebellion to its tongue-twisting Latin name, gardeners have dubbed these little blossoms Tommies.

It's a joy to know that at least this species finds Southern gardens congenial. Its amethyst flowers appear over a long season, from mid-January to early March. The reddish violet blooms, silver-gray in bud, make charming pools of

The buds of *Crocus tommasinianus*, naturalized in a lawn, open and close in response to winter sun.

Pale lavender forms of *Crocus tommasinianus* light up late winter borders. Photo by Lauren S. Ogden.

color as they multiply in ever-widening patches. Silver stripes accent the grassy, green foliage which rises to accompany the blooms in early March.

Carolina gardener Elizabeth Lawrence described the captivating movement of the Tommies in response to fickle Southern weather: "The flickering color is delightful in the pale sunlight of late winter and early spring, and as soon as the sun stops shining the petals are furled again into thin silver spears."

There are a few worthwhile color variations of *Crocus tommasinianus*, the most common of which is 'Ruby Giant'. This seems to offer all the vigor and adaptability of the species and has somewhat larger, more purplish blooms. 'Whitewell Purple' offers similar reddish purple blossoms on clumping plants. 'Roseus' and 'Lilac Beauty' are selections with silvered rosy and pale lilac blooms, respectively. 'Barr's Purple' is a richly colored violet with a gray exterior; 'Pictus' is deep violet with white throats and darker tips. 'Albus' is pure white. These selections of *C. tommasinianus* make ideal groupings for rock gardens, raised beds, crevices between stepping-stones, and other niches where the flowers can be appreciated close up. For more general garden purposes and naturalizing in lawns the common, light lavender seedling strains of the species remain unsurpassed, with just the right pallid tones to catch late winter sunrays.

Algerian Iris

The famous Algerian iris (*Iris unguicularis*) is another tuberous flower beloved for late autumn and winter blossoms. This Mediterranean native doesn't mind part shade, or even the drought and gloom beneath evergreen live oaks, but can be finicky about blossoming where winter temperatures regularly fall below 0°F. When coaxed to settle down in a well-drained position, the tough rhizomes of these evergreen irises send up short stems bearing a succession of frail, beardless blossoms from November to March. These sit down amid clumps of narrow, strappy, gray-green foliage and beg to be picked, although their short stems (actually the long tubes of the blossoms) suit them more for bowls than vases. A sweet, honeylike fragrance becomes noticeable on mild days or when blooms are brought into a warm room.

Iris unguicularis.

These delicate two- to three-inch blossoms are of typical iris form, feathered with yellow stripings at the haft. They come in shades of limpid purple, pale lavender, white, or, rarely, pale pink. As they are true flowers of frost, Algerian irises receive universal praise from gardeners, who are often surprised by the sporadic midwinter blooms. These seem to appear magically, expanding from the short buds almost overnight.

Low-angled winter light causes the translucent blossoms to fluoresce, yet these pale irises seem at their luminous best when winter weather is all gloom and fog. The blossoms come over a long season, with established clumps producing hundreds of flowers in periodic crops over the winter. Nevertheless, these irises are not the obvious color of drive-by suburban flowerbeds. They are better appreciated close up. In most forms the six-inch-tall blooms remain partly obscured by eighteen-inch-tall leaves. A variation of the species from southern Greece, *Iris unguicularis* subsp. *cretensis* produces four- to five-inch grassy foliage so that its large, deep violet flowers open above the leaves.

During summer *Iris unguicularis* withstands any amount of drought, thriving in the same situations that suit rosemary, but its leathery foliage may eventually become untidy. As with evergreen perennials like *Aspidistra*, dead or broken leaves need to be raked out of the clumps in early fall to prepare for the winter blooming season. The creeping rhizomes of *I. unguicularis* divide most readily in autumn when their wiry roots are white and active. Plants may sulk for months if disturbed at other seasons.

Several selections of this species are cultivated in English gardens. 'Mary Barnard' is one of the most floriferous, with slightly narrower leaves than typical plants and rich purple flowers that appear from early in November through March. 'Walter Butt' is a beautiful, large, grayed lavender form with neatly contrasted feathery markings over yellow crests, strong fragrance, and stiffly upright leaves. 'Marondera', a vigorous, light blue introduction from a Zimbabwe garden, offers handsome foliage and an unusually long season of bloom stretching from late October into April.

Iris lazica, an ally of *I. unguicularis* from the region around the Black Sea, should also succeed in the South. Preferring positions with partial shade, this species produces clumps of waxy, dark green leaves that bear heavily veined, purplish blue flowers in spring. Since it flowers later, *I. lazica* might be suitable for regions *I. unguicularis* finds unacceptably cold.

Roman Hyacinths

The wild forms of the hyacinth are surprisingly graceful flowers when compared to their highly bred, stiffly upright descendants. Most people wouldn't even recognize the old varieties as belonging to the same species. It's not until the sweet fragrance of the bell-shaped blossoms wafts through the air that the relationship becomes apparent. The earliest and most abundant of the hyacinths in the South is the French-Roman; a distinct white form of the common hyacinth (*Hyacinthus orientalis*), modern botanists recognize it as var. *albulus*.

Although some sources say these flowers originated in Greece, their princi-

French-Roman hyacinths (*Hyacinthus orientalis* var. *albulus*) flowering in late winter.

pal habitat today is southern France. In this region hyacinths have long played a role in the perfume industry, and were formerly exported widely for winter forcing. In addition to the common white French-Roman, there are pink and blue selections (Parisian hyacinths), which became popular in the nineteenth century.

Several of these old flowers have found their way to Southern gardens. The white form, especially, offers blossoms during the bleakest weeks of winter. The small, globular bulbs grow shallowly and multiply into thrifty patches topped with waxy, bright green leaves. Around the first of January these begin to produce slender spikes of pendant flowers. The pristine white blossoms are scattered loosely around the stems, and seem quite unlike the crowded, garishly colored mops of hybrid hyacinths.

What these graceful flowers lack in the bold form of their better known cousins, they make up for in generosity. Even small bulbs produce several spikes from between the whorled leaves. These appear in succession for six weeks or more, so that most clumps remain in flower from January through March. It takes a really large planting to get much impact from the small blooms, but the combination of fresh green leaves and snowy blossoms offers some of the liveliest of winter scenery. Their sweet, spicy fragrance is unsurpassable.

In mid-February, as the white French-Roman hyacinths peak, their blue-flowered cousins are just beginning. These old garden plants have dusky violet flowers and rather dark green leaves. This makes them difficult to discern from a distance. It's quite possible to smell these fragrant flowers before you see them. They commonly naturalize in wide mats on the front lawns of old Southern homes.

Pink Roman hyacinths are more rare, but there is a double pink variety found in some parts. Both forms are very old flowers. Gerard described both single and double hyacinths in his *Herball* (1597), reporting that the plants had been brought from the East. The Turks probably grew them for several centuries before Gerard made their acquaintance.

The single white French-Roman hyacinths are still popular in the bulb trade and command a good price, as Europeans value them for forcing even today. Blue and pink "Roman" hyacinths from commercial sources appear slightly different from the strains in old gardens, but they make worthwhile showings and seem permanent. A multi-flowering series of hyacinths, 'White Festival', 'Pink Festival', and 'Blue Festival', approximates the look of the old Roman hyacinths, but flowers later than older types.

Some of the earlier-blooming Dutch hyacinths will also settle into garden life if offered an opportunity. Their blossoms soon revert and look much like the wild Roman hyacinths. Louise Beebe Wilder described this transition in her classic treatise, *Adventures with Hardy Bulbs*: "These stout fellows, when left in the ground for several years with no notice taken of them until their starched pride is somewhat subdued, acquire a slender grace and modesty that is most becoming to them, and may then take their place among other spring bulbs."

Spring Starflowers

The same benignly neglected lawns that afford homes for the antique hyacinths often hold patches of grassy gray-green foliage. After the new year, any brief spell of sunny weather will coax these leafy clumps into bloom. The flowers are a cheerful pale blue and resemble simple six-pointed stars. Once they begin to appear, blossoms continue steadily onward through March.

These lovely blue flowers present a perennial mystery for gardeners who discover them in the grass. They seem to have created consternation for botanists as well. The usual questions are "What are they?" and "Where did they come from?" Everyone agrees the bulbs originated from Argentina and Uruguay, but that's as far as it goes.

Botanists have been shuffling these poor flowers back and forth for years. Their Latin names have included *Triteleia*, *Tristagma*, *Nothoscordum*, *Brodiaea*,

Spring starflowers (*Ipheion uniflorum*) naturalized on a lawn. Photo by Lauren S. Ogden.

Milla, *Beauverdia*, and *Leucocoryne*. Currently, they are resting under the title *Ipheion uniflorum*.

Although their short stature gives these little plants a crocuslike personality, all one need do is lightly bruise the foliage to reveal their true affinity, garlic. *Ipheion uniflorum* has the same acrid-smelling juice in its leaves as a wild onion. It's surprising that some botanist hasn't placed it in *Allium*.

Unlike *Allium* the inch-wide blooms of *Ipheion uniflorum* appear singly, one to a stem. The bulbs multiply at an amazingly rapid pace by offsets, seed, and droopers (short runners that form bulbs at their ends). These South Americans readily naturalize on almost any soil.

Although *Ipheion uniflorum* has no dislike of lime, on alkaline ground the bulbs should be planted where they will receive little summer water. This helps discourage rotting while the bulbs are dormant. On acid soils the natural chemistry discourages such problems, so they may be watered freely.

'Wisley Blue' is a supposedly improved selection of *Ipheion uniflorum* that seems hardly different from the old pale lilac types in Southern lawns. 'Froyle Mill' is more distinctive. Darker and earlier flowering than other clones, its rich purplish blue blossoms make it especially choice. 'Charlotte Bishop' is a recent selection with mauve-pink blossoms. 'White Star' and 'Alba' are near-white-flowered forms.

Jose Alberto Castillo of Buenos Aires, Argentina, has introduced several wild South American ipheions, including a lovely, oversized, white-flowered variety now offered by nurseries as 'Alberto Castillo'. These snowy, trumpet-shaped blooms are carried on strong stems among grayish leaves. 'Alberto Castillo' seems distinct enough from typical forms of *Ipheion uniflorum* to warrant recognition as a variety or even as a separate species. It shows much promise for Southern gardens. The white-flowered *I. sessile*, a smaller species from Argentina and Uruguay, bears pointed segments striped darker on the midrib and offers blooms over several weeks from late fall through winter.

Another distinctive ipheion, 'Rolf Fiedler', is a stoloniferous variety from northeastern Uruguay believed to be a selection of *Ipheion peregrinans* or, perhaps, an undescribed species. Nurseries usually list it as a form of *I. uniflo-*

Ipheion sp. 'Rolf Fiedler'. Photo by Lauren S. Ogden.

rum and occasionally as *I. pedunculata*. Whatever its ultimate name, 'Rolf Fiedler' is a show plant for Southern gardens, with luscious, cobalt-blue flowers bearing rounded, overlapping petals in the midst of flattened, pale green leaves. The spreading stolons help this plant quickly develop sizable clumps in the garden. Although not as cold hardy as most forms of *I. uniflorum*, 'Rolf Fiedler' seems to have little trouble with Southern winters. The remarkable flowers simply close and nod during cold spells, remaining undamaged with freezing temperatures to 20°F.

Windflowers

Like rain lilies, the little blooms of anemones have a long-standing association with the wind. Pliny remarked that they never opened, save when winter mistrals blew.

It's stirring to see a barren field dotted with these early blossoms. The pale, limpid blooms rest barely inches above the ground, so the earth itself appears to flower. Petals seem to open and close in concert with the shadows of each passing cloud. Although the winter grass may remain cheerless and dun, the lively flowers offer vibrant, living mirrors to the alabaster and azure of the heavens.

Botanists recognize anemones as inefficient flowers with redundant structures of ancient design. Along with waterlilies, magnolias, and other primitive blossoms, these plants display blooms which center around a cone-shaped reproductive organ composed of many individual stamens and pistils. True petals are absent or greatly reduced in *Anemone*; the brightly colored sepals are what we see instead.

After pollination, the central mass of the flowers ripens into a compact dome of dry, feathery fruits. These achenes disperse with the winds that arrive in early summer. The feathery seed heads recall the powder puffs of virgin's bower (*Clematis*), which also belongs to this ancient, peculiar family.

The tubers of most anemones appear brown and misshapen. They look quite lifeless after drying out during storage. An overnight soaking in fresh water before planting in autumn will restore plumpness and vitality. Even after this treatment, it is often difficult to discern the top of the root from the bottom. Fortunately, there will be no setback to plants if the tubers are accidentally placed upside down.

From Alabama westward into Texas the most familiar native windflower is *Anemone heterophylla*. Its white, pink, or blue daisy-shaped flowers appear singly above whorls of narrow, filigreed bracts. The parsleylike leaves are dark purple on their undersides and arise directly form the tubers. The foliage stands out prominently in dormant lawns, where it is often considered weedy. Nevertheless, when allowed to naturalize on rockeries or in unmown grass, these little wildflowers can be thoroughly charming. They thrive especially on heavy clay or limestone soils, ranging along the Gulf and northward in prairies and meadows.

Anemone heterophylla yields a succession of blooms from each tuber, and has a long flowering season from February through April. Since flowers come only one or two at a time, large groups of roots must be gathered and planted together in order to gain any effect. They look best in small groupings of a single color.

Anemone edwardsiana, a close cousin of *A. heterophylla*, bears two tiny blossoms on each stem. This is a localized central Texas species with a marked preference for rocky habitats and leafy, humus-rich soils.

Although neither of these native anemones is common in the bulb trade, the very similar Grecian windflower (*Anemone blanda*) is available in several color forms. In cooler sections of the South, this species naturalizes readily in leafy woodland wherever the winter sun shines to warm the soil. In warmer parts the tubers must be nestled in crevices between stones or placed in other situations guaranteeing a cool root run. Once established on well-drained soil with a bit of lime, the clumps spread steadily and increase in beauty each season. *Anemone apennina* is a similar, later-blooming relation from Italy.

More valuable than these on sandy, acid soils is another widespread native, the Carolina anemone (*Anemone caroliniana*). This species ranges through

Anemone caroliniana.

most of the South and Midwest, flowering in late winter. Its slender petal-like sepals run the usual gamut of white, pink, and blue colors, and its leaves are finely cut and unobtrusive.

In addition to their tubers, certain strains of *Anemone caroliniana* produce branching droopers that allow these beautiful flowers to creep gradually across an entire lawn. Each individual plant creates a pool of blue or white blooms, which can intermingle with neighboring colonies in an enchanting patchwork.

Another flower with a questing rhizome is the European wood anemone, *Anemone nemorosa*. This species belongs to the section of the genus with poppy-like blossoms. These are white in the common garden selection 'Grandiflora'. The loosely double 'Bracteata' is an heirloom variety from the 1600s. Its blooms have numerous white and green petal-like sepals. A few pink and lavender cultivars are popular in Europe but are seldom grown in America.

These anemones are easy and permanent in Southern gardens if given woodsy soil with a bit of lime. They especially enjoy a shady patch of ground where their triparted leaves and woody rootstocks can ramble. Wood anemones can be delightfully wayward, with flowers appearing anytime from November to April. The snowy whiteness of these blossoms shows beautifully under Japanese maples (*Acer palmatum*), whose early spring leaves emerge with a delicate tinge of rose, arriving in concert with the early flowers of the anemones. Their silky, nodding buds hover a few inches above the ground, then turn skyward as each opens in succession.

Another woodland flower, the rue anemone (*Thalictrum thalictroides*, formerly *Anemonella*) combines its tender white or pinkish blooms with thin, ferny, blue-green foliage. These little blossoms appear in clusters of three, bearing rounded petal-like sepals. Despite the delicate carriage of these plants, rue anemones seem surprisingly tough. During periods of drought they are capable of retreat to a clustered, tuberous rootstock.

The brightly colored poppy anemones of the Middle East, *Anemone coronaria* and *A. hortensis*, are so showy they are worth having even if they must be periodically replanted, which in much of the South is an unfortunate necessity. Their tubers are readily available and inexpensive, and the flowers ask for little beyond a sunny spot sheltered from winter gales.

It's this winter shelter that often determines the permanence of these anemones. Their fresh, parsley-green leaves emerge early in the fall and must successfully endure winter freezes if the plants are to prosper. In frosty parts of the South they may be dug annually and replanted in December to delay emergence and thereby improve cold tolerance.

These Mediterranean windflowers reach nearly a foot in height in common hybrid strains and make excellent cut flowers. They descend from plants domesticated by the Turks during the Middle Ages. Their precise ancestry is now obscure, but most are listed as forms of *Anemone coronaria*, a native species of southern Europe. The vigorous, single De Caen strain and double St. Bridgid group come in a wide range of colors including white, crimson, pink, violet, and lavender.

The St. Bavo anemones are usually considered to be *Anemone hortensis* derivatives. These are mostly lavender shades, but also vary to warm reds. Their leaves are less finely divided and their blooms have more petals than *A. coronaria*.

More in the province of rock garden specialties are *Anemone biflora* and *A. ×fulgens*. These have brilliant terracotta blossoms accented by black stamens. They enjoy dry summer bakings and gritty, lime-filled soil. Raised positions near the foot of a south-facing wall or boulder will suit these species, which come from Persia and the Mediterranean basin.

Ranunculus

First cousins of the anemones, and just as inclined to early bloom, are the various species of *Ranunculus*. These buttercups or marsh marigolds enjoy plenty of moisture during their spring blooming season, a characteristic alluded to by their Latin name, which means "little frogs."

Large-flowered buttercup (*Ranunculus macranthus*) is a Southwestern native that begins producing its inch-wide golden blooms in February and often continues into May. These waxy flowers are semi-double and appear in sizeable clusters, displaying the reflective sheen typical of their race. These long-lived perennials self-sow and naturalize in grass. In summer they retreat to the distinctive clawlike clusters of tubers that characterize this genus.

Like the large-flowered anemones, the popular bedding strains of Persian buttercup (*Ranunculus asiaticus*) are a legacy of ancient Turkish ingenuity

Ranunculus macranthus (large-flowered buttercup).

and were enormously popular flowers long ago. An English list from 1792 included over eight hundred named cultivars. Thomas Jefferson included both these and the poppy anemones in his spring bedding schemes at Monticello. With their feathery, green leaves and brightly colored and doubled blooms, these tuberous flowers bring a festive miscellany to spring gardens.

Persian buttercups suffer in severe cold spells, usually failing to return in regions where hard frost occurs annually. Late planting overcomes tenderness, so gardeners often lift and replant ranunculus tubers in December to delay their emergence.

Winter Cyclamen

From the Carolinas northward one of the most cherished cold weather blooms comes from the tiny *Cyclamen coum*. Gardeners in the subtropical South must forego these temperate flowers, as they dislike the warm soils that lie below the piedmont, but *C. coum* remains indispensable for winter gardens in the middle and upper South.

The petite flowers appear above the tight clumps of leaves on short, purplish stems, varying from near white through various shades of pink. Most are strong pinkish wine in tone. All have dark burgundy stains around the little teeth at the mouths of the blossoms. The nearly circular, smooth-edged leaves carry deep green undertones and are often decorated on the upper surfaces with a pewter overlay, sometimes with the dark green showing through in a Christmas tree pattern along the veins.

Native to Turkey and the Balkans, *Cyclamen coum* begins flowering at Christmas and continues through winter until the rush of flowers arrive in March. Although small, these little tuberous perennials slowly spread by self-sown seeds and can naturalize large areas at wood's edge, creating remarkable sheets of winter blossoms. Such small perky flowers do much to carry gardener's interests through some of the bleakest moments of the year.

Chapter 4
✍ Jonquils and Kin

ROUND THE FIRST OF MARCH, winter begins offering obvious signs of departure. Buds swell on the many-parted canopies of the elms. Grasses freshen perceptibly, and low rosettes of annuals show progress by adding new rounds of leaves. The final signal comes when the gracefully inclined blooms of daffodils paint gold over the awakening landscape.

In the South nearly any yellow narcissus may be affectionately pegged as a jonquil, whether or not it deserves this title, for *Narcissus jonquilla* and its hybrids have long been the most prominent of their race. These daffodils show a special fondness for these quarters, revealed through brave persistence and steady increase. Gardeners reciprocate tender feelings, rightfully doting on these early treasures.

It is customary in discussions of the genus to point out that *Narcissus* is the botanical name for the group, daffodil the common name, and jonquil a name for the small species, *N. jonquilla*. By tradition, however, gardeners persist in distinguishing the many-flowered white narcissi and the single white poet's narcissus from trumpeting golden daffodils. In the South several fragrant yellow varieties are best known as jonquils. Before dismissing these terms as simple synonyms, it's worth examining their origins.

The true poet's narcissus of the ancient Greeks, *Narcissus poeticus*, has an intriguingly original flower structure, which it shares with *N. tazetta* and other related species. In these plants the tubes of the blossoms are long and slender, surrounding six stamens. These come in two sets of three, one shorter than the other, inserted at separate points inside the tubes. The flowers open to small, shallow cups, which spread flatly in the center of six white petals. *Narcissus jonquilla* and its cousins have blooms constructed like the poet's narcissus, but they are usually brilliant yellow, with a memorable, honeylike fragrance. The leaves of these plants are narrow and rushlike.

In contrast, the wild daffodils (*Narcissus pseudonarcissus* and allies) carry bell- or trumpet-shaped cups, attached to shallow, open, floral tubes. The stamens are all one length and are inserted together near the base of the trumpets. These flowers come mostly in shades of yellow.

Garden hybridizers have blurred these fairly distinctive groupings with numerous intermediates, and all varieties are now officially labeled *Narcissus* by

93

botanists and daffodils by bulb fanciers. Nevertheless, the traditional groupings are not without meaning. A many-flowered daffodil is still a narcissus to most gardeners. In the South, where wild forms and hybrids of *N. jonquilla* are common, jonquil is the customary term for a yellow daffodil.

Narcissus jonquilla and its relations inherit tolerance to dampness, which suits them especially to the heavy clay soils of the South, as well as to seasonally moist sandylands. Their native haunts are centered in Spain and Portugal but extend to southern France and across the Mediterranean to Morocco. In these sunny countries moist, cool spring seasons give way to long, warm summers, and all of these bulbs receive a good baking.

The true jonquil (*Narcissus jonquilla*) is a tiny, golden flower that appears in scant clusters atop slender, jade stems. The powerfully scented blooms would seem out of scale if attached to the wide foliage of a common daffodil, but nature has designed elegant, tapered greenery to accompany the endearing blossoms. The upright leaves, rounded in cross section, provide inspiration for the specific epithet (*jonquilla* means "little rush"). In the South (and, one supposes, in their native habitats), jonquils naturalize in roadside ditches and other moist spots where their wild companions include true rushes (*Juncus* spp.). Perhaps their stiff, narrow leaves confer some disguise in this community that helps to protect them from browsing mammals or insects.

The true, early-flowering, sweet-scented jonquil (*Narcissus jonquilla*).

Another curious imitation of the jonquil is its blossom. Although designed along the same lines as *Narcissus tazetta*, jonquil flowers have a different personality, which comes from their more casually disposed umbels, their brilliant gold-waxed petals, and their remarkably strong fragrance. The redolent, honey-scented blossoms look and smell like flowers of barberries (*Berberis* spp.), which appear at the same early season. Apparently, the spiny, shrubby barberry and the tiny jonquil are out to attract the same precocious insects.

Several strains of *Narcissus jonquilla* appear in Southern gardens, differing primarily in blooming season. Early ones may arrive in January or

February during mild years, but more regularly come in March. As soon as the little flower stems rise above ground, the buds begin to open. The scapes reach ten to twelve inches by the time all the blooms have expanded. At this modest elevation they strike an elegant pose amid the narrow leaves.

These early jonquils last several weeks in cool weather and are particularly desirable for gardens, as the tiny blossoms can be enjoyed before the rush of spring flowers. They appear to be true heirlooms, unavailable in the Dutch trade, although common along rural roadsides. Usually offered by American dealers as early Louisiana jonquils, in the South they form large colonies on the same acid, sandy lands that support loblolly pines and sassafras.

Later jonquils continue appearing into April, making fragrant additions for an intimate nook or bend along a sunny pathway. One of the most famous is the double *Narcissus jonquilla* known as Queen Anne's jonquil. These old flowers reside in some of the historic gardens of the South. Like most doubles, they tend more to green than gold, and will blast (fail to open properly) except in cool, moist springs. Nevertheless, the lemony, many-petaled blooms possess a special daintiness. They are greatly treasured by those who know them. Nurseries offer this historic variety as the cultivar 'Pencrebar'.

Commercial suppliers often send out 'Baby Moon' in lieu of true species jonquils. This is a late-flowering hybrid between *Narcissus jonquilla* and a close relation, *N. rupicola*. Looking like an overly precise version of its parents, its one

Narcissus rupicola, a tiny cousin of *N. jonquilla*.

to three carefully fashioned blossoms stand stiffly, like small, golden yellow wheels. These are carried on short, six- to eight-inch stems among dark green leaves, sprawling more widely than in typical *N. jonquilla*.

With medium yellow petals, 'New Baby' is a very similar, late-blooming miniature, as are 'Chit Chat' and 'Kidling'. The pale yellow, gold-cupped 'Little Rusky' and all-yellow 'Chiva' are tiny varieties that flower in mid-spring. An unusual white-petaled cultivar with small, perfectly rounded yellow cups, 'Segovia' is a miniature hybrid of the Moroccan *Narcissus rupicola* subsp. *watieri*, a white-flowered jonquil native to the Atlas Mountains. Its solitary blooms appear in mid-spring. 'Xit', with small all-white flowers highlighted by dark green throats, is slightly later and has even more of the wild character of its species parent.

Rare dwarf relatives of *Narcissus jonquilla* include, in order of descending size, *N. jonquilla* var. *henriquesii*, *N. fernandesii*, *N. calcicola*, *N. willkommii*, and *N. scaberulus*. These interesting Iberian miniatures can succeed in the South and may sometimes be had from specialists. Except for the usefully early var. *henriquesii*, however, most are so small that a great number would be needed to produce any effect in a garden. They make charming additions to trough plantings or sunny rockeries.

True jonquil fragrance empowers all these flowers with a potency that goes beyond their midget proportions. The blossoms seem to speak directly, imploring gardeners to focus on the small, delicately fashioned blooms. Jonquil voices

Narcissus jonquilla var. *henriquesii*. Photo by Lauren S. Ogden.

may have spoken to Elizabeth Lawrence as she wrote of little daffodils: "When they are in bloom I feel as if I could not stop looking at them for a moment, and when they are gone I am almost ashamed of the sharpness of my regret."

Campernelles

The larger jonquils common to the South are actually old hybrids between *Narcissus jonquilla* and other wild daffodils. The favorite of all is an antique called the campernelle (*N. ×odorus*). It originates from southern France, Spain, and Italy where the range of *N. jonquilla* overlaps with the Lent lily (*N. pseudonarcissus*), creating the opportunity for chance hybridization.

Campernelles provide more springtime gold in the South than any other flower, and they have done so since the earliest days of European settlement. These richly colored blossoms flutter among groups of narrow, dull green leaves like troops of fragrant yellow butterflies. Their silhouettes always seem graceful and unobtrusive. More delightful and suitable bulbs for naturalizing could hardly be imagined.

The campernelle is another one of those gratifying old garden mules discovered by some alert flower lover of ages past. Clusius recorded it in 1595, and Parkinson discussed this variety in his *Paradisus* along with the single and double jonquils. The campernelle persists and thrives in gardens to this day, for it has that wonderful hybrid vigor (heterosis) common to many sterile crosses. Like

The campernelle, *Narcissus ×odorus*.

Narcissus jonquilla, these daffodils have a special affinity for damp conditions. They are the most successful of any yellow daffodil on clay.

Campernelle flowers appear in clusters of two to five on top of twelve- to fifteen-inch stems. They emanate the treasured jonquil perfume, though with less intensity than their tiny parent. The blooms often show slight imperfections on close inspection, and may be curiously dog-eared or bereft, with only four or five petals instead of the customary six. Although this keeps campernelles off the show bench and bans them from plantings of daffodil connoisseurs, it presents no barrier to their use in flower borders. If anything, this tattered appearance adds to their charm.

These old-time flowers begin to show around the first of March, which is early enough to make them welcome and late enough to avoid the most serious freezes. The fragrant blooms appear for a fortnight, or longer if weather remains mild. Their narrow foliage remains attractive after flowering is done, then draws minimal attention as it fades in early summer.

In addition to the familiar garden campernelle, several other strains of *Narcissus ×odorus* may be encountered when ordering bulbs from abroad. Some of these counterfeits are probably very old, for Haworth listed nine distinctly different variants of *N. ×odorus* in his monograph of 1831. However, these must not be enduring or free flowering in this country, for one seldom sees the other *N. ×odorus* cultivars in veteran plantings. 'Orange Queen', a supposed variant of the ancient variety 'Rugulosus', is one that may be had from nurseries, although it struggles in the fast-warming springs common to the South, and the small bulbs rapidly split up in warm Southern soils.

An exception, however, is the double form of the campernelle. These daffodils are just as fragrant, long-lived, and ready to flower as the singles. They open later, as their tightly packed buds require longer to expand. Like other doubles in the South, the cabbagey blossoms run to green shades and usually blast or open poorly. In certain springs, mild weather stays long enough to permit flowering. In gratitude, these old flowers will then unfold like perfect, golden rosebuds.

The Texas Star

In many old gardens there are strange-looking, sulfury jonquils that flower in March and April. Their homely, crimped blossoms sit on short stems, which keeps the flowers partly hidden in the foliage. You have to get down on your knees and part the pale green leaves to see them properly. If you smell the frail-looking blossoms, their fragrance seems pungently sweet, with an aroma that comes as much from Chinese sacred lily as jonquil.

These curious, light yellow flowers belong to another ancient hybrid, a cross between *Narcissus jonquilla* and *N. tazetta* known to botanists appropriately enough as *N. ×intermedius* and to gardeners as the Texas star. Unlike campernelles, which are known only from man-made plantings, botanists have located *N. ×intermedius* growing naturally in France, near Bayonne, in the foothills of the Pyrenees. Although still a wildflower in these regions, like other old jonquils, these seem to have been grown in gardens from the start.

The most endearing characteristic of Texas star jonquils is their unqualified toughness and persistence. They thrive equally on sand or clay, and accept a wide range of Southern climate extremes. One often sees them happily flowering in vacant lots without any care whatsoever.

The Texas star, *Narcissus ×intermedius*.

For best garden effect the rapidly multiplying clumps of *Narcissus ×intermedius* should be split and replanted every three years or so. This allows the bulbs to be spaced apart and keeps the overly generous foliage from crowding the blooms.

Montopolis

On the sandy uplands of the old Montopolis district in Austin, Texas, several old gardens include what appears to be yet another jonquil hybrid. The fat buds of these flowers open with distinctly rounded, sulfury petals set around lemon-colored cups, so as to resemble smaller, more yellow editions of *Narcissus tazetta* 'Grand Primo'. Only their honeyed fragrance and their slender, dark green foliage gives away their jonquil ancestry.

These may be narcissi of true Southern origin, for they do not answer to the description of any well-known daffodils. Similar plants discovered in plantings near Boston, Georgia, have been called 'Miss Sara'. The many references to seventeen sisters around the South may also refer to these hybrids. Perhaps some

"Montopolis," an old jonquil hybrid discovered in an Austin garden. Photo by Lauren S. Ogden.

industrious bee transferred pollen of 'Grand Primo' onto a jonquil blossoming in an old Confederate garden. The resulting seeds may have sprouted and bloomed for some lucky flower lover, who then shared bulbs with settlers moving west. These Montopolis daffodils may be among the first hybrid narcissi developed in the South.

Modern Jonquil Hybrids

Unfortunately, precious little in the way of narcissus rearing has been attempted by Southerners. This is understandable, for the brief, uncertain springs offer a poor breeding environment for most daffodils. To find flowers suited to warm-climate borders Southerners have had to lean upon the work of gardeners in regions where spring is a more predictable season. The mild climates of Oregon, Ireland, and New Zealand seem to have attracted most of the daffodil breeders.

Even in these gentle districts hybridizing is a daunting prospect, for daffodil seedlings require six or seven years to mature and bloom, and longer before bulbs multiply to commercial numbers. These flowers demand a lifetime of devotion, and the folk who undertake to breed them do so for love, rather than for any hope of profit.

In the system of classification adopted by the American Daffodil Society, hybrids that inherit rushlike leaves or honey fragrance from *Narcissus jonquilla* are grouped in Narcissus Division 7. Of all hybrid narcissi, these are the most fruitful for experimentation in the South, as most will settle into garden life if offered ordinary care. Many relish damp soils and summer heat.

Breeders have been active with the jonquils, and all the popular color combinations of white, pink, and yellow may now be secured for trial. The only general failing of this group in the South is their tendency to bloom late in the season. This attribute is welcomed in cool regions and has been actively developed by hybridizers. Although an asset in the North, in the fast-warming climate of the South such late narcissi often fade prematurely. They may still be enjoyed in this region, but should be carefully positioned to receive partial shade and shelter from hot winds.

There are, fortunately, several early- and midseason jonquil hybrids. All are excellent performers in the South and should be sought relentlessly. Of these, the preeminent variety is 'Trevithian', a 1927 introduction from Cornish breeder P. D. Williams. This breathtaking flower offers graceful, narrow, gray-green foliage, as a perfect foil for the blooms which appear in clusters of two or three together. These are precisely fashioned with rounded, golden petals surrounding a circular, butter-yellow cup. They are the picture of elegance, and make stunningly fragrant cut flowers.

It's surpassingly rare to discover a show-quality bloom with the garden vigor of 'Trevithian'. Around the Gulf, local wisdom often portrays hybrid daffodils as mere annuals for winter bedding, but with 'Trevithian' Southern gardeners have a perennial in the truest sense. These narcissi fill the role of refined, mod-

'Trevithian' is an elegant jonquil hybrid well suited to the South.

ern campernelles. Their clumps increase steadily, and a small investment in these bulbs will multiply tenfold in three or four years.

Although still a favorite commercial variety in New Zealand, 'Trevithian' has dropped off many nursery lists in recent years, displaced by more modern, later-blooming jonquil cultivars. These indispensable spring bulbs are no longer commonplace, but they are still available and are produced on a small scale by certain farms in the South.

Other jonquil hybrids that have settled into Southern life include 'Sweetness', 'Lanarth', 'Golden Perfection', and 'Golden Sceptre'. These have mostly solitary blooms with wide, deep golden cups and petals. They look a bit like standard large-cupped daffodils, but with heavy-textured petals, which are roughened and triangular in outline. This gives these flowers a starry appearance. They may be seen flowering faithfully in many gardens planted during the 1940s and 1950s. All but 'Sweetness' have since become scarce in the trade. Another older, early-flowering jonquil hybrid, 'Waterperry' displays a novel combination of white petals around an apricot cup, fading to ivory. It is still offered in quantity by a few bulb dealers.

The bright yellow, orange-cupped 'Suzy' is a showstopping flower, usually with three blooms to a cluster. Other jonquil hybrids such as 'Susan Pearson' have the same mix of reddish orange on yellow. 'Golden Dawn' is a flashy orange and saffron bicolor, usually classed with the tazettas. It is completely at home in the South, rather like an improved *Narcissus* ×*intermedius*, but later blooming,

Jonquil hybrid 'Sweetness'.

with petals that fade in the sun to pale yellow. 'Falconet', another tazetta-jonquil cross, provides blossoms in three-flowered clusters, garishly blending orange cups with gold petals. 'Martinette' is similarly bright, but with more blooms to the cluster. These spring-flowering hybrids have much of the spirit of the winter-blooming 'Soleil d'Or', and they also endure drought and heavy soils like their tazetta parents.

Several jonquil hybrids developed by Oregon breeder Grant Mitsch are worthwhile, including a number charmingly named for wild birds. One of the loveliest, 'Quail', is a rich self-colored yellow introduced in 1974. The cup of this variety is long and narrow, contrasting happily with flat, radiating petals. Blossoms usually come in groups of three, nodding slightly. This gives them a hint of grace in spite of their rather boxy form. Even a modest clump of 'Quail' will provide a great deal of color and fragrance.

'Pipit' is a Mitsch introduction whose cups open light yellow, then fade slowly to cream. This creates the avant-garde impression of a white cup against sulfur petals: in daffodil parlance, a reverse bicolor. The pale, fragile-looking blooms of 'Pipit' nod gracefully and appear toward the end of April. 'Dickcissel', 'Hillstar', and 'New Day' have analogous forms and color schemes, but possess darker, canary-yellow petals behind their milky coronas. 'Pueblo' opens pale yellow, but quickly fades to a beautiful all white. 'Bell Song' is white with a pink cup. 'Curlew' offers white petals around a long, trumpetlike yellow cup. 'Stratosphere' is a tall variety with tight clusters of two to three blooms bearing golden petals and cups.

Other American-bred jonquil hybrids include 'Fruit Cup', with precise white-petaled blooms bearing short yellow trumpets, and 'Kedron', with rounded, golden blossoms showing off small, deep orange cups. The late-bloom-

ing 'Intrigue' offers golden flowers nearly the size of standard daffodils, displaying a pale white halo around the base of its cup.

An unusual hybrid usually classed in Division 7, 'Sailboat' might as easily fit among *Narcissus cyclamineus* cultivars, as it seems intermediate in character with that early-flowering group. It is one of the best performers on the heavy, waterlogged clay soils of the Mississippi Delta, displaying pointed white petals, reflexed as if they were

Jonquil hybrid 'Golden Sceptre'.

catching the wind. These frame a flared yellow trumpet. 'Sailboat' makes small bulbs that multiply swiftly, blooming well in partial shade.

Brent and Becky Heath of Gloucester, Virginia, have been instrumental in promoting several of these novel jonquils and have also introduced a number of hybrids of their own. 'Golden Echo' offers white petals around long-nosed, golden cups similar to 'Curlew'. 'Sweet Love' shares this color scheme, offering strong fragrance and less protruding trumpets. 'Blushing Lady' is a delicate, soft

Jonquil hybrid 'Sailboat'.

Jonquil hybrid 'Sweet Love' flowering at Brent and Becky's Bulbs, Gloucester, Virginia.

yellow, haloed with white and blushing pink on the cup as it matures. 'Derrin-ger' is bright lemon-yellow with orange cups. 'O'Bodkin' offers precise white petals around small lemony cups. 'Pappy George' combines saffron-colored pet-als with vivid orange cups, bearing two to three blooms in a cluster. Although some varieties bloom too late in the spring to be of value for the lower South, the jonquil hybrids are treasures of form and color and seem entirely permanent.

Modern Daffodils

A number of gardeners in the South successfully cultivate the large trumpet daffodils (Division 1) as bedding flowers, but only a handful of these settle here with any permanence. During the Dutch narcissus embargo of the early twenti-eth century, American plantations raised thousands of bulbs of the best-known trumpet, 'King Alfred', in the sandy soils of Louisiana and east Texas. This huge, golden variety and a few other early bloomers such as 'Golden Spur', 'Robert Syndenham', 'Emperor', and 'Empress' may be seen in a few established gardens, blooming most reliably in the upper South. These historic cultivars differ little from wild trumpet-flowered species such as *Narcissus gayi*, represented by the ancient selection 'Princeps', and *N. hispanicus*, sometimes still seen in the culti-var 'Maximus', also known as Trumpet Major. Along the Gulf, a pearly-white-flowered variety introduced in 1938, 'Mount Hood', blooms successfully if given shade from hot afternoon sun. This surprisingly persistent daffodil seems to adapt to heavy soils better than most trumpets.

Bulbs offered in the trade today as 'King Alfred' seldom fare so well, and may actually be commercial substitutes of newer varieties such as 'Dutch Mas-ter'. Although these inexpensive flowers often grow magnificently their first year, they gradually give up blooming. After two or three seasons of dwindling performance, only gray foliage returns. The drab, flowerless clumps of these old trumpets persist indefinitely as winter accents to neglected suburban yards.

Incomparables

In the South better garden value comes from the large-cupped narcissi (Divi-sion 2), formerly classed among the primrose peerless, or incomparabilis, sec-tion. This varied group descends from wild and man-made hybrids of *Narcissus pseudonarcissus* and its allies crossed with various forms of poet's narcissus (*N. poeticus*). The section offers the greatest range of colors and some of the most graceful, showy blooms among daffodils. Many are excellent for mass planting on loamy or sandy ground.

In a few old gardens you may still see clumps of the starry-petaled 'Sir Watkin'. This famous flower is typical of many bicolors in this division, with buttery petals framing an orange-yellow cup. The corona is not so large as in the trumpet class but still makes a respectable show. 'Sir Watkin' follows the early trumpets in bloom, usually appearing in mid-March.

'Lucifer', another historic hybrid, shows more poeticus influence. Its narrower primrose petals, soon fading to cream, surround a shallow, chrome cup rimmed in orange. It's one of the few smaller-cupped daffodils suited to the South. Occasionally, two blooms appear on its stalk instead of one. 'White Lady', with fluted yellow trumpets and starry, primose petals fading to ivory, is another historic variety sometimes seen in old gardens. Its papery-textured blooms retain the grace of a wildflower, seeming close to the wild forms of *Narcissus* ×*incomparabilis* that occur where *N. pseudonarcissus* and *N. poeticus* grow together. 'Queen of the North', with rounded, snow-white petals around small, lemon cups, is another variety sometimes seen in Southern gardens. Although no longer common, 'Queen of the North' is one of the more readily available of these historic varieties.

Introduced in 1917, the orange-cupped, yellow-petaled 'Fortune' is well proven and popular for large scale plantings. In the South this old variety is

The historic daffodil 'Sir Watkin' may still be seen in Southern gardens. Photo by Lauren S. Ogden.

probably the best large-cupped daffodil for a good bolt of springtime gold. 'Carbineer', 'Ceylon', and 'Rustom Pasha', with orange-red on gold combinations, are all fine as well. 'Delibes' sets lemony petals around a large, flat cup banded in crimson. The oversized 'Fortissimo' combines large yellow petals with a garishly wide orange-red corona.

As an all-gold flower to substitute for the yellow trumpets, 'Carlton' has long been a favored choice. The slightly smaller 'St. Keverne' and much larger 'Gigantic Star' are other yellows good in the South. All of these are early bloomers, putting in an appearance around the first of March.

Among white varieties, most are too late blooming to be of much value, but the lemon-cupped, white-petaled 'Ice Follies' is reliable, early, and well loved by Southern gardeners. A double-flowered sport of this favorite, 'Obdam', is slightly later to flower but still successful, with gardenialike blossoms composed entirely of layered creamy white petals. Although very few pink-cupped daffodils do well in the South, 'Accent' is a midseason bloomer that has proven worthwhile in the Carolinas, making a graceful white-petaled garden flower with widely flared salmon coronas. As with all large-cupped daffodils, these profit from division every three years to keep the bulbs from becoming overcrowded.

A favorite large-cupped daffodil in the South, 'Ice Follies' adds spring interest to a garden otherwise devoted to a collection of daylilies.

Angel's Tears

Like many late jonquils, the Division 5 hybrids of *Narcissus triandrus* often flower into April. This only lessens their value in a small way, however, for they have great substance in their thick petals, and they last better than many other daffodils. They thrive in a variety of soils and prosper in partial shade. With their tilted or hanging blossoms, usually in clusters of two or three, these are the most graceful of narcissi.

Narcissus triandrus var. *albus*, a wild form of the species, has long been shared among gardeners under the charming name angel's tears. The grassy, gray foliage of this familiar daffodil increases happily in the South, although the blooms do not appear freely in all gardens. When they come, they appear in groups of three, on six- to eight-inch stems. The individual florets nod like fuchsias and have shallow, rounded cups. They are a uniform creamy white, which gives them a ghostly paleness.

Many *Narcissus triandrus* hybrids descend from the large, pale yellowish var. *loiseleurii*, known only from the Isles of Glennan, off the southwestern coast of Brittany. This rare form is hard to obtain, but succeeds in the lower South and flowers more freely than the angel's tears.

The best know of the larger triandrus hybrids is 'Thalia', a creamy white, exquisitely proportioned blossom commonly known as the orchid narcissus. This is a fine, fragrant, permanent garden flower, but, like many triandrus types,

The orchid narcissus 'Thalia' naturalized in a partially shaded lawn. Photo by Lauren S. Ogden.

it is slow to increase. More recent whites include 'Ice Wings' and 'Petrel'. The latter is especially floriferous, with as many as five or six boxy blooms to a stem.

'Tuesday's Child' is a graceful, pendulous daffodil with white petals and a yellow cup. 'Liberty Bells' appears dressed all in soft yellow, like a sunny version of 'Thalia'. One of the best performers along the Gulf, 'Lemon Drops' is a hybrid between *N. triandrus* and 'Fortune', with pendant clusters of sulfury yellow blossoms. All appear toward the end of April.

'Hawera' is a miniature *Narcissus triandrus* cross, whose other parent was a jonquil. This tiny daffodil inherits narrow foliage and a sweet fragrance. The starry rings of petals are luminous, pale yellow, and the modest little blooms show a graceful inclination to nod. Although not usually permanent on heavy soils in the South, this variety prospers on sand and will sometimes succeed on clay if planted in the dry, root-filled soil near the trunk of a pine tree.

The jonquilla-triandrus hybrid 'Hawera' combines handsomely with *Phlox subulata* 'Emerald Blue'.

Very different from this elf is the strong-growing 'Silver Chimes', a mighty descendant of *Narcissus tazetta* 'Grand Primo'. This late-blooming flower is one of the best daffodils for heavy clay soils. Its tall green foliage is much like its tazetta parent, but the clustered, milky blooms nod like good old 'Thalia'. It's one of the tried and true Southern daffodils, making a welcome April appearance in many gardens.

Reflexed Jonquils

There is an odd little Portuguese daffodil with extraordinary long trumpets and petals that turn back like a cyclamen blossom. Although the foliage accompanying the light, greenish gold bloom is flattened like a daffodil, it has the dark green slickness of a jonquil leaf. Gerard knew these miniatures as "reflex jonquilias." Botanists call them *Narcissus cyclamineus*.

These quaint little blooms need cooler, damper conditions than most of the South can offer, but they have sired a large race of hybrids that thrive on the acid sands of the Southeast. Most are early bloomers, so they are especially valuable in this climate. In gardens where the prevailing soil is a tight clay, they may be planted in raised beds of sand or decomposed granite. Under these conditions the cyclamineus hybrids (Division 6) will be long-lived and vigorous.

The most famous of this group are medium-sized bicolors, like the sulfur and yellow 'February Gold' and the white and yellow 'March Sunshine'. 'Auburn', 'The Alliance', and

Cyclamineus hybrid 'Jetfire'.

Cyclamineus hybrid 'Jack Snipe' with wild sweet William (*Phlox divaricata*). Photo by Lauren S. Ogden.

'Peeping Tom' are long-nosed, yellow types that may deputize for golden trumpets, although their petals sweep backward like those of their tiny ancestor. A sumptuous hybrid developed in New Zealand, 'Surfside' offers nodding blossoms with upswept, white petals and ruffled pale yellow trumpets that fade to ivory. 'Trena' and 'Tracey' are similarly colored Kiwi daffodils. 'Lemon Silk' is delectably sulfur.

In addition to these there are many small or miniature cyclamineus hybrids. 'Tête-à-tête' is a short, yellowish gold cross from *Narcissus aureus* 'Soleil d'Or'; it has become popular as a florist blossom, forced in small pots for Valentine's Day. 'Jetfire' has similar, but larger, orange trumpets. 'Jack Snipe' combines a gold cup with near-white petals. 'Beryl' is a delicate, straw-colored descendant of *N. poeticus* with an orange-banded cup. These need more certain watering during growth than the larger cyclamineus hybrids but are otherwise hardy. They prosper in leafy soil, and many will succeed in partial shade.

Poets

Most of the later-blooming tazetta and poet daffodils (Divisions 8 and 9) perform poorly in the South, although a few of them have been in gardens for a long time. The old hybrid called April beauty or twin sisters is actually *Narcissus ×medioluteus* (*N. biflorus*), a natural cross of *N. poeticus* and *N. tazetta* cultivated since the sixteenth century. The round, white-petaled blooms bear small, yellow cups, and appear mostly in pairs, but sometimes singly or three together. They often close the daffodil season in late April.

Another old hybrid, the silver jonquil (*Narcissus ×tenuior* 'Gracilis') is descended from a cross between a poet and a jonquil and inherits the tall, slender foliage of the *N. jonquilla* group. The pale yellow, sweet-scented blooms appear at the same late season as *N. ×biflorus*. These old flowers are best in gardens of the middle and upper South.

Some of the older poetaz hybrids, such as the orange-cupped, white-

April beauty or twin sisters (*Narcissus ×medioluteus*) is a late-blooming historic variety common in the upper South.

petaled 'Geranium', do well in the South, especially with partial shade from high-branching pines or pecans. The near-identical 'Cragford' also succeeds and is usefully early in bloom. 'Aspasia', 'Matador', 'Martha Washington', and 'Mrs. Alfred Pearson' are all dependable.

Double Daffodils

'Sir Winston Churchill' is a double poetaz variety that appeared spontaneously among a stock of 'Geranium'. Although certain to succeed here as a plant, it needs cool weather and an unfailing supply of moisture to keep from blasting. This is also true for double poetaz like 'Cheerfulness' and 'Yellow Cheerfulness'. A double-flowered sport of 'Cragford', 'Abba' is more reliable in bloom, appear-

"Eggs and bacon" (*Narcissus ×incompara-bilis* 'Orange Phoenix'), one of the historic double daffodils common to older Southern gardens.

ing very early in the flowering season in February and early March while temperatures remain cool. Another double poetaz, 'Bridal Crown' is also early and good, with fragrant, orange- and white-petaled blooms in clusters of three.

The unpredictable springs of the South try the patience of many double daffodils. Few open properly, even when the plants grow well. The same is true for many of the strange split-corona daffodils, in which the cups divide to form an extra row of petals.

An exception among doubles is the ancient incomparabilis selection 'Orange Phoenix', known in the South as eggs and bacon. These oddities are in many old gardens and, although ragged and tattered, offer an annual curiosity with their jumbled, yellow and golden orange blossoms. The same old gardens often include a double form of *Narcissus pseudonarcissus* called 'Telemonius Plenus' or 'Van Sion'. These march through the beds in tight rows, bearing fat, swollen buds above upright, gray foliage. If weather is favorable, they eventually open small blossoms stuffed with masses of irregular green and yellow petals, endearing, if not really beautiful.

Should the general failure of these bizarre types bring disappointment, Southerners may console themselves with C. L. Allen's comments from 1915:

> As flowers begin to be appreciated for their intrinsic worth, when we look into them rather than at them, when we see all their parts and their wonderful adaptation to each other, the beautiful necessity there is for each, our respect for double forms will be lost in our admiration for the single flower, perfect in all its parts as it was when it first beautified the earth, and there was none to admire it than the Power that gave it.

Snowdrops and Snowflakes

Southerners receiving bulb catalogs in early summer go through a perennial moment of consternation when deciding whether to order snowdrops (*Galanthus* spp.) or snowflakes (*Leucojum* spp.). These allies of the daffodils both carry pendant white blossoms marked with green, and their common names are similar enough that many people feel comfortable in interchanging them. Except in the damper, cooler parts of the South, though, this confusion soon resolves itself, for snowdrops rarely persist more than a season. The robust flowers merrily chiming out spring in Southern dooryards are those of the summer snowflake (*Leucojum aestivum*).

There are a few *Galanthus* species from sunnier regions that might endure in the South, but most come from soggy alpine meadows. Without melting snow to feed their succulent, early growth, they can hardly be expected to thrive. Any kind of prolonged drought means doom to these flowers, and knowledgeable nurseries avoid selling the bulbs in a desiccated condition. These little plants are best moved "in the green," with a good bit of moist soil surrounding the roots.

The most likely snowdrop to succeed in the South is *Galanthus plicatus* subsp. *byzantinus*, a vigorous flower native to western Turkey, where the bulbs inhabit mountain forests in heavy soil. This is one of the species with grayish foliage. *Galanthus elwesii* is similar and easy to bloom the first season, but it seldom establishes in Southern gardens. Both of these flower anytime from Christmas onward.

The common snowdrop (*Galanthus nivalis*) comes in several forms, all with lush, green foliage and snowy, pendant blooms. Vigorous selections such as 'Scharlockii' and 'Sam Arnott' are the most likely to succeed. They should be offered positions with shade and rich soil and should never want for moisture.

Summer snowflake (*Leucojum aestivum*) naturalized in damp woodland.

Flowers may be expected in February or earlier.

The spring snowflake (*Leucojum vernum*) is as ill-suited to Southern conditions as most snowdrops, but this failure is of little consequence. Although the species often appears on the lists of importers, they invariably ship the similar summer snowflake (*L. aestivum*) in its stead. This one positively thrives in the South, and you could hardly ask for a more appealing spring flower.

The name *leucojum*, an old one used by Theophrastus, translates as "white violet." These tiny, pure white, bell-shaped blooms have a subtle, sweet fragrance and appear in drooping clus-

Small green spots decorate the fresh white petals of *Leucojum aestivum*.

ters of two to six. They rise on twelve-inch stems directly from the robust, clustered bulbs. The six snowy petals are marked with unique thickened, green spots at the tips, and these give the fairy-sized blooms an air of unreality.

This is somewhat overcome by the tremendous bunches of lush green leaves that rise from the round, narcissuslike bulbs. This excess foliage is needed to set off the tiny sprays of bloom, and does a fine job if the bulbs are planted in clumps of at least six. 'Gravetye Giant' is a select large-flowered form that originated in the garden of English horticulturist William Robinson. Worth seeking out for its large blooms, it does not seem to be as rampantly vigorous as the ordinary strains common to Southern dooryards.

In their homes around the Mediterranean these bulbs grow in mucky soils along streams. In such situations they prosper on a surplus of spring moisture and a long summer baking. This prepares the flowers especially for the heavy clay soils of the South, but they perform well on moist sand, also, thriving equally in sun or full shade.

It seems hard to believe that summer snowflakes, so common and prolific in old Southern gardens, have become endangered in their home countries, but this appears to be the case. Overcollection for the bulb trade is one culprit, but widespread habitat destruction is another cause of decline. In your own yard, you can help these lovely, old-fashioned flowers by generous division and exchange with other interested gardeners.

Chapter 5
𝒟𝒪 Spring Treasures

EARLY BULBS like jonquils, irises, and tulips possess an extravagance of beauty that attracts all eyes. Smaller, more delicate flowers charm us with their frail countenances. A goodly measure of our delight comes from mixing the pallid, demure blooms with their bolder cohorts. Through several months each spring Southerners may revel in a diversity of bulbous flowers and combine them in an endless array.

Alliums

The wild onions (*Allium* spp.) include both bold and shy flowers with a great role to play in Southern gardens. Although the genus is best known for its pungently odorous edible members (onions, leeks, chives, and garlics), it includes a wide assortment of showy flowering types. All members of the tribe inherit the onion smell in their bulbs and foliage, and all hold blossoms in rounded clusters, or umbels. Beyond these common parameters, they achieve surprising diversity.

As a rule, hardy bulbs take several years to go from seed to flower, but many alliums grow rampantly, and seedlings frequently bloom only a season or two after planting. The tiny, black seeds may be scattered directly in the garden where bulbs are desired. This offers an inexpensive way to naturalize mass displays, which would be difficult to achieve through bulb planting alone.

March Snow

Even in this land where snows come rarely and tarry only for unpredictable instants, gardeners may blanket the ground in pristine purity. All we must do is introduce a few round bulbs or seeds of the Naples onion (*Allium neapolitanum*). Set in an untended bed beneath a grove of high-branching trees, these form a lush winter understory. During the first days of March swarms of loosely clustered blossoms rise to dance above the tapered foliage. Even while still closed tightly in bud, the clear white blooms reflect all light.

Although a small bulb, the Naples onion increases rapidly on any soil and soon extends in impressive patches. If it were not so well mannered about departing after its season, it might be regarded as a weed. The profuse, titanium-

116

white flowers silence any such concerns. These early flecks of snow afford one of the telling moments of Southern springs. Scarcely any other blooms seem so fresh and alive at this tender season.

The very earliness of these blossoms puts them at some risk from northers, which can nip the precocious buds. In most gardens the Naples onion benefits from a position near a south wall or beneath the protective canopy of a tree. Beyond this shelter, these bulbs ask only for restraint of the lawn mower prior to May, when the rosettes of long, tapered leaves yellow and die away for summer.

Like other ornamental garlics, the foliage of this Mediterranean bulb emits a pungent scent when bruised. Although some might object to the odor, this subtracts in no way from the beauty of the flowers, which themselves are sweetly scented, inspiring the name "daffodil garlic" in reference to their fragrance. Florists in Europe often set them in dye to color them.

The Naples onion has become well established in the Dutch bulb trade, despite its less than hardy inclinations. 'Grandiflorum' is a selection reputed to have large flowers. Also rather sizeable is a bulb sold as *Allium cowanii* (this name belongs to a variant botanists now include under *A. neapolitanum*). *Allium subhirsutum* is a related species with slightly hairy leaves and later-blooming, chalk-white flowers. All look so similar that no one would want them together in the same garden, but each seems well adapted to the South.

More distinctive are other white-flowered Mediterranean species such as *Allium triquetrum*, with milky, bell-shaped blooms on six-inch stems above clumps of leafy winter foliage. This moisture-loving species naturalizes happily

The Naples onion *(Allium neapolitanum).*   *Allium triquetrum.* Photo by Lauren S. Ogden.

in part shade, adding charm to spring plantings with its small, nodding flowers. *Allium paradoxum* can be weedy in the common bulbil-forming strain offered in the trade. Its variety *normale*, however, reproduces only by seed and offsets, making a well-behaved subject adapted to heavy clays. Its pendant white bells appear in mid-spring.

Drummond's Onion

One of the most charming of the small onions is *Allium drummondi*. It's hard to understand why this sprightly native of Texas, Mexico, and the Great Plains has not been used more often in gardens. It's hardy everywhere, and the little bulbs seem to accept anything from thin, rocky ground to damp bottomland. The dainty clumps multiply swiftly, naturalizing if allowed to mature their narrow, gray leaves. The blooms come in cheerful tones of rosy-purple, pink, or glistening white, arriving usefully in March, in time to join the displays of daffodils and hyacinths.

These wildflowers radiate a potpourri of spicy fragrances much like the scent of old-fashioned sweet William (*Dianthus barbatus*). This seems a bit out of place on a little member of the garlic clan but adds greatly to their charm. The interestingly detailed blossoms also attract attention for their color variations, for each petal darkens in tone on the keel while paling toward the edge.

Allium drummondi flowering in early spring on a north Texas prairie.

Even the bulbs of this onion have a surprising daintiness. They surround themselves in tawny, netlike coats (reticula, to botanists). These fibrous covers help the little bulbs survive the dry months of summer on their native prairies. As plants grow, they multiply by dividing in half. If you peel back the reticulations, you often discover that the bulb in your hand is really two bulbs held tightly together by these protective coats.

Allium drummondi is another wild onion that lends itself to naturalizing by seed. The tiny bulbs can be tedious to plant over large areas, yet seed can be readily sown anywhere. The young onions will flower the second spring after planting. *Allium drummondi* makes a wonderful early show when included in a buffalograss meadow along with other prairie flowers. This kind of semi-wild garden can be successful anywhere in the South.

Since both bulbs and seeds of this variety are scarce in the trade, gardeners may wish to mark a native stand during the blooming season and return to harvest seed in late April or May. Once you've got a patch blooming in your yard it's a simple matter to collect seed each season and spread the bulbs further.

An especially dark wine-colored form of *Allium drummondi* discovered by the author near Refugio, Texas; this specimen is blooming well in Tom Peace's garden, Lockhart, Texas.

Western Gold

The arid mesas and rugged basaltic mountains of west Texas are home to a surpassingly lovely garlic, *Allium coryi*. The leaves and bulbs of these little flowers resemble those of *A. drummondi*, but their blooms are rich, waxy yellow. Scattered among the dark volcanic rocks of their homeland, the tiny blossoms look like carpets of sunlight. One could never have too many of these glowing treasures, the only golden garlics in North America.

There are two or three yellow alliums native to the Old World, the most famous of which is the lily leek of southern Europe, *Allium moly*. This variety is showy and well loved in gardens elsewhere, but fares poorly in the warm climate of the South. The Mediterranean *A. flavum* does better, but blooms in June or July. By this time, temperatures have climbed too high for its meager, primrose flowers to last.

Of honestly golden alliums, only *Allium coryi* accepts Southern hospitality. This species increases rapidly through self-sown seed and bulb splitting. The one occasional pitfall seems to be rot during summer rains. This is particularly a problem in gardens with alkaline soils, which accelerate the activity of bacteria and fungi. The best remedy is usually a raised bed filled with acid sand or decomposed granite. This can be left to dry out in summer, or the bulbs may be dug and stored for replanting when cool weather returns.

In the wild, *Allium coryi* usually blooms in April, but in gardens it flowers a

The golden onion of west Texas, *Allium coryi*.

month earlier, along with *A. drummondi*. If both species are planted together (a delightful plan), they will hybridize. The offspring of this cross are pale straw, with pink tints on the keels of the petals. When viewed with sunlight shining through them, the colors suffuse and blend to warm apricot.

Canada Onions

Many native alliums would make excellent garden bulbs, yet most seem to have been intentionally ignored by gardeners. This is, perhaps, the fault of the notorious Canada onion, *Allium canadense*. The frightful weediness of this widespread bulb makes poor public relations for all our wild garlics.

This species produces tiny bulbils (miniature bulbs) in place of, or among its chalky flowers. In some strains the bulbils take on reddish casts and can be fairly attractive. Nevertheless, any show offered hardly apologizes for the bad habits of this species. When the bulbils ripen, they fall to the ground like hundreds of rice grains, and nearly every one sprouts. Even in a wild, naturalistic garden this onion soon makes a pest of itself by crowding less aggressive neighbors. The best revenge is to take these prolific herbs into the kitchen where they may be pressed as garlic and sent straight into the pot.

Inexcusably, taxonomists have attached the tainted reputation of these onions to a number of potentially useful garden flowers listed as varieties of *Allium canadense*. This is an extreme case of what is known in botanical jargon as lumping. Several distinct pink-, rose-, and white-flowered alliums, entirely lacking the treacherous bulbils, have been corralled and dumped into the same pile with a horrendous weed. One can only recall the couplet: "His is not to reason why. His is but to classify."

One of the "varieties" included in this morass is *Allium hyacinthoides*. This is a distinctive flower from north Texas and southern Oklahoma. The sweet, hyacinth-scented blossoms, held in small clusters, are shaped like miniature Grecian urns. They appear in early March, coming in strong shades of pink, old rose, or lavender. The gray-green leaves of *A. hyacinthoides* emerge wide at their bases, but taper quickly to narrow points. This is a hardy, fragrant allium, well suited to the middle and upper South. In the wild it grows in sun or shade, occurring on both sand and clay.

Near the Gulf, the April-flowering *Allium ecristatum* offers similar charms on plants especially suited to damp conditions. Like *A. hyacinthoides*, this onion has rosy blooms cupped upward like little bells or pots. The flowers, which smell like carnations or pinks, are accompanied by green, tapered foliage. They often bloom in standing water in their soggy native habitat on the Texas coastal plain.

Lilac spheres of *Allium mobilense* flowering on a sandy prairie along with crimson Drummond phlox and blue Carolina larkspur, late spring, south-central Texas.

This species relishes heavy clay soils, and multiplies quickly on damp ground. Although *Allium ecristatum* needs an unfailing supply of water during the spring growing season, it appears indifferent to drought during summer. The intriguing bulbs are covered in wide, thick reticulations, which look like miniature lattice work. They multiply by splitting in half.

Allium mobilense (*A. canadense* var. *mobilense*) is the common flowering onion in most of the South, with a range extending from Georgia west to Missouri. Its delicate lavender flowers appear in April on top of thin, twelve-inch stems. The petals spread out star fashion around the pale green ovaries. Although these individual florets are small, they mass together into attention-grabbing umbels. These lilac globes seem to float in the air as they perch above the slender leaves.

Through most of its range this species occurs on loamy prairies, which stay moist in spring and become dry in summer. In gardens *Allium mobilense* responds to damp conditions and acid soil. The bulbs multiply swiftly from offsets appearing around the base. For best effect these pale blooms should be used in large groups. They may be posed before a dark groundcover or among waving meadow grasses to highlight their pallid translucence.

The deep sand ridges of central Texas provide the home for an aristocratic variation of *Allium mobilense*. The big lilac spheres of this onion, rising above sparse, stiff leaves, sit atop stems that may achieve an extravagant eighteen inches. This elegant species was given the queenly name of *A. zenobiae* by botanists who knew it as a friend, although current taxonomic lumpers consign it to the same pile as *A. canadense*.

J. N. Giridlian glowingly described *Allium zenobiae* in the 1954 catalog of Oakhust Gardens: "A recent discovery from Texas, and to our way of thinking the finest of the alliums both for garden and for cutting. The large umbels consist of over 150 florets of satiny white tinged pink." These orphaned flowers deserve to have homes in Southern gardens, despite questions over their botanical pedigree. They make a lovely spring combination with *Phlox drummondii* and are excellent for sandy sites. Many gardens with poor, dry soil would profit from their inclusion.

Allium fraseri blooms on prairies and oak savannahs of Texas during April, and later as it follows spring northward to South Dakota. Its blooms are an alabaster white, like *A. canadense*, but the umbels lack the telltale bulbils of that species. *Allium fraseri* also prefers drier, better drained soils than the Canada onion. This species is an easy-growing spring flower that can be massed as a foil to vibrant blooms like Byzantine gladiolus or irises. The stems reach eighteen inches or more when well grown.

Even larger and better is the "white king," *Allium texanum*, a robust upland species from the hills of Texas and Oklahoma. Its blooms are chalk-white and similar to *A. fraseri*, but its wide, strappy leaves are gray-blue. The flowers assemble in big, dome-shaped umbels that expand near the end of spring, usually during the first weeks of May. Clumps of this allium provide fine companions for early daylilies.

Leeks

Every country person knows how a thriving row of leeks dresses up the vegetable plot. The stunning, tall foliage and big orbs of pinkish green blooms recommend these perennials for flower gardens, too, though they have seldom been invited to such places. Northerners may plead lack of room, but Southerners have no good reason to exclude leeks (*Allium ampeloprasum* var. *porrum*) from their plantings. The other big alliums common in the trade (*A. giganteum*, *A. christophii*, *A. aflatunense*, and their hybrids) perform dismally in this climate, save in cooler parts of the upper South. Of the really large-umbelled *Allium* species, only the short-statured *A. schubertii* blooms successfully without chilling, and this Mediterranean plant must be lifted or otherwise kept dry through summer to avoid rot.

Leeks are bold, architectural vegetables that seem to thrive in all regions. In many parts of the South, the wild ancestral leek, *Allium ampeloprasum*, has escaped from old farms and run wild through the countryside. These old-fashioned flowers look much like traditional culinary leeks, but make smaller stems. Multiplying at an extraordinary pace, they may be seen colonizing old fields and rough woods near former habitations.

Elephant garlic, another variant of the *Allium ampeloprasum* group, resembles an enormous version of its namesake. Its toe-sized cloves have garnered a considerable following and may be found in many supermarkets. One may debate their culinary value as compared to traditional garlic (*A. sativum*), but there can be little question as to superior productivity. Each clove swiftly multiplies into a leek-sized clump in the garden.

Gray-green sheathing leaves, overlapping like a stalk of corn, give the leek and its allies character, whether they are in flower or not. It's this leafy, edible stem that has brought them fame as vegetables. These noble potherbs have thereby earned their place in heraldry, for the leek is the emblem of Wales.

All *Allium ampeloprasum* variants grow easily and thrive even on poor soils. They are gratifyingly perpetual in Southern gardens, readily reproducing by offsets. The perfectly round clusters of flowers appear in May and last for a month in the garden, where they make a handsome focal point or tall backdrop. The blossoms may also be picked and put in a vase without water, where they will last indefinitely.

Egyptian Onions

Another culinary allium that may be put to service in flower gardens is the old multiplying type known in the South as the Egyptian onion. This variation of the common table onion (*Allium cepa*) shares its distinctive, hollow leaves. It differs by having replaced its blooms with fat heads of edible bulbils. These are often shared by gardeners over the fence.

Egyptian onions belong to the readily propagated proliferum group of onions. The true bulbs never get large, and for culinary purposes they are generally harvested and chopped green as scallions. They may be left in the ground over summer, unlike traditional onions, which easily rot away in warm climates.

As with the leek, the value of these bulbs for ornamental gardens is in their unique architectural line. The Egyptian onion produces several hollow leaves in a small cluster. These reach upward like pale green kelps around a Medusa's head of pinkish green bulbils. The whole assemblage looks as if some exotic sea creature had crept into the garden one early day in May.

Chinese Chives

The common chive (*Allium schoenoprasum*) is popular in herb gardens for its flavorful leaves, which are hollow, like those of table onions in miniature. Their charming domes of lavender, appearing in early spring, make a good showing as a border or low edging. During the protracted months of summer, however, these Alpine herbs decline. There is often little left to revive in the fall.

For this reason the chive of choice in most of the South is a very different bulb from Asia, *Allium tuberosum*. This species (fondly nicknamed the Chinese chive or garlic chive, in reference to its aromatic, strappy foliage) is a common herb in Asian cuisine. Its garlic-scented leaves are used in soups, salads, and other dishes for the same oniony effects as European chives, but are always added fresh, since cooking destroys their flavor.

The Chinese chive is a handsome plant, and one that takes happily to garden life. The bright green leaves are accompanied by flat umbels of starry, chalk-white blooms. These flowers are modest and unpredictable in their season, often beginning as early as May and continuing as late as November. Although entirely ordinary in appearance, the blossoms appear faithfully, last well when cut, and complement a variety of other flowers, both in arrangements and in the garden. In many ways they are among the most valuable of Southern garden blooms.

Unlike the strictly bulbous alliums described earlier, *Allium tuberosum* has developed a novel creeping rhizome from which individual bulbs sprout at close intervals. This allows these perennials to clump like dense, green grasses. They multiply swiftly, and may be divided and replanted at almost any time of year. The leaves die away briefly in winter, but are otherwise continuous. This is a reversal of the seasons observed by most alliums in the South.

Drumsticks

Other than the Naples onion, only a few European species seem happy in the South, and most are both dowdy and uncommon in the bulb trade. One that is rather attractive and available is *Allium sphaerocephalum*. The tongue-twisting bit of Latin used to name this species translates as "round-headed." Although vaguely descriptive, such an epithet offers little distinction in this genus of orb-topped herbs. The common name seems more definitive (and pronounceable): drumsticks.

The conical, wine-purple buds of

The drumstick onion, *Allium sphaerocephalum*.

Allium sphaerocephalum elongate slightly as the flowers open. This slowly warps the ball of blooms into a pear shape, so that the expanding umbel appears not unlike the tip of a drumstick in gross outline. The uniquely shaped clusters are one-and-a-half to two inches across. They sit atop stems reaching twelve to eighteen inches in height.

The flowers of the drumstick onion arrive late for Southerners, in mid-June, so they benefit from partial shade to prolong their display and prevent scorching. Otherwise, these alliums are easy and rapid of increase. The erect, blue-green leaves are so sparse and slender as to be invisible. The wispy plants may be mixed among shrubs and perennials without fear of intruding on the design. The rich purple blooms show well among gray artemisias or silver germanders (*Teucrium* spp.).

Society Garlic

A pretty South African ally of the alliums is *Tulbaghia violacea*, known as *wilde knoflook* ("wild garlic") in its homeland, and as society garlic in America. This is a marvelous bulb for Southern gardens, with a flowering season lasting the whole summer. The rich lavender-pink blooms, with tiny crests in the center of the petals, grow together in tight umbels on stems a foot high. The more or less evergreen leaves clump prolifically like Chinese chives.

Society garlic has a wide range from the Cape Province north to Zimbabwe and the Northern Province of South Africa, adapting to varied soils and temperate to tropical climates. It would make a fine cut flower if not for the rank juice in its stems and leaves. This slimy fluid smells like a mixture of onion and turnip, causing one to wonder in what kind of society these garlics would be appropriate. On the plus side, the acrid sap helps to preserve *Tulbaghia violacea* from browsing deer and rabbits.

In the garden, the common strains of *Tulbaghia violacea* are tough and enduring, readily recovering from drought and from temperatures as low as 15°F. Gardeners will be rewarded with better, more prolific bloom, however, if they give regular moisture through summer and modest shelter from frost during winter. This advice goes double for 'Silver Lace', a beautiful, white-variegated selection. Society garlics thrive best on a rich, well-prepared loam. They prove equally happy in open sun or part shade.

The pink agapanthus or sweet garlic, *Tulbaghia simmleri* (*T. fragrans*), is larger and more beautiful in most respects than *T. violacea*, but its winter flowering season prohibits use north of the lower South. Where frost is severe, these bulbs may be enjoyed in tubs on the patio. This species has very wide, gray foliage, which grows lavishly in summer but may flag and die away somewhat in winter. The dormant, leafless bulbs send up long-stemmed umbels of fragrant pink blooms. Appearing from November to April, they will last a week or more in a vase. Several additional *Tulbaghia* species are native to the summer rainfall regions of South Africa and would be worthy of trial in the South.

Crow Poison

In early March, before most flowers have awakened from winter sleep, roadsides and lawns begin to brighten with the small, creamy flowers and glossy, green leaves of crow poison (*Nothoscordum bivalve*). These tiny, yellow-centered blooms could be overlooked, if not for their welcome earliness and pleasant fragrance, which is sweet and spicy like old-fashioned carnations. On damp, protected banks near streams, the little blossoms appear in the company of lush green winter grasses and blue, purple, and wine-pink spiderworts. In such situations these precocious wildlings show their cheery blooms long before spring begins elsewhere.

Crow poison is a common native of the South, and grows also in Mexico and in South America, where it has several relations. The members of the genus *Nothoscordum*, or false onions, all have an onionlike build, but lack the pungent odor of true alliums. They bear fewer blossoms in their umbels, and the bulbs are white-coated, with a peculiar spongy texture unlike the hard skins of an onion. All the species flower over a long season in spring and early summer and thrive under ordinary care. Many, including *N. bivalve*, return to flower with fall rains. Although seldom showy, these small blooms are welcome.

The spreading tendencies of *Nothoscordum bivalve* offer little threat, but the same cannot be said of its weedy cousin, *N. gracile* (*N. inodorum*, *N. fragrans*). This Argentine species produces larger, more fragrant blooms than *N. bivalve*, but also forms myriad bulblets. In only a week's time a dried bulb set in a paper bag might produce fifty offsets, each prepared to rain down on the ground and begin to grow. Unless gardeners are wary, entire yards may be swallowed in the dirty white blooms and gray foliage of this aggressive plant.

Although *Nothoscordum gracile* should be avoided, there are several other South American *Nothoscordum* species of merit. *Nothoscordum nocturnum* has long, grayish leaves and nice-sized, whitish blooms marked with purplish keels. These remain partially closed in the daytime but open at dusk to emit a sweet, musky perfume. Although *N. montevidense* is small, it sends up a succession of bright golden blooms that would be an asset to any garden. *Nothoscordum arenarium* contributes starry umbels of pure white flowers in spring and fall.

Blossoms of the Harvest

As a rule, most things Californian fare poorly when brought to the South. The languid atmosphere here sets a different pace for life than the sunny breezes of the west. Still, there are a handful of onionlike westerners that persist, so long as they are offered spots where they may bask. In nature these flowers bloom at the onset of summer drought. On rolling hillsides dotted with evergreen oaks, they mix among masses of ripening grass. When hay is harvested, the blooms may be cut and baled.

In early classifications these papery flowers were grouped in the large genus *Brodiaea*, but now they may be met in such genera as *Triteleia* and *Dichelostemma*. Their six-petaled blossoms appear in sparse clusters that superficially favor alliums. The meager, unscented leaves are angular in cross section and rise from corms instead of bulbs. In California these plants are sometimes called fool's onion.

During the years between 1893 and 1945, an unusually capable plantsman, Carl Purdy, brought these western wildflowers into wide cultivation. A number of his introductions remain in commerce and are now available at modest prices. Most are permanent, but slow to increase in Southern gardens. They may be raised from seed more rapidly than from offsets.

One of the most widespread of this group is blue-dicks (*Dichelostemma capitatum*). Its natural range extends from Baja California to Oregon and inland to New Mexico, often appearing alongside sheets of golden orange California poppies. In mid-March, the washy, lilac blooms rise in tight clusters on twelve-inch stems. The individual florets bear tiny crests like blooms of society garlic. They last almost a month, while the leaves simultaneously yellow and wither.

'Pink Diamonds' is a cross between blue-dicks and a firecracker-red Californian species, *Dichelostemma ida-maia*, whose hanging, tubular flowers are pollinated by hummingbirds. This unusual hybrid is a true intermediate, bearing short-tubed, lavender-rose flowers in loose, semi-pendant umbels. Both *D. ida-maia* and 'Pink Diamonds' demand positions with good drainage and prefer to bake dry in summer, but are otherwise easy to accommodate in the South.

Other bulbs in this western group flower mostly in May and hold their cupped blooms in loose umbels like crowds of tiny shuttlecocks. One of the best of these later types is the wild hyacinth (*Triteleia hyacinthina*). Its blooms, usually with milky petals and green keels, occasionally shade to pale lavender. The flowers are sweetly fragrant and may be cut and dried for long-lasting winter arrangements. In the wild this species occurs from British Columbia to California. Unlike most of its kin, this species does well in low, moist areas.

Ithuriel's spear (*Triteleia laxa*) has more typical preferences. In nature it grows in areas of adobe soil. It doesn't mind waterlogged sites in the garden during winter, but when summer arrives it expects to be thoroughly dried and ripened.

These one-inch flowers awaken May gardens with an explosive charge of gentian-blue lined in dark green. Such rich hues are rarely available to gardeners in the South, so these blossoms may be forgiven for their sparse, yellowing foliage at bloom time. If planted among waving winter grasses, as in their native California and Oregon hills, the tattered leaves will disappear from view, and the deep violet flowers will shine like sapphires set in gold. Mexican feathergrass (*Nassella tenuissima*) turns to ripe tones of straw and chartreuse in late April and makes a suitable foil in the South.

Older selections of *Triteleia laxa*, such as the lighter blue 'Queen Fabiola' and blue-violet, purple-tipped 'Corrina', are widely available and worthwhile. 'Royal Blue' is a recently introduced double-flowered form. *Triteleia* ×*tubergenii*, a hybrid between Ithuriel's spear and a related species, *T. peduncularis*, looks like a lilac edition of *T. laxa* with darker blue rims. The novel *T. ixioides* 'Starlight' offers umbels of light yellow, up-facing stars on short-statured plants.

Spring Stars

A diminutive ally of these harvest flowers, *Androstephium caeruleum*, grows on undisturbed prairies from central Texas to Oklahoma and northward. Those who know this short, early flower sometimes call it blue funnel lily, but most people have never even seen it. The pale lavender blooms appear in March before the grass greens up, and it takes an observant eye to spot them hovering above the drab ground. Once discovered, they will not be forgotten, for the slender, starry petals have a succulent, transparent beauty. When numerous, they resemble fields of celestial anemones.

These little flowers favor gravelly areas with thin soil and fast drainage. In gardens they are useful for rockeries or troughs where their small stature will not be overpowered by taller, more aggressive flowers. They have never entered the regular bulb trade, but may sometimes be had from rock garden specialists. As with its relations, *Androstephium caeruleum* multiplies most quickly from seed.

Woodlanders

For a magical few weeks, certain Southern woodlands fill with carpets of spotted leaves. In February the delicate, marbled foliage unfurls into the frosty air and lays close against the earth. March brings ephemeral nodding blooms to join the dappled greenery. As April thunderstorms arrive, everything yellows and retreats into the ground to await another season.

This is the fleeting life cycle of *Erythronium albidum*, the trout lily, one of the well-loved forest flowers of America. The picturesque common name recalls the spotted skin of a brook trout, which the plant's mottled, elliptical leaves resemble. Fawn lily and adder's tongue also refer to this foliage. Dog's tooth violet is a quaint title inherited from the European *E. dens-canis*, whose long, pointed corm suggests a canine fang.

These small wildlings, because they nod and face the earth like tiny tiger lilies, can be viewed properly only with close inspection. Despite their unimposing proportions, the subtly colored flowers provoke delight in all who see them. The little blooms bespeak secret charm, as if they knew hidden groves where the forest fairies dance on moonlit nights.

Trout lilies are mostly native to places where spring is a longer, milder season than in the South. In consequence of this, their period of growth and flowering at these latitudes has been curtailed to a few brief weeks of spring. Only those who walk the woods on a regular basis know these flowers intimately.

The white- to lavender-flowered *Erythronium albidum* ranges through the middle and upper South, where the small corms seek out loamy terrace soils along watercourses. This is the easiest of our natives to bring into gardens, as it withstands drought and heavy soil. The yellow-flowered *E. rostratum* is also common in some parts of the South, but only in rich woodlands. It is a variation of the widespread yellow dog's tooth violet of the North, *E. americanum*. Its corms resemble the true bulbs of tulips and grow deeply in leafy, moist ground.

The trout lily, *Erythronium albidum*.

Both of these wildflowers have reputations as shy bloomers. This diffidence usually is blamed on their tendency to multiply by underground stolons, so that the plants develop into big patches of undersized bulbs, each with a solitary leaf. Only corms that mature and make two or three leaves will flower. Nestling them against rocks or trees will often encourage the corms to size up and bloom.

In addition to these native species, the creamy yellow *Erythronium californicum* may persist in cooler parts of the South. Up to three widely reflexed blooms accompany its mottled, glossy green leaves. These bulbs inhabit redwood groves in northern California and enjoy a rich, damp soil.

Dog's tooth violet (*Erythronium dens-canis*) may also be flowered in the South, but usually won't persist more than a few seasons. Since the species has a wide range through Europe and Asia, its numerous forms might be tested for permanence. This would be a worthwhile project for woodland gardeners in the middle and upper South. Several showy named selections are available in shades of white, pink, purple, and lilac.

Wake-Robins

As with erythroniums, wake-robins (*Trillium* spp.) are flowers of cool, moist forests. They put in an ephemeral spring appearance before leafy canopies fill in to block the summer sun. Although they might seem out of place in company with palmettos and magnolias, several species are native to loamy, neutral soils in woodlands south as far as the Gulf Coast. These grow readily enough in shaded gardens to recommend use even in the warmest parts of the South. Their creeping rhizomes slowly develop into good clumps, which may be divided and reset in any shaded position.

The most prolific wake-robins in the South are several similar species with purple-blotched foliage. *Trillium ludovicianum* of Louisiana, *T. gracile* of east-

Trillium ludovicianum with fallen live oak leaves and a dwarf ivy.

ern Texas, and *T. underwoodii* of north Florida closely resemble each other, and all three are allies of the more widespread eastern toadshade, *T. sessile*. Although less glamorous than the large-flowered northern trilliums, these species show the typical redundant pattern of three characteristic of this genus. Their attractively mottled leaves rise in early winter, expanding in whorls of three triangular blades. A greenish or maroon-flushed, three-petaled bud, sitting firmly in the center, persists in a closed position until late February, when it opens to reveal a maroon interior and three brownish red, upright inner petals. This somber color scheme is complemented by an unusual fragrance reminiscent of wild mushrooms.

These toadshades sometimes occur in pale greenish yellow phases as well as the typical dark maroon. Other varieties met in Southern woodlands include the purple trillium or bloody butcher (*Trillium recurvatum*), also with dappled leaves and purplish blooms, and the pink-tinged, green-leafed *T. pusillum*. Several rarer, showier species would be worth trying in northern Alabama and the southern Appalachians. Elizabeth Lawrence gives a tantalizing discussion of several trilliums successful in the Carolinas in *The Little Bulbs*.

Native trilliums are well worth acquiring for shady gardens. However, the delicate tubers should not be moved from the wild unless the forest is to be destroyed or developed. Several specialist nurseries propagate these wildflowers, and a variety of lovely species may be had in good conscience and at nominal cost. Patient gardeners may also raise them from fresh seed, which may be sown directly in moist, shady ground.

Solomon's Seals

The Solomon's seals (*Polygonatum* spp.) are leafy lilies whose associations are with the coolest, most boreal forests. They seem poor choices for warm climates like the South, yet several survive here and prove amazingly tough, thriving even on poor ground. The elegant, leafy arcs of foliage and tiny, drooping, bell-like flowers have much to offer any shady garden.

These hardy perennials spring from an elongated horizontal rhizome with annular rings like the roots of a bamboo. This is the source of the old Greek name of these herbs, *polygonaton* ("many knees"). This characteristic also explains their common name: each year a new ring appears on the roots after the leaves and flowers wither, and this is vaguely suggestive of a rounded seal.

The great Solomon's seal, *Polygonatum biflorum*, is the most common type in native woodlands. This handsome species is sometimes listed as *P. giganteum* in catalogs. It's an excellent grower, achieving three feet on rich, moist soil. It ranges through the South and down into the forested mountains of Nuevo Leon, Mexico. The delicate, greenish flowers of these plants make do with quiet beauty instead of loud color. When well treated, they ripen to purplish berries.

Polygonatum odoratum (often sold as *P. falcatum*) is usually cultivated in its choice variegated form, 'Variegata', which develops creamy edges on the leaves, beautifully accented by purplish colors on the stems. This tough native of Japan and Korea does surprisingly well in the warm climate of the South, returning faithfully each spring, even if subjected to scorching drought in summer. The rhizomes require several years to settle in before offering much bloom, but the lovely foliage offers a show from the outset. This combines happily with leafy banks of ferns and other woodland perennials. Other selections of *P. odoratum* introduced from Korea by Tony Avent are purple-stemmed 'Chollipo', light green-foliaged 'Lemon Seoul', and an unusual, large-leafed variant with gracefully twisted stems, 'Spiral Staircase'.

Several other *Polygonatum* species have been brought into gardens from Asia in recent decades and seem promising for the South. These include the dwarf groundcovering *P. humile* and an unusual orange-flowered form of the thread-leafed, climbing Solomon's seal, *P. kingianum*. A lushly vigorous species from southeastern China, *P. cyrtonema*, annually drapes hundreds of green-tipped white blossoms from its robustly branched stems.

Tulips

Tulips have long been features in the same gardens where the formal cult of azaleas and camellias holds court. These tall, majestic flowers are annually bedded in wide rows before glittering green shrubs, or may be massed in deep beds to bloom with dogwoods, redbuds, and wisteria. Less lively flowers would expose the artifice of these orchestrations, but the ravishing loveliness and rich color of tulips invariably bring off a grand show. In the South warm temperatures may advance and threaten their flowering season, but spring would be less magnificent if we did not at least try to grow these flowers.

Beyond these annually renewed displays, however, very few Southern gardeners give these blooms a second thought. Tulips are hardly ever advanced for use as perennials. The hybrid bedding varieties are casually selected by color, with little thought of their potential for long-term survival. While it is true that most tulip varieties are ill suited to Southern latitudes, a few are satisfactory, and more might be discovered or developed if gardeners made an effort to explore the genus instead of replacing bulbs each fall.

The first garden tulip, like the first anemone, hyacinth, and ranunculus, was the pet flower of some ancient Eastern sultan. Turkish horticulturists are often credited with their domestication, but Persians had tulips at an early date and also participated in their development. In both countries warm, dry summers follow spring. The old tulips grew in a much balmier climate than Holland, where our modern types have been bred.

Twelfth-century Persian poets praised the beauty of "multicolored tulips"; some historians have taken this as the first evidence of these flowers in gardens. Authorities disagree on the origin of the tulip, but consider *Tulipa gesneriana*, a scarlet species from Asia Minor, as the most likely progenitor. The first domestic derivatives were introduced to Europe from Turkey in the late sixteenth century. Our modern hybrids descend from this initial oriental infusion.

The Lady Tulip

It is possible that the old poems refer not to the hybrid tulip, but to what Parkinson and other early botanists called the Persian tulip, *Tulipa clusiana*. Modern gardeners know this red and white species as lady tulip or candy tulip. These cheery blooms rate among the most useful and permanent types in the South. They may also be the oldest of their race in gardens.

Like many bulbs that excel in warm climates, *Tulipa clusiana* is blessed with an added arsenal of DNA: technically, the species is a pentaploid, with five sets of chromosomes. Despite this anomalous condition, it sets viable seed and has

Lady tulip (*Tulipa clusiana*) with bluebonnets (*Lupinus texensis*) and annual golden corydalis.

naturalized in several countries around the Mediterranean. The vigorous bulbs also multiply by droopers (stolons), and in some strains by offsets or buds from the base.

Carolus Clusius (Charles d'Ecluse), author of *Rariorum Plantarum Historia* (A History of Rare Plants) and the man remembered in this flower's epithet, reported the introduction of *Tulipa clusiana* to the gardens of Florence in 1606. The original home of the lady tulip seems to have stretched from the mountains of Iran to Kashmir, but it has been cultivated for so long that the limit of this distribution is now unclear.

This history would mean little today if it concerned a drab, ordinary flower, but the lady tulip ranks as one of the prettiest species of its genus. The cheerfully marked blooms reach a respectable size yet always appear nimble and lithe. The twelve- to fourteen-inch stems carry a few slender, gray leaves with reddish margins. The upper two-thirds of the flower stalk remains bare, so as to show off the bright red and white blossom. Long stems may be cut without removing foliage, and buds may be guiltlessly harvested for indoor arrangements.

Vibrant cherry splashes appear over the lady tulip's outer petals. Only their margins show a bit of white, so the flowers appear entirely red when closed. Milky inner petals become visible as the bloom opens. When the long buds fully expand they reveal a cream-colored interior with a central blotch of carmine and six purple stamens.

One of the delights of the lady tulip and other members of this genus is their daily ritual of movement. Tulips show their love for the spring sun by tracking the heavens each day. In the cool of the morning, the buds nod to the east and slowly open wider as the day progresses. By noon they are spread flat and looking skyward; at four o'clock they lean toward the setting sun and begin to shut for the evening. In a clump of a dozen bulbs, this lively activity may repeat daily for a fortnight as each flower matures and runs its course.

Lady tulips have an undemanding nature, but they prosper best when offered well-drained, limy soils like those of their homeland. The small, brown-skinned bulbs bear a tuft of hair at the tip. This is part of a silky tunic surrounding the bulbs and preserving them through the arid summers of their homelands. Gardeners should take a hint from this natural device and offer these flowers a good summer baking. Beds filled with gritty, perfectly drained compost will be welcomed. This ensures the continuance of these Mideastern flowers for many seasons.

A form of the lady tulip from Afghanistan and Kashmir, var. *stellata*, differs in its shorter stature, narrower, more expansive petals, yellow stamens, and yellow central blotch. Another relation, *Tulipa clusiana* var. *chrysantha* originates

'Tubergen's Gem' in spring sunlight.

Tulipa 'Lady Jane' naturalized among cool-season grasses.

from Kashmir and has blooms with a bright yellow ground, marked red on the outer petals. An especially vibrant selection of this short-statured form, 'Tubergen's Gem', makes an ideal subject to nest among rocks in a raised bed.

Although formerly common in the bulb trade, *Tulipa clusiana* has been largely supplanted by several of its hybrids. These preserve many good characters of the species, although the wild form is still worth growing in its own right. 'Lady Jane' is a vigorous hybrid with rosy pink outer petals, stained yellow at the base, and showing a narrow white band along their edges. These alternate with three all-white inner petals around a cream-colored interior without the typical purple blotch of the species. 'Cynthia' is a six-to eight-inch hybrid with sulfury, red-flamed blooms, developed by crossing *T. clusiana* and its variety *chrysantha*. 'Tinka' is similar, but larger, reaching eight to ten inches. All enjoy the same culture as common lady tulips.

In the South the lady tulip and its cultivars may be planted in groups among clumps of summer snowflakes (*Leucojum aestivum*) and *Narcissus* 'Trevithian'. This triad of bulbs will bloom reliably together, usually in mid-April. Their slender grace complements one another, and they will all return and increase without need for disturbance. Bluebonnets (*Lupinus texensis*) and wild foxglove (*Penstemon cobaea*) are other good companions.

More Tulip Species

The Cretan tulip (*Tulipa saxatilis*) has a reputation for shy flowering, since some strains multiply to excess. All too often, only blind, undersized bulbs are produced. The lush, glossy foliage tells the tale when it comes up in December and makes its green sheet across the rockery. Nothing could frustrate a gardener more than the sight of a forest of solitary leaves, for this is a sure sign the bulbs will be too small to flower.

Like many species tulips, *Tulipa saxatilis* naturally propagates with droopers. Although nurseries have offered bulbs with these multiplicative habits in the past, recent selection efforts have sought to eliminate such traits. Instead of running, the improved *T. saxatilis* offsets. Nurseries usually offer it as the cultivar 'Lilac Wonder' or under the old synonym *T. bakeri*. Under any title these modern editions of *T. saxatilis* are improvements, offering bigger bulbs and surer flowering.

This is a happy turn of events for gardeners, since the blooms of *Tulipa saxatilis* are colored a delicious mixture of pink-lilac around a yellow center. The flowers are short, but open into wide bowls. When well grown, they arrive three to a stem. The bulbs resemble those of *T. clusiana* and seem equally permanent. As the epithet *saxatilis* ("rock dwelling") suggests, these Mediterranean flowers prefer gritty, well-drained compost with plenty of lime.

In more moist aspects of the garden, the species to try is the Florentine tulip (*Tulipa sylvestris*). Although the Latin epithet seems to imply a preference for woodland, this early flower is more often a denizen of fields and meadows. Its native range extends over Persia and Europe, where it is common in old pastures and vineyards. It has also escaped from gardens to run wild in the mid-Atlantic region of the United States. Thomas Jefferson reportedly had both this and *T. clusiana* in his garden at Monticello.

Tulipa sylvestris has a slender, lithe appearance, and a modest, twelve-inch stature. The medium-sized bulbs are covered with silky tunics that glow with the warm orange tone of sandalwood. There are two or three flowers to a stem, with several thick gray leaves

Tulipa saxatilis 'Lilac Wonder', flowering in company with the ferny foliage of love-in-a-mist (*Nigella damascena*). Photo by Lauren S. Ogden.

near the base of the stalks. The pale lemon buds are suffused with green and nod gracefully prior to opening. In mid-March they turn upward and expand into fragrant, yellow goblets. The pleasant scent of these blooms, vaguely resembling that of sweet violets, inspired the fulsome trinomial of a previous era, *Tulipa florentina odorata*.

Tulipa sylvestris is yet another tulip with a well-known spreading tendency. This may cause some loss of bloom, but if the soil is deep and rich, the bulbs should establish and yield enough flowers to justify the colonies of leaves. A selection from Iran called 'Tabris' and another called 'Major' are reportedly larger, more free flowering, and less colonial. *Tulipa sylvestris* var. *australis* is a Mediterranean variant with slightly smaller blooms.

The elegant Greek tulip (*Tulipa orphanidea*) has much of the slender grace of *T. sylvestris*, occurring commonly with muted, greenish apricot blooms or, in its popular variant 'Whittallii' (*T. whittallii*), with soft bronze-orange flowers. One to three lively blossoms appear atop its twelve-inch stems. These graceful Mediterranean flowers prefer drier, better-drained positions than the Florentine tulip, but otherwise seem equally adaptable.

Another curious tulip sometimes included on nursery lists is the horned tulip, *Tulipa acuminata*. No one seems sure about the origin of this plant, although it resembles some of the slender blossoms depicted in *The Book of Tulips* written in Turkey around 1725. The extraordinarily skinny blooms first showed up in gardens about 1816, reportedly as imports from the eastern Mediterranean. Their long, undulating petals are orange-red and long-lasting, but their thinness makes the flowers more odd than attractive. This species seems to have no need for winter chilling, but must be offered excellent drainage and a dry summer rest.

Somewhat similar to the horned tulip is the old *Tulipa retroflexa*, which was used to breed the modern lily-flowered varieties. These late-blooming tulips were developed from crosses with Darwin tulips. They were once included among the cottage tulips, a race of perennial types rediscovered and collected from old gardens during the nineteenth century. The lily-flowered tulips inherit graceful, vase-shaped blooms and strong, upright stems. Some, such as the orange-flowered 'Ballerina', show their legacy of antique breeding with a sweet fragrance.

Lily-flowered tulips have little need of winter chilling. In the South, vigorous selections, such as the glowing red-and-yellow 'Queen of Sheba', will perpetuate, so long as they are kept dry over summer. This may be accomplished with a raised bed of sand, or by lifting and storing the bulbs over summer. Since the lily-flowered cultivars are among the tallest tulips, deep planting is preferred to prevent rocking about in windy spring weather. A depth of six to eight inches is standard.

The Red Ones

Sometimes listed as *T. undulatifolia*, the gaudy red *Tulipa eichleri* is another tulip that endures in the South if sheltered from summer dampness. Although a natural species, its brilliant flowers compete in showiness with any hybrid. The magnificent blooms nestle between broad, gray leaves. Shiny brownish black, yellow-edged blotches gleam back from the center of the flowers. The plants don't always achieve their full twelve-inch height in unsteady spring weather, but this species is as reliable for early color as any tulip, and longer lasting than most. The native haunts of *T. eichleri* are in Turkestan and Iran, where the bulbs inhabit dry hillsides and fallow cornfields.

The showy *Tulipa linifolia* also provides red flowers without need for winter chill. This black-eyed miniature hails from Uzbeskistan in central Asia and is ideally suited to rock gardens. Its narrow leaves spread out like little gray starfishes. Eye-popping, silky red blossoms appear between the foliage in April. Several showy hybrids between *T. linifolia* and the soft yellow *T. batalinii*, with bronze, scarlet, or apricot flowers, may be had as well. If protected from summer wet, these will return for several seasons.

For general garden situations, however, the best of the red tulips, and perhaps the showiest of any tulip species in the South, is the early-blooming *Tulipa praecox*. About the same time the clustered blooms of *Narcissus tazetta* 'Grand

A fifty-year-old planting of early-flowering red tulips (*Tulipa praecox*) in a North Texas garden with equally old beds of *Narcissus tazetta* 'Grand Primo' just fading in the background.

Primo' begin to fade, the satiny, fawn-colored buds of this old garden tulip begin to open on stout, twelve- to eighteen-inch stems. These unique flowers sport three long, pointed outer petals set around a ring of inner petals that are significantly smaller. These also have distinct yellow bands marking the keels. The blooms expand to reveal brilliant scarlet-red interiors around shiny, greenish black eyes bordered in yellow, much as in *T. eichleri*. The undulating, grayish leaves, usually three to five from each blooming bulb, also resemble the foliage of that species. When spring sunlight passes through the succulent petals late in the day, a bed of *T. praecox* fluoresces in a sea of red unrivaled by any Southern blossom.

What makes this tulip such a success in plantings, however, is its prolific tendency to spread by short stolons, so that plantings increase by their own means into thrifty patches. In varied places around the South, old frame farmhouses will be found smothered in beds of *Tulipa praecox*. Even on the heavy clay soils favored for cotton production, these tulips persist and multiply. They seem miraculously indifferent to the summer humidity that frustrates other tulip species.

Tulipa praecox has a long history in gardens and is widely naturalized through southern France, Italy, and other Mediterranean countries. It is known in its native Turkey simply as *kaba lale* ("wild tulip"). First described botanically in 1811 from plants found near Bologna, Italy, *T. praecox* may actually represent an old garden selection, as all the plants known seem to be sterile triploid forms. It is close to several other red-flowered Mediterranean tulips such as *T. aleppensis* and *T. agenensis* (*T. oculis-solis*) and its subspecies *boissieri*, known in Israel as *T. sharonensis*. Unfortunately for modern-day gardeners, none of these species is common in the bulb trade, although they are frequent wildlings in olive groves and stony pastures around the Mediterranean.

Blue Bottles

One of the first flowers met by any child growing up in the South is the little blue muscari, known fondly as the blue bottle or grape hyacinth. These modest yet bright blossoms are in all the old lawns. They spread quickly by bulblets and seed, and have naturalized in all sorts of places. The dark green, wiry leaves come up in the fall, so the clumps make an obvious green tuft all winter. In early March the bulbs send up sweet-scented, violet-blue spikes. This is when children discover them and gather the blooms in tight handfuls to inhale their fruity perfume.

These old flowers have made themselves at home in our country and may be seen growing on many soils and exposures. They are the first spring bulbs that come to mind when anyone speaks about naturalizing. It's often taken for granted that any grape hyacinth will settle down and spread, just like the ones populating wayside gardens. In truth, the standard muscari of commerce seldom naturalize in the South, although nearly all flower well for a season or two.

The authentic dark blue bottle so widespread in old gardens belongs to a widespread European species that has never been common in the bulb trade. It is known by tradition as the starch hyacinth. Parkinson may have initiated this title when he described the fragrance of the small violet blooms as "like unto starch when it is hot and new."

The confusing botany of *Muscari* presents difficulty even for experts, and the dust has yet to settle on any listing that might be regarded as final, though perhaps DNA examination will offer a verdict in the future. In any case, the old grape hyacinth of the South displays characteristics readily distinguishing it from other varieties. Its globular, blackish blue flowers congregate in spikes, or racemes, with up to thirty downward-drooping blossoms. These sit on six- to eight-inch stems among the overly lush clumps of foliage. The lowest blossoms open first, revealing a rim of white teeth as they expand. At the top of the spike, a group of sterile florets shades to azure. These old-fashioned grape hyacinths, *M. racemosum* or *M. atlanticum* to past authors, are now better known as *M. neglectum*. This seems an appropriate epithet for a bulb so common about abandoned homesteads and untended meadows.

Although a select form of *Muscari neglectum* is available from Dutch nurseries, it does not seem to be the same persistent strain common to older Southern gardens. The more usual muscari imported from Holland are forms of *M. armeniacum*, which bloom well the year they are planted, but seldom persist in the South more than a season or two afterward. This species resembles the starch hyacinth, but has showier azure or purplish blue flowers without the distinctive pale rims. The Italian grape hyacinth (*M. botryoides*) is also close to these. It is commonly grown in its white variety, 'Album', which has the appealing nickname pearls of Spain. The beautiful sky-blue *M. tubergenianum* is another look-alike grape

Blue bottle or starch hyacinth (*Muscari neglectum*) blooming in an unmowed lawn.

hyacinth that reportedly originates from the mountains of Iran. Botanists suggest it may be a form of *M. aucheri*, a grape hyacinth from high mountains in Turkey, or a hybrid between *M. aucheri* and *M. armeniacum*. These and several other varieties of muscari may be coaxed to persist in the South if planted in raised beds of sand, but otherwise are likely to dwindle away and need replacing every few years.

Feather Hyacinths

Gardeners love a curiosity, as surely is testified by the prevalence of the feather, or plume, hyacinth in old Southern gardens. Other than *Muscari neglectum*, this novelty is the only grape hyacinth likely to be met in a naturalized condition. Thomas Jefferson recorded their bloom at Monticello on 25 April 1767.

These singular flowers, already well known in Parkinson's time, were probably introduced by the same ingenious Turks who developed the tulip and other Near Eastern bulbs. Botanists generally regard the feather hyacinth as a sterile form of *Muscari comosum* (tassel hyacinth). In its ordinary dress the species appears as a drab, loose, olive-green spike garnished with a topknot of dark purple.

The feather hyacinth hardly resembles this wild form. Instead of the bell-shaped blooms of ordinary muscari, its intriguing spike is transformed into an amethyst filigree. The branched, feathery tassels have a delicate translucence, which makes them seem glassy when lit by the April sun. They rise eight to ten inches above the curling, succulent, gray-green leaves.

Feather hyacinths bloom after the big rush of spring flowers, toward the end of April or first of May. Since the blossoms last for several weeks, they provide a useful accent at this transitional moment, when many early flowers are finishing and the blooms of summer have yet to begin. Their delicate lavender combines happily with broad, gray foliage, such as lamb's ears (*Stachys byzantina*). The shallow bulbs do well in sun or partial shade, so long as they are provided reasonably well-drained soil. They multiply swiftly and may be divided and reset every two or three years.

There has been a move on among some botanists to transfer the feather hyacinth, the tassel hyacinth, and a

Muscari comosum 'Plumosum' (*M. plumosum*), the feather hyacinth.

handful of other odd muscari into a separate genus, *Leopoldia*. If this view is followed *Muscari comosum* becomes *Leopoldia comosum* and the feather hyacinth should then be *L. comosum* 'Plumosum'. Most nurseries continue to list these flowers simply as *M. plumosum*. The most recent DNA analysis suggests they are correct.

Nutmeg Hyacinths

Another odd flower sometimes segregated from the herd of muscari is the nutmeg hyacinth, listed either as *Muscari* or *Muscarimia ambrosiacum*. This pale lavender and white flower is thought to be an old garden form of musk hyacinth (*Muscari moschatum*). Tiny spikes of barrel-shaped blooms rise above its thick-rooted bulbs toward the end of March. These pearly flowers can hardly be considered showy, but they are worth planting for their sweet fragrance. Gerard explained in 1597: "They are kept and maintained in gardens for the pleasant smell of their floures, but not for their beauty, for that many stinking field floures do in beautie farre surpasse them."

These old Turkish bulbs bloom readily in the South, persisting if planted in raised beds of sand so that they may bake dry during summer. Their flowers and foliage are so meager, however, that most landscape companions are likely to overpower them. An attractive niche among stones or a top dressing of crushed gravel or ultra-low groundcovers like the tiny Turkish stonecrop (*Sedum hispanicum* var. *bithynicum*) may be positioned to accommodate groups of *Muscari ambrosiacum* in rock gardens or raised beds, where their fragrance can be appreciated. The long-necked bulbs produce a perennial root system that takes much of their energy during the first season, so flowers should not be expected until the second spring. *Muscari macrocarpum* 'Golden Fragrance', an interesting relation of *M. ambrosiacum*, blooms with spikes of tubular yellow flowers topped with tufts of sterile lavender florets. Its strong scent is suggestive of bananas.

Hyacinth Squills

In old gardens, you may often see dark green rosettes marking winter beds like rows of lush, glossy starfishes. If you dig up the clumps, they reveal substantial, white, fleshy bulbs with large, visible scales. In many instances, these leafy perennials disappear mysteriously in early summer without ever having offered bloom, and gardeners are left to wonder for another season what curious flower belongs with this robust foliage.

Sometimes the solution to the puzzle is met along a nearby creek or stream.

On moist riversides these same bulbs escape cultivation to naturalize on the loamy terrace soils. Here they receive enough spring moisture to complete flowering. The big bulbs do not disappoint, for in late April they send up impressive, three-foot spikes of starry, lavender flowers. Arranged in loose, pyramidal racemes that open from the base, swarms of hazy lilac blooms and similarly colored flower stems expand below a tight spear of pale green and lavender buds.

This original and dramatic bulbous flower has long been known as the hyacinth squill (*Scilla hyacinthoides*). It's a Middle Eastern native commonly naturalized in southern Italy. It persists indefinitely in Southern gardens, but rarely blooms without coaxing. To encourage regular flowering, it's best to lift bulbs annually as the foliage yellows in early June. They may be replanted in autumn in rich, well-prepared ground. If irrigated generously through April, flowering will be ensured. Botanists, presently reorganizing the squills, have proposed a new name for this bulb, *Nectaroscilla hyacinthoides* (hyacinth squill).

This obscure, yet traditional, flower is often confused with a similar blue squill from South Africa, best known as *Scilla natalensis*, but in the recent squill reclassification, *Merwilla plumbea*. Although the two species are remarkably alike in flower, *M. plumbea* has fewer, wider leaves and normally grows with its succulent bulbs protruding from the ground. This subtropical bulb is a summer grower that flowers in July. It would be worth trying in warmer parts of the South.

The meadow squill (*Scilla litardierei*) is a slender relation of *Nectaroscilla hyacinthoides* with similar flowers, grouped in a more modest, eight- to fifteen-inch raceme. This hardy Dalmatian bulb was formerly known as *Scilla pratensis*, or *S. amethystina*, and will still be met under these names on nursery lists. Although native among limestone rocks, in the South it also grows and increases well on sandy soils, blooming in early summer. In the proposed *Scilla* split it becomes *Chouardia litardierei*.

Cuban Lilies

Another large squill successful in Southern gardens also carries an air of mystery, although not from shy flowering. At some point in history it acquired the curious common names Peruvian lily and Cuban lily and the Latin name *Scilla peruviana*. Botanists have proposed changing this to *Oncostema peruviana*. Since this plant grows naturally in hot, dry countries along the western Mediterranean, the epithet *peruviana* seems something of a misnomer. Reportedly, Clusius described this bulb from plants originally brought aboard the ship *Peru*. This, presumably, is the source of the confusion.

In gardens the Cuban lily sends up bright green leaves to form winter rosettes like hyacinth squills. In a sunny exposure on poor, stony ground this foliage remains hardened and resistant to frost. In too generous a spot, however, the leaves elongate and may be damaged with any serious cold. In late February dome-shaped clusters of buds begin to show in the midst of the leaves. At the first warm spell the eight- to ten-inch stems bolt upward and expand into a bee swarm of indigo-blue stars.

This prolific squill multiplies rapidly and usually needs dividing every two or three years. Although the Cuban lily has a reputation as a tender bulb, its foliage stands plenty of cold while still in a tight rosette. These Mediterranean bulbs may be grown anywhere in the South if they are planted on exposed positions to discourage dangerous early growth and bloom. A rare near-white form, 'Alba', is also worth having.

Spanish Bluebells

The flower that comes to mind for most Southerners when squill is mentioned is the Spanish bluebell or wood hyacinth. Although long known in garden literature as *Scilla campanulata*, botanists have shuffled these poor flowers about,

Spanish bluebells (*Hyacinthoides hispanica*) naturalized in a spring lawn with snowball viburnums blooming at wood's edge. Photo by Lauren S. Ogden.

first to the genus *Endymion*, and more recently to an uncomfortable resting place with the alliterative appellation *Hyacinthoides hispanica*.

None of these names do justice to the stately spikes of wisteria-blue that blossom in April gardens. The unscented, bell-shaped flowers of the Spanish bluebell hang down from twelve- to sixteen-inch stalks. Their thrifty bulbs seed and multiply in lavish pools, which spread out under the trees. This old Southern favorite is one of the finest spring bulbs for naturalizing in woodland, and will even succeed in the dark shade under live oaks. The round, white bulbs are happy anywhere they receive ample spring moisture. They have been popular since Elizabethan times and came to the South with the earliest settlers.

In addition to the common sky-blue strain of the species, there are several fine selections of Spanish bluebells with darker violet, pink, or white flowers. Nurseries sometimes offer these in a mix, but such combinations are best avoided or quickly separated following bloom, as the various colors combine in a gaudy pattern. Although beautiful, the related English bluebell (*Hyacinthoides non-scripta*) needs cooler, damper conditions than the South can provide.

Star of Bethlehem

Matted leaves of grape hyacinths often mix with low winter foliage from star of Bethlehem (*Ornithogalum umbellatum*) on the same old Southern lawns. The flowerless bulbs would be difficult to separate, if not for telltale silvery streaks marking the leaves of *O. umbellatum*. This is a sort of reverse color scheme of the flowers, which, as in all *Ornithogalum*, are white stars, marked down the back with green keels.

Dioscorides receives credit for the curious name of this genus, which translates as "bird's milk." The little round bulbs of common star of Bethlehem are theorized, also, to be the biblical, edible "dove's dung" sold during the Babylonian siege of Jerusalem. Other common names (sleepy Dick, nap at noon) refer to the daily openings and closings of these flowers in response to the spring sun. In France they are called *belle de onze heures* ("beauty of the eleventh hour").

Many gardeners regard *Ornithoga-*

Star of Bethlehem (*Ornithogalum umbellatum*). Photo by Lauren S. Ogden.

lum umbellatum as weedy, and, in truth, the green and white clusters of starry blooms are only modestly showy, at best. Nevertheless, these small Mediterranean bulbs have proven faithful in adversity, and disappear after spring flowering with little fuss. This is one of the few early flowers suited to naturalizing in lawns. It makes a fine companion for *Allium drummondi, Crocus tommasinianus, Anemone caroliniana, Ranunculus macranthus,* and other low-growing, hardy flowers.

Showier, but less common in Southern gardens is the drooping star of Bethlehem (*Ornithogalum nutans*), known to Parkinson as the "Starre-flower of Naples." The satiny flowers of this species appear on six- to ten-inch spikes among four or five straplike leaves. These graceful blooms are strung upward along one side, and open from the bottom up, like small, flaring bells. Moist, shady positions suit these European natives better that most plants, and they grow well in borders of deciduous shrubs. In the upper South these bulbs occasionally run wild in rough grass and woodland, although with less passion than *O. umbellatum.*

The greenish black ovaries of *Ornithogalum arabicum* stand out like shiny beads against the pearly flowers, and give this star of Bethlehem a personality entirely distinct from *O. umbellatum.* Like the Cuban lily, this Mediterranean bulb is often regarded as tender, but will stand cold if planted on a sunny, exposed position in gravelly soil. Its gray leaves spread flat against the ground over winter and send up a two-foot stem in April. This carries a compact grouping of creamy round buds, which open gradually from the outside. These pleasant blossoms have a sweet fragrance and last well when cut.

Although *Ornithogalum arabicum* is widely available and commonly planted, colonies seldom establish in the South. This failure is probably the fault of gardeners who are too generous to these desert flowers. They thrive on the most barren sands and rocky soils, kept dry over summer. They would be an excellent choice for seaside gardens.

The chincherinchee or wonder flower of South Africa (*Ornithogalum thyrsoides*) grows readily on either sand or stiff clay, but its fragrant white blooms come in winter when they are liable to damage from frosts. In the South this

The orange chincherinchee, *Ornithogalum dubium.*

Virgin's spray, *Ornithogalum narbonense*, flowering with prairie phlox (*Phlox pilosa*).

long-lasting cut flower survives in the warmest parts of the Gulf Coast and Florida. Although not scented, the related *O. maculatum* and *O. dubium* (yellow- and orange-flowered, respectively) are hardier and seem to perform well even with occasional temperatures in the low twenties, displaying clusters of fifteen or more cheerful green-centered blooms on eight- to twelve-inch stems in mid-spring. These species produce tight winter rosettes of slick green foliage and seem to be permanent if planted in raised beds allowed to dry in summer. The common name chincherinchee is said to derive from the sound made by the dry flower stalks rubbing together in the wind.

Rising up fifteen to twenty inches, the graceful, upright wands of *Ornithogalum narbonense* open into loose spikes, like a milky white version of the hyacinth squill. The gray foliage is flattened and sparse as in *O. arabicum*, but always stands erect. Even the heaviest clay soils present no difficulty for the brittle, long-necked bulbs of this species, which may often be found naturalized about older gardens in the middle South. *Ornithogalum narbonense* has been in gardens for many years, but is now uncommonly listed. In their homeland along the Mediterranean in France these graceful white flowers are known as virgin's spray.

The blooms of *Ornithogalum narbonense* perform the same daily openings and closings seen in others of this group, but still make fine cut flowers and good focal points for a herbaceous border. Wine-pink *Penstemon triflorus* is a fine April companion, and the coral-pink asparaguslike buds of *Hesperaloe parviflora* also rise and mix with these flowers while they are at their peak. Colonies increase well from self-sown seed and soon cover large areas.

Wild Hyacinths

Remarkably similar to *Ornithogalum narbonense* in general build are the American camas lilies or wild hyacinths (*Camassia scilloides*). In the South these may be found on prairies and rich grasslands from Georgia to central Texas. These native bulbs vary in color from lead-white to violet, but most often appear in light lavender tones. Such pale colorings require skill to properly show off in the garden, but carry with them some of the wild beauty of Southern meadows. The tender lavender stars of the wild hyacinth make an elegant complement to the pale *Tulipa* 'Lady Jane' and other hybrids involving *T. clusiana* and are worthwhile in any bedding scheme, if used in good clumps. They have a delicate, sweet fragrance.

Other *Camassia* species available in the trade, such as *C. quamash* and *C. leichtlinii*, seem to be universal failures in warm parts of the South, but might be tried in cooler, damper places along the Mason-Dixon line. These natives of western North America are famous for

The wild hyacinth of Southern meadows, *Camassia scilloides.*

their edible bulbs, which fed Chief Joseph and the Nez Perce during their war with the United States. The generic name derives from *quamash*, the Nootka Chinook word for the bulbs. Although their bluish flowers resemble hyacinths, these American wildflowers belong to the agave family (Agavaceae).

White Camas

The South also has several creamy, lilylike flowers that bear a vague similarity to the wild hyacinths. These blossoms are known as wand lilies, white camas lilies, or zygadenes; a more treacherous name, death camas, may be attributed to the poisonous alkaloids found in the leaves and bulbs of several varieties. The odd generic name *Zigadenus* (Greek for "yoke gland") refers to the floral glands found at the bases of the crimped, starry flowers. These have something of the appearance of *Camassia* blooms, but their fragrance is heavy and cloying, like privet or wild plum.

Since these wildflowers carry reputations for toxicity and come mostly in drab off-white tones, they attract little attention from gardeners. Nevertheless, the white camas lilies are among the most graceful of our natives. They adapt well to cultivation, so long as their thin-skinned bulbs or tubers are returned to the ground promptly after division, so as not to dry out.

The large-flowered zygadene (*Zigadenus glaberrimus*) grows from a blackish, creeping rhizome and occurs in coastal savannahs, bogs, and damp pinelands through the Southeast. Its whitish yellow flowers have purple spots in the centers, and appear from June to September in loose, pyramidal clusters. These summer growers thrive on abundant moisture and acid soils, often in the same habitats that favor carnivorous pitcher plants (*Sarracenia* spp.). *Zigadenus leimanthoides* is similar, but bears smaller flowers on a more widely branched inflorescence.

Earlier blooming and better suited to dry situations is *Zigadenus nuttallii*. This rugged uplander grows from a true bulb, rather than a horizontal rhizome. It does well on neutral or alkaline soils, and enjoys mucky black clays. The bright green, grassy leaves rise in three ranks in early spring, and are as valuable in the garden as the flowers, often looking like some exotic sedge. The blooms follow in late April, packed in dense spires on two-foot stalks. These ragged, milky blossoms have the texture of crumpled tissue, and display yellow blotches at the base of each petal. This quaint color scheme inspired the charming common name merryhearts, which is certainly preferable to death camas.

Fly poison (*Amianthium muscaetoxicum*), bunchflower (*Melanthium virginicum*), and featherbells (*Stenanthium gramineum*) are three allies of the zygadenes native to the acid sandylands of the South. Their four-foot spikes of porcelain-white bloom appear from May to July, and would make fine additions to the back of a damp border. The white-flowered false asphodel (*Triantha racemosa*) and the apricot-yellow sunny-bells (*Schoenolirion croceum*) are smaller Southern natives suitable for foreground plantings. Like their relatives, some of these lilies are considered to be toxic. Early settlers crushed the bulbs of *Amianthium* and mixed them with sugar to attract and destroy houseflies.

The Green Lily

For drier gardens the green lily (*Schoenocaulon texanum*) offers an interesting April accent. Like the fall-flowering coconut lily (*S. drummondii*), this Texas native throws feathery, pinkish green wands above its evergreen clumps of foliage. These unscented blooms lack true petals and produce the same bottlebrush effect as the coconut lily.

With their draping, grassy leaves, these hardy bulbs look well at the top of a stone ledge. The spires of clustered stamens provide a sort of miniature fireworks display in the spring border, and the leaves remain attractive all year. The brownish, spindle-shaped bulbs endure any amount of drought, and seem to thrive on the poorest soils. As with many other neglected natives, the carefree vigor of these graceful Southern lilies recommends them for wider use.

Chapter 6
Irises, Gladioli, and Shellflowers

OUTHERNERS LOVE the elegant iris, or fleur-de-lis, as much as gardeners in any part of the world, but the peculiarities of the territory emphasize a unique range of blooms. The tall bearded hybrids popular in other sections of the country do not wholly adapt to the South, requiring careful placement in this warm, humid climate. They take second place to races whose affinity for warmer gardens makes for real opportunity, if only Southerners resolve to seize it. Instead of lamenting the failure of some of the tall bearded irises, gardeners may bravely delve among neglected subtropical beauties of this genus: Louisiana hybrids, spurias, Spanish and Dutch irises, historic bearded irises, remontant irises, and many others.

When Old Is Better Than New

In spite of their obvious merit elsewhere, many newer iris creations remain suspect in the South. This warm climate promotes bacterial soft rot (*Erwinia carotovora*) and other pathogens that threaten the starchy tubers borne by these perennials. The disease causes a basal rot of the rhizomes, and whole plants often seem to melt away in the middle of the summer. Bacterial rots become progressively worse as one goes south, so that while many bearded irises thrive along the Mason-Dixon line, few endure in the climate of the Gulf Coast. Avoiding heavy fertilizers and keeping flower beds dry and well drained through the summer reduces afflictions, but only up to a point.

A few exceptional irises have proven themselves less susceptible to bacterial rots: these are the types best suited to gardens in most of the South. Many originate from regions surrounding the Mediterranean. Like other flowers from these territories, they perform best on mellow soils with a measure of lime but will give faithful service if offered less. These irises endure even on the poorest, driest soils.

The usual way to acquire these resistant varieties is as divisions shared by other gardeners or collected from old, abandoned homesteads or cemeteries. Many lovely types lurk in neglected corners of the South and are worth seeking out. Although the old irises lack the size, substance, and color range of modern hybrids, they make up for this in vigor, tenacity, and historical value. Several

151

varieties common in the South have had a presence in gardens dating to the Middle Ages.

White Flags

The first perennial irises to bloom in spring are several antique bearded types of dwarfish stature. Because their height is modest, they are usually included in the median iris group (*Iris* Barbata-Media) in modern classifications. The "beards" of these species are formed by long rows of feathery stamens, which mark the centers of the three outer petals, or falls. The inner petals, or standards, curve upward and inward to create the familiar fleur-de-lis seen as a motif in historic art and architecture.

Like all bearded irises, these heirloom varieties grow from fat, starchy rhizomes. The tubers creep along close to the soil's surface and multiply swiftly with side branches and by forking. The plants may be easily divided for increase at any season but customarily are separated in fall or immediately after spring bloom. To ensure flowering, at least one good-sized fan of leaves should accompany each division.

The most familiar of the historic irises in the South is the old white flag, *Iris albicans*. The Latin epithet, which translates as "off-white," was given to plants found growing in Spain during the mid-1800s. Although these irises are now

The early white flag, *Iris albicans*.

common waifs in many warm countries, their original homeland appears to be on the Arabian Peninsula. Tradition holds that the Moors carried this iris wherever they traveled in conquest, planting the flowers as memorials on the graves of fallen Muslim soldiers. When Spanish colonists came to Florida and Mexico, they brought this Mediterranean flower with them and continued the tradition of planting them in cemeteries. These are now the most common irises in the South.

The leaden flowers and gray, sword-shaped leaves of *Iris albicans* line paths and fill graveyards and vacant fields in March. They are often accompanied by early blue flags, thought to be variants of the same species: on some occasions a blue flower may be seen sporting from the side of an old clump of white *I. albicans*. In all respects, save color, these two forms appear identical. Officially, the blue flags may be called by their cultivar name, 'Madonna'. They supposedly originate from Yemen.

For as long as *Iris albicans* has been in gardens, it has suffered confusion with a near relation, the pale white *I. florentina* (Florentine iris). This famous plant is the preferred source of orris, a fixative used in the perfume industry. The rhizomes are harvested, dried, and grated, or distilled to release a fragrance resembling sweet violets. This iris is still raised for this purpose in Tuscany and has been grown for its aromatic roots since Gerard's time. In previous centuries many irises were valued as much for their supposed herbal or medicinal virtues as for their showy flowers.

The Florentine iris differs from *Iris albicans* in its taller, more open spikes of bloom. These carry papery bracts that often dry and turn brown by the time the flowers open. Although the blossoms are larger than those of *I. albicans*, they open sparsely and are less effective in the garden.

Early garden writers described *Iris florentina* as a natural species, but botanists now regard it as an ancient hybrid. Like *I. albicans*, it has a blue variant. Although less common and prolific in Southern gardens than the early flags, *I. florentina* tolerates the climate better than many modern bearded irises. It appears occasionally in old gardens and may be seen blooming in April, several weeks after *I. albicans* finishes for the season.

Italian Iris

Even if the Southern climate defeated all varieties save the red-purple Italian iris (*Iris kochii*), gardens here would be rich and enviable. Like *I. florentina*, this tenacious flower is another old pseudospecies inherited from the gardens of antiquity. Tradition holds that the first plants were found growing on hills above Lake Como. These lovely blooms are now widely distributed and may be seen in mild-climate gardens all over the world.

The compact, fragrant blossoms of *Iris kochii* glow with a warm reddish violet, and are striped creamy yellow by the short, dainty beards. The vibrant flowers display that rare intensity of color that mixes happily with almost any hue. Blossoms appear in earnest during March, along with the white and blue flags, and just as the early campernelles and other narcissi are fading. Italian irises may also give a reprise performance in autumn, and in mild years they sputter in bloom right through winter.

No more beautiful flower grows than these short-statured irises. The vibrance of their Tyrian purple is unmatched, and it can be telling mixed among bright-hued California poppies (*Eschscholzia californica*) or soft lavender *Phlox subulata* 'Emerald Blue'. These irises also look well in combination with gray foliage or white April blooms like those of *Ornithogalum narbonense* or *Ipheion uniflorum* 'Alberto Castillo'.

German Iris

Nurseries formerly grouped several of the old garden irises as varieties under *Iris germanica*, the German bearded iris. These plants were not strictly of German origin, but during the Middle Ages they were commonly cultivated in northern Europe and naturalized along stone walls surrounding castles. Botanists now understand that these irises, too, arose as early garden hybrids, rather than as natural species. Like *I. albicans*, *I. kochii*, and *I. florentina*, they are sterile horticultural mules with abnormal complements of forty-four chromosomes, rather than the customary numbers of forty or forty-eight.

The most prominent of these border stalwarts is an early-flowering iris with tall stems and rich violet-purple blooms. In old catalogs it was listed as 'Atropurpurea' or 'Purple King'. During the 1800s collectors discovered the same variety in the gardens of Kathmandu and introduced it as 'Nepalensis'.

These old purple flags bloom a little after *Iris kochii*, and along with *I. florentina*. They have taller, better-branched stems than the earlier irises, and the flowers achieve better size and proportion. The deep mulberry falls and upright signals reflex entirely, so the flowers present the greatest possible surface to the viewer. This shows off the pale beards, which shade from yellow at the throat to creamy white in the center of the petals.

These rich, succulent blooms emit a heavy, honey-sweet fragrance, and they attract a steady procession of large, black and yellow bumblebees. Their appearance signals the arrival of high spring in the South, and coincides with the blooms of bridal wreath (*Spiraea prunifolia*), dogwoods, wisteria, and the first flushes of the red and pink China roses. 'Nepalensis' may be seen in nearly all the old gardens, and in many modern ones as well. Gardeners still share these prolific plants with one another, as they have for centuries.

Dalmatian Iris

The fine broad foliage and tall, lightly branched stems of *Iris pallida* give this old garden species a more graceful aspect than is typical among bearded iris. 'Dalmatica', the common strain in the South, seems all the more elegant for its deli-

Iris pallida 'Dalmatica' with musk rose.

cate amethyst, white-throated blossoms. These appear in April, a little later than the purple *I. germanica*. Erect stems hold the blooms above the pointed leaves and bear short bracts, which dry to a silvery translucence at bloom time. Blue-gray foliage, opalescent petals, white beard, and yellow pollen all harmonize in an extraordinary way.

Although resident in gardens for as long as *Iris germanica*, the Dalmatian iris appears little changed from its wild form. The species is common on the southern foothills of the Alps and ranges eastward as far as the Crimea. In Italy it is raised to produce orris in the same way as *I. florentina*.

In addition to 'Dalmatica', nurseries offer a beautiful cream-striped *Iris pallida* with pale blue flowers. This selection, dating from 1901, is aptly called 'Variegata'. The showy foliage makes it one of the most valuable of border plants, although it is shy with its porcelain-blue flowers. 'Variegata' seems more prone to bacterial rots than 'Dalmatica', but is worth attempting for the sake of its milk-streaked swords.

More Intermediates

The good foliage, large flowers, and noble deportment of *Iris pallida* may be seen in many of its descendants. This species and *I. variegata*, a central European

Iris 'Madame Chereau', an old plicata.

species with yellow standards and brown-stippled falls, are believed to have been the principal forerunners of garden irises. The early crosses between them developed mixed purplish or bicolored blooms. In the Victorian catalogs of English nurseryman Peter Barre, these were listed in various "species" classes based on the patterns of their flowers. Lavender to violet blooms, such as the old variety 'Princess Beatrice', were grouped with the pallidas, while yellows and maroons fell among the variegatas. *Iris amoena*, a strain with white standards and purple falls, was nicknamed the agreeable iris for its pleasant mix of colors. The plicatas bore white blooms frilled with edgings of lavender or purple, as did the elderberry-scented *I. sambucina*. The indescribable *I. ×squalens* group included bronze varieties and fantastic yellow-purple blends and combinations.

So many hybrids have been made among these old sections that it is impossible now to find one's way with these antique names. In humble country gardens, one still sees irises that look no different from those painted by Redouté, as they grew for the Empress Josephine at Malmaison. 'Madame Chereau', a nineteenth-century plicata, may still be seen in the South. An assiduous search through April gardens and countrysides will reassemble several of these old varieties, as well as many more recent hybrids of value.

During the first half of the twentieth century, intermediate strains of irises received serious attention from breeders for the first time. Several irises from this period are now common denizens of Southern gardens.

A yellow hybrid often seen in the South is 'Shekinah'. This favorite shows a light brown thumbprint at the throat, but is otherwise a rich buttery tone. A famous old bronze, 'Ambassadeur', blooms along with it and the early lemon-yellow daylilies. This vigorous hybrid was introduced by the Vilmorins, who bred irises near Paris before World War I. They regarded 'Ambassadeur' as their masterpiece. Its translucent lavender standards combine with yellow beards and deep plum falls, which are striped and penciled white and purple at the throat.

Remontants

Several of the intermediate iris hybrids descend in part from *Iris kochii* and inherit its inclination to fall and winter flowering. This ability to bloom again in autumn is one of the most desirable traits an iris may possess in the South. Brief, erratic springs sometimes play havoc with early flowers, but the mild weather of autumn generally encourages long-lasting blossoms. In favorable years these reblooming irises offer a succession of blooms through the entire winter.

The old yellow 'Golden Cataract' is a compact-growing variety gracing many established gardens. Its warmly colored blooms often put in an appearance on Christmas Day. One of the few true dwarfs worth attempting in the South, the old yellow bicolor 'Jean Siret' is another late fall rebloomer. 'Crimson King' and 'Eleanor Roosevelt' bear deep red-purple blooms like their ancestor, *Iris kochii*, but are even more regular in fall bloom. 'Black Magic' offers an autumn reprise of its dark blackish purple blossoms. In certain favorable years the old purple *I. germanica* will throw a few November spikes of bloom, as well.

Among the most valuable of all the rebloomers is 'Pink Classic'. In cold springs this old selection begins flowering with *Iris albicans* and *I. germanica*, but in a forward season it may appear even before these early types. With favorable weather, the spikes of bloom continue intermittently through the entire year, with concentrations in fall and early spring. The clear pink flowers, with their lively, tangerine beards, offer one of the best sources of these warm colors. 'Pink Classic' displays its sizeable, well-formed blooms on tall, symmetrically branched stems.

In addition to these proven rebloomers, many newer irises may be tried for fall flowers. Hybridizers have recently married the fall-flowering habits of the intermediate race with the modern forms and colors seen in the tall bearded. One may now choose among hundreds of rebloomers with all the qualities of modern breeding. Few of these have been tested for resistance to bacterial soft rot, but they seem the most promising of modern irises for the South.

During the years before World War II, breeders strove to develop tall bearded irises with pendant falls and erect standards like those in the old purple *Iris germanica*. This style of blossom gives a great deal of color in gardens and the blooms display a striking profile. More recent efforts have focused on enlarging individual flowers and bringing up falls toward a horizontal plane. This upright carriage and many new color patterns give modern iris hybrids a decidedly different appearance, designed especially for its bold effect in a vase.

The orchidlike quality of bearded irises comes into its own when mixed in a sizable collection. One, two, or three colors blooming together seems mundane, but a dozen multicolored irises together in a patch looks as if a flock of gigantic butterflies had descended. If a liberal sprinkling of blue cornflowers, crimson poppies, and violet larkspurs can be seeded among the rhizomes in early fall, and if shrubby musk roses can be set nearby, these will join the irises in April to complete a charming scene.

Aril-breds

The strange mourning iris (*Iris susiana*) is another bearded type that has been in gardens for several centuries. Its globular blooms bear heavily veined and stippled patterns. The background color of the rounded falls is a light cream, but the markings themselves are a dark brownish purple. The beard and standards verge on black.

These somber characteristics show that these blooms belong to the oncocyclus, or aril group of irises. The members of this curious section come from parts of the Middle East where winters are mild and damp and summers are rainless. They have always been difficult to grow in humid climates such as the South, but the odd markings of the flowers are so extraordinary that devotees maintain collections by lifting the rhizomes over summer and storing them in dry sand for replanting in autumn.

Breeders have been active with this section and have made several crosses between these Middle Eastern irises and the more moisture-tolerant tall bearded irises. The hybrids, known as aril-breds, show more vigor than the aril species. Few of these have been widely tested in the South, but it seems likely that some will eventually prove permanent. Their unusual patterns and mysterious colors are reason enough to try.

Spuria Iris

During the first weeks of May, many older gardens boast clumps of narrow, dark green leaves topped with tall white and yellow irises. These are the old Turkish salt marsh irises (*Iris orientalis*), well known to a previous generation of gardeners as *I. ochroleuca*. In the South these enduring perennials flower just as the tall bearded varieties fade, in concert with the old, fragrant, white and red flecked peony 'Festiva Maxima'. Their vanilla-scented blossoms have a slender elegance, which makes them ideal for cutting.

Iris orientalis and its relations comprise a group known popularly as spurias. These Near Eastern plants seem particularly successful in the South, ranking among the most adaptable irises for warm climates. Less common, but also to be seen in old yards, are some allies of *I. orientalis*, the dark golden *I. crocea* (*I. aurea*) and the pure, bright yellow *I. monnieri*. This last has been known as the iris of Rhodes, but seems to be an early French sport or hybrid from *I. orientalis*, rather than a native species of the eastern Mediterranean. Louis-Guillaume Lemonnier grew it at Versailles, and it is his name which is commemorated in the Latin title of this flower.

The white *Iris orientalis*, yellow *I. monnieri*, and the violet-blue *I. spuria* have combined in a wide range of hybrids. Many of the first crosses made in this group had narrow petals and pale colors, but the shapely yellow hybrid 'Wadi Zem Zem' has since given rise to fine varieties with deeper hues and better-formed blossoms. All seem to thrive in the South, and gardeners may have their pick among the latest, most beautiful spuria creations.

One old species spuria is worth retaining for its dwarfness. The plum-

The salt marsh iris of Turkey, *Iris orientalis*.

scented iris (*Iris graminea*) is a short central European native with narrow leaves. Its violet-purple blooms are marked with yellowish streaks. They rest down among the grassy foliage, so gardeners must stand near to appreciate them. These favorite flowers appear two to a spike in early May and smell delightfully of ripe plums.

If your garden includes roses as well as irises, by the time the spuria hybrids come to bloom, you may well have a thriving population of fig beetles (*Cotinus* spp.). These large, greenish insects love to bury themselves among freshly opened flowers, especially soft-petaled blooms of old roses and irises. This usually ruins blossoms just as they reach their peak.

In a small garden these beetles can be controlled by hand picking, but if your collection is large, you will need to treat the ground around the roses to rid the soil of overwintering grubs. Milky spore, a natural fungus enemy of these in-

A modern hybrid spuria iris.

sects, may offer some control. If you plan to use your irises mainly as cut flowers, they may be harvested while in tight bud to prevent entry of the beetles, solving your problem, also.

All spurias are easy to grow from divisions, and most will bloom in three or four years from fresh-planted seed. Unlike bearded irises, spurias enjoy a covering of two or three inches of soil over their rhizomes and may be mulched freely with leaves or compost. The clumps dislike frequent division; they may be separated for increase every five to seven years.

When the big bunches of spuria leaves die down in late summer, they leave sizeable holes in the garden. It is good idea to have nearby perennial or annual flowers to fill their places during the July and August interregnum. With fall rains the beautiful leaves return to add their bold upward sweep to the garden melee.

Short Stem Iris

There is another beardless iris common to Southern gardens with tall, narrow foliage just like the spurias. Unless the plants are in bloom, it's nearly impossible to tell them apart, but the late April to May flowers tell the story. These are a ravishing blue marked with bright yellow eyes, and they have a flattened fullness unlike any spuria.

The dark green leaves of these irises are particularly attractive; this plant was once named for them as *Iris foliosa*. It is now properly known as *I. brevicaulis* ("short-stemmed") because the blooms sit on ten- to twelve-inch zig-zagged stalks set down among the leaves.

This flower is one of the South's most beautiful garden irises—and one of the most valuable, as it tolerates shade. Average garden soils suit them perfectly, and they will thrive under all but the most arid conditions. The clumps will even continue flowering in an aggressive matted groundcover like English ivy. This is something few perennials of any kind can promise.

Apart from its place in older Southern gardens, *Iris brevicaulis* is best known to iris lovers as one of the parents of the Louisiana hybrids. Although not a true water iris like others of this group, *I. brevicaulis* is closely related and crosses freely among them.

Water Irises

When J. K. Small published his *Manual of the Southeastern Flora* in 1933, he listed dozens of different irises as natives of the bayous and swamplands of the lower Mississippi Delta. Most of these plants have since been identified as natural hybrids, and subsequent botanical treatments have reduced Small's original number of species down to only four or five. Although taxonomists no longer recognize many of these varieties, the Louisiana irises are gaining wider recognition in gardens. In only a few decades, flower lovers have generated an entire garden race from these beautiful Southern wildlings.

These indigenous blossoms grow well under ordinary damp garden conditions as well as in bogs, and now come in a wide range of colors, including the most vivid reds seen in the genus. In size the flowers vary from elegant three- or four-inch miniatures, such as the old, wild *Iris fulva*, to gargantuan blossoms seven to eight inches across, like the monstrous 'Godzilla'. The velvety petals may droop or flare, remain separate or overlap, and, in modern types, show ruffling or bicolor effects. All the Louisiana hybrids have lovely, narrow green foliage to complement their April blooms. With tall, slender stems, many make choice cut flowers.

In addition to modern cultivars, several of the original species may be seen in Southern gardens and are still worthwhile. The copper iris (*Iris fulva*) is famous for its unique, warm red blossoms. This species occurs as a wildling from the Gulf north to southern Illinois. Although the flowers are on the small side and the petals droop as if they were sad, blooms of the copper iris make an effective, relaxed display. These irises also thrive in damp shade, which makes them doubly valuable.

The copper iris, *Iris fulva*.

Very similar, but much larger is *Iris nelsonii*, a robust species known to collectors as the Abbeville red. This iris, ranging from crimson to yellow in various wild forms, has been used extensively in breeding. Many of its descendants show good vigor and broad, overlapping petals.

The dark blue, purple, to cream or white *Iris giganticaerulea* is an early-blooming species with especially lush, blue-green foliage. This is a common flower in the marshes of the central Gulf Coast. It seems less hardy to cold than some of the other Louisiana irises, but is one of the most vigorous types. Along with *I. brevicaulis*, it is the source of blue and purple pigments seen in many hybrids.

In addition to these wild forms, the rich violet 'Dorothea K. Williamson' is common in many old gardens. This tough, hardy hybrid from *Iris fulva* and *I. brevicaulis* was introduced in 1918. It thrives on damp, heavy ground, and rapidly propagates by vigorous rhizomes. Another iris hybrid from the same parentage is also typical in older plantings. Formerly called *Iris vinicolor*, this naturally occurring form offers deep claret-purple blooms.

The roots of most Louisiana hybrids run about incessantly, and it is futile to try to separate varieties in the garden if they are planted near each other. After a good season of growth, many types will travel as much as three feet from their original location. Any collection quickly becomes confused, with the labels left in the dirt, far from the young fans that will flower the next spring.

All the Louisianas thrive as bog or aquatic plants, so one way to keep varieties separated is to plant each one in an individual plastic or stainless steel tub. These may be sunk in the ground or disguised with leafy perennials, so as to blend in the garden. Under these conditions culture is simple, and all the flowers require is an occasional topping up with water from the hose.

In addition to the species used to breed the Louisiana hybrids, the South has two other native aquatics of value. Both have attractive blue, beardless flowers marked with small spots of yellow at the haft. *Iris hexagona* (prairie blue flag) grows around the Gulf of Mexico to Florida, and north to South Carolina. Found in flooded ditches and bogs in sun or shade, it needs a moist, acid soil to prosper.

The Virginia iris (*Iris virginica*) grows in swamps, moist meadows, and salt marshes throughout the Southeast. Although these habitats usually have acid soils, some forms of the species tolerate alkaline conditions, if given plenty of moisture. In addition to the common blue *I. virginica*, there are also white and pink selections. 'Socastee Strain No. 1' appears to be a hybrid of this species with either *I. tripetala* or *I. versicolor*. The young spring fans and flower stems emerge dark purple. Flowers appear in April, along with the Louisiana hybrids.

The yellow water iris (*Iris pseudacorus*) is a European species often seen as an escape on the sides of streams and ponds in the South. It produces absolutely enormous masses of upright foliage like big clumps of cattail, reaching five to six feet or better. The yellow blooms top the leaves in April and have a flounced, orchidlike appearance. Nurseries offer an old, heirloom double and a variegated form of the species, although in the South the attractive variegation fades quickly with warm weather. All need abundant water to thrive, but are otherwise easy and tolerant of limy or acid conditions. Thomas Jefferson had these irises at Monticello, where he knew them as flower-de-luces.

The Japanese irises (*Iris ensata*) are the glamorous cousins of *I. virginica* and *I. pseudacorus*. They have been widely hybridized in the Orient and include many magnificent varieties. Unfortunately, they are not so easily grown as other water irises. They demand partial shade and acid, damp conditions. They quickly fail if subjected to drought.

In the lower South these irises usually sulk in summer heat unless immersed in the cool waters of a garden pond. The most satisfactory varieties for general use are old, tested hybrids such as the white 'Gold Bound' and purplish 'Mahogany'. These flower after the Louisianas, extending the water iris season. Several unusual hybrids of *Iris ensata* with *I. pseudacorus* may also be expected to be adaptable and vigorous.

Siberian Iris

The title "Siberian iris" is something of a misnomer, for *Iris sibirica* has a much wider range in Europe and Asia than the frostbitten region for which it is named. Several color forms and hybrids with white and purple blooms may be had from perennial dealers, but only an old dark violet sort is common in the South.

These are moisture-loving irises, best suited to heavy soil and low ground. They may be grown in water-filled tubs or at the edge of ponds, like Louisianas. Most of the whites and blues tolerate slight alkalinity, but the red-purple strains need acid soils. The Siberians resemble spurias, but reach only half their height and size, becoming fully deciduous in winter. They are especially valuable for positions in partial shade and will flower happily under tall pines.

Piedmont Iris

The miniature blue *Iris verna* is a delicate woodlander native to the hills and mountains of the Southeast. Although fussy about receiving a moist, acid soil, it is worth having for its dainty, sweetly fragrant flowers. These are beardless, coming in lilac-blue, marked with wide blotches of orange. The entire plant, blooms and all, remains under a foot. The very early flowers appear in March, so these understory plants can complete growth before trees leaf out for summer.

Gladwyn Iris

Another type valuable for shade is the Gladwyn iris (*Iris foetidissima*). This species is a native of limy soils in Mediterranean countries and in western Europe. The unflattering botanical name translates as "stinking," but this seems a bit harsh, as the flowers are not unpleasant, and the leaves and stems only produce an odor if crushed. The blossoms of this iris are small, marked only in quiet tones of fawn and washy lilac. It is the lustrous evergreen leaves that make the plants an asset in the garden.

Another show comes in autumn when the capsules ripen and split to reveal the orange-red seeds. Looking like small, bright marbles, they last well in the garden or in a vase for winter decoration. A slow-growing variegated type ('Variegata'), a yellow-fruited selection which also has yellow blooms ('Golden Gobbet'), and a variant with white fruit ('Albo-Fructo') are available from specialists. Like *Aspidistra*, these irises prosper in dry, deeply shaded positions where few other flowers succeed.

Crested Irises

The crested irises mostly lack the thickened rhizomes, bulbs, corms, or other means of storage common to the genus. They get along, instead, on wiry, running roots and evergreen fans of foliage. The flowers bear slightly elevated crests intermediate between a bearded and a beardless condition. All the members of this group enjoy leafy, humus-rich soil. Although they stand some drought, their appearance is better with regular watering. In the South they perform best with partial shade.

The Japanese roof iris, *Iris tectorum*, is famous in its native country as a flower for planting on sod roofs, just as houseleeks (*Sempervivum* spp.) are used on the cottage roofs of France. In gardens the silky, green fans of leaves form large patches, making fine subjects for a wooded slope or the foreground of a shady border. In April the ruffled, orchidlike blooms appear among the handsome leaves. In common forms these are a rich, mottled blue, with white crests. Even lovelier are the white, yellow-crested blooms of *I. tectorum* 'Alba'. 'Woolong' is an especially large-flowered, vigorous blue selection. *Iris tectorum* 'Variegata' has leaves attractively striped with cream in spring, fading to green in summer.

The native dwarf crested iris of the Smoky Mountains, *Iris cristata*, looks much like *I. tectorum*, but is less vigorous in Southern gardens. It needs a thoroughly cool, shady position and must never be allowed to suffer drought. Plants recently exported from China as *I. wattii* appear to be easier to grow in the South, with lush, upright fans of velvety green foliage and blue, mottled blooms closely resembling *I. tectorum*.

More in the vein of subtropical flowers are several other crested irises of the Far East. *Iris japonica* produces branching stalks of pale lavender blossoms flecked with deeper lavender and orange spots. These appear above glossy, green fans in April. 'Eco Easter' is an especially floriferous form selected by Don Jacobs of Atlanta; *I. japonica* also comes in two stunning variegated strains, 'Variegata' and 'Kamayana'. This species multiplies vigorously from slender stolons, which run just under the surface of the ground. Although fairly frost tolerant, the attractive fans of foliage benefit from a mulch of pine straw when temperatures dip below 20°F.

Such care will also be appreciated by 'Nada', a hybrid of *Iris japonica* developed in the 1950s by California nurseryman J. N. Giridlian. The other parent of 'Nada' was *I. confusa*, an obscure iris from Sichuan and Yunnan. A tremendous grower in the lower South, 'Nada' sends up tall sprays of ruffled, white blooms marked with orange speckles. Where frost is severe, the early-rising flower spikes may be nipped, but this spectacular iris is otherwise easy to grow in a shady bed. 'Darjeeling' is a second-generation child of 'Nada', with larger, more

Iris 'Nada' with columbines.

lavender-toned blossoms. 'Fairyland' is a delicate hybrid of *I. japonica* 'Uwodu' and *I. confusa.*

Bulbous Irises

Perhaps because Dutch and Spanish irises are so common in the windows of flower shops, these honestly bulbous types are less appreciated in gardens than they might be. The florist industry forces these beautiful flowers by the thousands, so they may be had cheaply and in variety year-round. They offer gardeners one of the best bargains among bulbs adapted to the South. The narrow-petaled blooms, with the same elegant proportions as spurias, come in several good colors, especially rich blues, strong yellows, and warm bronzes.

Gerard and Parkinson knew the Spanish iris as the onion-rooted fleur de luce or Barbary fleur de luce, and these bulbs have played a role in gardens since at least the late 1500s. Botanically, these bulbous irises belong to *Iris xiphium* (*Xiphium vulgare*) and its allies, which are native to Spain and surrounding countries. The Latin comes from the Greek *xiphos* ("sword"), a reference to the slender foliage of these irises. The translucent, grayish green leaves of xiphiums reflex gracefully, making the plants look like diminutive leeks when they are not in flower.

A spring display of Dutch irises, *Iris ×hollandica*, with poppy anemones, Chinese pinks, and gerbera daisies.

The modern Dutch hybrids (*Iris ×hollandica*) are derived mostly from the yellow, white, or blue Spanish iris (*I. xiphium*) and the deep blue Moroccan *I. tingitana*. Both species grow naturally in seasonally wet areas on granite or limestone. They enjoy plenty of water while in growth during fall and winter, and they value a long summer baking afterward. Both clay and sandy soils suit them. The similar, but leafier English irises (*I. latifolia*) derive originally from moist, cool meadows high in the Pyrenees. They sulk in Southern heat, flowering poorly, if at all.

Strong-growing Dutch iris varieties, such as the ultra gentian-blue 'Prof. Blau', will naturalize and may be seen in many older gardens in April. Paler blues, like 'Wedgwood', descend from *I. tingitana* and usually flower several weeks earlier. An especially large-growing hybrid, 'Blue Magic', not only offers beautiful violet-blue flowers in April, but also makes a show for weeks with its architectural fountains of channeled leaves. These display pearly white upper surfaces that glisten in the spring sun, a character typical of *I. tingitana*. The basal leaves, or cataphylls, of this unusually cold hardy clone are also intriguingly suffused with purple.

The older, seldom-offered strains of Spanish iris are similar to these Dutch hybrids, but bloom later and have more slender, delicate appearances. The most common ones in gardens are narrow-leafed, small-flowered yellows. A wide collection of all these bulbous irises will provide bloom through a period of two or three months.

Both the Dutch and Spanish varieties make foliage early in the season, so bulbs should be planted in fall as soon as they can be obtained. The slightly built leaves and stems are often inadequate foils for the jewel-like flowers, so these slender irises may be planted in groups against backgrounds of hardy shrubs or perennials, or mixed in winter bedding schemes with violas and dianthus. Since the bulbs do not mind compacted earth, they offer an excellent solution for winter borders where

In a dry corner of the author's Austin garden, winter sun gleams off the reflective foliage of *Iris ×hollandica* 'Blue Magic'.

large clumps of subtropical crinums disappear after frost. The irises may be set nearby to fill in during the cool season. They will bloom in April, then disappear under the emerging leaves of the crinums in late spring.

Junos, Hermodactylus, and Reticulatas

Iris persica is a frail, translucent flower in the mysterious Juno group of irises. With its slate-colored petals appearing above very short leaves early in the season, it is one of several old flowers that share the nickname fair maids of February. Parkinson grew this small, fragrant iris four hundred years ago, and it has been shared among gardeners in America since colonial days. Thomas Jefferson planted it at Monticello in 1812.

Although fairly well suited to the upper South, *Iris persica* seldom persists near the Gulf. In its Middle Eastern home, this species grows in dry oak scrub where the plants receive little rainfall in summer. In the South these bulbs prosper when planted under the eaves of houses or against sunny walls, where they may bake dry over summer.

Although it is closely related to other bulbous irises, botanists usually give another iris, with similar wants, a genus of its own: *Hermodactylus tuberosus* (*Iris tuberosa*), the widow or snake's head iris. The somber blossoms of this Mediterranean species, with black falls and olive-green signals, appear in the midst of long, sparse, four-cornered, gray leaves. The weird roots creep about

and resemble long, white worms. The generic name *Hermodactylus* ("Hermes' finger") refers to these tubers.

The snake's head iris establishes readily and can be very free of increase with its long, spiky foliage. Flowering is unpredictable, however, unless the bulbs are well ripened over summer. Raised beds of sand, decomposed granite, oystershell, or lime rubble will provide the fast drainage necessary, with an arid summer, to prepare flower buds for the following spring. The gardener's reward will be a bouquet of sinister, blackish green blooms in early February.

The widow iris or snake's head iris (*Hermodactylus tuberosus*).

Miniature reticulata irises (*Iris reticulata*), coming from the cold, dry uplands of Turkey, are reliable perennials only in the upper South. They return and bloom easily, however, if dug and stored dry over summer; a raised bed of gravelly soil may harden and preserve the bulbs in the same way. They are worth any minor trouble, for the tiny, violet-scented blooms are valuable at their early February blooming season.

There are several color forms of *Iris reticulata* in shades of violet, lavender, and blue, all marked with a bright yellow eye. Another commonly offered iris in this group, *I. danfordiae*, has clear

Iris reticulata. Photo by Lauren S. Ogden.

golden blossoms. It is less reliable in its flowering than *I. reticulata*, and the bulbs usually split into multitudes too small to bloom after their first year.

Iris vartanii is a related dwarf iris from Israel, where it is especially abundant around the city of Nazareth. The pale blue or white blossoms are striped with light yellow and customarily appear in December. Only the white 'Alba' is in the trade, but it is the most vigorous form of the species, and the best variety to establish on a sunny bank.

Spanish Nuts

The little blue irises called Spanish nuts belong to a group of cormous irids native mostly to the Cape Province of South Africa. The sole Mediterranean representative of the section is one of the few species suited to the South. Formerly classed in *Iris*, and for many years known as *Gynandriris sisyrinchium*, botanists now place this flower in the genus *Moraea* along with its relations from southern Africa. The species name is from an old Greek word for iris, and perhaps this is the same flower that the ancients knew.

If planted in the fall, the brown-coated corms send up several narrow, channeled leaves over winter. In April and May the pale or deep blue flowers follow on slender stems set among the leaves. The ephemeral blossoms bear creamy blotches, and several open in succession from each spike. These short-lived blooms expand in the afternoon and fade by midnight.

Moraea sisyrinchium comes from regions with shallow, rocky soil and little summer rain. Raised beds or dry, sunny positions under the eaves of the house are best. Winter cold is no trouble for them.

Butterfly Irises, Cape Tulips, and Fortnight Lilies

In the mildest parts of the South, a few of the South African butterfly irises may be tried, although only the most vigorous will establish and return. Like the Spanish nut, these *Moraea* species develop corms and were once included in *Iris*. Most of the South African members of this group operate on a winter growing schedule. For this reason many species are hardy only where frosts are light.

The most generally successful species is *Moraea polystachya*, a native of the *karoo*, or dry region, of the Cape Province. In late summer its small corms send up several sparse, narrowly channeled leaves. These are joined in mid-fall by two-foot branched stalks dotted with handsome, lilac blossoms. The flowers resemble miniature irises with orange eyes in the middle of the outer segments, appearing a few at a time from October through February. In California and the Southwest, this variety seeds itself into great patches, but in most of the South it is slow to increase, unless gardeners intervene to gather the seeds and save them for fall planting. These irislike plants prosper with gritty, well-drained soil and a dry summer rest.

Several *Moraea* species have simple blooms with six nearly equal petals in the style of a crocus; these species (formerly classified in *Homeria*) will sometimes flower in the South after mild winters. The muted salmon and yellow blossoms of the most common species, *M. collina*, are fragrant and enchanting, and

Moraea polystachya.

they warrant an attempt, even at the risk of occasional failure from unseasonable cold. If set in well-drained soil, the corms send up a single, wiry leaf in fall, with the crocuslike flowers following on branched stalks in March and April. In their South African homeland, these little blooms are known as Cape tulips or *rooitulps* ("red tulips"). The flowers close at night and during cloudy weather, but appear over a period of four or five weeks in spring.

Gardeners often apply the name moraea to the summer-growing fortnight lilies, now placed in the genus *Dietes*. These clumping irises are more at home in the humid South than many of their corm-bearing relations, but they still run some risk of damage during cold winters. Their swordlike, evergreen leaves rise from a sturdy, creeping rhizome and arrange themselves in slender fans like spuria or Louisiana irises. This exceptionally handsome foliage makes fortnight lilies popular landscape specimens in mild climates.

In their South African homeland, the fortnight lilies often grow along margins of ponds or in damp, shaded forests. Although tolerant of some drought, they are more regular and generous bloomers if regularly fed and watered. The individual flowers last only a day, but they appear over a long season from spring through fall. Intermittent crops of bloom come in bursts separated by two-week periods, hence the name fortnight lily.

Two *Dietes* species are common in gardens along the Gulf Coast. *Dietes grandiflora* (the one more often seen, usually sold as *D. vegeta* or *Moraea iridioides*) bears distinctively broad, three-foot evergreen leaves. Glistening white or light lavender, iris-shaped blooms appear in small groups against the dark foliage. 'Lemon Drops' and 'Orange Drops' are selections with creamy blossoms and bright blotches of yellow and orange, respectively.

The yellow African iris (*Dietes bicolor*) has narrower, paler green leaves and light yellow flowers marked with maroon spots. The elegantly slender foliage combines strikingly in a variety of settings, making this rugged plant a favorite subject for pots. Mixed with bright orange *Zinnia angustifolia* and rich purple *Setcreasea purpurea*, *D. bicolor* offers a resilient subtropical display through the entire summer. This species is fairly hardy, remaining evergreen to 15°F or less. It also resists browsing deer and is more tolerant of drought than *D. grandiflora*.

Cape Bulbs

The Cape Province of South Africa has one of the richest floras in the world. The iris family, in particular, has undergone an explosion in diversity there. Many South African irids have fantastic blossoms marked with brilliant colors and iridescent spots like the feathers of peacocks. These are some of the bulb world's finest flowers.

However, many of these beautiful bulbs come from mild, winter-rainfall regions. Garden hybrids of *Freesia*, *Sparaxis*, *Tritonia*, and *Ixia* often balk at the South's hot, damp summers, and frosty, unsteady winters. For Southern gardeners the summer-rainfall regions that extend from the Eastern Cape through KwaZulu-Natal and the highveld around Johannesburg are the most promising areas of South Africa to prospect for bulbs.

Painted Petals

One dainty, warmly colored irid that especially thrives in the South is called painted petals in its African home. The bright scarlet flowers have darker reddish spots at the base of the lower petals, which account for the charming appellation. Formerly listed as *Lapeirousia laxa* or *Anomatheca cruenta*, these days botanists call this species *Freesia laxa*.

The flowers of these little irids appear in loose, one-sided spikes up to a foot or two in height. They usually arrive in spring but may come at almost any season, depending on when the corms break dormancy. Some start into growth in fall, others in early spring, so a succession of flowers may be secured; furthermore, no weather disaster will befall all the colony at one time. The small, light green fans of foliage remain attractive even without bloom.

Painted petals (*Freesia laxa*) nestled near the maplelike leaves of Turk's cap (*Malvaviscus drummondii*). Photo by Lauren S. Ogden.

Around Johannesburg and south to the East Cape, the little corms of painted petals grow in rich woodland. They thrive in leafy shade in the South. Sun will not harm them as long as they receive plenty of moisture while in growth. The corms usually enter dormancy in summer, after the flowers swell into oval pods. The hard, round seeds that form inside may be planted in pots or left to naturalize in the garden, where they will germinate in the coming winter. Corms multiply in this fashion into thriving patches.

Freesia grandiflora is a similar species with somewhat longer, more slender petals. It flowers in late winter slightly before *F. laxa* and is not usually hardy north of the Gulf. In addition to the shrimp-red of this and the common painted petals there is a good white form of *F. laxa*, 'Alba'. This comes true from seed, bearing ivory-colored blossoms decorated by small, rosy blotches at the base of the three lower petals. A lavender-flowered variant may also be had, but this does not seem as vigorous.

Another freesia sometimes encountered in Florida gardens, *Freesia corymbosa*, was one of the varieties used to breed the large-flowered florist's freesias. The species itself has slender, grassy foliage and rather small, pale yellow blossoms marked with gold on the inside of the lower petals. These have crimped edges that partly close the mouths of the flowers like little snapdragons. Although not especially showy, the slender spikes of bloom are mildly fragrant and have a wildflowery grace reminiscent of *Ixia*. When left to naturalize in lawns, they glow against the bright spring grasses as the sun shines through their primrose buds.

Freesia corymbosa.

Also incorporated into the hybrid strains of *Freesia*, *F. alba* and *F. leichtlinii* are dwarf species with showy, mostly white flowers that exude delicious fragrance. The outsides of their funnel-shaped blooms sometimes have

Freesia alba. Photo by Lauren S. Ogden.

a slight purplish flush, their throats may bear a few darker pencilings, and the lower lips usually display a flash of yellow, but the overall effect of the blossoms remains white. Unlike larger hybrid freesias, these wild species seem entirely hardy and at home in the South, returning faithfully each winter to offer their flowers in early spring along with *F. laxa*. With fresh, white blooms and tidy clumps of grassy leaves, these species make charming additions to raised rockeries, where their sweet fragrance can be enjoyed close up.

Harlequin Flowers

Hybrid garden strains of the fantastically colored harlequin flower, *Sparaxis*, often bloom in the South for a season or two, but tend to dwindle away after that. Surprisingly permanent, however, is a colorful species from meadows on the Bokkeveld plateau, *S. elegans*. The salmon-orange, overlapping petals of this

One of the harlequin flowers of the Bokkeveld plateau, *Sparaxis elegans*.

showy variety have purplish bases edged with black bars and yellow spots, describing a bold circle in the center of the one-inch-wide blooms. These appear in March, borne a few at a time on short fans of green leaves. *Sparaxis elegans* is native to heavy clay soils in a region of South Africa that receives hard winter frosts and at least some summer rainfall. It grows readily from seed and may also be multiplied from small corms that form at the base of the parent tuber.

Montbretias

The common name montbretia commemorates French botanist Antoine François Ernest Coquebert de Montbret, who accompanied Napoleon on his invasion of Egypt in 1798. Gardeners still attach his name to a lovely old hybrid now classed in *Crocosmia*, although for a while it was placed under *Tritonia*. The present generic name means "crocus-scented": the colorful blooms, if dried and placed in water, develop a strong smell of saffron.

The old montbretia of Southern gardens ranks as a first-class border flower, thoroughly hardy and undemanding in rich, moist soil. Its bright green sheaves of flattened, grassy leaves send up a succession of brilliant, nodding, lilylike flowers held in graceful, arching sprays. These are orange-red on the exterior but glow with yellow from the inside, where their throats are marked with reddish brown streaks. Spreading by means of short stolons, the corms multiply rapidly in good neutral or acid soil, so there are always plenty to share or move about.

This vigorous exotic descends from an 1882 cross made by French nurseryman Victor Lemoine, of Nancy. The parents of the hybrid were the orange *Crocosmia aurea* and the rich crimson *C. pottsii*. When Lemoine introduced his creation, botanists gave it the confusing name *C.* ×*crocosmiiflora* ("crocosmia-flowered crocosmia"). This certainly offered sufficient excuse for gardeners to continue calling them montbretias.

A great number of *Crocosmia* hybrids have been created since, and several different ones may be had in a range of colors through cream, yellow, orange, and crimson. 'Solfatare' is a famous late-nineteenth-century hybrid with apricot-yellow blooms and bronze-tinted foliage. It's one of the most beautiful, although it is less vigorous than the common montbretia. Other good hybrids include the soft orange 'Star of the East', mango-colored 'Jenny Bloom', and fiery orange 'Golden Ballerina'.

Nurseries sometimes offer the golden swan montbretia (*Crocosmia masoniorum*), but this high-altitude species and its hybrids sulk in the summer heat of the South. Fast-multiplying forms such as 'Lucifer', a popular flaming orange-red hybrid between *C. masoniorum* and the pleated-leafed *C. paniculata* (in Afrikaans, *waaierlelie*), perform well in colder areas, but their bulbs generally split up and fail to bloom in the South after the first season.

Falling Stars

One of the species Lemoine used to create his hybrid is itself a fine garden plant in the South. Known commonly as falling stars, *Crocosmia aurea* ranges naturally from the Eastern Cape through Mpumalanga, KwaZulu-Natal, and Swaziland, growing along stream banks, wooded cliffs, and forest margins. In gardens this is a fine flower for shaded or partly sunny positions, slowly rambling on short runners that periodically send up slender, eighteen-inch fans of light green foliage. In late summer these carry clusters of nodding, golden orange, star-shaped blooms. In the fall the spent blossoms ripen into surprisingly attractive, leathery, orange-red pods carrying shiny, black seeds. These may be planted directly in the garden and will bloom in their second season.

Like all *Crocosmia* species, falling stars enjoys rich, moist soils. Its flowers appear over several weeks, providing vibrant tones to mix with summery blue Cape plumbago, buttery cannas, or tall white phloxes. In the South, hummingbirds fill in for the absent

Falling stars (*Crocosmia aurea*) flowering in late summer among aloes, author's garden, Austin.

African sunbirds, swarming around the glowing orange blooms in August and September.

Gladioli

The gladiolus, or sword lily, is the best known of all the African irids. It has been a popular bedding flower since the mid-1800s, when florists bred the first tall varieties suited for cutting. All the members of this large genus bear sword-shaped foliage (*Gladiolus* translates as "little sword" in Latin).

The modest requirements of the modern gladioli include rich, moist soil and early planting. In the South it is customary to set out fresh, blooming-size corms at biweekly intervals from mid-January until mid-March. This assures a succession of bloom extending through early May. Later plantings are usually futile, since thriving populations of thrips and sweltering heat do these flowers in during the summer. If flowers are cut for the table, at least four or five leaves should be left to feed the large, flattened corms. With good care, these plants easily multiply from tiny offsets called cormels.

Although many hybrid gladioli are perfectly hardy in the South, most deteriorate and cease bloom without annual replanting in fresh, prepared soil. A few old species exhibit sufficient vigor to be considered true perennials. All are choice, and among the most desirable of garden flowers.

The parrot gladiolus, *Gladiolus dalenii.*

One of the old plants seen in the South is the parrot gladiolus, or Natal lily (*Gladiolus dalenii*, formerly *G. natalensis* or *G. psittacinus*). This is one of the principal species used to breed the modern hybrid gladioli, and its stiff, veined leaves and tall stature have a familiar appearance. The brilliant orange, hooded blooms are very showy, and they appear on three- to four-foot spikes in early May. Each flower has three upper segments forming the orange hood, while the lower three petals reflex and glow with a buttery yellow tone. Four or five blooms open at any one time.

These robust plants fend for themselves on the poorest soils, but their beauty increases dramatically with generous feeding and watering. The large corms soon multiply into attractive stands, and may be set in groups of five or six to punctuate the rear of an early summer border. Either sun or part shade is satisfactory, but it is well to keep in mind that the one-sided flower spikes usually face south, and will be most attractive if placed to the north of viewers. Setting the corms at least four inches down in the soil will overcome any need for staking.

The Maid of the Mist

Around the turn of the twentieth century, engineer F. S. Thompson was engaged to build a bridge over the Zambezi River below Victoria Falls in then Rhodesia. On the rocky slopes below the waterfall, he spied a clump of clear yellow gladioli. These had graceful blossoms with the upper petals bent over to form hoods. Thompson noticed that the specialized blooms protected the flowers' reproductive organs from the continuous spray of the waterfall. Excited collectors soon gathered and introduced corms of this new flower, dubbed the maid of the mist (*Gladiolus primulinus*), nearly exterminating it in the wild in their enthusiasm. Botanists now regard this gladiolus as a pale-flowered variant of *G. dalenii*.

When bred to various large-flowered hybrids, this light yellow gladiolus sired a race with extraordinary, graceful blooms. The delicate colorings of the hooded blossoms ranged from pale yellow through apricot, salmon, saffron, and orange-red. Flowers of primulinus hybrids also spaced themselves farther apart on the stem than other gladioli.

These orchidlike flowers have tremendous vigor, and their lighter, airier appearance and graceful, arching stems make them especially beautiful in gardens. They make lovely, permanent additions to a May border. Modern butterfly gladioli descend from the original primulinus hybrids. Their frilled, satiny flowers have vivid markings of red or rose in the throat. 'Atom' is one that is still in the trade with satiny red florets dressed by a white picotee edge. Heirloom, pastel-colored gladioli such as 'Bolivian Peach', 'Carolina Primrose', and 'Boone' appear close to the original maid of the mist.

Acidanthera

The fragrant Abyssinian gladiolus (*Gladiolus callianthus*) has long been known to gardeners as *Acidanthera bicolor*. Long-tubed, creamy blooms give this nocturnal flower a distinctive appearance. In its native east African home, this summer grower inhabits rich, marshy ground. Since the blooms open in the

Gladiolus callianthus sends out powerful fragrance at dusk.

evening, they escape the heat stress experienced by day-flowering gladioli.

These fragrant flowers thrive in damp borders, and rooted corms may even be immersed in shallow water, where they will revel in the abundance of food and moisture. The sweet, primrose-scented blooms open one at a time over several weeks. The strain sold as *Acidanthera bicolor* has creamy blossoms marked with chocolate-brown spots. The robust 'Zwanenburg' flowers early, with handsome dark blotches. *Gladiolus murielae* is taller, with purplish markings.

Along the Gulf Coast, Abyssinian gladioli may be expected to return if they have been well fed and watered. In the upper South, they may be dug and stored over winter. *Gladiolus callianthus* is a delightful, fragrant companion for summer phlox, Virginia saltmarsh mallow (*Kosteletzkya virginica*), and other moisture-loving perennials.

Corn Flags

Although most gladioli are African, several hardy species are also scattered around Turkey and the Mediterranean, the most famous of which is the old-fashioned Byzantine gladiolus (*Gladiolus byzantinus*). The magenta spires of this invaluable flower appear at the same time as bearded irises, reaching above the deep green clumps of swordlike leaves. Each claret-cerise blossom curves beautifully and fits tightly into a showy spike. Creamy flashes mark the lower three petals.

These tough, old flowers, thriving on heavy clay soils, may be seen in many gardens in the South, where they persist indefinitely without attention. They are often set in large rows to edge paths or borders of roses, but they also complement informal borders, where they flower along with the yellow, blue, or white false indigos (*Baptisia* spp.). Byzantine gladioli have been cultivated since ancient times in Europe. Dioscorides began the tradition of calling them corn flags, and they may often be seen growing in fallow cornfields around the Mediterranean.

The corms of *Gladiolus byzantinus* should be planted in the fall if they are to bloom on schedule. Tiny cormels may be set out along with blooming-size corms to add foliage, or they may be grown on in rich soil, where they will flower after three years. The frost-hardy foliage usually shows above ground in January, with blossoms following in April. The papery leaves, ripening toward the end of May, may be disguised among leafy perennials or allowed to develop their natural straw tones in a grassy meadow.

The true strain of *Gladiolus byzantinus* is well represented by 'Cruentus', a robust, upright plant with dark-colored flowers. American growers sometimes offer this heirloom, but Dutch suppliers more often send out smaller, paler flowers under the same name. These are usually related, inferior species, such as *G. communis*. These counterfeits may establish in Southern gardens, but they fail to provide the impact

The corn flag, or Byzantine gladiolus (*Gladiolus byzantinus* 'Cruentus'), a common heirloom of Southern gardens.

of 'Cruentus'. Other allied gladioli, such as *G. imbricatus*, *G. italicus*, and *G. segetum*, are hardy, small-flowered varieties suited to rock gardens and may be had from specialists.

'Alba', a delightful white sport of *Gladiolus byzantinus*, is found in some older gardens in the South. Although slow in growth, it is permanent and ideal for planting designs in which the strong magenta of 'Cruentus' would be overly harsh. In Europe this lovely gladiolus is raised for the cut flower trade.

In addition to these denizens of old gardens, a variety of modern hardy glads will perennate in the South, although some bloom too late in the season to be of much value. The baby glads (*Gladiolus* ×*colvillei*) descend from the yellow marsh Afrikander (*G. tristis*) and the waterfall gladiolus (*G. cardinalis*), hardy miniatures from the Bokkeveld plateau and the mountains of the southwestern Cape. The numerous cultivars have pink, rose, peach, or white blooms, charmingly flashed with darker spots. They bear enchanting, descriptive names such as

Gladiolus byzantinus 'Alba'.

Gladiolus tristis (marsh Afrikander).

'Blushing Bride', 'Peach Blossom', and 'Charm'. The small, slightly fragrant flowers appear six to a stem on wiry, graceful plants. They do well in rich soil, if planted in the fall so that the corms have time to grow and flower before the onset of summer heat.

Gladiolus tristis itself is also successful in the South, preferring a sunny, damp position for its clusters of slender stems and rushlike leaves. The pale greenish yellow blossoms arrive in April, looking like flocks of small butterflies. They emit a sweet nocturnal fragrance. Hybrids between G. tristis and G. watsonianus (formerly Homoglossum watsonianum) are known as homoglads and seem more cold hardy and vigorous than G. tristis itself. These have muted, coppery peach blossoms with pale yellow throats and maroon splashes on the lower petals, inheriting the night fragrance of G. tristis.

Shellflowers

When Gerard wrote his Herball (1597), he related the tale of a fantastical flower, "a kinde of Dragons not seene by any that have written thereof." He doubted the existence of this bloom, "the floure of Tigris," but described it for his readers to expose the fraud:

> The root (saith my Author) is bulbous or Onion fashion, outwardly
> blacke; from the which spring up long leaves, sharpe, pointed, narrow,

and of a fresh greene colour: in the middest of which leaves rise up naked or bare stalkes, at the top whereof groweth a pleasant yellow floure, stained with many small red spots here and there cast abroad: and in the middest of the floure thrusteth forth a long red tongue or stile, which in time groweth to be the cod or seed-vessel, crooked and wreathed, wherein is the seed. The vertues and temperament are not to be spoken of, considering that we assuredly persuade ourselves that there are no such plants, but meere fictions and devices, as we terme them, to give his friend a gudgeon.

Having seen a tigridia in actual blossom, a gardener can well imagine how difficult it must have been for Gerard to believe such a flower could be real. The bulb is ordinary enough, but the foliage is strangely pleated, like the seedling leaves of a palmetto. The wiry stalk holds up gaudy, carmine, reddish orange, yellow, pink, or white triangular blossoms. With a glowing, silky texture, like the pearly interior of a conch, the blooms carry an indescribable pattern of yellow and purple dots and blotches. These are distributed about the base of the three largest petals, and entirely cover the three smaller ones, which form a depressed cup. From the midst of this dazzling display rises the long, three-pronged staminal tube, with the stigma protruding like some exotic antenna reaching out to the stars.

The Mexican shellflower, or tiger flower (*Tigridia pavonia*) is one of the marvels of the plant kingdom. These gorgeous iris relations once grew in the ancient gardens of the Aztecs, who cultivated them not only for their beauty, but also for their edible bulbs. Their name in the Aztec tongue, *oceloxochitl* ("ocelot flower"), seems to be the direct antecedent of both the English common name for the genus, tiger flower, and the Latin *Tigridia*. Since the blooms are spotted and not striped, the Aztec comparison to the ocelot seems more apt.

Shellflower refers to the delicate, shell-like appearance of these blossoms, which belong to a large group of American irids. All these "tigridioids" share pleated foliage and true bulbs covered in papery, brownish coats. Their beautiful, spotted flowers last

The Mexican shellflower, or tiger flower (*Tigridia pavonia*).

only a day, but new buds continue to open in succession over several weeks of the summer.

The common strains of *Tigridia pavonia* available in the bulb trade descend from the original stocks cultivated by the Aztecs in the high, eternally fresh climate of the Valley of Mexico. In Southern gardens these are unhappy in the heat of summer and must be given rich, well-watered soil to see them through. Partial shade is welcome, and the bulbs should be set at least four or five inches deep to assure a cool root run. If treated generously, *Tigridia* may return as a perennial, but it is customary to lift the bulbs, gladiolus-fashion, and store them in a dry place over winter. After frost they may be tied in bunches and suspended in the air to prevent predation from hungry mice.

Many lovely species of *Tigridia* are scattered over Mexico. Although most are high-elevation plants suited to cool climates, a few, including some strains of the showy *T. pavonia*, grow at lower altitudes. A form with six-inch orange-red blooms introduced by Carl Schoenfeld from a very hot area in Tamaulipas has done well in the South.

In addition to the common up-facing, iris-shaped blooms, some *Tigridia* species bear nodding, bell-shaped flowers. These types often come in brownish tones, checkered with spots so as to resemble the European *Fritillaria meleagris*. *Tigridia ehrenbergii*, one suited to the warmth of the South, produces attractive yellowish buff bells from July through September. It comes from the oak-covered Sierra Madre Oriental in northeastern Mexico.

The pine woods lily (*Alophia purpurea*).

The Pine Woods Lily

The South has a native tiger flower with blooms inclined to one side, sort of halfway between a nod and an upright stance. This displays the rich, purple glory of the pine woods lily (*Alophia purpurea*) to perfection. The larger violet petals surround a shimmering cup flecked with warm brown spots. Three yellow and white eyes sit at the tips of the smaller petals.

This exotic color scheme must have special meaning for the pollinators of this flower. Botanists believe these shell-flowers actually mimic insect appearance with their blooms. This strategy is also pursued by some orchids, usually to entice male wasps, who fertilize the blossoms as they attempt to "mate."

In the sandy soils of eastern Texas and Louisiana, and south along the Gulf into Mexico, these vigorous irids may be seen flowering in damp places among grass or under pines. Depending on rains, they may flower over the entire summer. The blooms open freshly each morning, lasting until noon, or later if the weather is overcast. The pleated leaves die down for winter, but emerge early in spring. Pine woods lilies grow readily from seed, naturalizing in sun or part shade. Their slender foliage is never obtrusive, and their fleeting blooms are invariably astounding.

Botanists once included the pine woods lily in the genus *Eustylis*, and these flowers may still be listed under this name. In addition to the rich purple of the common Southern species, several *Alophia* species from Mexico seem equally permanent; one, *A. vera-cruzana*, is a vigorous species with lovely, pale lilac-blue flowers. The drought-tolerant *Eleutherine bulbosa*, an ally of *Alophia* from tropical America, opens its fragrant, white blooms in early evening.

Alophia veracruzana.

Celestials

A blue shellflower worthy of a favored place in any garden is the celestial, *Ne-mastylis acuta* (*N. geminiflora*). These crocuslike Southern natives have for-saken the irregular form and spots of their allies, but they retain the pleated, grassy foliage and deep-rooted bulbs typical of other tigridioids. The hardy

The celestial, *Nemastylis acuta.*

leaves rise during late winter, with the ephemeral, sky-blue flowers following in April and May.

Celestials, looking best when planted in large groups, grow well in partial shade as well as sun. The bright yellow anthers give the delicate blue of the petals an extra zest, setting them apart from more ordinary blooms. Although seldom offered for sale, celestials may be marked in fields and roadsides during May, so that gardeners can return to harvest seed in June. The seed should be held for fall planting in pots or directly in garden beds. Although the hard, round seeds are slow to germinate, *Nemastylis* seedlings grow rapidly with good treatment.

In addition to the blue-flowered *Nemastylis acuta*, a celestial of northeastern Florida, the violet, white-eyed, fall-flowering *N. floridana*, would be an attractive prospect, with blooms opening in late afternoon. The purple *N. tenuis* subsp. *pringlei*, a summer grower from the Southwest, may also prove hardy. The yellow, starlike *N. revoluta* of western Mexico would be worthy of trial.

Prairie Nymphs

Many gardeners along the Gulf discover the April blooms of the prairie nymph, *Herbertia lahue*, appearing spontaneously in their lawns. These tiny, exotically spotted, blue irises grow in the heavy coastal clays where sod is raised; they often pirate their way into gardens along with St. Augustine grass. Since their narrow foliage comes in winter, they are at little risk from lawn mowers. The up-facing, one-inch blooms scarcely top six inches in height but make up for their small size in mottled glamour. As with most of these American iris relations, the blossoms open freshly each morning, and close up promptly each afternoon.

Herbertia pulchella is a similar-looking cousin from South America, where many small tigridioids grow on the subtropical savannahs. It offers especially large, orchidlike, deep blue blossoms held on four-inch stems, growing readily on moist sandy soil or reddish clay-loam.

The orange-gold *Cypella herbertii* is also hardy and reliable on acid clay or sand. Its flowers are exotically spotted like *Tigridia* blossoms, but appear more orchid-shaped and a good deal smaller, with three noticeably drooping petals. Carried in branching clusters above the one-inch-wide, pleated leaves, the flowers of *C. herbertii* last well into early evening before falling smartly away to prepare for their replacements the following morning. Blooming begins in April and continues through most of the summer. The similar *C. peruviana* bears its larger orange-yellow blooms on solitary stems later in the season. Another summer bloomer, *C. aquatilis*, needs an unfailing supply of moisture to provide its golden blossoms. *Cypella coelestis* sends up fleeting, three-inch, gun-metal-blue blossoms, marked yellow at the base. These arrive on two-foot stems in mid-summer, continuing into the fall above clumps of bluish green, pleated foliage. This comes from northeastern Argentina, where it grows on acid red clays that stay very moist while the bulbs are in growth.

Gelasine elongata, another beautiful blue-flowered irid, produces substantial clumps of handsomely stiff, blue-green foliage, looking like thickly planted seedling palmettos. The one-inch, cae-

The prairie nymph (*Herbertia lahue*).

rulean flowers show white stars and violet flecking in their throats. They appear on glaucous, two-foot stems in May, lasting only a day each, but new blooms continue to appear for several weeks. The striking leaves contribute their distinctive form to the garden most of the year.

Other unusual bulbous irids worth growing in the South include several small *Tigridia* species formerly placed in the genus *Rigidella*, with orange-scarlet blooms reflexed like shooting stars, and *Cipura paludosa*, with tiny, glistening white blossoms held in sprays like a miniature gladiolus. *Herbertia amatorum*, *Kelissa brasiliensis*, and *Onira unguiculata* are South American rarities with flowers like tiny lavender orchids. All prosper on damp, acid soil.

The palmlike foliage of *Gelasine elongata* adds texture to a mixed border.

Bartram's Ixia

Among the rarest of all these little irids is a Southern native from a small, curious region west of Jacksonville, Florida. The ephemeral flowers are known to locals as violets and to botanists as Bartram's ixia (*Calydorea coelestina*). They occur in a sort of refuge area for unusual North American plants. Their closest relatives are Mexican and South American.

The tiny, autumn blossoms of these irids resemble *Cipura*, but they are violet-toned, with white eyes. Only early risers may appreciate them, for the flowers open with the sunrise and close by eight in the morning. These rare, fleeting beauties were discovered in the 1760s by John Bartram of Philadelphia. This intrepid gentleman, America's first native botanist, discovered and introduced an amazing number of Southern rarities. His son William, who later described the bulbs botanically, gave an especially romantic account of their explorations in Florida. After sleeping in a bed of soft Spanish moss at their lakeside camp, they awoke to "behold the azure fields of caerulean Ixea!"

Walking Irises

More commonly seen in Southern gardens are several walking irises (*Neomarica* spp.) of the American tropics. These grow from clumping, perennial rootstocks, instead of bulbs, but they show relation to tigridioids in their ephemeral, spotted blossoms. After flowering, the flattened scapes sprout leafy plantlets. As the stems bend over, these form roots and "walk" about the garden. Since these flowers propagate themselves, they are often shared. The evergreen foliage of walking irises is tender to hard frosts, but the rootstocks will usually recover from freezes if the plants are well mulched.

The white and blue flowered *Neomarica gracilis* is easy and popular, not only for its blooms but also for its glossy fans of leaves, like those of *Iris japonica*. The apostle plant (*N. northiana*) sends up similar white, violet-stained blossoms with a sweet fragrance. The three-foot *marica*, or Brazilian walking iris (*N. caerulea*) prefers good, acid soil. Its pale green, leaflike stems produce a succession of richly blue, spotted blossoms, barred with yellow-brown, and equal to the loveliest tigridias.

The yellow walking iris (*Trimezia martinicensis*), the most drought tolerant of the group, stands hot sun as well as part shade. It also endures alkaline soils and seems indifferent to heavy clays. The crimped, three-quarter-inch, orange-yellow blossoms resemble *Cypella*.

Blue-Eyed Grass

The blue-eyed grasses (*Sisyrinchium* spp.) are miniature interpretations of the walking iris theme, with grassy clumps of foliage and tiny, short-lived blue, white, or yellow blossoms. They are wholly American in distribution, with ninety species distributed from Canada to Tierra del Fuego. Although several attractive, blue-flowered natives occur in the South, these little flowers are largely overlooked in regional garden making. There is no good reason for their neglect, as all make good dwarf plants for April and May bloom.

The most common varieties on nursery lists are selections of *Sisyrinchium bellum*, either the common blue or the white ('Album'), and the yellow *S. californicum*. These western species usually prove temporary in the South, but are not difficult during the cool part of the year. From the warm, humid island of Bermuda, *S. bermudianum* would seem to be an attractive prospect for Southern gardeners, but many plants sold under this name prove to be forms of *S. idahoense*, a species better adapted to the mountain west. When it can be had, the true *S. bermudianum* makes tidy, eight-inch tufts of grassy foliage, carrying small lavender-blue blossoms in spring and early summer.

'Lucerne', a selection of the eastern American *Sisyrinchium angustifolium*, performs happily as a garden plant in the middle South, offering three-quarter-inch lavender-blue flowers from May until hot weather sets in. Another native, 'Suwannee', is a blue-eyed grass originally collected from chalky banks along the Suwannee River by Charles Webb. This undetermined Florida species makes vigorous clumps of eight-inch foliage that disappear under masses of sky-blue flowers in late spring. As with many plants from limestone habitats, 'Suwannee' adapts to both dry and wet soils. It also succeeds in sun or shade.

More unusual sisyrinchiums include 'Quaint and Queer', a hybrid with tidy tufts of foliage carrying muted, chocolate-brown flowers. Also uniquely colored, the Patagonian *Sisyrinchium striatum* sends up two-foot spikes of pale straw, purple-keeled blossoms. Although this species is not long-lived in the South, it makes impressive clumps of foliage and may be had in a showy variegated form, 'Aunt May'. The South American *S. palmifolium* offers golden blossoms held above equally large clumps of blue-green foliage. Its sizeable flowers open in early evening on two-and-one-half-foot stems. *Sisyrinchium tinctorium* 'Puerto Yellow', a summer-blooming species from northeastern Mexico, is another beautiful yellow-eyed grass, reaching just a foot in height.

A South African cousin of the blue-eyed grasses, the *blousterre* (*Aristea ecklonii*), ranges along humid foothills of the Drakensberg escarpment north into Tanzania. In late spring, zig-zag stems arch upward to two feet, carrying sprays of one-inch, cobalt-blue flowers like a gigantic sisyrinchium. Remaining evergreen to 15°F, this handsome subtropical offers lush, irislike fans of apple-green foliage ideal for plantings in full to partial shade.

Blackberry Lilies

There is a speckled Asian irid that offers something of an analog to the American tigridias. The old botanical name for the plant is *Pardanthus* ("leopard flower"). In the South these rich orange, purple-spotted blossoms have long been familiar as blackberry lilies, for the round, black seeds that persist clustered like blackberries after the fat pods open. Most garden literature refers to these perennials as *Belamcanda chinensis*, a Latinized version of their Asian name, *balamtandam*, and their home country, China. Recently, however, DNA-wielding botanists have assigned this distinctive plant the more pedestrian title *Iris domestica*.

This flower was once common in gardens, but is now more often seen as an escape, growing on damp, acid soil. Like many other deserving plants, this easy-growing irid has yielded its place to more obvious blooms. Jefferson had it at Monticello, where he knew the colorful blossoms as Chinese ixia.

The ephemeral flowers, appearing on slender stems above short fans of matte green foliage, continue over a long summer season. After the pretty flowers fade, the capsules enlarge to form the handsome "blackberries," which persist over winter and as cut decorations for autumn vases. The fleshy roots develop offsets that may be divided for increase, and the seeds, when sown, often flower the first season.

In addition to the common purple and orange of the wild *Iris domestica*, nurseries provide a pale yellow selection, 'Hello Yellow', and several hybrids with the Mongolian *I. dichotoma* (formerly *Pardanthopsis dichotoma*). Usually sold as pardancandas or candy lilies, they come in a wide range of exotic, warm-colored pastels. All grow readily on damp ground and make showy, but short-lived perennials. They grow easily from seed and mix cheerfully in borders of white phlox, yellow daylilies, and blue mistflowers (*Eupatorium coelestinum*).

Chapter 7
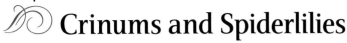 Crinums and Spiderlilies

A^t some point in May, the freshness of spring finally gives way to the steady warmth of summer. There can be no further pretense about gardening in a temperate clime. The subtropical season has arrived, and the South hereafter takes on an exotic ambience. The heat of the day sends gardeners cowering under porches or hiding beneath their hats. At dusk this uncomfortable warmth yields gradually to a pleasant humidity. A palpably thick atmosphere pervades the evening, seeming as if it were specially created for the sweet fragrances of jasmine, gardenia, and magnolia. If you walk among the borders at nightfall, you may spy the expanding buds of the most wondrous flowers of Southern summers, the powerfully fragrant blossoms of a freshly opened crinum or the delicate, fringed cups and dangling petals of a spiderlily.

Of all the bulbs cultivated in the South, none seems more Southern than these, and none is more important to regional gardens. Both *Crinum* and spiderlilies (*Hymenocallis* spp.) display special affinity for this region, and their lavish foliage marks many gardens. The sword-shaped leaves of spiderlilies appear in two opposite ranks, like those of amaryllises. Crinum foliage is distinctively whorled in lush rosettes.

Crinums

The flowing fountains of crinum leaves are a hallmark of traditional plantings. Their powerfully scented flowers, cherished since colonial times, have been shared, bred and improved by enthusiastic Southerners up to the present day. Old clumps of *Crinum* embellish antebellum estates and sharecroppers' hovels with equal abandon. Often, the deep-rooted bulbs have outlived their associated architecture, and they may be seen marking sites of old homes, plantations, and cemeteries. Through their robust vigor, endurance, and showy, fragrant blooms, these virtuous bulbs have carved a niche in regional landscapes like no other flower.

Crinums are noteworthy not only for their incomparable, exotic blossoms, but also for an amazing ability to perform in the poor soils and erratic climate of the South. Seemingly intractable heavy clays and nutrient-poor sandy soils grow fabulous crinums. In nature these bulbs are often found in seasonally

189

flooded depressions, swamps, arid sandylands, or among coastal dunes. Their growth cycles respond to the irregular supplies of moisture they receive in these difficult habitats. Many *Crinum* species behave as true opportunists, producing leaves and flowers following each downpour. After blooming and making seed, they rest until the next shower. Like giant-size rain lilies, these bulbs bloom many times over the year in response to precipitation. Few flowers contribute so much and ask so little.

When summer downpours moisten the ground, awakening their enormous bulbs, crinums erupt with lush fountains of straplike foliage. Leaves are quickly joined by thick flower stalks, which appear at the sides of the bulbs, then rise above the foliage. About ten days after the rains, the first buds open atop the tall scapes. Blooms may number fifteen to twenty or more in an umbel, so plants remain in flower for several days as blossoms open on successive evenings. If cut and set in a vase, the thick scapes will continue to open new flowers each night, just as if they were in the garden.

In garden borders these robust plants perform services more akin to peonies than to lilies. Their vast clumps of foliage provide an important focal point or anchor, whether the bulbs are in bloom or not. Like peonies, crinums dislike unnecessary disturbance and should be treated as long-lived perennials, rather than bedding flowers. They develop an enduring system of fleshy roots, which spreads as much as six feet in all directions. For this reason, crinums flower

Crinum variabile in habitat along a seasonal stream in the Bokkeveld escarpment of South Africa.

more prolifically and continuously when left in the ground for several years. When well treated they develop large clumps with numerous flowering-size bulbs.

Crinums will benefit from good soil preparation and should be set deeply, at least twelve to eighteen inches down. The plantings may then receive a thorough mulching of rotted leaves, pine straw, or other organic materials, giving them a moist, cool root run in summer and protecting them from penetrating frost during the winter. Mulching and deep planting also encourage the bulbs to size up, rather than offset, so that individual plants flower more freely.

Like other subtropicals, crinums respond with dramatically larger, more abundant blooms if dressed with rich compost or manure. The practice of making manure tea or liquid manure is also beneficial. It's a tradition in the South to take a brew of manure or grass clippings steeped with water and pour it over the leaves of crinums so nutrients may be absorbed as a tonic. This not only feeds the plants, but also stimulates them to throw up bloom spikes.

Many crinums grow well as partial aquatics, and potted bulbs may be set in pans of standing water through the entire growing season. Slow-release fertilizers or water-soluble plant foods will encourage prodigious growth on bulbs receiving this bog culture. Most crinums also thrive if planted near the margin of a garden pond.

When dividing an established clump, it is best to dig a trench around the entire group before attempting to undercut the deep-rooted bulbs. It is a good plan, also, to lift and separate all the bulbs, rather than risk slicing them to pieces by digging off the sides one at a time. The largest two or three bulbs may then be returned to the hole and replanted to make a quick show, while the offsets can be planted elsewhere or shared with friends. Dividing these big perennials requires considerable effort and a sharp, sturdy spade. The plants usually take a year or two to reestablish and resume full flowering, so this is a task best performed infrequently; once every three to five years is often enough.

Methuselah

Part of the allure of crinums stems from their mysterious, antediluvian origins. Many gardeners in the South maintain large collections of these border stalwarts, but even the most meticulous record keepers face a challenge telling names of bulbs in their charge. More often than not, these sturdy plants have been inherited as heirlooms, obtained from a kindly neighbor, or liberated from a vacant field or cemetery. They may have persisted unnoticed, unrecognized, and with little or no attention for decades.

The origins of several garden crinums lie shrouded in the mists of nine-teenth-century horticulture. Quite a few appear to be products of casual back-yard hybridization, and such ignominious births may never have received proper christenings. Nurserymen and inventive flower lovers have provided their own titles for these bulbs, and names like lily of the dawn or snow white angel will be met in the lists and market bulletins offered by the farm ladies of the South.

The history of crinums as garden plants is a long one, and *Crinum* species were among the first flowers to be deliberately crossed by early breeders. The Hon. and Rev. William Herbert, Dean of Manchester, compiled a list of hybrids in 1837. This tally included nearly thirty varieties, many of which probably re-main in cultivation, although their identities have been lost. These early hybrids were widely distributed by sailors who carried bulbs home on their ships. Their continued presence in gardens is a living testament to the movement of peoples through the warm climates of the world. Several old crosses are so robust and vigorous that they have outlived their creators and, like Methuselah, seem des-tined to outlive us all.

The Deep Sea Lily

The most prolific and abundant crinum in Southern gardens is a distinctive spe-cies with tapered, blue-green foliage. Each leaf reaches as much as two feet in length and three or four inches in width at the base. These wrap around each other to form a thick column topped with gracefully arching fountains of foli-age. In the center of the rosettes, there are usually a few thin, wispy, blue leaves just emerging; this unique appearance makes this crinum easy to distinguish wherever it grows.

Some country folk know these old garden flowers as deep sea lilies. In their native South Africa they are called *Oranjerivierlelie* ("Orange River lily"), *Vaal-rivierlelie* ("Vaal River lily"), or *vleilelie* ("pond lily"). They may be found grow-ing along the banks of streams from the Northwest Cape east to the Northern Province, KwaZulu-Natal, Mpumalanga, Lesotho, Swaziland, and the Free State. These robust amaryllids are also common escapes in the South and in other warm parts of the world, where they may be seen flowering in April in the shallow water of roadside ditches.

Old garden literature named this species for its long leaves (*Crinum longifo-lium*) or its homeland (*C. capense*), and these defunct epithets are still occasion-ally seen in nursery catalogs. Botanists, meanwhile, have settled on the un-romantic epithet *C. bulbispermum* ("bulb seed"), a reference to the peculiar, fleshy capsules of this plant. They swell and ripen into large pods, which split and tear open as they mature.

All crinums bear peculiarly large, fleshy seeds, which makes most varieties easy to raise. If left on the surface of the soil in a humid, shady position, the thick, green embryos germinate and form perfect miniature bulbs. These usually send down long roots, which pull the young plants deeply into the soil. Three or four years' growth on rich earth will mature the fledgling bulbs enough to begin flowering. Because of its prolific seed bearing, *Crinum bulbispermum* has sired numerous hybrids: this species is the forerunner of many of the old garden flowers of the South.

The succulent leaves of *Crinum bulbispermum* stand more frost than most other crinums, and this is the best species to plant where freezes regularly penetrate the ground. The bulbs thrive anywhere in the South and are hardy in protected situations as far north as Denver and Long Island. Blossoms are most prolific in April and May but come almost any season if stimulated by rains. In sheltered gardens *C. bulbispermum* flowers welcomely through December and January.

Flowers vary widely from plant to plant; they may be all white or pale pink with darker pink or wine markings on the keels. A dozen or more trumpet-shaped blooms cluster together, with five or six open at any one time. These lustrous flowers emit a peculiar, spicy odor, a wintry fragrance something like musk and anise mixed together. This is pleasant to some noses, but not all gardeners appreciate it.

The ordinary pinkish forms of *Crinum bulbispermum* may seem a bit homely, but they return with the trusted loyalty of a cocker spaniel. Even the poorest offers good, gray foliage to mix in a border. Improved selections include some of the finest flowers that may be grown in the South. The old pure white 'Album' reflexes luminous,

A dark wine-colored form of the Orange River lily, *Crinum bulbispermum* 'Sacramento'.

waxy blooms over a period of four or five months. It soon increases into impressive clumps. The wine-flamed 'Sacramento' is a show plant with deeply pigmented blossoms. This variety, descended from a reddish strain of *C. bulbispermum* collected near Kimberley, South Africa, inherits a reluctance to offset from its colorful parent. It may be readily propagated by seed, though, to develop a spectacular group in the garden.

The Sabie Crinum

Another crinum seldom, if ever forming offsets is *Crinum macowanii*. This species has a wide range from the Eastern Cape of South Africa to Zimbabwe and is especially common along the Sabie River near Kruger National Park in Mpumalanga. Its big rosettes of tapered foliage are as rank as those of *C. bulbispermum*, but they are dull green in tone, with none of the blueness of the Orange River lily.

The May blooms of *Crinum macowanii* are tulip-shaped and open widely at the throats to display thick, black anthers set against pale interiors. Light rose stripes line the backs of the petals, so that the buds resemble groups of pink-striped balloons. A sweet fragrance radiates from the rounded blossoms as they open in early evening. Each night several big flowers open and pose in an outfacing circle. The next morning they nod and fold their heads toward the ground. Since the petals recurve at the tips, these pendant, clustered blooms look like bunches of ruffled bells all through the following day.

Crinum macowanii.

This species is uncommon in the South, but may be found occasionally in old gardens, usually growing as a solitary bulb. It grows easily from seed and, when cared for, assumes enormous proportions. Certain tetraploid strains of *Crinum macowanii* hold the record for excessive size among hardier crinums. The fountains of leaves exceed five feet in height and spread, while the necks of the bulbs come to look like the trunks of young trees. Despite a near-tropical homeland, this species seems fairly frost tolerant. It performs well on heavy clay soils as well as deep sands and is remarkably resistant to drought.

Creole Lilies

The rough-margined, undulating leaves of *Crinum scabrum* make this old garden treasure easy to recognize even when out of bloom. Although similar to *C. macowanii* when young, this species produces foliage of a brighter green. The wavy rosettes of leaves frequently lie prostrate against the ground and writhe about like lively vegetable snakes.

In the first weeks of June, the globular bulbs send up fat bloom stalks. Each stem carries five or more milky blossoms, which expand into shapely bells marked inside and out with deep stripes of crimson. Scented with a fantastic, spicy aroma, they attract all the hawk moths in the neighborhood and bring to mind visions of lush jungle landscapes illuminated by a gibbous, tropical moon.

Although *Crinum scabrum* is clearly an African flower, the precise origin of the species has long been in doubt. The bulbs described by Dean Herbert and other early botanists were collected from low ground around Rio de Janeiro. Presumably, they had been carried to Brazil along with slaves imported from West Africa. It seems likely that the presence of these beautiful flowers in the South marks the legacy of the African slave trade, as well.

Crinum scabrum thrives on rich, loamy ground where the bulbs do not lie cold or damp during winter dormancy. This deciduous, semi-tender species suffers in hard freezes but will tolerate temperatures as low as 10°F if planted on acid, sandy soil. Such loose earths hold warmth better than clay and help to discourage bacteria, fungi, and consequent winter rots.

When well situated, *Crinum scabrum* multiplies into large clumps that flower generously through early summer. Each bulb produces several spikes of showy flowers, with an occasional late bloom following autumn rains.

Crinum scabrum.

This spectacular species is the ancestor of many modern hybrids, and its brilliant wine-red coloring has passed to several beautiful descendants.

Tender Species

In the warmest parts of the South, gardens often boast prolific clumps of *Crinum zeylanicum*, a showy native of tropical India and east Africa. This is a variable, frost-tender bulb. The darkest forms are nearly as brilliant as *C. scabrum*, but more ordinary types are only lightly striped with pink. These markings are darkest toward the ends of the petals, which are drawn out in distinctively pointed mucro tips. The leaves of *C. zeylanicum* may undulate like *C. scabrum* or spread in flattened rosettes. They develop a strong central ribbing like leaves of corn, and this character passes to some hybrids. All forms of *C. zeylanicum* have a fine, spicy-sweet fragrance.

Another prominent group of tropical crinums in the South are the forms and hybrids of *Crinum jagus*, an evergreen species with spoon-shaped leaves and creamy, tuliplike flowers. The name *jagus*, a corruption of *gigas* ("gigantic"), refers to the lush, dark green foliage of these bulbs. The fragrant blooms appear in small umbels in early summer. The best forms of this tropical African crinum, such as the cultivar long grown in the South as 'Rattrayi', smell deliciously of vanilla. Another variant known as the "Christopher lily" or "St. Christopher," multiplies prolifically, but is less free with blooms. 'Maya Moon' is a tender dwarf with oversized, tulip-shaped blossoms introduced from Guatemalan gardens.

These are choice bulbs for positions in partial shade, valuable for their fine foliage, even when they are out of bloom. They resent hard freezes, however, and need rich, acid soil to prosper. They are most valuable in mild, protected gardens near the Gulf and in Florida. They also make fine subjects for large tubs on a warm, shady, patio or for perpetually soggy soils near the edge of a pond.

Moore's Crinum

The forests of the Eastern Cape province provide the home to a half-hardy relation of *Crinum jagus* that has become a favorite wherever it can be grown. It first flowered in Europe from seeds planted at the Glasnevin Botanical Gardens in Dublin. These had been sent to Dr. David Moore, the director there, by a British soldier serving in South Africa around 1863. Unlike its tropical allies, most forms of *C. moorei* cycle leaf growth to climax in late winter, with flowers following in early summer. The plants often die down entirely in July and August to await fall rains.

The lush, cornlike rosettes of foliage sit on tall necks, which project from the big bulbs. Glossy, whorled leaves provide fine complements to the tall scapes of bell-shaped blooms. With mild weather the fragrant flowers last several days and assume rich tones of rose, pink, or white, without any of the striping seen in other colored crinums.

In most of the South, winters are a bit too cold and summers much too hot to do justice to these princely bulbs, but a few *Crinum moorei* variants succeed in shady gardens along the Gulf. The warm temperatures prevailing in early summer bleach the flowers to a pale semblance of their appearance in California or other cool climates, where this species is better adapted.

For Southern gardens the most successful variety of *Crinum moorei* is a snowy white form, var. *schmidtii*. This variant comes from areas in the northeastern range of this species where summer rainfall is prevalent. Its growth is more in tune with the South, and var. *schmidtii* flowers more reliably. The goblet-shaped blooms, opening one at a time in late May, radiate an ethereal fragrance. A few pale-pink-flowered forms, including an attractive variegated selection, 'Mediopicta', also succeed in the South.

The white-flowered *Crinum moorei* var. *schmidtii*.

Swamp Lilies

The native crinum of the South, *Crinum americanum*, is a surprising rarity in gardens, although several of its hybrids are common. This stoloniferous wildflower inhabits estuaries in the darkest Southern swamplands and demands similar conditions in the garden. If given adequate flooding in a pond or artificial bog, the leafy bulbs

The native swamp lily of the South, *Crinum americanum*.

offer fragrant umbels of four to eight spidery flowers in late summer or autumn. Pure white, with reddish stamens, they have a delicious fragrance.

An old garden plant recognized by many collectors as *Crinum americanum* 'Robustum' is in reality the South American *C. erubescens*. These two species are so close in appearance, it's a wonder botanists ever separated them. Both share blunt-tipped leaves, uniquely marked with paired longitudinal creases. The one important distinction between them is that *C. erubescens* grows happily under average garden conditions, while the native Southern swamp lily must stand in water if it is to blossom. The name *erubescens* ("blushing") is a reference to the purplish tint of the buds and flower stems in the Brazilian form.

In gardens *Crinum erubescens* continues in flower from July till frost, and is well worth having for its sweet-scented blossoms. It quickly runs about the garden to make large patches and will even come up in lawns if conditions are to its liking. It is wise to plant the bulbs in a tub sunk in the ground if the questing roots might present a problem.

Crinum erubescens.

There is also a tiny ally of *Crinum erubescens* imported originally from gardens in St. Croix. Identified as *C. oliganthum*, this miniature travels underground just like its larger brother. Bulbs as small as a scallion will flower. They yield one, two, or three small blossoms on six-inch stems. Patches of this crinum resemble clumps of spidery white rain lilies. *Crinum oliganthum* is hardy in the middle and lower South and may be used as a small-scale groundcover like liriope or ophiopogon.

Other relations of *Crinum ameri-*

A miniature crinum from the West Indies, *Crinum oliganthum.*

canum include *C. loddigesianum*, a tropical species from mangrove swamps along the Gulf Coast of Mexico and *C. cruentum*, from cool-running streams in the Mexican highlands. These resemble the other species of swamp lilies, but *C. loddigesianum* has blossoms with extra long tubes and strongly recurving petals; *C. cruentum* displays showy umbels flushed rosy-pink on the exterior. Neither species is very hardy, although both grow successfully in the lower South as emergent aquatics.

The St. John's Lily

In seaside gardens along the Gulf and Atlantic, the old frame houses often have lush plantings of positively enormous crinums. These obviously tropical bulbs develop huge necks topped with broad, green, spear-shaped leaves. The stout stems hold the foliage in a stiffened rosette, which spreads like a big, succulent agave. Several times each year, but especially in fall and winter, these noble bulbs send up scapes topped with clusters of spidery, white blossoms.

These gigantic leeklike plants are forms of *Crinum asiaticum*, a species whose natural range extends across the Indo-Pacific. Variants and near allies of this crinum occur from Japan south to Australia and east to Madagascar, and it's a popular garden plant over much of the Asian tropics. Since the big, green seeds float, they have the capacity to spread from island to island over the waves. Mariners brought this noble bulb to the Gulf and Caribbean basins during the sixteenth century, where they became known as St. John's lilies.

Like many crinums, the succulent stems and leaves of *Crinum asiaticum* contain an acrid, bitter juice. This has earned these flowers a wide reputation as poisonous plants, and they are called poison bulbs in their native Indonesia. In spite of this ominous title, Southeast

The St. John's lily, *Crinum asiaticum*.

Crinum procerum 'Splendens' provides a leafy foil for flowers of a native Southern grass, *Stipa avenacea*.

Like its foliage, blooms of *Crinum procerum* 'Splendens' display purplish overtones.

Asian children often pluck the tubular blooms to drink the sweet nectar, just as Southern children do with honeysuckle blossoms.

Crinum asiaticum is one of the few crinums that have entered successfully into the landscape trade. Since it propagates easily from seed and makes a fine foliage plant, it has become popular for poolside landscaping in Florida and other frost-free regions. The wide-necked bulbs of this species do not form offsets in the usual fashion, but multiply by dividing into two halves. They also grow more shallowly than other crinums. For this reason *C. asiaticum* is not reliably hardy where temperatures below 20°F visit on a regular basis.

In addition to the common large green-leafed *Crinum asiaticum*, collectors of exotic bulbs also cultivate several variegated relatives of this species. A dwarf ally with spreading foliage, *Crinum japonicum*, sometimes occurs in an intriguing variation with yellow-spotted foliage. An aquatic cousin from Queensland, *Crinum pedunculatum*, displays nearly erect leaves, while a leafy species from Tahiti, *C. xanthophyllum*, shows off foliage that turns from lime-green to golden yellow as it matures. The stunning *C. procerum* of Indonesia has several forms such as 'Splendens' with showy pink flowers and dark, bronze-red foliage. All display similar narrow-petaled blossoms, and all require shelter from hard freezes.

Queen Emma's Lily

The last native monarch of Hawaii, Queen Emma, included several favorite bulb flowers in her garden at Lawai-kai. She is remembered for her love of these plants, especially a huge, treelike crinum, the residents of Kauai call Queen Emma lily. Lawai-kai is now a part of Allerton Garden, managed as part of the National Tropical Botanical Garden, and botanists there know the Queen Emma lily as a purple-leafed form of *Crinum procerum* commonly cultivated on Kauai. This beautiful

The Great Mogul of Barbados, *Crinum augustum.*

plant is also popular in Florida, where it has become a prized specimen for containers and patio plantings.

Nevertheless, "Queen Emma lily" is a name also associated with a very different crinum, an old pink-striped hybrid of *C. asiaticum* called *Crinum augustum*. This distinctive bulb is common in coastal gardens of Florida, the Gulf, and the southeast Atlantic as far north as Charleston; in Barbados it is a famous tropical flower called the great mogul. Herbert recorded that sailors brought the first bulbs of this exotic to Calcutta from the small island of Mauritius. A similar plant from Sumatra was introduced around the same time and named *C. amabile*. Both of these appeared to be spontaneous hybrids from *C. zeylanicum* and the gigantic *C. asiaticum*.

Enormous, trunklike bulbs hold the leaves of *Crinum augustum* in an erect whorl. Several times each year they send up tremendous, empurpled stalks, which expand into huge umbels of spidery, wine-striped blooms. The fat stems usually lie on the ground, but this does not deter the succulent, twelve-inch blossoms from opening and scenting the air with narcotic sweetness.

Although tropical, *Crinum augustum* survives modest frost if planted in a sandy bed near a south wall. The shallow bulbs should be mulched or periodically reset at depth to protect against disastrous freezes. Otherwise, they require only a large space in which to sprawl. When well grown, the leaves of this crinum may exceed six feet in height and spread. Offsets form slowly but steadily and, since they grow shallowly, may be carefully removed without disturbing the mother bulb.

Milk and Wine

The most familiar garden crinums in the South have trumpet-shaped blooms striped with wine on the keels as in *Crinum augustum*. Known as milk and wine lilies, these trusted flowers descend from *C. bulbispermum*, which conveys its tall scape and rugged constitution, and *C. scabrum*, which imparts more or less reddish striping. The hybrids radiate a musky-spicy fragrance recognizably derived from both parents. Although varying from ordinary to extravagant, blossoms nearly always appear on vigorous, floriferous plants. Foliage is impressively rank, tapered, and grassy green.

Dean Herbert originated the first milk and wine lily in 1819. His achievement is commemorated in the grex name *Crinum ×herbertii*, which applies to any hybrid of *C. scabrum* and *C. bulbispermum*. Many crosses involving these fruitful parents have followed, and *C. ×herbertii* now exists in a multitude of forms. It is impossible to know exactly which clone came first, but it seems entirely probable that Herbert's original still grows in gardens. He described the milk and wine lily in 1836: "A plant of great beauty, bearing 11 flowers on a scape three feet high . . . blush with deep red stripes. It requires a warmer situation where the wall is a little heated to make it flower finely, which it does several times each year."

In 1888 J. G. Baker published a handbook of the amaryllis family, listing many new *Crinum* species. Nurserymen seized on several of Baker's varietal names, applying them to the many different milk-and-wine forms at hand. As a result, such botanical titles as *sanderianum*, *kunthianum*, and *virginicum* became attached to various milk and wine clones. Bulbs still pass under these mistaken names in market bulletins and nursery lists. Since these hybrids rarely produce seed, they make themselves obvious in collections that include honest, fertile species such as *C. bulbispermum* or *C. scabrum*.

Many *Crinum ×herbertii* variants

Crinum ×herbertii (milk and wine lily) flowering in a cemetery near Beeville, Texas.

bear light-pink-striped blossoms, but a few are marked nearly as dark a burgundy as in *C. scabrum*. In most clones the stripes are strongest in color near the center of the blossoms, fading gradually toward the petal tips. 'Carroll Abbott' is one of the darkest, with large umbels of wine-marked blossoms. It's an old heirloom flower of Southern gardens, originally imported from England during the nineteenth century. The vibrant blooms appear in late spring and early summer. 'P. F. Reasoner' has pale pink stripes, but offers its large umbels of bloom in effective masses following summer rains.

'Gowenii' is a milk and wine hybrid with tapered foliage like *Crinum ×herbertii*, but its reversed color pattern shows that it descends from a union of *C. bulbispermum* with *C. zeylanicum*, rather than from *C. scabrum*. The recurved petals, with pointed mucro tips like the elongated fingernails of a mandarin, bear pale exterior stripes, fading toward the center of the flowers, oppo-

Crinum ×herbertii 'Carroll Abbott'.

The striped flower buds and tapered leaves of *Crinum* 'Gowenii'.

Among the most common milk and wine lilies of Southern gardens, *Crinum* 'Gowenii' can be readily distinguished by the clawlike tips of its curling petals.

site the pattern seen in *C. ×herbertii*. The blooms open several at a time, so that the spikes almost always fall over to the ground before they have finished flowering unless they are staked. These lightly striped blossoms look nearly white when seen in strong sun. Especially deep-rooted bulbs make 'Gowenii' tough and hardy. Clumps persist, flower, and slowly increase under the most rigorous conditions. Gardeners know these pale trumpeting amaryllids as August lilies, for they often appear after late summer showers.

Bred in England by J. R. Gowen, this unique and distinctive hybrid dates from around 1820 and was pictured in several Victorian treatments of garden flowers. Bulbs of this crinum probably first came to the South in the mid-1800s. South Carolina nurseryman Jenks Farmer has reintroduced 'Gowenii' to the trade as 'Regina's Disco Lounge', for the source of his original stock.

Nassau Lilies

There is another, more exotic section of the milk and wine lilies quite different from these hardy trumpets. Their flat, star-shaped blooms begin to appear in the second half of the summer. As they open in early evening, they send forth an intense, delightfully sweet perfume.

The most prolific of these star lilies is a half-hardy hybrid whose presence in the South dates back over a century. At Round Lake, a historic Irish settlement along the Texas coast, settlers planted long rows of these crinums. The bulbs they set around their homes came from the nearby convent of San Patricio, where sisters cultivated the fragrant flowers as early as 1876.

Reasoner Brothers' Royal Palms Nursery of Oneco, Florida, advertised this variety in their catalog of 1900:

C. fimbriatulum,
The Nassau, or Milk and Wine Lily.

A strong grower; not particular as to soil. Flowers in umbels; very large and showy, striped white and carmine; 3 to 4 inches in diameter. Exceedingly choice and desirable as a pot plant or for bedding out during the summer in the North. The fragrant flowers are so different from any of the more common flowers grown North that they produce a sensation when seen.

Twelve years later, Florida plantsman Henry Nehrling lamented the misnaming of this and other crinums. He then compounded horticultural error by making his own guess at the proper name of this flower:

There is great confusion in the nomenclature of these plants, scarcely half a dozen being correctly named in the various catalogues . . . . *C. erubescens* (usually advertised as *C. fimbriatulum*). One of the most common species in Florida gardens. Increases rapidly by offsets. Leaves long, thin and narrow, 2 to 3 feet long: flower stem 2 to 3 feet tall, purplish green, carrying usually four to six very beautiful fragrant flowers, pure white with a faint pink keel, outside purplish red. Does not bear seeds, and is useless for cross-breeding. Found everywhere in gardens.

In truth this old, sterile hybrid is neither *Crinum fimbriatulum* nor *C. erubescens*, although something close to the latter is one of its parents, the other parent being *C. scabrum*. As evidence for this, the slick, lime-green leaves of the Nassau lily bear the longitudinal creases characteristic of *C. americanum* and its allies. The Nassau lily may be reasonably surmised to be a child of *C. americanum* and *C. scabrum*, a cross officially named *C. ×digweedii* in 1820. Nevertheless, in collections this old favorite appears under varied names including *C. erubescens*, *C. fimbriatulum*, *C. submersum*, and 'Royal White'.

The spindle-shaped bulbs of the Nassau lily multiply by short stolons to form compact, upright clumps. With good care the bulbs offer fine blooms over a long season from July till frost. Near the coast these classic Southern perennials may be seen marking old property lines from which hurricanes have removed "permanent" structures. There could hardly be a more romantic encounter than stumbling upon a blooming clump among the dunes, with the intoxicating fragrance of the succulent flowers wafting on the sea air.

The deliciously fragrant Nassau lily, *Crinum ×digweedii* 'Nassau'.

Modern breeders have introduced hybrids similar to the Nassau lily and all are showy and worth growing, although none can compete in vigor or fragrance with the original. 'Stars 'n Stripes', 'William Herbert', and 'Carioca' are three showstopping hybrids from Thad Howard with wine-streaked, starry blossoms. 'Sundance' is a pink-striped, frilly hybrid from *Crinum scabrum* and the long-tubed Mexican *C. loddigesianum*. It likes plenty of water, but is otherwise easy.

More Star Lilies

Crinum zeylanicum has also sired striped hybrids with *C. americanum*, and these may be seen in many gardens in the lower South. 'Maureen Spinks', 'Southern Belle', and 'Blockade Runner' are named varieties which may be had from collectors. These crosses, officially known as *C. ×baconi*, usually prove less cold-hardy than the Nassau lily, but are fragrant, beautiful, and useful for gardens in the lower South. They follow the typical *C. zeylanicum* color scheme, with darkest striping on the exterior of the petals, becoming paler toward the center and interior of the blossoms. The petals bear long clawlike tips and the flowers invariably have a deliciously spicy scent. The rounded, globular bulbs should be set deeply to protect them from hard frost and discourage over-rapid multiplication, to which these hybrids are prone. 'Veracruz', 'Maximilian', and 'Marinero' are similar crosses of *C. zeylanicum* with *C. loddigesianum*.

Crinum 'Veracruz', a spontaneous hybrid of C. zeylanicum and C. loddigesianum.

The Empress

In 1906 Reasoner Brothers imported a colorful, fragrant crinum, 'Empress of India'. This honestly Victorian hybrid (Queen Victoria *was* the empress of India) bears huge, wine-striped, powerfully scented blossoms, which rise on tall, dusty purple stems above nearly prostrate, channeled, green foliage. The nine-inch nocturnal flowers are at their best on moon-filled nights, for they fold promptly and wither at first light.

The straplike leaves and night-flowering habit make 'Empress of India' one of the most distinctive milk and wine lilies in Southern gardens. These characteristics imply descent from *Crinum zeylanicum* crossed with one of the tender, nocturnal Indian species such as *C. pratense* or *C. amoenum*. Herbert listed several hybrids of these Indian species in 1836, 'Paxtoni', 'Louisae', and 'Cooperi' among them. He also reported exchanging bulbs with a horticulturally inclined missionary friend, Dr. William Carey, of Serampore, India. It seems quite possible that one of these varieties persisted in India and was imported by Reasoner Brothers at the turn of that century.

Although not especially hardy, the small, night-flowering Indian crinums are themselves intriguing garden plants, bearing rosettes of flattened, prostrate leaves and slender stalks of white blossoms much like those of *Crinum americanum*, except for their strictly nocturnal habits. *Crinum amoenum* succeeds in the South on moist, acid soils, but is little grown.

Crinum amoenum.

Twelve Apostles

The oldest building on Mustang Island is the historic Tarpon Inn, a long frame structure built in 1886. Its twenty-six small, efficient rooms once housed sportsmen intent on capturing trophy fish from the nearby bays. The pugnacious, silvery tarpons are mostly gone from these estuaries, and this weathered compound is all that remains of the former town of Tarpon, presently included within the city of Port Aransas, Texas.

Along the cypress-post foundation of the inn grow several large specimens of *Crinum augustum*, and, interspersed

Crinum 'Twelve Apostles'.

with them, a fragrant hybrid crinum familiar to gardeners as 'Twelve Apostles'. The scent of these narrow-petaled, pink-tinged blossoms is sweet, but also carries a hint of anise or musk. This odd fragrance and the tapered foliage of the plants identify these old flowers as products of *C. bulbispermum*. The other parent is thought to be *C. asiaticum*, as may be seen by the robust size of the bulbs and by their slow rate of increase through vertical fission.

'Twelve Apostles' is a remarkably apt name for this plant, for that is the usual number of blooms found in the umbel. The somewhat homely flowers come periodically through the entire year, so this crinum eventually wins favor by its persistence. The pallid, spidery blossoms do not always show to good effect in gardens, but they last well and will pervade the house with a pleasant fragrance if cut and set in a tall vase. 'Pecan Tree Inn' and *Crinum ×eboracii* are other names sometimes applied to this hybrid.

More glamorous cousins of 'Twelve Apostles' such as the spectacular 'Sangria' descend from crosses of the bronze-leafed *Crinum procerum* 'Splendens' with *C. bulbispermum* 'Sacramento'. I first discovered this unusual crinum as an unflowered seedling in the garden of Marcia Wilson of Brownsville, Texas. Now available through tissue culture, 'Sangria' displays deep wine-red foliage and iridescent pink blossoms reflexed gracefully as in *Nerine*. With its *C. bulbispermum* ancestry, this crinum is fairly cold hardy, but can be slow to increase

The dark wine-colored foliage of *Crinum* 'Sangria' rises from a patch of prairie phlox (*Phlox pilosa*).

unless bulbs are sliced to induce multiplication. Gardeners can readily raise their own red-leafed hybrids by placing bulbispermum pollen on blooms of *C. procerum* 'Splendens'.

Miss Elsie

Much more generous with offsets are several old hybrids of *Crinum bulbispermum* and *C. americanum*. With narrow, whitish, spreading petals and clusters of violet-toned filaments, these fragrant crinums have a character similar to 'Twelve Apostles', but on shorter, leafier plants. Carolina plantsman William Lanier Hunt describes the flowers as bearing a "decided odor of anise." Elizabeth Lawrence says the blooms have the "delicious scent of waterlilies." They are certainly pleasant to smell, in any case.

'Miss Elsie' is the best known of these near-white hybrids and is common to gardens of Georgia and the Carolinas. 'Catherine' (originally from the Natchez garden of Catherine Winston), 'Seven Sisters' (selected by Grace Hinshaw of Mobile), and 'Carolina Beauty' are similar types well distributed in the South. 'Ollene' is a beautiful ivory-toned descendant of 'Seven Sisters' introduced by Thad Howard. All are very hardy, succeeding everywhere below the Mason-Dixon line if given enriched soil and unfailing moisture.

Blush Wine

One of the most intoxicatingly lovely crinums is an old blushy hybrid from Theodore L. Mead of Oviedo, Florida. Around 1900 Mead imported a collection of nearly a hundred crinum varieties from India and set about making crosses. The bulbs were planted near a small bog, which overflowed during the rainy season, inundating the beds of seedlings. When the waters receded, one of the surviving crinums was rescued and moved to higher ground. Although the exact parentage was lost, this hybrid proved outstanding, with tall stems of huge, pinky-white, scented blossoms. Mead named his cross 'Peachblow'. Although somewhat tender and inclined to flop unless staked, it is one of the most beautiful crinums, with an exotic appeal similar to 'Empress of India'.

Mead's contemporary Henry Nehrling introduced another handsome blush-colored hybrid around 1915. This exquisite flower, 'Mrs. James Hendry', ranks among the most beautiful and rewarding of Southern perennials. The superb, pink-tinged blossoms appear in tidy umbels, which open so that the flowers face forward together. The buds are set on sturdy scapes amid lush, compact, green foliage, with none of the untidiness seen in other hybrid crinums. The flowers

A group of *Crinum* 'Mrs. James Hendry' graces a shaded nook in the author's garden, Austin.

An heirloom bulb of Southern gardens, *Crinum* 'Alamo Village'.

possess one of the most delectable fragrances of any summer blossom, spicily scented but never overpowering. They grace garden borders with their tender colorings from May till frost. 'Mrs. James Hendry' multiplies at a steady pace and seems hardy anywhere frost does not penetrate the ground.

'Alamo Village' is another blush-colored hybrid from various older Southern gardens. Its graceful umbels of narrow-petaled, near-white flowers radiate an intense, spicy fragrance. The bulbs are vigorous, everblooming, and surprisingly hardy. Deep wine-colored buds and long, claw-tipped petals suggest *Crinum zeylanicum* was a parent.

Although not yet widely grown in Southern gardens, the Luther Bundrant hybrid 'Jubilee' is another beautiful blush-colored crinum. This hybrid of *Crinum loddigesianum* offers large, fragrant, pale pink blossoms and good foliage in the style of 'Mrs. James Hendry'. It seems equally hardy. 'Jubilee' should be available from nurseries in the near future via tissue culture.

'H. J. Elwes' is a famous blushy pink selection raised by the British horticulturist Henry John Elwes. In the lower South, this fragrant offspring of *Crinum moorei* and *C. americanum* makes a fine border plant, with short rosettes of thick, spreading leaves. In colder areas it does well in pots—and is one of the few sufficiently compact crinums for this use. In 1908 it received an RHS Award of Merit. A modern duplication of this cross, 'Hannibal's Dwarf', is also a fine garden plant, bearing richer, rose-pink flowers.

'Summer Nocturne', a Thad Howard hybrid of *Crinum moorei* and *C. erubescens*, is similar to Elwes' plant, but has paler, whitish blooms and blunt, grass-green foliage. The sweet-scented flowers begin appearing in early July following summer rains and continue till frost. Other, larger blush-toned hybrids from *C. moorei* include 'Maiden's Blush' and 'White Mogul'. The especially lush foliage of these varieties makes them outstanding choices for edging a bed in semi-shade.

Crinum 'Jubilee', a Luther Bundrant hybrid of *C. loddigesianum.*

'White Mogul' is unusual in that it descends from *Crinum yemense*, a rare variety from the deserts of the Arabian peninsula. The foliage of this species resembles *C. zeylanicum*, but its blooms are entirely white, with long petals and olive-toned floral tubes. After flowering in early summer, this remarkable plant ripens several lumpy seeds the size of tennis balls. In its desert homeland this allows this crinum to reproduce in periods of extended drought, for the seeds germinate and form sizable bulbs without need for rain. Although better adapted to Mediterranean climates, such as California, *C. yemense* succeeds in the South if planted in deep, sandy soil.

Powellii

When *Crinum moorei* is bred to other crinum, whether striped or plain, the offspring usually develop self-colored flowers, rather than a milk-and-wine pattern. This can be seen clearly in the numerous pink or white forms of *C. ×powellii*. Like the *C. ×herbertii* hybrids, these crosses of *C. moorei* and *C. bulbispermum* are hardy workhorses among crinums. Their tapered, lush green clumps of foliage may be seen in many older gardens.

Crinum ×powellii 'Album' is a plant of superlative quality, with tall scapes bearing large umbels of shapely, snowy blossoms. Introduced as early as 1888, it is now common in gardens, performing equally well in sun or shade. The rich pink 'Cecil Houdyshel' was selected in the 1930s from among thousands of seedlings by the California nurseryman of the same name. The tremendous vigor of this outstanding tetraploid hybrid has earned it a niche in Southern

An old clump of Crinum ×powellii 'Album'.

gardens. Large bulbs of 'Cecil Houdyshel' reliably send up eight or more stalks in a season, remaining in almost perpetual bloom.

Other valuable hybrids of ×*powellii* form include a dusty-rose cultivar developed by Grace Hinshaw called 'Summer Glow'. This is a robust plant with usefully tall scapes, ideal for a position in the back of an early summer border. The pale pink 'Mrs. Horace Kennedy' shows its *C. bulbispermum* ancestry in its narrow foliage and waxy-petaled, trumpet-shaped blooms. 'Claude Davis', a prolific, wine-purple powellii type with contrasting brownish floral tubes, descends from Les Hannibal's colorful, but rare and slow-to-offset *C. yemense* hybrid, 'Cape Dawn'.

White Queen

The famous plant breeder Luther Burbank worked his genius on crinums as well as on many other flowers, and a few lucky gardeners still grow some of his creations. 'White Queen', arguably the loveliest crinum ever bred, is a frilly, snow-white hybrid of *Crinum* ×*powellii* 'Album' and *C. macowanii*. The blossoms retain the bell-like petals of *C. macowanii*, but have the fine form and fragrance of *C. moorei*. These large bulbs are tough and long-lived, with good fountains of glossy, green foliage. Offsets appear slowly, so this fine white has remained a collector's item for decades. However, tissue culture may soon make this beautiful plant more common in Southern gardens. With its indomitable constitution,

Luther Burbank's famous hybrid, *Crinum* 'White Queen'.

Crinum 'J. C. Harvey'.

architectural foliage, and pristine umbels of bloom, it deserves to be widely
grown.

Shell-Pink

The most ubiquitous of all the *Crinum
moorei* offspring is 'J. C. Harvey', a late-
nineteenth-century cross with *C. zeylanicum*. This half-hardy hybrid displays
clear pink, goblet-shaped blossoms and
lush foliage. The foliage is heavily
ribbed, like leaves of corn, making these
crinums easy to identify even when
they are out of bloom. With only a little
encouragement, 'J. C. Harvey' multiplies like the devil, so it has become
especially common in Southern gardens. Partial shade and deep planting
in rich soil are needed to encourage free
blooming, but this old, shell-pink crinum is otherwise fantastically easy to

Crinum 'Pink Mystery'. Photo by Lauren S. Ogden.

grow. 'Pink Mystery', a similar pale pink variety with starry, narrow-petaled blooms, appears to be a hybrid of 'J. C. Harvey' and *C. americanum*.

Reds

'J. C. Harvey' is a probable parent of the famous wine-red clone 'Ellen Bosan-quet', first listed in the Reasoner Brothers' catalog of 1930 as 'Mrs. Bosanquet'. This lovely plant was bred by a British plantsman, Louis Percival Bosanquet, residing in Fruitland Park, Florida. Mr. Bosanquet named his creation for his wife. Although American gardeners may be tempted to pronounce this obvi-ously French-titled crinum *beau-zan-KAY*, in true English fashion the breeder pronounced the last syllable of his Gallic surname phonetically: *KWET*.

The lush foliage of 'Ellen Bosanquet' resembles 'J. C. Harvey', and the two plants can be readily confused when out of bloom. The rich burgundy flowers of 'Ellen Bosanquet' are distinct, however, and appear punctually in the first weeks of June. This timing points to *Crinum scabrum* as the other probable parent of this colorful hybrid. Slightly ruffled leaves, spicy fragrance, and short, sturdy scapes support this theory, as well.

This invaluable crinum multiplies nearly as well as 'J. C. Harvey' and is even more tolerant to cold and drought. Shade from the hottest sun will allow the big, wine-colored blooms to open to perfection. You could hardly wish for a showier, more affable garden flower, and 'Ellen Bosanquet' must be considered one of the

The sumptuous June blooms of *Crinum* 'Ellen Bosanquet' combine with palms, cycads, and gingers in the author's Austin garden.

South's great horticultural treasures. Although flowering is heaviest in June, established clumps continue to blossom into autumn. 'Burgundy', a nearly indistinguishable clone, flowers slightly later.

In attempts to exceed 'Ellen Bosanquet' in depth of coloring, breeders have continued to hybridize with *Crinum scabrum* and other colored crinums. 'Elizabeth Traub' is a tall, wine-tinted variety nearly as dark as 'Ellen Bosanquet', but with foliage more like *C. ×powellii*. Probably descended from a cross of 'Cecil Houdyshel' and *C. scabrum*, it makes a fine, hardy plant for the rear of a summer border, useful where 'Ellen Bosanquet' would prove too short.

Other showy dark-toned hybrids include 'Birthday Party', 'Lorraine Clark', 'Fay Hornbuckle', and 'Rose Parade'. 'Mystery', a plant originally distributed by Oakhurst Gardens of California, appears to be a cross of 'Ellen Bosanquet' with *Crinum erubescens*. Its fragrant, narrow-petaled flowers are deep rose-red around white centers, appearing on short stems above arching, glossy foliage much like the pink-blossomed 'Hannibal's Dwarf'.

Bicolors

Katherine Clint of Brownsville, Texas, crossed 'Ellen Bosanquet' with *Crinum ×powellii* 'Album' to produce 'Walter Flory', an unusual bicolor with exquisite pink blossoms accented by burgundy stripes and green petal tips. This early-flowering hybrid has excellent lush, green foliage, and, like its parents, succeeds

Modern *Crinum* hybrids: *C.* 'Rose Parade' is at lower left, *C. ×worsleyi* at upper right.

in both sun and shade. *Crinum ×worsleyi*, a cross of *C. moorei* and *C. scabrum*, provides similar pink, wine-striped blooms later in summer. The tremendous fountains of glossy leaves and waxy blooms of this hybrid are at their best in half-day sun or partial shade. 'Carnival' is a novel *C. ×herbertii* hybrid from Thad Howard with rather untidy leaves and spectacularly variegated red blooms.

Walking Sticks

H. B. Bradley, a barrister residing in Sydney, Australia, developed several colorful crinums that received Awards of Merit from the New South Wales chapter of the RHS in 1927. 'Bradley', with deep wine, open-faced blossoms on tall, slender scapes, helped inspire the Australian colloquial name for these plants, walking stick lilies.

These waxy flowers bear spreading, rounded petals, and the bulbs produce curling fountains of bright green, narrow foliage. Together with the rose-

The rare yellow-flowered form of *Crinum flaccidum* from South Australia.

A walking stick lily, *Crinum* 'Bradley'.

red color of the blossoms, this suggests descent from *Crinum scabrum* and the rare Australian native *C. flaccidum*, a species famed for its rounded blooms that vary from sulfur-yellow to white and pink. *Crinum flaccidum* itself seems ill at ease in most of the South, but its hybrids thrive, and breeders have used it to bring novel yellow pigment into their crosses.

In addition to 'Bradley', two other Australian hybrids are offered by American dealers. 'George Harwood' is one with slender leaves like *Crinum flaccidum* and wine-red, white-centered blooms. These goblet-shaped flowers open one at a time like *C. moorei*. 'Bradley Giant' has larger, redder flowers and lush, spreading foliage. All Bradley's hybrids are vigorous garden performers, multiplying with long-necked, globular bulbs.

Emma Jones

If forced to choose among the colored crinums, the most satisfying flower might belong to 'Emma Jones'. This blousy pink hybrid originated in the Corpus Christi garden of Fred Jones from an improbable cross of 'Peachblow' and 'Cecil Houdyshel'. Although saturated with the deep pink, velvety color of its *Crinum* ×*powellii* parent, the ruffled blossoms also carry the exotic fragrance of Mead's old Florida hybrid. The tall stems and large umbels inherit the 'Peachblow' fault of flopping over, but who could imagine a more cheerful necessity than to be forced to tend to the huge, pink buds as the scapes rise in succession through the summer?

Amarcrinums

When temperatures climb to near 100°F in mid-July even the heartiest flowers lose their enthusiasm. By midmorning most crinums fold up and limply hang their heads. Any fragrance left from the night before steams away on the noon air, and the best colors of the succulent blossoms swoon away.

At such times it is congenial to have garden blossoms such as those of ×*Amarcrinum* who defiantly surmount the trials of summer. These tough, lily-like blossoms belong to an intergeneric hybrid of *Crinum moorei* and a related bulb from South Africa, *Amaryllis belladonna*. Heat and strong sun are the very conditions they savor, and their delightful fragrance could cool the fiery breath of a dragon.

The most famous of the several ×*Amarcrinum* clones is a pale pink developed by and named for California plantsman Fred Howard. It's one of the finest flowers any Southerner can hope to bloom, regardless of weather. A flowering stalk of this ×*Amarcrinum* lasts for a month in the hottest season. Sixteen or seventeen buds appear on each two-foot scape. These open to waxy pink, blunt-petaled blossoms, accented with white throats and radiating a refreshing bouquet that smells like a gentle mixture of vanilla and lemon chiffon pie.

The oversized bulbs of ×*Amarcrinum* 'Fred Howard' seem a little clumsy attached to their modest tufts of straplike leaves. Inheriting the character of their belladonna parent, these leaves set themselves in more or less opposite ranks, rather than in rosettes. It takes a hard freeze to knock this compact, glossy foliage down, and in mild winters these plants remain nearly evergreen. Lean, sandy soil seems to encourage more generous growth and flowering.

In California, where *Amaryllis belladonna* and various *Crinum* ×*powellii* clones often grow together, several additional ×*Amarcrinum* have been discovered by alert gardeners. 'Lon Delkin' is a fast-offsetting pale pink with well-formed flowers. 'Born Free' is a near white. 'Dorothy Hannibal' is an elegant, late-flowering selection with raspberry blossoms, fading to light pink in strong sun. These hybrids lack the size and intense fragrance of 'Fred Howard' but are valuable additions to this section.

A common bulb of California gardens and a native of winter-rainfall areas in the Western Cape, *Amaryllis belladonna* (Cape belladonna) is itself sometimes planted in the South, but may rot from excessive summer moisture unless planted by a dry foundation or in a raised bed. If winter temperatures fall below 20°F, leaves may be damaged and this, along with the lack of a dry summer to ripen the bulbs, often prevents bloom in the South.

Southerners sometimes succeed with the more vigorous hybrids of the Cape belladonna such as *Amaryllis* ×*parkeri* ('Hathor', 'Rubra Bicolor', or 'Purpurea Major', for instance) but flowering is hardly a consistent event. It is often necessary to lift the bulbs in early summer to enforce a dry dormant period. If replanted in September, blooms appear quickly. The lovely blossoms are like elegant versions of ×*Amarcrinum*, with ruffled clusters of pink or white, scented blooms. They appear on bare stems unaccompanied by foliage, so, like *Lycoris*, they are often called naked ladies. Related hybrids such as ×*Amarine* (*Amaryllis* × *Nerine*) are equally lovely but ill suited to the South.

Several species of the similar genus *Brunsvigia* grow in the subtropical, summer-rainfall regions of the Eastern Cape and KwaZulu-Natal in South Africa, and these ought to succeed in the South, although they have been little tried. Known as *kandelaarblom* ("candelabra flower"), the pink, rose, red, or wine-colored *B. natalensis*, *B. radulosa*, *B. grandiflora*, *B. gregaria*, and *B. undulata* would all be worth growing on the acid soils of the Southeast. These spectacular plants flower with massive, globe-shaped umbels of bright blooms held above prostrate, strap-shaped foliage. It would be desirable to breed them—and related genera such as *Nerine, Ammocharis,* and *Scadoxus*—with crinums to develop a range of hybrids suited to humid climates.

Ballerinas of the Garden

The uniquely graceful evening flowers of the spiderlily clan (*Hymenocallis* spp.) offer some of the garden's most exquisite fragrances. Like crinums, these easy-growing flowers are characteristically Southern. Although neglected and overlooked by many horticulturists, native *Hymenocallis* species include the most elegant and beautiful of wild bulbs. The subtropical American forms contribute some of the most pleasing and dependable perennials to summer borders. Common names for the various species include spiderlily, basket flower, crown beauty, Peruvian daffodil, and chalice lily. In Latin America they are often called *flor de San Juan* ("St. John's flower"), a name widely applied to any fragrant, nocturnal bloom.

Hymenocallis derives from the Greek *hymen kallos* ("beautiful membrane"), a reference to the gossamer cups of webbing centered inside the spidery white petals. These bizarre blossoms have an exotic, mysterious quality, which makes them especially choice. Although several amaryllids share the common name spiderlily, *Hymenocallis* deserves first claim on this title. With slender petals, rounded cups, dangling stamens and style, it would be hard to imagine a blossom built more like an arachnid.

Each flower has a tapered, usually greenish tube, which expands to six slender segments. These are ordinarily white, but one or two yellow or greenish flowered species are known. The petals surround spidery, dark green stamens, which in turn unite to form the diaphanous, white or yellowish cup, or corona. On the tips of the stamens, maneuverable anthers dusted in orange or yellow pollen dangle and swivel with each passing breeze or buzz from a hawk moth's wings. From the center of the cup rises the greenish style, tipped by a drop of clear, sticky liquid.

Once pollinated, these amaryllids rapidly ripen their seed. Fleshy and green, like those of crinums, they usually have the capacity to float. As the seeds swell, they burst from the pods at the ends of the long stems. During the heat of the day, the stalks lie flaccid on the ground, releasing a few seeds at a time. At night the flower stems become turgid and rise upward. As they repeatedly move up and down over several days they describe a small circle, releasing seeds at intervals to assure an even distribution around the mother bulb.

If placed in a humid, shady position free from marauding slugs, seeds quickly germinate to form miniature bulbs. Evergreen *Hymenocallis* species begin growth immediately, sending out leaves and roots, and pulling down into the soil. Deciduous types usually remain dormant, waiting till the following spring before leafing out in earnest. With three or four years' growth, the young bulbs come into flower.

Like other warm-weather bulbs, *Hymenocallis* species relish rich soils. Most thrive under boggy conditions, and several Southeastern species prefer aquatic culture for best growth. Heavy clays are to their liking, but sandy ground is usually fine, so long as it is well watered.

Spiderlilies range from big, bulky tropical evergreens to tiny, daffodil-like miniatures. Nearly all make fine foliage plants. The blossoms of the various species have much the same appearance but differ in fragrance and in season of bloom, so it behooves gardeners to include a wide array. With careful selection, Southerners may enjoy these flowers from early March till frost. It's thrilling to watch the nightly ritual of the blossoms as they actively swell, cling for a moment, half-open by the petal tips, and then burst wide apart to admit the first hawk moths of the evening.

Ismenes

The most common *Hymenocallis* species in horticulture are the deciduous Peruvian daffodils. Botanists sometimes place these South American flowers in the genus *Ismene*, so named after the daughter of Oedipus and Jocasta. These Andean species differ from other hymenocallis in their large, trumpetlike coronas and short stamens. Their anthers bend inward over the centers of the flowers, instead of sprawling outward. The overlapping leaves of the bulbs also form a unique neck or pseudostem.

In the warm climate of the South, these mountain-dwelling bulbs require deep planting and heavy mulching to assure a suitably cool root run. The bulbs should be reset every other year in fresh, well-manured ground to discourage splitting to less than flowering size.

Small species, such as *Hymenocallis pedunculata* (*Ismene macleana*), are now and then offered in the bulb trade, but the best known and most readily available of the ismenes is the large-flowered *H. narcissiflora* (*I. calathina*). The common horticultural strain is sterile and routinely produces blooms with five petals instead of the customary six. The funnel-like coronas, attractively fringed, are shaded with green along the ribs of the stamens. The blooms radiate a thickly sweet, nocturnal fragrance.

Because they are naturally deciduous, these subtropical natives of Peru and

Bolivia may be grown in cold climates by digging and storing, as with gladioli. In this fashion, bulbs may be scheduled to bloom on command. They reliably flower within a week if planted during warm weather.

The famous clone 'Festalis' was bred by English bulb fancier Arthington Worsley from a cross of *Hymenocallis narcissiflora* and the strange, greenish-flowered *H. longipetala*. This curious species was once segregated into its own genus, *Elisena*, an ancient word meaning "romance." Although *H. longipetala* is more intriguing than beautiful, it imparts a graceful, orchidlike curling to the petals of 'Festalis'. Unfortunately, this hybrid tends to increase at the expense of bloom. 'Advance' is a better-behaved seedling of 'Festalis' backcrossed to *H. narcissiflora*.

'Sulphur Queen' is a popular, light yellow selection descended from a cross of *Hymenocallis narcissiflora* and the lily of the Incas (*H. amancaes*). This three-flowered species and its one-flowered cousin, *H. heliantha*, are the only golden flowers in this otherwise ghostly white, nocturnal genus. These bright-colored species, denizens of high deserts around Lima and Cajamarca, Peru, are ill-suited to the humid lowlands of the Southern United States. 'Sulphur Queen' is more forgiving and rates as the most reliable of the ismene group in the South, forming impressively large bulbs. 'Sulphur Queen' has a pleasant primrose scent to complement its attractive flowers.

During the 1960s Cincinnati, Ohio, breeder Len Woelfle created a series of flowers from the same parents as 'Sulphur Queen', the finest of which was a yellow and white bicolor named 'Pax'. He also developed several graceful, greenish gold flowers from crosses between *Hymenocallis amancaes* and *H. longipetala*. These long-necked plants (known as the dancing dolls) have never become com-

mon in the bulb trade, but they are grown by a few fanciers of the genus. They seem to thrive in the South, and are entirely hardy.

In the mildest parts of the Gulf Coast and Florida, the magnificent hybrid 'Daphne' is also worth planting. This treasure, raised by the Dutch bulb firm Van Tubergen before 1900, descends from a surprising cross of *Hymenocallis narcissiflora* and the Caribbean *H. speciosa*. It combines the large cup of its ismene parent with the elegant form and evergreen foliage of *H.*

Hymenocallis 'Daphne'.

speciosa. The lush, spear-shaped leaves renew themselves in autumn; they should be protected from strong sun and hard frost. The ravishing clusters of sweet-scented blossoms appear in early summer.

Tropical Spiderlilies

Most of the cultivated hymenocallis in the South are old heirloom flowers, originally brought from the tropical shores of the Antilles and the Spanish Main. The early explorer Oviedo initiated the long garden history of these bulbs when he encountered his first *lirios blancos* ("white lilies") growing on beaches near Porto Bello, Panama, in 1535. Spiderlilies were also reported by later English and French explorers, and they were soon spread widely by sailors. As with crinums, the identities of many of these flowers have been obscured in the tangled web of horticulture. Although naturally evergreen in frost-free climates, the more vigorous tropical spiderlilies endure the annual loss of their foliage in winter.

The most widespread hymenocallis in gardens is also a variety for which there is the least certain information. This frustrating plant, distinctive enough to be readily recognized anywhere, matches none of the descriptions of known species. It might be one of Herbert's old Puerto Rican or Jamaican species, *Hymenocallis expansa* or *H. caymanensis*, but unless a botanist arranges an expedition to visit the Caribbean, he or she can do little to resolve this question.

Early descriptions of spiderlilies are imprecise, and dried *Hymenocallis* specimens in herbaria are so shriveled and distorted they bear little resemblance to the living plants.

All that can be done is to note everything that may be observed in garden cultivation, in hopes that others may some day fill in the gaps in our knowledge. We can attempt to arrange our cultivated hymenocallis into more or less sensible species, but Nature incessantly reminds us, "I own not any name, / Neither order nor degree."

Botanists and nurseries generally list these familiar garden flowers as *Hymenocallis littoralis*, *H. caribbaea*, *H. rotata*, or *H. tenuiflora*, titles rightly

The common spiderlily of Southern gardens, *Hymenocallis* 'Tropical Giant'.

applying to four unrelated plants. Since no honest botanical name is forthcoming for the venerable spiderlilies of Southern gardens, the most acceptable and least confusing tag to apply to these cultivars is an old horticultural one, 'Tropical Giant'.

'Tropical Giant' is a favorite landscape ornamental, one of the finest foliage perennials in the South. The lush fountains of glossy, sword-shaped leaves arch gracefully, and the generously proportioned bulbs soon multiply to form imposing clumps. The abundant foliage sets off the sweet, spicily fragrant, white blooms, which appear in early July. These blossoms sit atop flattened, sharp-edged scapes, which are typical of Caribbean hymenocallis. Their moderately long tubes and large, spreading coronas are distinct, well proportioned, and lovely. The slender petals, set in two ranks of three, one recurving and one spreading, are unique to the species. 'Tropical Giant' might be an old garden hybrid, but when well grown it ripens glossy green seeds, like other wild hymenocallis, which sprout and grow up to look much like their parents.

Queen Emma cherished this plant in her Hawaiian garden, and it is widely distributed around the world in warm climates. The bulbs, apparently hardy anywhere the ground does not freeze deeply, may be planted on any damp soil. In addition to the ordinary luxuriant 'Tropical Giant', a few gardeners maintain stock of a rare double-petaled variety. The extra set of petals makes the flowers less graceful, but they are worth including in gardens for the sake of novelty.

Island Beauties

On the white coral sands of the Florida Keys, large, succulent-leafed hymenocallis are often the first plants to colonize the salty, wave-tossed beaches. When they flower in July and August, the thick bulbs send up elegantly long-tubed blossoms. These support erect, gobletlike cups and trail spidery, dangling petals that swirl around the tubes. In September, the stalks ripen large, gray-green seeds, which may soon be seen floating among the waves and drifting up on the beaches.

This bulb occurs widely over the Caribbean, flowering from midsummer till autumn. It escapes and persists around old settlements near the Gulf. Botanists have attached the name *Hymenocallis latifolia* ("wide-leafed")—an apt description of some forms of this species, but in natural colonies the foliage is diverse, varying from blunt to pointed, flattened to rolled, and from glossy green to ashy sage tones. Although typically a denizen of sunny beaches, this species is as apt to be met in shady mangrove swamps and along freshwater ponds.

A wonderful old garden form of *Hymenocallis latifolia* is commonly planted in sandy beach gardens along the Gulf. This cultivar has stiffly erect, bright green leaves and exceptionally long (seven or eight inches) floral tubes, for which characteristic it is sometimes segregated under the name *H. pedalis*. The enchanting fragrance of the blossoms, suggesting vanilla or buttered pecans, scents the evening air for nearly a month in late summer. This old garden form remains seedless unless planted near other clones of *H. latifolia*.

Another selection of *Hymenocallis latifolia*, 'Variegata' (usually listed incorrectly as *H. caribaea* 'Variegata'), develops beautiful ivory stripes along the leaves. Unfortunately, it lacks sufficient strength to survive the open sun and inclines to rot if left cold and damp over winter. It is most useful in honestly tropical gardens, or as a pot or greenhouse subject, given rich, acid soil. A popular bulb in Thailand, this variegated spiderlily is offered in the aquatic plant trade as an emergent plant for ponds.

The Big Fatty

Several gardens around Jacala, in the eastern Mexican state of Hidalgo, include a large, early-flowering spiderlily with especially fine blooms and foliage. This spectacular species, *Hymenocallis imperialis*, was apparently collected by gardeners from the local region, for it may occasionally be seen growing on nearby hillsides. The huge bulbs and enormous, spear-shaped leaves resemble 'Tropical Giant', but the foliage has a slight grayish tinge. The late April or May blossoms of *H. imperialis* have wide, snowy petals, which makes them particularly showy.

When given rich soil and partial shade, this species is among the largest which may be grown. Aficionados of *Hymenocallis* know *H. imperialis* by the nickname big fatty. Like other Mexican plants, it seems rather hardy. Well suited to garden use through the South, it reproduces easily from large, gray-green seeds, as well as offsets.

Even tougher is an old spiderlily common to early-twentieth-century gardens in south Texas and northern Mexico. Named for the state of Nuevo Leon ("new lion"), Mexico, this variety blooms in May, like *Hymenocallis imperialis*, but the snowy flowers show themselves against foliage that is particularly blunt and dark green. Bulbs are enormous, with a squared, globular form and thick blackish coats. The flowers never set seed, so this may be an old hybrid. It is of special value for its drought resistance, an uncommon attribute in this genus of water-loving flowers.

The Clumper

One of the mystery plants of subtropical gardens is an old hymenocallis with lushly narrow, arching leaves. This glossy foliage makes a striking fountain effect in gardens, like an exotic giant liriope, but the globular bulbs remain perpetually desolate, without a hint of bloom. This old variety is one of the most hurried offsetters, and it seems likely that the lack of flowers is the price exacted for hasty multiplication. The many offsets assure wide distribution, and "the clumper" is ubiquitous in gardens of the subtropics. Although flowerless, it merits use as a foliage plant.

In the benevolent climate of Iberia Parish, Louisiana, the tropical *Hymenocallis littoralis* is widely naturalized in swamps. This glossy-leafed species is similar in foliage to "the clumper" and is probably the species that Oviedo met in Panama. The slender petals adhere to the cups of the bloom and make *H. littoralis* easy to distinguish from other tropical spiderlilies. The snowy blossoms appear in August, accented by filaments tipped with bright orange pollen.

Hymenocallis littoralis is fairly tender to cold. It comes into its own in the South only when set in a watery tub or shallow pond. When grown aquatically, it shows gratitude by forming dense, tangled mats of underwater roots, which completely envelope the pots. The bulbs may be left submerged through winter, so long as ice forms only on the surface of the water. Some nurseries offer this fast-multiplying spiderlily for use in landscaping, but the trade generally confuses it with *H. caroliniana*, a native Southern species.

A hardy cousin of *H. littoralis* from southern Mexico, Guatemala, and adjacent countries flowers in October and November—usually the last spiderlily to bloom in Southern gardens. This species is aptly named *Hymenocallis acutifolia* for its long, pointed leaves. The grand, frilled cups and drooping or spreading petals look sensational against the slender, dark green foliage. They are especially welcome during their late season.

Like *Hymenocallis littoralis*, this species may be grown aquatically, but also performs well when planted on damp soils. In its native habitat *H. acutifolia* grows along jungle streams in

A late-flowering spiderlily, *Hymenocallis acutifolia*.

deep shade, and it enjoys shade in cultivation, as well.

The river spiderlily, *Hymenocallis acutifolia* var. *riparia*, is a smaller, earlier-flowering edition from western Mexico. Remarkably hardy and prolific, it self-sows under ordinary garden conditions. Nice frilled blooms appear in early summer.

Mexicans

The seasonally dry hills of western and southern Mexico are especially rich in deciduous *Hymenocallis* species, including some of the gems of the genus. Native habitats extend from just south of the Arizona border down to the volcanic mountains of the Isthmus of Tehuantepec, where more than twenty species of spiderlilies grow in varied conditions among forests and scrublands. The bulbs remain dormant during a long winter season. They leaf out briefly to flower and set seed with summer rains. Like all others, these *Hymenocallis* species are more or less poisonous and bitter. Tarahumara Indians are reported to consume bulbs of their local *lirio del rio* ("river lily") by boiling them twice to rinse away and destroy toxins, and slicing and frying them like potatoes.

Most of these fascinating plants are hardy in the South, if given sun or part shade and ordinary garden soil. Perhaps because of their diminutive stature, they remain rare in cultivation. Although slow to offset, many Mexi-

Hymenocallis maximiliani flowering in early summer.

Hymenocallis maximiliani opens fresh buds each evening.

can hymenocallis set abundant seed, and several may be propagated quickly by slicing or coring the bulbs.

Hymenocallis maximiliani is a narrow-leafed species from the state of Guerrero, superficially much like *H. acutifolia* var. *riparia*, but with long, shiny, green foliage and petals that dangle freely from the cups. The graceful, white blooms appear prolifically from May into July or later, ripening generous clusters of seed. This robust variety thrives in the South as if it were native. The botanical name recalls a tragic figure of Mexican history, the Emperor Maximilian.

Although hardly common, the most cultivated Mexican species is the *estrella de San Nicola* ("star of St. Nicholas"), *Hymenocallis harrisiana*. This modest dwarf was originally described in 1840 from plants imported by a Mr. T. Harris, Esq., of the Grove, Kingsbury. These probably came from the Valley of Mexico, where this species once grew abundantly on swampy plains. Much of the natural range of these bulbs has been covered in the sprawl of Mexico City, but these flowers still occur in a few adjacent valleys and southward to near Acapulco.

The tongue-shaped leaves of *Hymenocallis harrisiana* cluster together, forming a short false stem, which is typical of several of the Mexican spiderlilies. Foliage is a dull, dusty green in the common garden strain, but forms from lower elevations have glossier green leaves. A pair of longitudinal folds or creases marks the foliage of *H. harrisiana* and helps distinguish this species from others. The truly spidery blossoms carry pendulous, dangling petals crowned by

Hymenocallis harrisiana.   *Hymenocallis eucharidifolia.*

ridiculously tiny, white cups. They appear in May in slender groups of six or less and later ripen abundant seed.

Showier for garden use is the gray-foliaged *Hymenocallis glauca* (*H. choretis*). The large-cupped, snowy blossoms of this southern Mexican species appear in pairs in early summer, while the emerging stems are still quite short. Gray, spear-shaped leaves elongate afterward, eventually reaching two feet in length and offering an interesting accent for a shady or partially sunny corner. The attractive flowers have orange pollen and smell strangely of ammonia or chlorine. *Hymenocallis chiapasiana*, from the beautiful uplands of the state of Chiapas, is similar, but smaller in all parts.

The fabulous *Hymenocallis eucharidifolia* is a rare, shade-loving species with rosettes of unusually broad, green, hostalike foliage. Although mostly unknown to cultivation since its description in 1884, this remarkable bulb has been imported from Oaxaca in recent years and is available in limited numbers from nurseries. The snowy flowers are held in up-facing groups of three or more, showing effectively against the large, glossy rosettes of leaves. The vigorous bulbs thrive in rich, leafy soil and part shade. They offset at a steady pace and seem as hardy as other Mexican species, so they may one day become more common in gardens.

Hymenocallis leavenworthii and *H. azteciana* are exotic species from high, cool woodlands near Patzcuaro and Guadalajara. They have unusual, spreading, long-stemmed, or petiolate, leaves, and this beautiful foliage has an elegant, satiny dusting of gray overlaying dark green. Small clusters of erect blooms, rising between the flaccid foliage, open together like miniature, midsummer bouquets. These species enjoy shade and cool, loamy soil.

Hymenocallis guerreroensis is a delightful miniature with slender, paired leaves like a tiny daffodil. One to three good-sized blooms appear in early summer. *Hymenocallis araniflora* and *H. sonorensis* produce larger clusters of long-tubed, sweet-scented blooms, and somewhat wider, pale green or grayish foliage, respectively. These species proliferate locally on coastal prairies and upland volcanic soils in western Mexico, reproducing readily from seed. Like all the smaller Mexican spiderlilies, these rarities make intriguing subjects for early summer borders.

Native Spiderlilies

When Mark Catesby wrote his *Natural History of Carolina, Florida, and the Bahama Islands* in 1731, he described an exotic flower found blooming in a bog "on the Savannah River within the precinct of Georgia." Catesby noted that the plants resembled the sea daffodil (*Pancratium maritimum*) of southern European coasts but had deep, shining green foliage, rather than gray leaves.

This American spiderlily eventually became known as *Hymenocallis caroliniana*. Since Catesby's work, over twenty additional *Hymenocallis* species have been described as natives of the South. Most are more or less aquatic, and several are small plants of modest garden merit. There are at least a half dozen, however, with good-sized, showy blooms. Some of these plants adapt to general garden culture as well as to ponds and bogs. They are some of the most elegant blooms which may be grown, and these wildflowers deserve to be planted with pride in Southern gardens.

Lily-scented Hymenocallis

From Mobile Bay westward to Texas, the most abundant spiderlily on the coastal prairies is *Hymenocallis liriosme*. This early-blooming species is distinctive for its yellow-centered, frilled cups. The glossy, dark green leaves, emerging in spring along with the blooms, vary in length from a modest eight inches to nearly three feet in the most vigorous forms.

The white blooms of *Hymenocallis liriosme* have distinctive yellow throats.
Photo by Lauren S. Ogden.

This species often stands in shallow water and invariably grows in thick, heavy clays. Although most common near the Gulf, this beautiful flower ranges as far inland as southern Arkansas. The black-coated bulbs seem entirely hardy, and will succeed anywhere in the South if given ample moisture through spring and early summer. The lovely blooms appear during March and April. The clusters of buds sit atop razor-edged stems, which range from less than a foot to two feet tall. They have the fragrance of Easter lilies and make a fine complement to Louisiana irises, which flower at the same season. If summers are wet, *Hymenocallis liriosme* may rebloom sporadically in summer and autumn.

Hymenocallis liriosme flowering in a coastal marsh near Refugio, Texas.

Galveston Lilies

There is a long-standing confusion between *Hymenocallis liriosme* and another widespread spiderlily, *H. galvestonensis*. Both were collected originally by Thomas Drummond in the vicinity of Galveston Bay. Dean Herbert successfully grew one of Drummond's bulbs long enough to observe its gray-green, deciduous leaves. Herbert reported, "Having been forced early out, it has gone to rest before the end of July." Although he saw no fresh blossoms, one of Drummond's sheets bore a pressed flower stalk, so Herbert was able to describe the plant, as *Choretis galvestonensis*. J. G. Baker later transferred this species to *Hymenocallis*, but in doing so he included another Drummond specimen with both leaves and flowers together. Unwittingly, he had combined the dark green-leafed, spring-flowering *H. liriosme* with this very different, gray-leafed, summer-flowering species.

The true *Hymenocallis galvestonensis* is a native Southern bulb that often behaves like the oriental *Lycoris squamigera*, putting up foliage in spring, dying away, and then blooming in response to summer rains. The species is unique in the genus for flowering on rounded, naked stems, and this makes it especially exotic and beautiful in gardens. Although locally common in parts of the South, *H. galvestonensis* is generally considered to be rare. It may sometimes be seen in July flowering in thick clumps around old homes or cemeteries in open woods of loblolly pine. The jaunty, angled petals and lavish, spreading cups make a memorable summer show.

Culture for this species is different from other Southern spiderlilies, for *Hymenocallis galvestonensis* naturally grows on reddish, friable, upland soils. It needs plenty of water during the spring growing season, but may be left to dry out after May. It has no tolerance for heavy, waterlogged clay or for alkalinity.

Hymenocallis eulae, originally described from near Tyler, Texas, seems to be a synonym of *H. galvestonensis*. References to summer-blooming spiderlilies from other parts of the South such as *H. occidentalis* and *H. moldenkiana* may refer to environmental forms of *H. galvestonensis*. With ample rainfall, these bulbs sometimes retain foliage while flowering, presenting a very different appearance and leading to misidentification.

River Lilies

The showiest of the strictly aquatic native spiderlilies is *Hymenocallis coronaria*, named for its especially large, frilly cups. This species grows in clear, flowing streams with its bulbs nestled firmly between rocks, bound against the current by masses of strong twining roots. It is locally common on watercourses from Alabama to North Carolina. The early summer flowering of these Cahaba lilies along Alabama's Cahaba River creates an annual floral event.

In the brackish water of the Everglades and south Florida, *Hymenocallis palmeri* (alligator lily) is the most common aquatic spiderlily. This very fragrant species has odd, green-tinged blossoms that appear singly along with sparse, narrow foliage. The bulbs are stoloniferous, so they multiply into patches among the native reeds. Coronas of the alligator lily usually display several prominent teeth, but this is a character that varies widely in *Hymenocallis*.

In eastern Florida's lake country two dwarf spiderlilies, *Hymenocallis floridana* and *H. traubii*, proliferate in calm freshwaters. Both are lovely, with large fringed cups appearing in early summer. Of the two, *H. traubii* is the miniature, usually flowering with just two oversized blossoms to each six-inch scape. Both species have narrow, dark green leaves and multiply steadily by stolons like the alligator lily. Botanists sometimes lump these together as dwarf variants of *H. rotata*. *Hymenocallis puntagordensis* is a similar, small-cupped species from Florida's west coast. Other Florida natives suited to damp positions include *H. henryae*, *H. duvalensis*, *H. choctawensis*, and *H. godfreyi*.

Hymenocallis floridana is common to lakesides and marshes around Gainesville.

Luther Bundrant, of Poteet, Texas, crossed the tiny *Hymenocallis traubii* with *H. narcissiflora* to create 'Excelsior'. This beautiful hybrid inherits the tiny stature of *H. traubii*, but displays frilled, fragrant blossoms to eight inches across, with four-inch cups. 'Excelsior' thrives under boggy conditions and makes an excellent subject at the edge of a garden pond, perfectly hardy as long as the bulbs themselves are preserved from frost.

Sea Daffodils

The barren, sandy beaches of the Greek islands are home to one of the hardier members of the Old World genus *Pancratium*, the *krinos tis thallasas* ("lily of the sea"), *P. maritimum*. These interesting bulbs, cousins of the American hymenocallis, bear flowers like small Peruvian daffodils. Their seeds are flat and black, and their thick, evergreen foliage is fleshy and straplike. Often tangling in a spirally twisted mass, the unique leaves are dusted in a silvery gray bloom, which helps conserve moisture.

Pancratium maritimum (sea daffodil).

In the South, sea daffodils are easy to grow on sandy soil in full sun, but they only flower if kept fairly dry over summer. They need very little moisture to get along and make excellent subjects for beach plantings. The sweet-scented blooms appear in July. Seed ripens in autumn, and may be planted immediately to sprout and grow through winter. This very odd bulb is fairly easy to locate in nursery lists. Dioscorides reported using it medicinally to control asthma and coughs.

Although the hardier Italian forms of another Mediterranean species, *Pancratium illyricum*, might succeed in the South, these have not been introduced. Other related plants such as *P. canariense* are mostly winter-growing, deciduous bulbs suited to near frost-free conditions. *Vagaria parviflora* and *Calostemma purpureum*, allied bulbs from the Mediterranean and Australia, grow and flower in winter and enjoy poor sandy soils. Their small, somberly colored blooms resemble the clustered flowers of *Narcissus tazetta*.

Amazon Lilies

In tropical Florida and in protected areas along the Gulf, the Amazon lily (*Eucharis grandiflora*) is a popular perennial for shady beds. Its hostalike leaves form thick clumps. Modest-sized, waxy, ismene-like blooms appear in fall and winter and emit a powerful, sweet fragrance. Plants weaken if they lose their evergreen foliage, so Amazon lilies must be relegated to pot culture where frosts visit regularly. The common form in cultivation appears to be an old, sterile hybrid. Several smaller species are native to the forests of South America.

Chapter 8
 Summer Glories

I F TRUE LILIES (*Lilium* spp.) possessed ordinary bulbs like daffodils and could withstand the same rough handling, they might rank as the most popular of summer bulbs. As it is, the majority of these aristocratic perennials call for more careful treatment. Lilies come primarily from temperate woodlands, and their primitive, loose-scaled rootstocks suffer if allowed to dry excessively, either in the garden or in storage. Some of the most beautiful, such as the golden rayed lily of Japan (*L. auratum*), are famous for their exacting requirements: well-aerated, humus-rich, unequivocally acid soil, and generous positions in cool, filtered sun.

Not all members of this genus are so particular, and several are suited to ordinary garden situations, even on heavy clays or on limy soils. If Southerners dedicate their efforts toward these more vigorous lily varieties, their plantings can be gloriously enhanced with nominal effort. The fussier Oriental hybrids can usually be accommodated in the same beds that house azaleas. This combination works well for the lilies, which enjoy rooting among the bushes, while their tall, elegant blooms help relieve the tiresome summer greenery of the shrubs.

Most lilies require several seasons to mature before giving their best performances. With good care the bulbs become truly enormous, and they will send up proportionally large stalks of bloom. If for some reason they must be moved, it is best to treat established lilies as if they were mature shrubs: a generous portion of earth should be taken up along with the delicate roots. As long as this is done, the clumps may be moved at any season, even while in full bloom.

Lilies look their best when planted in groups, so that the towering stems do not appear overly gaunt. The initial expense of bulbs might dissuade gardeners from planting enough for good effect. Fortunately, these bulbs are among the most readily propagated flowers.

Many lilies grow quickly from seed, and all varieties may be started from bulb scales. In addition, several types form tiny bulbils in the axils of the leaves, which may be carefully removed to start new plantings. By peeling away the outer sections of the bulbs as if preparing an artichoke, several scales may be procured. Scales, seeds, or bulbils should be set in pots of rich, leafy soil and grown on for the summer. They may be set in permanent quarters in autumn. After three seasons of good care, the young bulbs will be large enough to begin blooming. Such homegrown plants establish readily and often outproduce purchased bulbs.

When propagating these flowers it is important to secure virus-free parent stock, for mosaic disease is a serious problem of some lilies. Viruses express their presence in visible streaking of foliage, followed by loss of vigor. There is no remedy, and infected plants will need to be destroyed to prevent the spread of disease.

Choice lilies may be preserved by growing new, virus-free bulbs from seed. Keeping a fresh batch of seedlings coming along at all times provides an excellent long-term strategy to defeat disease. Many commercial lily growers follow this ploy, producing named strains from seed, rather than from clonal hybrids.

Due to their tall, weighty stems, most lilies benefit from planting with three or four inches of soil above the tops of the bulbs. The emerging stalks often develop bulblets and roots in this zone, which help to anchor the plants against wind and rain. After a season in the ground, the bulbs adjust themselves to their preferred depth. The Madonna lily (*Lilium candidum*) is an exception: it should be set with its bulb just below the soil surface.

In spite of, or perhaps because of their temperamental reputations, lilies occupy a special place in the hearts of all lovers of floral beauty. With their leafy stems and loosely built blossoms, they unabashedly reveal the primordial structures of their family. Stamens, pistils, petals, and leaves all combine in a fascinating array of colorful designs, as if they had been painted and assembled from separate pieces by troops of imaginative children.

Madonna Lilies

The white, funnel-shaped blooms painted on the walls of the Minoan palace of Knossos belong to the Madonna lily, *Lilium candidum*, and this sentimentally romantic flower has been pictured innumerable times since. These fragrant, immaculate blossoms have long been emblematic of purity. Medieval depictions of Mary usually show her clutching a bouquet.

Lilium candidum is unique in the genus for its habit of leafing out in fall, and the species is also unusual in its preference for limy soils. The frostproof foliage, forming tidy rosettes like small green hostas, is an asset to winter gardens all by itself. In April the leafy stems elongate, eventually reaching two feet or more in height. These are topped by several waxy blossoms, which scent the air sweetly in all directions.

In the middle and upper South, wherever soils include a measure of lime, the Madonna lily features in old, country gardens. It often keeps company with blue cornflowers and pink or wine-purple shrub roses. In April or May the chaste torches of glistening white bloom may be seen lighting the grayed monuments of colonial cemeteries.

Unlike most other lilies, these natives of the eastern Mediterranean flourish on the same dryish, sunny slopes as bearded irises. They sometimes prove mysteriously difficult to establish in new gardens, even in districts where ancient colonies flourish. Viruses may be the culprit, so it is useful to look for bulbs raised from seed. This oldest of garden flowers prospers on benevolent disregard—and on the liberal dousings of soapsuds, tea slops, and rotted horse manure that ordinary gardeners offer their most cherished possessions.

There is a very old hybrid of the Madonna lily, the lovely, apricot *Lilium* ×*testaceum* (Nankeen lily). Six to twelve blooms appear on top of its tall stems and nod like *L. chalcedonicum* (Turk's cap), its other parent. The soft chartreuse 'Limerick' and pale yellow 'Uprising' are more recent cultivars of similar parentage. These are seldom planted in the South but should succeed in the same gardens in which *L. candidum* prospers.

Trumpets

Nearly all the trumpet-shaped lilies of the Far East flourish in the South, and many of their hybrids do, also. The most famous of this group is the old Bermuda or Easter lily, *Lilium longiflorum* var. *eximium*, formerly raised commercially on the island of Bermuda and forced by florists for its pure, fragrant blooms. Although slightly tender, this showy flower performs well in Florida and the lower South. Any soil, including heavy clay or barren chalk, seems suitable. The bright grassy green leaves and snowy blossoms fill Gulf Coast gardens in April.

Lilium longiflorum naturally inhabits subtropical brushlands in Japan and Taiwan. Bulbs often grow in shallow pockets of soil formed over volcanic or coral rocks. They sometimes

Lilium longiflorum var. *eximium* (Bermuda lily).

appear just above high tide line, where the spray from the waves splashes on the foliage and impregnates the soil with salt. In the South these flowers make excellent choices for seaside plantings.

Modern cultivars of *Lilium longiflorum*, such as the dark green-leafed 'Croft', have supplanted the Bermuda lily (var. *eximium*) in greenhouse culture and are now the Easter lilies most popular for forcing. Although hardier and later blooming, they are not so vigorous as the Bermuda lily.

The most prolific Asian trumpet in the South is *Lilium formosanum*, sometimes listed as a variety of the similar, but more tropical *L. philippinense*. No lily could be easier to grow than this fragrant flower, known traditionally in the South as the Philippine lily. The narrow-leafed stalks are dressed in slender, bright green leaves, which recurve gracefully up the stems. These stalks reach upward to seven feet and carry a dozen or more ten-inch, elegantly declined trumpets that look and smell like Easter lilies. These appear in late summer.

After blooming, the architectural plants turn upward to ripen their attractive capsules of papery seeds. These remain through winter and make interesting dried arrangements. If left to stand, the seeds sow themselves into any partially shaded corner. The robust seedlings grow rapidly, often flowering in their second year. The Philippine lily naturalizes widely on sandy soils; its creamy blooms may often be seen peeking out from the edges of pine woods in August, and periodic whiffs of its sweet fragrance often accompany nighttime drives on Southern country roads.

Dwarf Philippine lily, *Lilium formosanum* var. *pricei*. Photo by Lauren S. Ogden.

In its native home on the island of Taiwan, *Lilium formosanum* ranges from near sea level up to twelve thousand feet, inhabiting both tropical and temperate climates. In 1912 R. Price gathered seeds of a dwarf form of *L. formosanum* found high on Yu Shan (Mt. Morrison), the tallest peak in Taiwan. Introduced as var. *pricei*, this is a more cold-hardy strain of the species, showing red-purple markings on the outsides of its petals in cool climates such as the

Pacific Northwest. These pigments fade in warm Southern summers, however, so the blooms may remain Easter-lily white. Nevertheless, var. *pricei* grows well in the South, making an effective display for smaller gardens. It usually blooms slightly before the tall strains of Philippine lily. *Lilium formosanum* var. *pricei* received Awards of Garden Merit in England in 1921 and 1929.

Other members of the trumpet group include *Lilium brownii, L. sargentiae, L. leucanthum, L. sulphureum,* and *L. regale*—the types that have been most developed through hybridizing. All were collected from the Chinese mainland by explorer E. H. Wilson, who discovered and imported nearly one thousand Chinese plants in the early 1900s.

The regal lily (*Lilium regale*) is the member of this group most planted in its natural, unhybridized form. This beautiful flower deserves its royal title, for it is at once easy to grow and thoroughly lovely. The vigorous, sturdy stems reach three or four feet in height. In May they bear several pearly, funnel-shaped blossoms. These are flushed with lilac-purple on the backs of the petals, and are warmed by a yellow zone at the throat. In the heat of the sun these colors often fade, so it is customary in the South to provide partial shade for these and all other lilies flowering after mid-May. 'Album' is a snowy cultivar that lacks the external striping.

Lilium regale (regal lily). Photo by Lauren S. Ogden.

In the mid-twentieth century, Oregon breeder Jan De Graf began hybridizing trumpet lilies, bringing into existence a spectacular race of garden flowers. The trumpets themselves were intercrossed to produce the Olympic hybrids, or centifolium lilies. These were larger, more vigorous versions of their wild predecessors, but inherited susceptibility to virus.

A better, healthier race came into being with the Aurelian lilies. These bowl-shaped flowers descend from crosses with the vigorous oriental Turk's cap, *Lilium henryi*. This small, brown-freckled, orange-yellow blossom imparts virus resistance to its offspring; most of the Aurelians inherit strong constitutions. The first breeder to develop this section, M. E. Debras, named the group for his hometown, Orleans, France.

Lilium henryi is itself a fine garden lily in the South and tolerates a wide range of soils and positions. When established, the tall stems bear several nodding, apricot-yellow blooms, curiously marked and relieved with papillae, or small bumps. The petals completely recurve in typical Turk's cap manner, with the orange-tipped anthers projecting merrily downward.

These blossoms appear in early summer and combine well with snowy 'Mt. Fuji' summer phlox. The selection called 'White Henryi' is a sport with larger, ivory blooms. It sometimes reverts to the ordinary form, which is only a small disappointment, since both versions of this plant are lovely. This species was introduced by Dr. Augustine Henry, an Irish physician and forester who explored central China and Taiwan in the late 1800s.

The Aurelian hybrids are often sold as strains named to designate their various color forms. 'Pink Perfection', 'Green Magic', and 'Golden Splendor' describe themselves. 'African Queen' is a rich golden yellow. 'Black Dragon' is streaked darkly on the petal exteriors, but in the warmth of Southern summers often fades to white. 'Gold Eagle' thrives in the South, offering June flowers with the aspect of a large, butter-yellow *Lilium henryi*.

'Thunderbolt', a huge, strong-growing Aurelian with fragrant, wide-open apricot-orange blossoms, is no longer common in the bulb trade, although breeders have used it to sire valuable offspring. Some of these belong to a new class of lilies called Oriental-Trumpet hybrids, combining the vigor of Aurelian lilies with the wide-open blooms and brilliant color patterns of Oriental lilies. Parallel crosses using Easter lilies and Philippine lilies as substitutes for the Aurelian parent are known as Longiflorum-Asian hybrids and Longiflorum-Oriental hybrids. Although all are just now making their way into gardens, these new lily classes seem to have great promise for the South, offering blooms that range from delicate pastels to shocking bicolors. As with other summer-flowering lilies, shade will help prevent their large, waxy blossoms from scorching and fading.

Lilium 'Thunderbolt'.

Tiger Lilies

The familiar spotted orange tiger lily, *Lilium lancifolium*, is a sterile hybrid that has been grown for centuries in Japan. It is probably a cross of *L. leichtlinii*, an oriental Turk's cap, and *L. ×maculatum*, an old Japanese garden flower with up-facing blossoms. Tiger lilies carry extra chromosomes (a triploid set), with resultant vigor and resistance to virus. Gardeners still call this beloved flower by its old name, *L. tigrinum*, and they cheerfully share and multiply their stocks by means of the prolific, dark green bulbils that form along the stem.

This most reliable of all the spotted lilies in the South accepts the widest range of conditions. If offered any modestly prepared soil, tiger lilies will flower freely through summer. They ask for little added attention beyond shade from the hottest sun. Up to twenty nodding blossoms appear on strong stems above the handsome, dark green leaves.

In addition to the common bright orange-red tiger ('Splendens'), there are a rare double form and an unusual variegated selection. A race of varicolored tiger lilies may also be had from bulb dealers. 'Yellow Tiger' ('Yellow Star') is bright, buttery yellow with black dots. 'White Tiger' has maroon speckles and stamens; 'Pink Tiger' ('Tigrinum Rose'), 'Red Tiger' ('Red Fox'), 'Cream Tiger' ('Torino'), 'Orange Tiger' ('Tigrinum Fortunei'), and 'Gold Tiger' ('Sunny Twinkle') are additional, colorful variations of this old garden flower.

Some of the well-known Asiatic hybrids are descended in part from the tiger lily. A few of the most vigorous, such as 'Enchantment', succeed in the middle and upper South. For the most part, however, these up-facing candle-stick lilies perform better in cold climates.

The Oriental hybrids of the pink and red showy Japanese lily (*Lilium speciosum* var. *rubrum*) and the yellow and white gold-rayed lily (*L. auratum*) are better in cool climates, also. Nevertheless, vigorous selections of these beautiful lilies sometimes succeed in the South without undue difficulty.

The tiger lily, *Lilium lancifolium*, forms numerous bulbils along its leafy stem.

Well-drained, acid soil and partial shade are requisite. Some gardeners also employ the technique of tilting bulbs slightly when setting them out. This prevents the loose scales from collecting water and remaining overly moist or soggy.

The same kind of careful treatment suits the rare native lilies of the South, for they are denizens of rich, peaty woodlands in the southern Appalachians, sandy pinelands of the coastal plain, and acid pitcher-plant bogs. The Southern red lily (*Lilium catesbaei*), Carolina lily (*L. michauxii*), royal lily (*L. superbum*), pot-of-gold lily (*L. iridollae*), and roan lily (*L. grayi*) are widely distributed through the Southeast. All have spotted, fragrant, Turk's-cap-style blooms in early summer, produced from small, often stoloniferous bulbs. Wild colonies should not be disturbed, but bulbs may be raised from seed or obtained from wildflower specialists who propagate their own stock.

Climbing Lilies

Some of the most exciting lilies adapted to the South have adopted the novel habit of vines, and will climb on a trellis or post. These spectacular flowers offer an exotic way to dress up a wire mesh fence. Their generic name is *Gloriosa* ("glorious"), and so they are.

The glory lilies include several forms native to subtropical Africa and India, once classified under as many as thirty separate names. Botanists presently include all these as variations of a single species, *Gloriosa superba*. The weak, trailing stems of the glory lilies carry elliptical, tendril-bearing leaves and sprout from odd, L- or V-shaped tubers, which travel slowly under the ground. These may be dug and divided, making sure that each severed piece includes an eye, or growing point. The tubers replace themselves each season, so they should be disturbed only after the plants have completely ripened their foliage.

In the wild these rhizomatous flowers grow in semi-arid scrubland, where they remain dormant through a long, dry winter season. In gardens they thrive on rich soil and summer moisture. They may be left in the ground over winter if sheltered from cold, damp conditions.

One showy form, *Gloriosa superba* 'Rothschildiana', may still be met in horticulture under its older name, *G. rothschildiana*. These climbing lilies reach three to six feet in height, enjoying full sun or partial shade. The flowers are like bizarre Turk's cap lilies, with yellow, undulating petals, flamed red on their upper two-thirds. The fleshy, green stamens and pistil curve and splay outward from the center of the nodding blooms. This popular form originates from Uganda.

Gloriosa superba has a wide range from South Africa through tropical east Africa and India. Some forms have the red and yellow rothschildiana pattern, but the variety typically offered by nurseries as *G. superba* is a rich orange with yellow edges. Another well-known cultivar, 'Lutea', is valued for its lemony yellow blooms. All forms of *G. superba* have especially narrow, crisped petals.

A variant formerly called *Gloriosa simplex* (*G. plantii*) is a dainty flower from the Eastern Cape, KwaZulu-Natal, and tropical east Africa. Its orange and yellow blooms undulate only near the tips of the petals. The flowers open with a pale greenish yellow tone, for which reason it is sometimes called *G. virescens*. The vining stems reach about three feet in length.

Florida nurseryman Wyndham Hayward used a rare yellow gloriosa discovered in an old Trinidad garden by the flower painter Wilhelmina Greene to create a series of tall, late-blooming hybrids. The other parent of this cross was the central African *Gloriosa carsoni*, a medium-sized species with prominent claret markings on the petals. The strain 'Wilhelmina Greene' includes clear sulfuryellows and selections with slight wine featherings. Although rare in the bulb trade, these are still grown by some Southerners. Similarly beautiful plants were once bred by Sidney Percy-Lancaster and his son, Alick, and may persist in the gardens of India.

All the glory lilies ripen large pods of reddish, marblelike seeds. These may be saved in autumn for planting in pots in March. They are slow to germinate, and it is wise to allow at least four months for them to sprout. The young plants rapidly form tubers and will be ready to bed out in their third season.

Littonia modesta (climbing bell lily, or *geelklokkie*) is a rare relation of

Gloriosa superba 'Rothschildiana'.

Gloriosa with similar wants and habits. The flowers are bell-shaped, with six tapering petals of a beautiful golden yellow. These ripen to form decorative seed pods. 'Keitii' is a robust selection of this South African perennial. Another *Gloriosa* ally from the same region, the Christmas bell, or Chinese lantern lily (*Sandersonia aurantiaca*), produces small, clear orange blooms that puff out like little bells. These appear in midsummer (Christmastime) in its South African homeland.

Parrot Lilies

Tropical America, too, has unusual vining lilies, but these lush perennials ramble about, rather than honestly climb. Their thickened rootstocks wander vigorously under good conditions. Best known are the florist's Peruvian lilies (*Alstroemeria* cvs.), mostly natives of the cool, high Andes mountains with multicolored blooms suggestive of exotically marked azalea blossoms.

These high-elevation species do not generally succeed as garden plants in the warm South, but their lowland cousin from Brazil, the parrot lily (*Alstroemeria psittacina*), prospers mightily. This curious flower has six petals compressed laterally so that the blooms resemble orchids. The coloring of the flowers is a Christmasy red with green tips and chocolate freckling on the interior. This mix of tones seems fairly lackluster in the garden, but serves to attract hummingbirds, who are the principal pollinators of these flowers.

Parrot lilies grow vigorously in moist soil and partial shade, and they are

The parrot lily, *Alstroemeria psittacina*.

quite capable of taking over an embankment or other rough position. They are perfectly hardy in the South and flower reliably in early summer. The whorled, green foliage grows during the winter months and remains attractive until after the June bloom cycle, becoming dormant for a brief period in late summer. There is also a beautiful variegated form, which is less rampant and more easily managed in the garden. *Alstroemeria psittacina* is sometimes listed as *A. pulchella.*

A few hybrids, such as the golden-flowered 'Sweet Laura', descend from another Brazilian species, *Alstroemeria caryophyllaea*, with fragrant pink blooms. 'Sweet Laura' inherits the perfume of this species and its heat-tolerant constitution, but has yellow blossoms marked with orange-tipped petals and chocolate specks. 'Glory of the Andes', a variegated sport of 'Sweet Laura' with leaves edged in a creamy picotee, also shows promise for the South. Other low-elevation Brazilian species such as *A. brasiliensis*, *A. sellowiana*, and *A. radula* would no doubt succeed in the South as well.

Also hardy and adaptable in the South, but rarely grown is the Chile arrowroot or *salsilla*, *Bomarea edulis*. This is a cousin of *Alstroemeria* from Mexico, the West Indies, and tropical South America. It forms a leafy, semi-vining plant that rises from a thickened tuber. The outer petals of the flowers are pink, the inner, yellowish green with purple spots. This upland species prefers rich, moist soil and partial shade, but is tough and long-lived once established. The pliant stems benefit from the support of a fence or trellis.

Blue Gingers and Dayflowers

Many perennials of the dayflower family (Commelinaceae) have thickened roots, but these rhizomes are usually poorly developed. Only in the so-called blue ginger (*Dichorisandra thyrsiflora*) of Brazil are the tuberous roots really substantial. Although not a true ginger, this South American is as glamorous as any summer flower, with smooth, shiny green leaves arranged spirally along a stiff two- to three-foot, jointed stem. At the top, five-inch heads of rich blue-violet, white-centered blooms appear in late summer. This tender perennial grows easily in rich soil, sprouting stems from its creeping rootstock like *Alstroemeria*. It is hardy along the Gulf, but resents freezes. When cut back by winter cold, it needs most of the summer to build up strength for bloom. *Dichorisandra reginae* and *D. pendula* are additional blue-flowered species sometimes available from dealers in tropical plants.

Although it is overly free with self-sown seed, the related, native dayflower *Commelina erecta* (widow's tears) is sometimes admitted to gardens. The celestial-blue, two-petaled blossoms are certainly worth having in early summer borders, although they remain open only during the cool morning hours. The nutlike tubers have strong roots, which tend to pull down into crevices and other hard-to-weed places. Some varieties also root from trailing, jointed stems, forming a sort of succulent groundcover.

Potato and Madeira Vines

Potato vines (*Dioscorea bulbifera*) and Madeira vines (*Anredera cordifolia*) are old-fashioned, tuberous climbers popular in the South for their lush, green summer foliage. In the era before air conditioning, these fast-growing vines provided the very functional service of screening and shading porches. They are still popular for this purpose among country people.

The potato vine, or air potato (*Dioscorea bulbifera*), is remarkable for its production of aerial tubers. Looking like small, brown, Irish potatoes, they develop over summer along the vining stems. They remain hidden behind the glossy, heart-shaped leaves until fall, when this foliage yellows and dies away. The "potatoes" may then be gathered and saved for planting the following season or left to fall in place. They will sprout on their own if not frozen during winter.

Potato vines belong to the tropical yam family, which includes several lily-like, tuberous climbers. The tiny flowers of all species are insignificant for garden display. Roots of the edible Chinese yam, or cinnamon vine (*Dioscorea batatas*), may sometimes be found in Asian or Latin markets. If set in rich soil after danger from frost, these make attractive, leafy vines for summer gardens. The drought-loving elephant's foot vines of Africa and Mexico (*D. elephantipes, D. glauca, D. sylvatica,* and *D. macrostachya*) are also easily grown in summer, but their exotically corky, protruding tubers must be sheltered from damp and frost over winter.

The Madeira, or mignonette vine (*Anredera cordifolia*), has succulent, glossy foliage similar to the air potato, but lacks the prominent, parallel veining of *Dioscorea*. This South American also imitates the air potato in forming occasional aerial tubers, although these are not so large or prolific. The sprays of flowers are pale, greenish white, and too small to be noticeable, but they emit a penetrating, nocturnal fragrance that endears this plant to all. Rude vigor and heat- and drought-tolerance are other valuable attributes of *A. cordifolia*.

Asparagus

Asparagus is a large genus of lily-type perennials, many of which bear attractive, feathery foliage and showy berries. The true leaves of these plants are tiny and scalelike, and their function is largely replaced by modified branchlets called cladophylls. Fleshy roots support the matted crowns; these perennials may be cut apart with a sharp knife for increase. All varieties grow readily from seed.

Along the Gulf several evergreen asparagus ferns are popular for landscaping. Basket asparagus (*Asparagus densiflorus* 'Sprengeri') is best known. Its sprays of prickly, emerald-green cladophylls, resembling pine foliage, cascade gracefully to form mounds three feet across. These rugged natives of KwaZulu-Natal endure drought and poor soil and thrive in seaside gardens. Their root-stocks are rather hardy, but slow to recover when frozen. If the prickly stems and tender foliage are sheltered from frost, small, creamy blooms appear in spring and form bright red berries in autumn. Foxtail fern (*A. densiflorus* 'Myers') is a stiffer, more compact cousin valued for its architectural form. Native to the same region, the ming fern (*A. macowanii*) is equally tough and hardy, with especially beautiful, delicate sprays of dark green foliage.

Asparagus setaceus (climbing asparagus) is another rugged African species popular in Florida and Gulf Coast gardens. Its flattened sprays of luxuriant, dark green foliage form horizontal pyramids at intervals along the wiry, twining stems. These leafy sprays look good trained on trellises in deep or partial shade, or they may be cut for floral arrangements. Like *A. densiflorus*, climbing asparagus resprouts if frozen, but is most valuable in gardens where freezes seldom visit. The tiny, sweet-scented flowers ripen to black berries.

Sickle thorn (*Asparagus falcatus*) is another half-hardy climber suited to the lower South. Although beautiful and robust, it should be planted with caution. The dark green, yewlike foliage disguises vicious thorns, which make this robust plant unfriendly to garden around.

One of the most beautiful of the many South African *Asparagus* species is *A. virgatus* (broom fern), a feathery, sprawling plant with dark green sprays of foliage. Although delicate in appearance, the tough, wiry cladophylls stand up to hot sun and remain evergreen to frosts as low as 18°F. The stems carry small, greenish white blooms in spring and summer, with the pea-sized, orange-red fruits following in autumn. Any soil seems satisfactory. Over time, the spreading roots of this species colonize large areas. Broom fern is common in older gardens near New Orleans, where it was once raised for florist's greenery.

The hardy, deciduous *Asparagus* species are seldom planted in flower gardens, although they often escape and persist around old plantings in the South. Common table asparagus, *A. officinalis*, makes a beautiful plant, with waving, ferny foliage that turns a fine yellow in autumn. The shiny, red berries are showy, also. There is no reason why plants grown for their tender spring shoots cannot be sited where their summer greenery can contribute to the garden as well. For those not interested in harvesting for the table, a Romanian form, *A. officinalis* vr. *pseudoscaber*, may be planted strictly for ornament; 'Spitzenschleier' is an especially graceful German selection of this.

Asparagus filicinus is a charming dwarf species from India and China with low, compact mounds of fresh green foliage, like a small, upright version of *A. densiflorus* (nurseries sometimes offer it as a compact selection of that species). Although deciduous and hardy, in the South this asparagus remains dormant for only a short time. The lush, thornless stems are very suitable for bordering beds in sun or partial shade. The fruits of *A. filicinus* are reported to be black, but neither blooms nor berries form on the common garden strain. Several additional *Asparagus* species native to South Africa and the Mediterranean region would be worthy of trial in the South.

Equestrian Star Flowers

The American belladonna (*Hippeastrum puniceum*) was long ago robbed of its birthright by Dean Herbert, who maintained that the South African belladonna, instead, should bear the beautiful name *Amaryllis*. The strange substitute name for the genus, *Hippeastrum* ("horse star"), was apparently inspired by the two-parted spathe valves surrounding the thick buds. These open "like ears [to] give the whole flower a fancied resemblance to a horse's head."

Gardeners are rightly skeptical of such foolishness and still universally refer to these beloved flowers as amaryllises. Within the ranks of this vast tropical American genus may be found the most splendid of flowering bulbs. In the native Quechua tongue of the Andes, where many amaryllises grow wild, they are known as *aputika* ("flowers of God").

St. Joseph's Lily

In 1888 Henry Nehrling, just beginning his teaching career, traveled to Houston to assume a position with the Lutheran schools. This was the future nurseryman's first trip to the South, and, as he stepped off the train from chilly Chicago, he was thrilled by the lush gardens greeting him.

Nehrling enjoyed his first experience of Southern magnolias and sweet-scented gardenias. He marveled at the lush, tea-scented China roses and long borders of aspidistra that filled every neighborhood. What especially caught his fancy was a clump of flaming red amaryllises. These beautiful flowers later became the focus of his career; Nehrling eventually moved to Florida and authored a treatise, *Die Amaryllis*, on these favorite blooms.

The flowers Henry Nehrling beheld in those early gardens still grace Southern plantings, although they have long since disappeared from most nurserymen's catalogs. They belong to a familiar, deep crimson, trumpet-shaped amaryllis with white keels and bronze-tinted foliage. Sources differ on the date of introduction (Baker records 1799; Herbert says 1810), but they agree that this is the earliest of all amaryllis hybrids. Raised in a Lancashire garden by an English watchmaker named Johnson, it is known in horticulture as *Hippeastrum ×johnsonii*. Gardeners call these beautiful flowers St. Joseph lilies.

Several *Hippeastrum* species were discovered during the eighteenth-century explorations of the wild territories of South America. These were introduced to Europe, and Johnson used two of them to create his lovely hybrid. The queen's amaryllis (*H. reginae*) from Peru contributed its gorgeous, satiny red petals to the cross, while the Brazilian *H. vittatum* gave its hardy con-

The St. Joseph lily, *Hippeastrum ×johnsonii*, with *Phlox pilosa* subsp. *ozarkana* and cornflowers.

stitution, many-flowered umbel, and white, central stripes. This species also seems to be responsible for the trumpet shape of the blooms and for the tolerance of heavy clay soil evidenced by the black-coated bulbs.

After nearly two hundred years, *Hippeastrum ×johnsonii* remains the most prolific and hardy of garden amaryllises. Its bold, crimson trumpets rise in clusters of four to six atop two-foot stems. In most of the South, these blossoms appear in early April. They make exotic companions to irises, columbines, and other hardy perennials of the season.

Hippeastrum ×johnsonii is one of the most cold-hardy amaryllis cultivars, succeeding wherever the ground does not freeze deeply. Partial shade suits the bronze foliage best, but the handsome fountains of leaves will accept direct sun if watered generously through the summer. A good bulb will frequently throw up four spikes of flowers.

Garden Amaryllises

Amaryllises respond readily to the gardener's hand, and the many beautiful species intercross with ease. Large bulbs can be swiftly raised from the papery black seeds, so long as these are very fresh. Half-sterile hybrids, such as *Hippeastrum* ×*johnsonii*, may be shy to bear seed, but most amaryllises will ripen fat pods like gigantic rain lilies.

Fanciers of *Hippeastrum* customarily float seeds in cups of water for a few days to induce germination. Sprouted plantlets may then be potted individually, rather than in flats. This avoids disturbing the young bulbs as they grow.

Seedling amaryllises flourish in containers filled with rich, well-drained compost and topped by a thin layer of sphagnum moss. The pots of tiny bulbs should be set in a warm, brightly lit area, such as an interior windowsill, or outside in bright shade. The seedlings may be covered with plastic bags to retain humidity until they have formed their second sets of leaves. With generous feeding and shelter from frost, seedlings may reach flowering size in two years or less.

In the garden a raised position in good, rich loam, heavily manured and sheltered from strong sun, gives the best results. In the lower South most amaryllises may be left in the ground over winter, if provided good drainage and protective mulches of straw or bagasse. Where the soil remains cold and damp for long periods or where frost penetrates to any depth, only hardier types, such as *Hippeastrum* ×*johnsonii*, may be trusted.

An heirloom garden amaryllis of the Mead strain with *Penstemon tenuis*. Photo by Lauren S. Ogden.

Most garden amaryllises are hybrids descended from various South American species. Some of the pioneer work with these plants was performed by Henry Nehrling at his nursery near Gotha, Florida. Nehrling's plants were developed further by Theodore L. Mead of Oviedo, and eventually became the Mead strain of amaryllises. These tough, hardy plants became popular during the early twentieth century. Their small- to medium-sized, mostly pink-striped blooms may still be seen in gardens throughout the South.

A particularly common Mead hybrid with green-throated flowers and white petals, penciled lightly in red, is sometimes passed along by gardeners as the similarly colored species, *Hippeastrum vittatum*. This old cultivar also seems similar to the hippeastrum offered in the Dutch trade as 'Ambiance'. By whatever name, it is a fine garden flower, with good, coppery-stained foliage and abundant flowers in April. Unlike many amaryllises, these are of a usefully pale shade, mixing well with other spring flowers.

After World War II, nurseries began distributing the fabulous, large-flowered amaryllises of Holland. These descend from *Hippeastrum leopoldii*, a huge, scarlet-flowered species originally collected around 1870 by Richard W. Pearce, who journeyed to South America on behalf of Veitch, the famous English horticultural firm. These immense, showy Dutch hybrids have become the common amaryllises of gardens. In addition to fine reds, pinks, salmons, and whites, the modern hybrid strains include colorful doubles and unique picotees. When properly grown, most send up at least two four-flowered scapes.

Although this group has been bred mainly for pot culture, vigorous clones

St. Joseph lilies (*Hippeastrum ×johnsonii*). Photo by Lauren S. Ogden.

Red Dutch hybrid amaryllises with baby blue eyes (*Nemophila phacelioides*).

such as 'Appleblossom', the favorite pink, make good border flowers in the lower South. Similar crosses developed in South Africa also show excellent vigor and work well in gardens. Home-grown hybrids between the Dutch or African strains and *Hippeastrum × johnsonii* or the hardy Mead strain are usually excellent landscape performers.

Species and Species Crosses

Of the fabulous wild amaryllis species, the American belladonna lily (*Hippeastrum puniceum*) is the most cultivated in gardens along the Gulf Coast. Its lilting, scarlet blossoms, usually appearing in pairs, have an exotic, orchidlike personality. In the wild this species ranges from the West Indies to Bolivia and varies in color from red to pink and near-yellow. The common, orange garden strain appears to be a sterile triploid; 'Semiplenum' ('Albertii') is a very old double selection. Although bulbs of *H. puniceum* endure considerable cold, they often flower poorly after harsh winters.

The yellow-flowered belladonna of Bolivia, *Hippeastrum evansiae*, was used by California breeder C. D. Cothran to create the sulfury hybrid 'Yellow Pioneer'. This unique color break in amaryllises has been further developed through such cultivars as 'Lemon Lime' and 'Green Goddess', with creamy, yellowish petals around green throats. 'Germa', another primrose-toned selection, exhibits trumpet-shaped blooms and seems to descend from the desert-dwelling Argentine *H. parodii*. It should tolerate more drought and cold than most amaryllises.

Hippeastrum striatum is a nasturtium-red variety from the Cerro del Mar of southeastern Brazil. The old selection 'Fulgida' is marked with radiating bands of scarlet, creamy keels, and a pale star in the center of the blooms. This strain has been a popular houseplant in America for generations and may be seen in subtropical gardens around the world. Another variant of the species, var. *crocatum*, has pale yellowish flowers and sometimes persists in old Florida gardens.

The easy-growing bulbs of *H. striatum* spread by short stolons and summer happily in the ground, but may rot over winter if conditions become overly cool and damp. *Hippeastrum blossfeldiae* and *H. petiolatum*, related species from southeastern Brazil and northeast Argentina, are sometimes included as forms of *H. striatum*.

The miniature Dutch amaryllises often referred to as gracilis hybrids, such as 'Pamela' and 'Scarlet Baby', descend from *Hippeastrum striatum* and have similar grace and beauty. These make excellent garden flowers in the lower South, reaching twelve to fifteen inches in height. They offer a more natural-looking habit than the large,

Hippeastrum striatum.

sometimes stiff, Dutch hybrids, making them easier to blend into mixed plantings.

Although spectacularly prolific as a parent of hybrids, the original *Hippeastrum leopoldii* disappeared from cultivation before the close of the nineteenth century. Nothing like the species was seen again in the wild until the 1960s, when Dr. Martin Cardenas collected bulbs in the department of La Paz, Bolivia. With his re-collected *H. neoleopoldii* and the related *H. pardinum* (leopard amaryllis), he developed a gorgeous hybrid, which he christened 'Sumac Pinini' ("most beautiful flower" in the native Aymara language of Bolivia). Dutch nurserymen have propagated this lovely amaryllis and made it widely available under a less romantic name, 'Spotty'. The spreading blossoms are dotted and dashed all over with terracotta freckling. The small bulbs grow easily and offset swiftly. Another modern hybrid, 'Santa Cruz', also shows some of the wild character of the Andean amaryllises.

Even more exotic are species such as *Hippeastrum cybister* (spider amaryllis), with naked stems topped by narrow-petaled, tan to maroon, insectlike blossoms. This is native to dry areas of southern Bolivia. Fred Meyer of California actively developed this species, and several of his introductions have become available as novelty amaryllis. 'Chico', 'Reggae', and 'Rosario' are spidery bicolored hybrids of *H. cybister* with twisted, bronze-red and green petals. 'Ruby Meyer' offers dark, wine-colored petals like a somber orchid. 'Lima' and 'La Paz', providing spidery green blooms suffused with rose and wine colors, are among several hybrids of *H. cybister* with the winter-growing butterfly amaryllis, *H. papilio*; they will sometimes flower in fall as well as spring. 'Emerald' is another in this group that affords pale, green-throated, star-shaped blossoms, lightly penciled in red. 'Merengue' is a luscious, coppery apricot of orchidlike form. 'Inca' offers arresting dark crimson blooms, like a multi-flowering sprekelia.

The aquatic *Hippeastrum angustifolium* has a similar spidery appearance, but with a more scarlet tone. This odd species comes from southeastern Brazil and looks like a bright red, narrow-petaled orchid. Although difficult to obtain, it is easy to grow immersed in a garden pond and seems entirely hardy in the lower South.

With its long-tubed, white flowers, the fragrant *Hippeastrum brasilianum* resembles an Easter lily more than an amaryllis. It is one of several long-tubed species that may be hybridized to create novel, trumpeting amaryllises. 'Amputo' is a scented cultivar of this type, with graceful, pure white trumpet-shaped blooms on plants similar in stature to the gracilis hybrids. 'Pink Floyd', another Meyer introduction, seems to have much of the character of the Venezuelan trumpet-flowered *H. doraniae*, with sweet-scented, rose-pink blossoms, lightly striped with white.

'Mrs. Garfield', an old tropical evergreen cultivar, bears small, pink-flecked white blooms and wide, oval leaves with distinctive ivory stripes down the center. It is common in Florida gardens and makes a beautiful planting for shaded borders, handsome in leaf even when it is not in bloom. This tender amaryllis descends from a cross of the Brazilian *Hippeastrum reticulatum* var. *striatifolium* and an old red hybrid, 'Defiance'.

Hippeastrum 'Sumac Pinini' ('Spotty').

The greatest challenge to growing all these amaryllises lies in their susceptibility to mosaic viruses, for *Hippeastrum*, like *Lilium*, often succumbs to this disease. Strong-growing hybrids such as *H. ×johnsonii* may continue to multiply and flower even when leaves are visibly streaked with mosaic, but their performances will pale in comparison to uninfected bulbs. Diseased bulbs should be discarded and replaced with healthy seed-grown stock at the earliest opportunity.

The Lily of the Palace

One section of *Hippeastrum* seems resistant or tolerant to virus infection and offers hope for developing healthier hybrids. These are the forms and relatives of the winter-growing *H. aulicum* (lily of the palace), comprising the subgenus *Omphalissa*. 'Ackermanii', the result of a cross between *H. aulicum* and *H.* ×*johnsonii*, is a forerunner of the Mead strain and probably accounts for the vigor of these old varieties. This old hybrid is a common garden plant in the South, nearly as hardy and well loved as the St. Joseph lily, with similarly bright red, but less trumpet-shaped blooms.

The rich red, modern hybrid 'Voodoo', also known as 'Naughty Lady', is readily confused with *Hippeastrum* 'Ackermanii' or even *H.* ×*johnsonii*, as it shares their dark crimson petals and white starlike throat patterns. This suggests similar ancestry, and 'Voodoo' seems to adapt well to garden life in the South. The richly colored flowers appear in late April, slightly after *H.* ×*johnsonii*. 'Pasadena', a double-flowered hybrid, and 'Baby Star', a smaller variety, are otherwise similar to 'Voodoo'.

Hippeastrum aulicum itself is an easy-growing, odd flower with a muted red and green color scheme. The thick, sturdy foliage comes up in autumn, with the blooms following before Christmas. With its winter growth cycle, *H. aulicum* must be protected from hard frosts.

Butterfly amaryllis (*Hippeastrum papilio*), a spectacular mahogany-and-chartreuse cousin of *H. aulicum*, has become popular as a pot plant and as a garden flower in near frost-free regions. Like *H. aulicum*, it prefers a winter growth cycle and often flowers in late autumn. This amazingly striated blossom was discovered in the state of Santa Catarina, Brazil, by the Argentine collector Dr. Carlos A. Gomez Rupple. 'Jaguar', a robust hybrid of *H. papilio* with similarly striated blooms, and 'Giraffe', a pale green hybrid of the species marked with beautiful reddish

Double-flowering *Hippeastrum* 'Pasadena' threads through stems of the white tea rose 'Mme Joseph Schwartz'.

pencilings, have proven successful in Southern gardens; unlike *H. papilio*, these flower in the spring and quickly multiply into attractive clumps.

Hippeastrum bukasovii, another beautiful relation of *H. aulicum*, should become popular when better known. It is an arresting Peruvian amaryllis with petals changing abruptly from dark red to greenish yellow at the tips. Another aulicum type, *H. calyptratum* (green amaryllis), is a bizarre evergreen with orchidlike, chartreuse blossoms. Although this species is a tree-dweller and entirely frost tender, it may be intercrossed with garden amaryllises to produce intriguing hybrids.

Hippeastrum 'Jaguar'. Photo by Lauren S. Ogden.

More in tune to the South's summer schedule of growth is the spring-flowering *Hippeastrum iguazuanum*, a rare species from Iguazu Falls on the Rio de La Plata. The parrot amaryllis (*H. psittacinum*), which grows in the region between Rio de Janeiro and Sao Paulo, is similar. These species have waxy foliage like *H. aulicum*, but are deciduous in winter and may be counted hardy. Their flowers look like gigantic versions of *Alstroemeria psittacina*, which inhabits the same region.

Best of all is a cross of *Hippeastrum aulicum* and a rare miniature, pink-flowered belladonna, *H. traubii* f. *doranianum*. The result, 'San Antonio Rose', is a tough, vigorous plant with glossy, flattened, red-edged leaves and gorgeous twin-flowered scapes of rosy red blooms. These appear following rains in early summer, long after most amaryllises have finished for the season. This hybrid has handsome foliage ideal for the foreground of a subtropical border and is hardy all along the Gulf.

Hippeastrum 'Giraffe'. Photo by Lauren S. Ogden.

Aztec Lilies

The Aztec lily (*Sprekelia formosissima*), one of the most beautiful flowers of the Americas, can often be found in the wild growing along with crowds of rain lilies, lording over the hillsides like motherly orchids set among the rocks. The deep-rooted bulbs seek out shallow pockets of soil, enjoying the same rugged terrain and semiarid conditions as many zephyranthes.

The Aztec lily ranges widely across Mexico, as well as through the mountains of Central and South America. Orchidlike, crimson blooms rise from the sides of the black-coated bulbs in response to rain, appearing in both spring and fall. When seen in the sun, these appear to be dusted with gold. The specific name *formosissima* ("most handsome") is apt.

Long, green, upright leaves sprout from the necks of the bulbs all summer, and offsets appear at a steady

Hippeastrum 'San Antonio Rose' blooming with a feathery backdrop of broom fern, *Asparagus virgatus*.

Aztec lilies, *Sprekelia formosissima*.

pace. If differing clones are intercrossed, seed readily ripens and grows off quickly, in the same way as amaryllises.

'Orient Red' is a rich-colored selection that bears white stripes on the keels of its petals in fall, but not in spring. 'Peru' is a dark, velvety red throughout. Both are good garden plants in the South, performing better than the common commercial cultivar, 'Superba', which was developed for pot culture and often must be dug and stored to induce bloom. Like most Mexican plants, *Sprekelia formosissima* is hardy in the South.

A bigeneric hybrid, ×*Hippeastrelia* 'Mystique', derives from a surprising cross of *Hippeastrum* and *Sprekelia*. Its broad, red flowers show both the orchid-like beauty of *Sprekelia* and the size of Dutch amaryllises. Surprisingly, 'Mystique' sets abundant seed when pollinated by plants of either genus. Although this curious flower has not been in gardens long, it seems vigorous and hardy in the South.

Veld Lilies

The summer-rainfall regions of South Africa around the Drakensberg ("dragon mountains") house a number of intriguing bulbs adaptable to the South. Most respond to more careful care than crinums and prefer richer soils and abundant moisture. They thrive with cool root runs in the warm season, preferring sheltered, well-drained positions in winter. Partial shade is usually helpful.

Cyrtanthus obrienii (Ifafa lily) is a showy amaryllis relation from KwaZulu-Natal with grassy leaves like rain lilies and curved tubular blossoms colored an electric orange-red. This is one of over fifty *Cyrtanthus* species from South Africa, several of which seem adaptable to the South. The blooms and foliage of *C. obrienii* appear together in early summer following showers. *Cyrtanthus mackenii* is a similar species available in numerous color forms, most with a delightful fragrance. Both species seem to perform best in the South if given well-drained soil and fairly dry conditions in winter.

Cyrtanthus obrienii (Ifafa lily).

Scadoxus multiflorus, the torch lily or *bloedblom* ("blood flower"), has similar wants. Its magnificent globes of spidery red florets appear in late spring, followed by attractive rosettes of dark green, oval leaves. These appear on top of a short false stem formed by the leaf bases. In full shade the beautiful foliage remains dark, glossy green all summer. In autumn the stems ripen bright orange-red globular fruits.

The spectacular *Scadoxus puniceus* (paintbrush lily) is one of Africa's most striking bulbous plants. Native to shady areas in coastal bush, ravines, and forest, it offers its glowing cinnabar blooms in large, dome-shaped clusters, cupped by several purplish red bracts. These appear with rains in early summer, with the leaves expanding afterward. The paintbrush lily ranges from the Northern Province of South Africa through the Free State, KwaZulu-Natal, the Eastern Cape, and into tropical Africa. There is a beautiful white-flowered form as well.

These showy tropical bulbs were formerly included in the genus *Haemanthus*. *Scadoxus multiflorus* is still listed by many nurseries under its old name, *H. katherinae*, and *S. puniceus* under *H. magnificus*. Gardeners usually keep these showy bulbs in pots, bedding them under trees for summer, but in the lower South they are hardy and permanent on well-drained soils. Their whorled leaves appear atop short false stems, making attractively lush rosettes through the summer.

Although most *Nerine* species perform poorly in the South, the thread-leafed *N. filifolia* has proven successful. The eight-inch, chivelike foliage sprouts from thick clusters of small, white bulbs. In October and November these send up slender stalks topped with clusters of wavy-edged, narrow-petaled blooms like a miniature, rose-pink lycoris. The plants seem to prosper on damp soils, replacing their leaves continuously so as to be almost evergreen. This hardy species grows along the Drakensberg range in the Eastern Cape, Free State, Swaziland, and Mpumalanga.

The pineapple lily, or *wildepynappel* (*Eucomis* spp.), is a curious member of the hyacinth family. Its long-lasting, clustered summer blooms resemble the fruit of a pineapple, complete with rosettes of leaves on the top. The globular bulbs are easily grown on well-watered ground, either clay or sand, and remarkably hardy to winter cold.

Scadoxus multiflorus in a raised bed, Mercer Arboretum, Humble, Texas.

Introduced from KwaZulu-Natal in 1878, *Eucomis bicolor* is the most common species in cultivation. Its ample flower stems reach eighteen inches and bear many tightly packed, greenish, nodding blossoms. These are edged in purple, and topped with a tuft of green leaves. The wavy-edged basal rosettes are attractive and structural in appearance. This is a choice specimen plant for a sunny, damp position, and makes a good underplanting for clematis, enjoying the same cool root runs as these flowering vines.

The wine eucomis (*Eucomis comosa*) has some of the most beautiful flowers in the genus, varying from white to pink or wine-purple. Foliage also varies in tone; and the variety *striata* has given rise to several showy bronze-leafed forms such as 'Sparkling Burgundy'. Leaves of the wine eucomis are more flaccid than those of *E. bicolor*, but still make a good summer showing. This species was formerly known as *E. punctata*.

Several others of the roughly fifteen species of *Eucomis* would be worth planting in the South. *Eucomis pole-evansii*, the tallest of the pineapple lilies, reaches up to six feet in the wild, but usually less in the South; *E. zambesiaca* has some of the loveliest pendant white flowers; chartreuse-flowered *E. autumnalis* makes a striking all-green architectural subject; *E. vandermerwei* is a charming dwarf with purplish blooms and splotched foliage.

Another useful lily from the eastern provinces of South Africa is *Ornithogalum saundersiae*. This species has big, grayish rosettes with blunt leaves, appearing much like *Eucomis* in foliage. Soaring, three-foot stems carry globular clusters of milky, up-facing flowers in midsummer. Plants grow easily on any soil, but winter best on dry, sandy ground.

Several South African bulbs belong to the similar genus *Albuca*, recently included by some botanists in *Ornithogalum*. Its members offer white- or yellow-petaled flowers striped green on the reverse, as in *Ornithogalum*, but in *Albuca* the blooms remained partly closed and often nod gracefully like

The wine eucomis (*Eucomis comosa*).

fritillaries. Some of these make intriguing garden bulbs in the South, and many might be experimented with.

A plant often sold as *Albuca nelsonii* (candelabrum lily) may actually be *A. fastigiata* or *A. batteniana*, as it grows with its large, green bulbs exposed above the ground. (True *A. nelsonii* has a buried bulb.) Whatever its identity, this plant is a strong grower, resistant to drought, with attractive, succulent, green rosettes and showy white flowers in late spring and often again in fall. The bulbs seem perfectly hardy into the high teens, and the leaves remain evergreen into the low twenties. With pendant, yellow blossoms, and leaves that smell of anise when crushed, *A. shawii* is another native of the northeast Cape and KwaZulu-Natal that might prosper in the South.

In the semiarid regions of South Africa, a number of scilla-like lilies have evolved bulbs to store water. In nature these usually rest above the surface of the soil, as in the *Albuca* species just described. At least one such plant, *Drimiopsis maculata*, thrives in the lower South, enduring modest frost. The bulbs of *Drimiopsis* are fleshy, primitive affairs, with large, visible scales like true lilies. In summer they carry nondescript spikes of small, white blooms and attractive rosettes of hostalike foliage. The leaves, speckled prominently with maroon dots, luxuriate in full or partial shade. With rich soil, the bulbs multiply at a terrific pace. The clumps stay low, six inches or less, and make an intriguing edging for summer borders.

Ledebouria is a similar South African genus with bulbs either above or below the soil level. Deciduous types with mostly below-ground bulbs such as *L. cooperi* and *L.* sp. 'Gary Hammer' are thoroughly hardy in the South. Varieties with above-ground bulbs and evergreen foliage such as *L. concolor*

A pineapple lily, *Eucomis pole-evansii*, flowering at Plant Delights Nursery in North Carolina, with silvery leaves of *Hibiscus grandiflorus* as a background.

Drimiopsis maculata with dwarf *Aloe* 'Crosby's Prolific' and daylily foliage.

and *L. socialis* (better known as *Scilla lutea* and *S. violacea*, respectively) make good subjects near the Gulf. These have intriguing mottled or striped foliage, like *Drimiopsis*, and rather poor, muscari-like spikes of bloom.

Lily of the Nile

The splendid *Agapanthus* (lily of the Nile, flower of love) is the best known and most cherished of South African blossoms. Invaluable stems of blue or white blooms bring a cool, bright loveliness to summer gardens unmatched by other flowers. The lush tufts of slick, green leaves are an attractive feature in themselves and make a perfect foil for the globular clusters of bloom. Set in a tub on a terrace, a flowering agapanthus always looks smart, and requires no companion or ornament to enhance its beauty. The botanist Charles Louis L'Heritier de Brutelle, with appreciation for the special qualities of these plants, named the genus from the Greek words *agape* and *anthos*, meaning "flower of love."

The individual blossoms of *Agapanthus* resemble lily blooms but sit in large umbels like *Allium*. Some varieties have more or less drooping, tubular florets; others have blooms that spread widely like bells or funnels. The blue coloring is usually darkest on the keels. Flower stems may reach from two to up to six feet. In most varieties they arch gracefully toward the strongest light, so this should be taken into account when positioning clumps in the border. Fleshy roots spread widely over the surface of the soil and support a short, more or less tuberous rootstock holding several leeklike false stems.

Few genera are as badly confused in horticulture as *Agapanthus*. Navigating the treacherous botany of this genus is, however, a necessity for Southerners. Only a handful of varieties truly prosper in this climate, and these have many impostors.

The more common nursery strains in America derive mostly from the evergreen *Agapanthus praecox* subsp. *orientalis*, which is found on stony slopes and in grassland from the southeastern Cape to KwaZulu-Natal; in horticulture this species is often sold as *A. africanus* or *A. umbellatus*. Although certain forms of subsp. *orientalis* and also *Agapanthus praecox* subsp. *minimus* cultivars, such as the dwarf 'Peter Pan', succeed in mild parts of the South, they tend to rot away during the winter if subjected to hard frost or planted on heavy soil. Large-statured cultivars, such as the old, white 'Albus', cream-striped 'Variegatus', or double blue 'Flore Pleno', are slow growing but more enduring than common seedlings; these robust forms are sometimes listed as varieties under the names *A. umbellatus* var. *maximus* or *A. giganteus*. California nurseryman J. N. Giridlian developed several hybrids from *A. praecox* subsp. *orientalis*, including 'Albatross', a gigantic white with over one hundred fifty blooms to a cluster, and the brilliantly colored five-foot-tall 'Blue Skyrocket'.

Gardeners in the South often treat these evergreen agapanthus varieties as summer annuals, keeping their roots in pots, or bedding fresh plants out for summer in part shade. Mulching sometimes helps to bring clumps through winter, but it may do more damage than good if the ground remains soggy.

More cold-hardy, deciduous agapanthus such as the Headbourne hybrids descend from *Agapanthus campanulatus*, a species found in moist grasslands and on rocky hillsides from the Eastern Cape to the Northern Province of South Africa. *Agapanthus campanulatus* demands rich, peaty ground and unfailing moisture in order to provide its blue summer flowers. Although winter hardy, these are only likely to succeed in the coolest, most temperate parts of the South.

Garden forms of hardy agapanthus include 'Mooreanus', an old selection made by Sir Frederick Moore of Glasnevin in 1879. Some authorities list this semi-deciduous dwarf variety, also known as 'Minor', under *Agapanthus campanulatus*. The narrow leaves are deep green and in midsummer send up several straight, eighteen-inch spikes topped with radiant clusters of exquisite blue flowers. 'Mooreanus' grows readily on rich, well-watered soil and makes a beautiful summer companion for orange montbretias.

The most successful garden agapanthus for Southerners, however, is a 1990 introduction bred and released by Archie Amate through the Los Angeles State and County Arboretum. Called 'Ellamae', this beautiful semi-deciduous plant makes three-foot clumps of deep green, straplike, pendulous leaves, topped by loose, eight-inch umbels of blue-violet flowers. The richly colored blooms appear in late June, several weeks after common cultivars of *Agapanthus praecox* subsp. *orientalis*. Held on thick, three- to five-foot stems, projecting well above the tapered foliage, several of the intensely colored flowers hang down from the tall stalks like bluebells.

The refreshing semi-pendulous blooms of *Agapanthus* 'Ellamae'.

The pendulous character of these flowers seems to be an inheritance from the drooping agapanthus (*A. inapertus*), an attractive, tuberous species native to open grasslands along the Drakensberg escarpment. The beautiful, dark blue to violet (or occasionally white) flowers of *A. inapertus* are pollinated by sunbirds, who perch on the thick stalks in order reach up into the drooping blossoms. Its gray-green, strap-shaped foliage occurs in groups of six to eight leaves per shoot, forming thick false stems at the base of the plant. In its

The tapered, leeklike foliage of *Agapanthus* 'Ellamae' shows the influence of *A. inapertus*.

homeland *A. inapertus* is naturally deciduous and goes completely dormant during the dry winter months.

'Ellamae' seems to combine the leeklike foliage and tolerance for winter cold of the drooping agapanthus with a capacity to endure in warm climates typical of evergreen *Agapanthus praecox* subsp. *orientalis* cultivars. 'Elaine', a similar plant from the same California breeding program, is shorter, with darker violet blossoms in slightly smaller clusters and light green, upright foliage more typical of *A. inapertus*. 'Storm Cloud' is another hybrid in this group with open clusters of deep blue-purple nodding blooms. 'Mood Indigo', with three-foot stems of deep violet, tubular blossoms in mid to late summer, is winter-deciduous like its *A. inapertus* parent.

Divisions of any of these agapanthus may be made in spring or fall, or immediately after flowering, as long as care is taken to avoid unnecessary damage to the fleshy, white roots. Plants may take a year to settle in before blooming at full capacity, but are otherwise simple to grow in part shade. Seedlings are also easily raised and may be expected to flower in their third year. Good soil preparation and ample watering will be repaid in a refreshing abundance of cool, midsummer blossoms.

Tuberoses

In 1519 the army of Cortez descended to the beautiful, lake-filled Valley of Mexico. The Spaniards walked in wonder over well-built causeways ushering travelers to the fearsome, skull-topped walls of the Aztec capital, Tenochtitlan. As they entered the gates of the city, the soldiers marveled at lush gardens and wondrous markets filled with fruits and flowers. One of the blossoms they encountered was a surpassingly fragrant, waxy white bloom that grew from a clustering, spindle-shaped bulb.

The Aztecs cultivated many flowers; they appreciated the poetic contrast of beautiful, ephemeral blossoms with the gruesome traditions of their religion. Captives were taken in mock battles called "wars of flowers," then prepared by priests for sacrifice with obsidian knives. Glistening white *omixochitl* ("flowers of bone") were associated with these rituals, and were held sacred to Xochiquetzal, the goddess of art, beauty, and love.

The Aztec's universe crumbled at the hands of the conquistadores, but the flowers of their gardens continued to grow and blossom, and soon passed to many other lands. Ninety years after the conquest of Mexico, Clusius wrote the first full account of the omixochitl, now known to gardeners as the tuberose, *Polianthes tuberosa*.

As early as 1530 a missionary returning from the Indies, Father Theophilus Minuti, introduced tuberoses to his garden at Toulon, France. The variety he grew, 'Mexican Single', has narrow, grassy foliage and long, tubular florets. The individual blossoms, radiating stiffly from the tall, slender stems, expand six short petals at their tips, forming a small white star. Parkinson knew this flower as the "greater Indian Knobbed Jacinth" and said that it had a "very sweet scent, or rather strong and heades."

In addition to the single tuberoses, early gardeners grew a variegated sport with creamy margins on the leaves. The first double originated as a seedling raised by M. Le Cour of Leyden, Holland, who considered the plant to be the finest flower in the world and hoarded his stock for many years. In 1870 the Flushing, New York, nurseryman John Henderson discovered a dwarfer, larger-flowered double tuberose with especially broad, dark foliage. This he named 'Pearl', and it soon became the most popular of all Victorian blossoms.

The lovely, waxlike flowers of 'Pearl' are fully double and resemble spikes of miniature gardenias. Their rich, exotic fragrance makes them highly prized cut flowers, as well as garden ornaments. Both the single and double tuberoses have been embraced by flower-loving countries such as India, where they are cultivated for use in religious ceremonies. Although centuries old, 'Mexican Single', 'Variegata', and 'Pearl' are all still widely grown.

Each flowering tuberose produces many offsets in a season, and any reaching or exceeding thumb size may be expected to flower in the following summer. One common pest, the soil nematode, or eelworm, sometimes attacks old clumps of tuberoses in the garden, preventing the bulbs from properly sizing up and ripening for the following year. As long as the bulbs are annually dug up and reset in fresh, well-manured ground, this pest can be kept at bay, and blossoms may be expected in abundance.

The fragrant tuberose, *Polianthes tuberosa* 'Mexican Single'.

In summer heat 'Mexican Single' is the most reliable variety; this is the most "perennial" type suited to the South. Doubles respond to more careful handling. Large bulbs of 'Pearl' should be held for delayed planting in June, so that the blossoms will not open until cool, autumn weather prevails. Small bulbs may be set out earlier, and will have time to mature before September flowering. Nothing could be more wondrous than the fragrance of these evening flowers wafting on fresh autumn breezes.

Around the town of Grasse, in Provence, the French perfume industry annually harvests over 2.2 million pounds of tuberoses. Within hours of picking, the blossoms travel to nearby factories, where they are laid between layers of refined Italian lard. There the petals remain for forty-eight hours, so that the blooms may continue to manufacture and exhale their perfume for the fat to absorb. This is then slightly melted and reformed and frozen into the waxy concentrate known as pomade. From pomade the perfumeries produce alcoholic washings of fragrance, which are in turn distilled to obtain the pure flower oils. Only the most perfect blossoms are used for this process. Tuberose is usually extracted at night, since it is especially fragrant after sunset.

Although widespread in gardens, *Polianthes tuberosa* has never been collected in habitat; it may have been driven to extinction in pre-Columbian times. It has, however, several beautiful wild relations that are little grown but adaptable to Southern conditions. Some of these, such as *P. nelsoni*, *P. palustris*, and *P. pringlei*, are fragrant, white, night-bloomers, like small versions of 'Mexican Single'. Others, such as the scarlet Mexican twinflower (*P. geminiflora*), have colorful, paired blossoms designed to attract hummingbirds. *Polianthes ×blissii* is a sunset-colored hybrid.

Polianthes ×bundrantii 'Mexican Firecracker'.

Polianthes howardii, a unique tuberose species from the state of Colima, Mexico, is especially easy-growing and garden-worthy. It produces two- to three-foot wands of solitary, red and green blossoms with near-black interiors. A vigorous pastel orange, red, and purplish hybrid with 'Mexican Single' is *P.* ×*bundrantii* 'Mexican Firecracker'. These are easy garden flowers in the South and multiply rapidly with good care. The shallow-growing bulbs may be protected from hard frosts by resetting at depth each autumn or covering with thick mulches of straw.

Rattlesnake Master

Gardeners are usually surprised to learn that a close cousin of the tuberose is native to the South. The rattlesnake master, or American aloe (*Manfreda virginica*), is a very neglected wildflower. It is known to botanists mostly as a step-child of the century plant genus, *Agave*, and to gardeners hardly at all. Although tough, interesting, and attractive, manfredas have yet to be widely appreciated.

These relatives of *Polianthes* prosper in the South and are especially enduring in drought. Nematodes occasionally cause difficulty, inhibiting proper blooming and growth, but may be simply and easily discouraged by planting the massive, tuberous roots on raised beds of lime rubble or decomposed granite.

The odd nicknames of this plant derive from its use among native peoples of Mexico and the southeastern United States. The Catawba of North and South Carolina mashed the starchy rootstocks of the local *Manfreda virginica* and drank its juice as an antidote to snakebite, hence rattlesnake master.

Huaco and *amole* are aboriginal Mexican names. Tradition holds that a snake-eating bird called the huaco uses manfreda to cure itself when it has been bitten. Amole refers to a cleansing lather made by crushing the swollen roots. Commercial preparations of amole soap harvested from native manfredas were once sold in Texas for use as shampoo.

Tall, honey-scented, green and cinnamon bottlebrushes rise from the succulent, leafy rosettes of *Manfreda virginica* in early summer. These odd flowers lack obvious petals, but thickened, waxy stamens project to form the feathery blossoms.

The substantial, pointed leaves offer an attraction, perhaps greater than the blooms, forming neat rosettes like dwarf aloes or agaves. This waxy, deciduous foliage is usually slick and gray, but may be marked with interesting maroon blotches or dots. Clumps multiply and serve admirably as edgings for beds in partial shade. In the wild, *Manfreda virginica* ranges from the Atlantic seaboard to central Texas. It grows happily on poor, dry soil and frequents mixed oak woodlands, prairies, and railroad embankments.

Even more beautiful are the evergreen, succulent-leafed manfredas of south Texas and Mexico. Their fleshy rosettes are uniquely handsome and their spicily scented blossoms develop thick, waxy petals like tuberoses. In the tall-growing varieties these are further enhanced by long-projecting stamens. These manfredas endure frost as low as 20°F with little damage to their fleshy foliage. They recover quickly if frozen back to the bulb. A winter mulch of straw will see them through more severe cold.

Manfreda maculosa (spice lily), the most widespread species in southern Texas, may be seen blooming in summer or fall following periods of rain. Fragrant blossoms open creamy petals, which fade gradually to somber purplish olive, so that the two-foot spikes grade from dark to light as the buds open from the bottom. The very fleshy foliage usually has rows of soft teeth on the margins and abundant brownish red spots.

In nature *Manfreda maculosa* grows in the shade of shrubs and dwarf trees, but it will accept sun if given plenty of water. The same conditions suit Runyon's manfreda (*M. longiflora*), a rare miniature variety from the lower Rio Grande Valley. It has night-scented blooms like *M. maculosa*, but with long tubes and starry petals that fade to pink, rather than brown. The foliage is very slender and striated with tan pencilings.

The large-growing manfreda of the lower Rio Grande, *Manfreda sileri*, bears oddly flaccid, bluish leaves, marked with large purple blotches. The five-foot spikes of flowers are especially beautiful, carrying dozens of upward-facing, chartreuse blossoms, which open gradually over a period of three weeks.

Night-flying hawk moths are frequent visitors to these summer or autumn blooms. Hummingbirds too seem to love them, often perching on the stalks in early morning. The stiff, slightly woody flower stems never need staking and are a welcome addition to windy gardens, where these elegantly tall plants provide some of the most graceful flowers that can be grown.

Several manfredas from Texas and Mexico send up equally tall stems topped with modest groups of brownish green blooms. One variety has been grown in Texas gardens for many years as *Manfreda variegata*, making valuable clumps of evergreen leaves that are more succulent and narrow than *M. sileri*. This old garden plant refuses to set seed and displays all the vigor one might expect from a garden hybrid: it may be an old cross of *M. sileri* and *M. maculosa*.

Farther south in Mexico in the lush Sierra Madre, plants with very different, unspotted foliage grow on the rugged slopes. An especially beautiful form with undulating, silvery green leaves is common in oak woods near Monterrey. In 1903 J. N. Rose applied the name *Manfreda undulata* to a plant that flowered in a Berlin greenhouse in 1869. It seems hard to imagine a more appropriate epithet for the Monterrey manfredas, and they may be the rightful owners of this old binomial.

In the state of San Luis Potosí, spots return to leaves. The manfredas that grow in this area show great vigor and the capacity to multiply by stolons. An old horticultural strain of this type, distributed by J. N. Giridlian of Oakhurst Gardens as 'Maculata Gigantea', has had wide circulation and is also known as 'Helen Wynans'. Like *M. virginica*, 'Maculata Gigantea' is naturally deciduous and seems very cold-hardy. Its grayish blue leaves are heavily spotted with brown and make a showy patch of succulent herbage, useful for covering dry banks.

Strange as it may seem, the weirdly beautiful manfredas confirm their relation to the tuberose by hybridizing if offered the opportunity. The black, flattened seeds grow easily and flower in their second or third year, so this is a good project for home gardeners. Hybrids recorded so far involve *Manfreda virginica* and *Polianthes tuberosa* 'Mexican Single'. Although these "×*Manfredanthes*" are not always showy, they are vigorous and sometimes inherit the wonderful tuberose fragrance. A cross using the maculate, yellow-green *M. sileri* might be spectacular.

Manfreda sp. 'Maculata Gigantea' ('Helen Wynans').

Naiads

There are some tuberous flowers whose personalities are so sprightly and lithe, one is loath to consign them to the garden border. Even when planted en masse, the slender stems and leaves of the Mexican star (*Milla biflora*) practically disappear from view until their flat, white blossoms expand. Ordinarily, such gracefully carried flowers would be best displayed in pots, but they seem to grow more successfully if plunged in cool ground for summer.

The growth of *Milla* species is geared to the alternating wet and dry cycles of their homes in Mexico and the Southwest. Most need a profound winter rest and a sudden jolt of summer rain to get them growing and flowering on schedule. Although these flowers are hardy in the South, the flattened corms should be dug in autumn and stored over winter to enforce dormancy. Otherwise, even large, healthy roots may fail to leaf out, sleeping quietly underground for years, until they finally waste away.

A gigantic, night-flowering species from southern Mexico, *Milla magnifica*, is one of the few types successful without winter storage. Gray, hollow, onionlike leaves reach three feet in height. Equally tall umbels carry a dozen or more long-tubed blossoms, which are white, with green stripes on the reverse of the petals like *Ornithogalum*. Their fragrance is rich and cloying. Both leaves and flower stems flop over untidily if not supported, but this is a minor fault in an otherwise glorious summer flower. If well treated, the corms reach the size of gladiolus roots. They offset freely, and usually multiply by self-sown seed.

A beautiful companion for *Milla* that enjoys the same treatment is the coral drop (*Bessera elegans*). Dealers in bulbs occasionally offer this native of western Mexico, and gardeners should jump at any opportunity to possess them. There is nothing like a bessera in the floral kingdom.

Threadlike foliage and wiry stems suspend small umbels of incredibly graceful, drooping flowers. These are marked like little birds with bright scarlet or rich purple. Creamy white stripes run through each tiny petal. Slender, dangling, purple stamens and a miniature corona protrude from the center of the blossoms to complete the fantastic accouterments.

Coral drops, reaching twelve inches in height, appear for several weeks in summer. They need the same dry rest as most *Milla* varieties and may be kept in pots or dug and stored. Although rather hardy on sandy, acid soils, they are too beautiful and too difficult to obtain to risk leaving in the ground over winter elsewhere. The tiny, black seeds grow readily and will bloom in their second or third season.

Coral drops (*Bessera elegans*).

Another small Latin American treasure, the glory of the sun (*Leucocoryne ixioides*), offers exquisite, satiny blue blossoms. These have the fragrance of freesias and appear in April or May if corms are planted in January or February. As the roots tend to pull the plants deeply into the soil over the growing season, it is useful to contain them in a mesh or wire bag to make retrieval of the corms easier in early summer. These beguiling Chilean flowers must be kept dry after their leaves die down in summer, but they are otherwise hardy and unparticular. Increase comes by seeds, rather than offsets.

Star Grass

Although not a flower of great glamour, the yellow star grass (*Hypoxis hirsuta*) is a stalwart performer in Southern gardens, quietly blossoming through spring and summer, with an occasional appearance in fall or winter, as well. The little star-shaped blooms have six petals, which are green and slightly hairy on the back but clear yellow on the face. They appear without protest on the heaviest clays and poorest sandy soils. Shade and competition from oak roots hardly slow them down.

The entire plant scarcely passes a foot in height, and the leaves resemble hairy, green clumps of grass. The cheery, yellow blooms, coming in small groups, stand out in spite of their small size. These cormous plants ripen small pods of seeds, which look like black grains of sand. They grow throughout the eastern United States and are entirely hardy.

The showier members of the star grass family come from Latin America and Africa. The Argentine *Hypoxis decumbens* seems nearly as tough as our native yellow star grass, but forms lush clumps with much larger, richer, golden blossoms. In early summer these appear in masses large enough to smother the foliage. *Hypoxis decumbens* makes a superb foreground specimen, beautiful associated with mounds of sky-blue *Plumbago capensis*.

With leaves held in ranks of three like a large, ground-hugging sedge, *Hypoxis hemerocallidea* displays butter-yellow flowers similar to *H. decumbens*, but larger. This is an attractive garden plant with slightly hairy leaves, silvered underneath and recurved in a striking sicklelike pattern. Previously known as *H. rooperii*, this species has a long history in traditional South African medicine. The large, hairy corms (popularly known as ape's armpits) contain substances that help boost the immune system, presently of critical importance in treating the effects of HIV.

The red star, *rooisterretjie* (*Rhodohypoxis baurii*), is a related, rose-colored flower from South Africa that has become popular as a subject for pots. Charming, solitary, rosy pink blooms appear all summer on stems only four inches high. Although rather hardy, the tubers are liable to rot over the winter if not kept dry, so they should be lifted or placed in raised beds of gritty soil. In the summer growing season they enjoy damp conditions.

Orchids

The South has several beautiful wild orchids that grow from tubers. Unless you garden in a boggy meadow filled with insect-eating pitcher plants, however, or a deep, shady glade beneath gigantic stands of beech, these shy blossoms are unlikely prospects for cultivation. Even with care, most transplant poorly. Wild stands should be noted and cherished in place, left to bloom unmolested. These shy blossoms are happier without undue human attention.

One tuberous orchid that takes kindly to the gardener's hand is the Chinese ground orchid, *Bletilla striata*, and this should be in every garden. All it asks is a bit of shade in the hottest part of the summer and an annual dressing of autumn leaves. This helps to shelter the precocious spikes of bloom, which come too early in spring to be safe from late frosts. In return the gardener will enjoy several dainty, true orchid blossoms and a long summer of attractive, pleated leaves. These look like rich green, dwarf aspidistra foliage, and they spread luxuriantly in any shady position.

The common form of the ground orchid is a vibrant rosy purple, but there is also a good white, 'Alba'. Some forms offer an added attraction of creamy-white picotee margins on the foliage. 'Albostriata' is a pink-flowered variegate of this type; 'First Kiss' is a white-blooming variety with striped foliage and just a touch of rose-purple on the lip. 'Innocence', an exquisite selection from Harlan Hammernick, has lush green foliage and pearly white blooms, delicately blushed lavender on the lip. The blooms of all these cultivars have a typical orchid shape, with furrowed lower lips and five spreading petals. They appear in March or April, held in clusters of five or six just above the leaves.

In China these robust flowers grow on the margins of thickets, and occur

Chinese ground orchid (*Bletilla striata*).

from sea level up to ten thousand feet in the mountains of western Yunnan. The fleshy, U-shaped tubers divide annually, so the clumps increase at a steady pace. *Bletilla* orchids are entirely charming and rewarding flowers. They are almost foolishly easy to grow, yet convey an air of distinction to shady borders, where they make a handsome textural combination with ferns, boulders, or other natural features.

Several rarer species of *Bletilla* inhabit eastern Asia. Although these are less vigorous than *B. striata*, they can be accommodated in cool, shaded positions with rich, peaty soil and generous, leafy mulches. *Bletilla formosana*, a native of Taiwan, offers pale rose-colored flowers on spikes a foot tall. *Bletilla ochracea* bears its small, light yellowish flowers about two weeks after *B. striata*. Lavender or red markings sometimes show on the lips, although these may also be dark yellow.

These, and other unusual species such as *Bletilla szetschuanica* and *B. yunnanensis*, have been used to create hybrids with beautiful blends of rose, yellow, or peach-colored petals, and fanciful red- or purple-flecked lips. The crosses seem more vigorous than the species themselves and make better garden perennials. 'Aurea', sold by Dutch nurseries as a selection of *B. striata*, displays creamy petals with contrasting yellow lips dappled in purple. 'Penway Dragon', a variable cross with purplish pink petals, shows white lips, margined and spotted with orchid. The light yellow petals of 'Penway Sunset' flush pink on their reverse, combining with golden lips splashed in light purple. 'Yokohama' offers lilac petals around a yellow, lavender-streaked throat. 'Brigantes' shows rose-purple petals and a purple lip marbled with yellow.

Magic Flowers

It is hard to imagine anything more appealing than a brimming potful of blooming achimenes. Gardeners show their universal approval of these flowers in the many nicknames they bestow upon them: magic flowers, widow's tears, cupid's bow, monkey-faced pansies, Japanese nut orchids, kimono plants. These hardy relatives of gloxinias and African violets are of easy culture. In the South they have long been popular for pots and porch boxes. Although tropical in origin, the underground bulbs remain safe from frost, so achimenes may be used as perennials in shady beds filled with rich soil.

Achimenes are leafy, hairy herbs that grow about a foot tall. Species come mostly from Mexico and Guatemala, with a few introduced from the West Indies. The long-tubed flowers, varying from an inch to three inches in diameter, resemble pansies or petunias. In color they are always vibrant, with a velvety, substantial depth and intensity. More popular formerly than they are now (nineteenth-century bulb dealers offered some four hundred cultivars), they may be seen in a pleasant, naturalized condition about older gardens.

The oblong tubers are composed of many scales, which overlap in a unique design like the pollen-bearing cones of a pine tree. With warmth, shade, and rich, moist soil, they begin growth in early summer. After several weeks, flowers begin to appear and continue until the plants are dried off in early fall.

It is important to provide a constant supply of moisture through the blooming season, for drought signals the plants to rest and begin forming tubers. These develop not only in the soil, but also at nodes along the stems. The fragile bulbs may be gathered in autumn and saved for replanting in rich compost the following summer. They store best in pots or bags of soil, sphagnum moss, or vermiculite to prevent desiccation.

The common magic flower seen everywhere in older gardens is a large, hyacinth-blue, trailing selection of the Mexican *Achimenes longiflora*. This easy, vigorous old cultivar is 'Galatea', also called 'Blue Beauty' or 'Mexicana'. Another old purple-blue, *A. grandiflora* 'Atropurpurea', is distinctive for the bronzy green tone of its heavy foliage. 'Ocampo', a selection of *A. grandiflora* from northeastern Mexico, has proven especially hardy in the South. *Achimenes coccinea* 'Major', the original rosy scarlet introduction, is a selection of a Jamaican species with smaller petals and a longer tube than most achimenes. *Achimenes candida* is a large-flowered white species from Guatemala. All these and several others have been widely hybridized, so that these blossoms are now more often seen as colorful strains than as named species or varieties.

A notable development is the double-flowered race known as the Rose series. These hybrids come in lavender, pink, and white, as well as a lilac picotee; the blooms look like varicolored miniature gardenias and compete in beauty with any summer bedding flower.

Tuberous relations of *Achimenes* include several species in *Sinningia*, the florist's gloxinia. Native to subtropical South America, these make hardy, summer-flowering perennials in the lower South, sprouting from thick, potatolike tubers. The white-flowered *S. tubiflora* makes a superb addition to evening gardens with soft, hairy leaves and clusters of long, tubular white flowers scented of jasmine all summer. *Sinningia aggregata* is one of several Brazilian species with orange or pink tubular blossoms attractive to hummingbirds; other species offer flowers reminiscent of foxgloves.

Begonias

Many exotic begonias thrive on porches and in summer window boxes in the South, but these are not tuberous members of the genus. Tuberous begonias descend from species native to the cool mountains of Bolivia, which were collected originally for Veitch by Richard Pearce, the same gentleman who introduced *Hippeastrum leopoldii*. As might be expected, these Andean species and their hybrid progeny usually sulk in the sultry climate of the lowland South.

There is a tuberous begonia from Asia that may be planted as a hardy perennial, and it is so unique and vigorous that it deserves to be in all Southern gardens. This is the famous *Begonia grandis* (*B. evansiana*). The modest sprays of tiny pink blooms are not as showy as those of the hybrids, but the luxuriant, embossed foliage, red-tinted beneath, makes a fine addition to any shady nook. 'Alba' is a rare white-flowered form, and 'Simsii' is a selection with reportedly larger blossoms. 'Heron's Pirouette', a Dan Hinkley introduction collected in Japan, offers especially large clusters of rose-pink blooms.

Begonia grandis enjoys a cool position with rich, leafy soil and abundant moisture. Where it is happy it quickly spreads to form large patches. In late summer small tubers form along the stems, and these may be gathered and potted immediately for increase. The plant yellows and dies down entirely in autumn. Since this hardy begonia emerges fairly late in the spring, it is a good choice to follow early-blooming woodlanders such as trilliums.

In the lower South gardeners may experiment with some of the rhizomatous begonias. These are mostly Mexican plants, and they endure heat and heavy soil better than other begonias. Their creeping rootstocks rest on the surface and should be protected from hard frost with a mulch of straw over winter. All varieties propagate readily from leaf cuttings, so gardeners can quickly produce spare plants to set out for trial. They are among the most beautiful of foliage plants, and have a uniquely succulent, watery character.

Begonia heracleifolia (star-leaf begonia) is a tremendous, vigorous species with deeply lobed, pale green leaves held above the rhizomes like parasols on bristly, pinkish stalks. Light pink blooms arrive in late winter or earliest spring. An especially beautiful form of this species, var. *nigricans*, offers dark, heavily veined, bronzy foliage. Although these are tender evergreens, they resprout readily even when the leaves are frozen.

The lotus-leaf begonia, *Begonia nelumbifolia*, is similarly hardy, with rounded, glossy green leaves to fifteen inches across and pale pink to white blooms. *Begonia crassicaulis* is naturally deciduous, so it should not mind occasional frost during its dormant period. The pink sprays of bloom appear in early spring before the deeply cut, shining green leaves.

Dahlias

The hybrid dahlias of summer gardens descend from plants originally domesticated by the natives of Mexico. Like tuberous begonias, they are flowers for cool, pleasantly mild regions and do not generally thrive in the torrid, steamy weather of the South. Since these daisy-type blooms are closely related to annual *Cosmos* and *Coreopsis*, both of which thrive in heat, it is tempting to forego this genus altogether. Purists will point out that *Dahlia*, like other tuberous genera, has a unique succulent quality. This gives the blooms a translucent depth and color not found in other daisylike blooms.

Although hybrid dahlias are poorly suited to the South, some of the Mexican species may be tried. *Dahlia merckii* is a modest-sized plant with lilac ray florets, pointed at the tips. *Dahlia coccinea* is scarlet with a bright yellow central disk. These two species were the forerunners of the modern single and collarette dahlias, and both might perform acceptably in the upper South. *Dahlia imperialis*, a tall-growing plant offering white flowers with reddish disks, is suitable for shady gardens in the lower South. Most species grow easily from seed. The clustered tubers may be separated with a knife in early spring, if care is taken that each division has a growing "eye."

Yellow Show and Coral Flowers

Other summer-flowering Mexican tubers are better suited to the warmth of the South, but these are little known as garden plants. They are most commonly grown by succulent enthusiasts, who pot the enlarged roots in an exposed position to display their gnarled, bonsai-like swelling. As long as the tubers are planted safely underground in well-drained soil, these plants may be treated as perennials. They revel in heat.

Yellow show (*Amoreuxia wrightii*) is a small plant that belongs to a curious, tropical American family, the Cochlospermaceae. It makes a round tuber the size of a walnut. After summer rains, short stems with gray-green, palmate leaves come up and bear bright yellow, nasturtiumlike blossoms. These open freshly in the morning and fade in early afternoon. Interesting, egg-shaped capsules with transparent windows follow, containing numerous hard, brown seeds. If planted in ordinary garden soil, these grow rapidly, forming flowering-size plants in their first season. Old tubers sometimes succumb to nematodes, but this plant is easy to keep coming from fresh seed.

Tougher and equally exotic is the coral flower, or *jicamilla* (*Jatropha cathartica*). This relative of the common bull nettle foregoes the painful thorns of its cousin. Instead of fragrant, white blooms, it sends up a succession of small, coral-red blossoms. These ripen into three-sided capsules bearing nutlike seeds.

If gathered before the capsules burst, the seed can be set straight in the border where the plants are desired. Growing well in dry, sandy soil in full sun, they have attractive, gray, palmlike leaves. The tubers are long-lived and eventually become six to eight inches in diameter. The coral flower is hardy wherever the soil does not freeze.

Wood Sorrels

With over eight hundred species, *Oxalis* is a huge genus that has scarcely been explored by gardeners. Although several common horticultural species prefer cool, maritime climates, a goodly number come from warm regions, especially Mexico and South America. These revel in the Southern climate, and make fine garden material.

Nearly all oxalis have ornamental, divided foliage, either cloverlike or much dissected, resembling tiny windmills. Leaves are often further ornamented with markings of bronze or purple. The attractive clusters of five-petaled blossoms furl themselves tightly while in bud, and both leaves and flowers exhibit strong sleep movements, twisting and closing at night. Flowers ripen to oblong pods that burst as they dry, scattering the seeds.

The common name shared by *Oxalis* species is wood sorrel, a designation apparently borrowed from true sorrel, which is a very different-looking plant in the dock genus, *Rumex*. What sorrel shares with *Oxalis* is the pleasantly acid, mustardlike flavor in its leaves. True sorrel is often harvested for use as a potherb. The more strongly flavored wood sorrels may be used in small doses as a condiment, but the concentration of oxalic acid in the leaves is usually too high to permit more liberal consumption. *Oxalis* comes from the Greek *oxys* ("sour").

South Americans

One oxalis in particular is outstanding for its widespread use in borders and as low edgings for beds or pathways: *Oxalis crassipes*. Most gardeners simply know this ubiquitous, mounding species as pink wood sorrel, but this risks confusion with several other varieties. The epithet *crassipes* ("thick foot") refers to its swollen, tuberous roots. Although many oxalis develop simple bulbs composed of scales, *O. crassipes* goes beyond this with its starchy rootstock and potatolike swellings. These storage structures help make this species especially drought-tolerant. The thick roots can be easily divided at any season, and it is a simple matter for gardeners to propagate all they might desire.

Gazing out at plantings of the small, rounded clumps of *Oxalis crassipes* on a frosty February morning, a hasty observer might fail to notice the folded, nodding buds. With the warmth of the noonday sun, these turn upward to display cheerful, magenta-pink funnels. This resolute bloomer graces gardens in earliest spring, and continues well into summer where it receives shade from the western sun, opening its flowers progressively earlier in the day and closing them in afternoon heat.

A tough, thrifty native of the Argentine pampas, *Oxalis crassipes* often returns to bloom in the fall, persisting through the winter on sheltered sites. This

Pink wood sorrel, *Oxalis crassipes*, makes a nearly indestructible border flower.

is an invaluable plant for Southern gardens. Its lightly felted, cloverlike leaves make handsome mounds even when not in bloom.

The common form of *Oxalis crassipes* has especially vibrant, wine-striated blooms. These sometimes clash with other flowers (or red brick), but the lovely white forms, 'Alba' and 'Snowflake', can be used in any scheme. These have fresh, green foliage, and replace the wine pencilings in the petals of the common form with light gray striations. Growers also occasionally offer attractive pale pink forms of this species.

Oxalis braziliensis is a beautiful ally of *O. crassipes* with a dwarfer, more spreading habit. Instead of thickened roots, this species spreads from small, scale-covered bulbs. The leaves have the same mounding quality as *O. crassipes*, overlapping like shingles to form a solid groundcover. The handsome foliage has a lustrous, waxy greenness which bespeaks the tropics, and it is indeed tender to hard frost. The rounded leaflets provide an ideal background for the glowing cerise blossoms that appear from March through May.

Oxalis braziliensis is one of the most beautiful species if given its preferred moist, acid soil. It makes a charming filler for crevices between stone pavers, although no one would want to step on its leaves or flowers. Like *O. crassipes*, this species grows in winter, becoming dormant with the heat of June. The small bulbs should be planted in the fall.

Oxalis regnellii is another South American that takes to the climate of the

Early spring sun glances across an awakening tuft of white wood sorrel, *Oxalis crassipes* 'Alba'.

South. It has become fairly popular as a bedding item for its attractive three-parted foliage. If watered and shaded from hot sun, the leaves hold up through summer as well as winter. The white flowers of common *O. regnellii* look rather ordinary, but they show off against the triangular green leaflets, which are purple underneath. 'Triangularis' is a splashy introduction with brilliant reddish purple leaves throughout and pale pink blossoms. *Oxalis regnellii* subsp. *papilionacea* and *O. regnellii* 'Fanny' supply green, butterfly-shaped leaflets marked with an attractive pewter pattern. 'Irish Mist' splashes tiny silvery flecks across it foliage. 'Mijke' and 'Francis' are purple-leafed selections with bright, almost iridescent foliage compared to the darker 'Triangularis'.

These varieties grow easily on rich, moist soil, and spread steadily to form dense patches in full or partial shade. The fresh green or purple, flattened foliage contrasts happily with river fern (*Thelypteris normalis* var. *lindheimeri*) or orange shrimp plant (*Justicia fulvicoma*) and makes good filler for foregrounds of shady bedding schemes.

Oxalis corymbosa (*O. martiana*), the common houseplant oxalis, is a native of tropical America. It is like a taller, looser *O. crassipes* with pale pink blossoms and small nutlike bulbs. In the South this species survives in shaded, protected nooks. The most interesting form to grow is 'Variegata', an old selection with yellowish, reticulated veins.

The golden-flowered *Oxalis lobata* of Chile and Bolivia is a winter grower that

Oxalis regnellii 'Triangularis' flowering with purple violas in Tom Peace's garden, Lockhart, Texas. Photo by Lauren S. Ogden.

dies down in May, but may be safely left in the ground through its summer dormancy. Hardy in the middle and upper South, the showy blooms of this species appear over several weeks during winter, along with lush green tufts of foliage.

Bermuda Buttercups

In the lower South the light yellow blooms of the Bermuda buttercup (*Oxalis pes-caprae*) are a regular feature of late winter. They often punctuate old lawns and are almost as common as *O. crassipes*, although they are less prominently used in borders. This South African species makes lax clumps that lean nonchalantly in the direction of the February sun. The leaves have the same cloverlike appearance as *O. crassipes* but are peppered all over with brown freckles.

The clustered yellow blooms are at their best at ten in the morning and look especially pretty when massed under the gaunt bareness of a rugged, old elm. Unless it is a misty, overcast day, they fold up and rest after midday. An old epithet for this flower, *cernua* ("nodding"), refers to this afternoon siesta; the present, *pes-caprae* ("goat foot"), refers to the heart-shaped leaflets.

Although this species is a vigorous spreader, hard frost is its enemy, and in cold years it is a struggle to see the tender foliage through the winter. The beautiful double form 'Flore Pleno', which tends to rich, golden yellow, is a choice, early flower, and makes a deserving subject for a sheltered position at the foot of a south-facing wall.

More than two hundred species of *Oxalis* grow in South Africa, but many of these prefer a winter growing cycle, making them a challenge to grow in the South. The candy-striped oxalis (*O. versicolor*), native to Namaqualand in the Western Cape, is one of these cool-season species. Its heavily divided leaves are usually so furled and tousled that the clumps of foliage look like moss. In late winter, flowers begin expanding on warm days. The backs of the petals are deep pink, the faces white, so in opening and closing an unusual peppermint effect predominates.

This winter-growing species seems entirely hardy in the middle and lower South, but it has no tolerance for summer rains during its period of dormancy. It is best grown in a pot plunged into the ground over winter. This may be lifted and dried off in early summer for replanting in the coming fall. If used in this way these pink-and-white beauties are valuable for cool-season color.

The beautiful apricot-pink *Oxalis obtusa* is a long-blooming species from some of the same regions in South Africa, but it also grows in areas where summer rains occur. Its bright-colored pastel flowers appear from late winter to spring and are especially appealing. Selections from the eastern part of its range

Double-flowered Bermuda buttercup, *Oxalis pes-caprae* 'Flore Pleno'.

may adapt to Southern conditions and would be choice subjects for sunny rockeries. Another good species, *O. bowiei*, is a fall-bloomer from the Eastern Cape, where summer rains are common but hard frosts are rare. Its oversized rose-pink flowers appear with large, shamrocklike, green foliage in late winter in Gulf Coast gardens.

A more adaptable species with a range extending from the dry areas of Namaqualand to the Eastern Cape, *Oxalis purpurea* displays colorful blooms ranging from purple and rose to yellow and white. Its shamrocklike foliage, hairy and purple beneath, bears tiny cilia along the margins, making attractive clumps. Many named selections of this species with varicolored blooms are popular as pot plants. At least one of these, the purple-leafed selection 'Garnet', seems adaptable to Southern conditions. It provides mounds of dark purple leaves as foils for showstopping clusters of lustrous, rosy blooms with yellow thoats. These appear from December to April and seem proof against frosts to 20°F or less. The attractive foliage dies down in summer, returning with fall rains. The Israeli cultivar 'Nufar' is similar.

Southerners

A delightful woodland flower, the wild purple wood sorrel (*Oxalis violacea*) makes a dainty spring garden subject, useful to combine with the yellow star grass. The cloverlike leaves are pale green, and the blooms are rosy purple (not violet). The small, scaly bulbs spread by rhizomes but are seldom invasive.

More glamorous is the Southern yellow wood sorrel, *Oxalis priceae*. This has foliage and build like *O. violacea*, but the blooms are rich, golden yellow. The root is a slender, creeping rhizome. Flowers appear in April and May on poor, sandy ground.

This fine flower should not be confused with the ubiquitous *Oxalis corniculata*, which makes a taproot instead of a tuber and often has purple-tinted leaves. This cosmopolitan species is too well known to most gardeners to need more definite introduction. Well-nigh ineradicable trailing stems make it a frightful weed, and it is capable of seeding itself through an entire bed in short order. Any decent garden will inevitably endure its onslaught, for *O. corniculata* seems to come as a free plant in every nursery pot.

Texicans

Southwestern and Mexican *Oxalis* species carry the blooming season into summer and fall. Many of these are especially choice flowers suited to a special niche on the rockery. All grow from true bulbs and tolerate considerable drought. They enjoy rich, clay soils with a measure of lime, but will succeed on sand, also.

Oxalis lasiandra sends up charming, many-parted leaves on tall stems like little palm trees. This species is widespread over the semiarid uplands of Mexico. Some forms reach nearly a foot in height, but others remain much shorter. The blooms appear on six- to eight-inch stems carried among the leaves in early summer. They are a very bright, almost electric cerise-pink. The slender carriage of these plants suggests display against lichen-covered boulders, so that they will not be hidden by leafier neighbors.

The iron cross oxalis, *Oxalis tetraphylla*, produces foliage like a four-leaved shamrock, but with dark purple stains marking the base of each leaflet. This coloring highlights the iron cross pattern, making the mounds of leaves stand out boldly in the garden. In May and June satiny, rose blossoms join the foliage. *Oxalis deppei* and *O. nelsonii* are similar, but with deeper red and purplish blooms, respectively. All are natives of western and southern Mexico.

Oxalis latifolia is a fast-spreading, tropical American species with leaves composed of three wedge-shaped leaflets. In the common form, these are green, but there is a striking burgundy-leafed selection that looks much like the purple-leafed *O. regnellii*. It is smaller and more drought-tolerant, with lilac-pink blossoms in late summer and fall.

A Texas relation, *Oxalis drummondii*, also spreads vigorously, and may be unwelcome in some gardens for this attribute. Nevertheless, it sends up redeemingly large, lilac-rose blooms in September and October. The foliage comes up at the same time and remains through the winter. It is so low growing that it is only a nuisance in the most manicured gardens, and the blooms are pleasant if allowed to naturalize in a rough lawn.

Oxalis drummondii var. *vespertilionis* ("batlike"), from the mountains of western Texas and northern Mexico, has narrow, V-shaped leaves that sometimes look like the wings of bats. This form is worth cultivating for its unusual foliage, as well as its autumn blooms. In some clones the leaves are also marked with bars of purple.

Chapter 9
⌘ Cannas, Gingers, and Aroids

I**N THE BENIGN CLIMATE** of the South certain families of tuberous plants venture beyond ordinary parameters. With impressively substantial foliage, cannas, gingers, and aroids sometimes make their garden presence felt in such a way as to rival woody shrubs. The succulent stems of these robust sub-tropicals die back with hard frost, but while in summer growth they afford basic garden architecture as well as exuberant bloom. Their brave performances through the summer help redeem this sweltering season.

Cannas

The original garden cannas were not planted for their flowers at all, but for their exotic, bananalike foliage. Victorian growers favored tall, leafy varieties for summer bedding schemes, proudly combining them with castor beans, begonias, and other bold growers in a dramatically tropical style.

Wild *Canna* species hail from moist, upland forests in the tropics of Asia and the Americas, with two yellow-flowered aquatic species, *C. flaccida* and *C. glauca*, venturing north along the Gulf and Atlantic coasts into Southern swamps. All cannas produce thick, branching rhizomes, and these carry stout upright stems, sheathed by large, alternating leaves with the clustered flowers eventually emerging at the top. New shoots rise at intervals from the slowly creeping roots like sprouting stems of bamboo, giving the plants a continuously lush appearance.

In the South these robust flowers can be tremendously free growing. Since gardeners know this, they often relegate cannas to less than ideal conditions. Although they will endure occasional droughts and poor soil, cannas prefer steady, abundant water and rich ground. They amply reward good care with luxuriant performances and prove perennial in any climate where frost fails to penetrate the soil deeply.

The blossoms of cannas are curiously built affairs in which enlarged, sterile stamens (staminodia) take the place of petals and sepals. The true petals remain tiny, forming a narrow tube from which the showy, orchidlike staminodia protrude. There are usually four of these petal-like structures together, with one bent and reflexed to form a sort of lip.

The first hybridizer of cannas, Mons. Thré Année, was the French consul-general at Valparaiso, Chile. When he returned to Europe in 1846 he brought along a collection of species that he used as breeding stock. Some of Année's early crosses and the wild species used to create them may still be seen lurking in older Southern gardens.

Indian Shots

The best known of the cannas from Année's breeding stable is the Indian shot (*Canna indica*), so called for its hard, round seeds resembling buckshot. Typical forms of this tropical American species have glossy, coarsely veined green leaves and grow between two and six feet tall. Narrow-"petaled," up-facing blooms appear at the tops of the stems. These have yellowish to orange lips and are frequently spotted with red.

Année also used the tall, bronze-leafed *Canna indica* var. *warscewiczii* in his breeding, and this tropical American variety may be the source of colored foliage seen in many garden cannas. The slender blossoms of var. *warscewiczii* are bright scarlet, but they appear very small in relation to the tremendous foliage.

An especially fine, purple-leafed canna, perhaps the old cultivar 'Robusta', is in many gardens in the South. It is among the tallest, achieving nine to twelve feet on rich soil. The substantial, veined leaves hold their color in sun or shade, and ask only for shelter from

The native yellow water canna of the South, *Canna flaccida*.

Canna indica var. *warscewiczii*.

strong wind. This selection makes an ideal specimen plant, with graceful, outward-arching stems; it is superb as a dark-colored centerpiece among bright summer flowers or feathery grasses.

A slightly different canna, 'Red Stripe', bears broad, fluted leaves tinged red on the midribs and stems, a color pattern that matches the description of another tropical American species, *Canna edulis*. A similar plant is cultivated in English gardens under the name *C. indica* 'Purpurea'. These make exotic foliage accents and bear slender clusters of rich red or orange blooms.

Several old green-leafed cannas are nearly as tall as these bronzy types. One of Année's famous hybrids, 'Imperator', was such a plant, and derived from a cross of two other South American forms of *Canna indica*, var. *musaefolia* and var. *gigantea*. All three were popular nineteenth-century companions for the large purple-leafed cannas. Although leaf rolling insects plague many modern canna hybrids, they usually ignore these old, tall varieties, which bear much tougher, more leathery foliage.

The Iris-flowered Canna

The largest blooms among the tall cannas belong to the pendant, rosy crimson

Canna 'Orange Punch' has pendant blooms like its parent *C. iridiflora*.

Canna iridiflora. This distinctive Peruvian is one of the few wild types still in cultivation. Its epithet *iridiflora* ("iris-flowered") refers to the showy, large-"petaled" blooms. The broad, smooth leaves have a handsome blue-green tone, and are especially sturdy. They appear along five-foot stems, topped by the long-tubed, cardinal-rose blossoms. These dangle on slender stalks that curve like a swan's neck. Throughout summer a succession of warmly colored blossoms suspend themselves like bright butterflies over the foliage. Swarms of hummingbirds follow the brilliant blooms.

Around 1860 Année used *Canna iridiflora* to produce the hybrid 'Iridiflora Rubra', better known in horticulture as 'Ehemanii'. This had the same brilliant rose-crimson flowers as *C. iridiflora*, but engravings from the period show that the vigorous plants held their blooms in upright clusters. 'Ehemanii' became popular in the late 1800s for its rich, heavy foliage and abundant bloom, and was soon used to breed other large-flowered hybrids.

Cannas commonly offered by nurseries as 'Ehemanii' seem to represent a sterile clone of *Canna iridiflora*, as they bear the pendant blossoms typical of the species. What appears to be actual 'Ehemanii' is a common heirloom in Southern gardens, with handsome, slightly waved, blue-green foliage and fully upright clusters of quite fertile, rose-red blooms. Both cultivars make fine garden plants, whatever their names. A modern hybrid of *C. iridiflora*, 'Orange Punch', is an introduction from Arkansas breeder Kent Kelly that carries glowing orange, yellow-throated blossoms on modest three- to four-foot stems. This showy dwarf retains the gracefully pendant floral habit of its species parent. All *C. iridiflora* cultivars seem to prefer cooler conditions than most cannas, performing best if their tubers are not allowed to dry out completely when dug and separated for increase.

Crozy Cannas

Several nineteenth-century French gardeners worked to develop cannas for their floral beauty. Mons. Crozy of Lyon is usually credited with developing the large-flowered hybrids that now dominate gardens. Showy Asian species such as the tiger canna (*Canna childsii*), with yellow, crimson-spotted blooms, and the dwarf *C. limbata* (*C. aureo-vittata*), with slightly variegated foliage and red and yellow blossoms, probably contributed to Crozy's hybrids. Typical of the old French cannas, the dwarf cultivar 'Lucifer' bears brilliant red blooms with striking yellow borders in an irislike form. Another canna still in cultivation, the five-foot, orange- and yellow-flowered hybrid 'Florence Vaughn', is thought by some to be the famed old selection 'Madame Crozy'. (It is, perhaps, suspect that Vaughn's nursery of Chicago made their introduction in 1893, the same year 'Madame Crozy' was awarded a bronze medal at the Chicago World's Columbian Exposition.)

The Harlequin Canna

Another old Crozy-type canna may be seen everywhere in Southern gardens, and is always an attraction. The four- to six-foot stands of leaves are topped abundantly in early summer by massive, orchidlike blooms. Normally, these flowers have yellow petals covered with red dots and accompany clear green foliage.

Canna 'Cleopatra'.

With amazing regularity, however, various shoots develop spontaneous variegations in which the leaves become wholly or partly purple. At the same time, the blooms change to vermilion. Individual stems may sometimes be found with bronze and red on one side, green and yellow on the other, as if they had been cut vertically and sewn together from two separate plants.

No one seems sure of the proper title or ancestry of this harlequin canna, or Spanish emblem, as it is sometimes called, but it is widely sold as 'Cleopatra'. In its green-leafed phase this fascinating canna answers the description of the old Crozy hybrid 'Admiral Courbet'; the red-leafed form could be another nineteenth-century variety, 'Edouard Andre'. Under any title this is one of the most rewarding cannas, outstandingly brilliant and exotic, no matter which aspect it chooses to display.

Asiatics

The pinstriped variegation seen in 'Bangkok' ('Striped Beauty') suggests that this Asian cultivar may be close to the wild *Canna limbata*. In America this beautiful dwarf is also sometimes sold as 'Nirvana' or 'Minerva'. The lance-shaped foliage is attractive in itself and usually remains under two feet. The yellow, white-striped blooms are lively and refreshing—bright, yet without the gaudiness of common canna hybrids.

Striped foliage seems to have appeared spontaneously on cultivars distantly descended from *Canna limbata*, and several dramatic variegated plants have been discovered as sports. Brilliant orange flowers top the ruddy, five-foot stems of 'Bengal Tiger', better known as 'Pretoria' and sometimes listed as 'Imperialis' or 'Aureostriata'. This favorite introduction from India displays obvious golden pinstripes, pale midribs, and darkly penciled edges on pale green leaves, glowing when backlit. Although 'Bengal Tiger' exhibits no more love for water than other cannas, its vibrant color has made it especially popular for poolside plant-

ings, where it may be grown as an emergent aquatic.

An even more opulent selection,
'Durban', carries bronze-toned leaves
decorated with yellow and apricot-
tinted stripes; these glow against its
purplish foliage and vibrant red-orange blooms. 'Pink Starbust' is similar,
but with shorter two- to three-foot
stems and pink flowers. 'Mactro' (Tropicanna Gold) closely resembles 'Bengal
Tiger', but bears yellow-edged, light orange blossoms atop ivory-toned stems.

The apogee of variegation belongs,
however, to 'Phaison', popularly marketed as Tropicanna and sometimes
listed as 'Orange Durban'. The sizeable
leaves of this South African introduction, a sport from the bronze-leafed
'Wyoming', emerge with fluorescent,
purplish pink undertones, contrasted
with alternating yellow and bronze

Canna 'Bengal Tiger' ('Pretoria') flowering
with *Curcuma* sp. 'Scarlet Fever'.

stripes. Glowing orange flowers complete an overwhelming scene and make
'Phaison' a popular subject for containers or special niches suited to its unchal-
lenged brilliance.

Orchid-flowered Cannas

In the marshes of the coastal South two species of wild canna offer graceful, pale
yellow flowers amid slender, upright leaves. These are bluish in tone on *Canna
glauca* and fresh green on *C. flaccida*. These native species naturally set their
slender rhizomes in water alongside quiet streams and lakes. Breeders have used
them to develop the beautiful orchid-flowered cannas, varieties that often inherit the upright, lance-shaped leaves of the wild species and the elegant, long-
tubed aspect of their flowers. Not surprisingly, the hybrids show a preference for
moist or even aquatic conditions.

The first cannas of this type were bred from *Canna flaccida* and introduced
in the 1880s by Dammann & Co. of Naples, Italy. Few of the originals remain in
general commerce, but renewed appreciation for Victorian-era cannas has

Canna 'Endeavour' shows the attractive blue-gray foliage of *C. glauca*.

The delicately colored, orchid-flowered *Canna* 'Panache'.

brought back several varieties that retain floral qualities of the orchid-flowered race, sometimes known as Italian cannas. The ravishing pink 'Madame Paul Caseneuve', luscious apricot 'Madame Angèle Martin', and glowing orange 'Sémaphore' ('Pacific Beauty') are late-nineteenth- and early-twentieth-century selections that continue to be worthwhile garden subjects. All offer attractive grayed-purple foliage as a foil for their elegantly shaped blooms.

Breeding by Robert J. Armstrong at Longwood Gardens, Pennsylvania, added a modern series of orchid-flowered varieties with the attractive blue-gray foliage of *Canna glauca*. An especially choice clone is 'Erebus', with delicate, salmon-pink blossoms; 'Endeavour' is a robust red. Like all the Longwood cannas these may be planted as aquatics. Herb Kelly of California has expanded this group with fine clones like 'Panache', which bears handsome blue-green foliage and pale, nodding blooms suffused with rich coral-pink at the base. Another Kelly hybrid, 'Intrigue', carries its orange flowers over upswept, lance-shaped leaves deeply suffused with purple.

Modern Varieties

Many cannas have been developed for use as summer bedding plants. Shapeless masses of brilliantly colored blooms have been the breeders' principal aim. Although most varieties remain more or less dwarf in Northern gardens, in the generous climate of the South it is not unusual for bedding cannas to exceed four or five feet. Standard, green-leafed selections such as the rosy pink 'City of Portland', golden yellow 'Richard Wallace', and scarlet 'President' achieve good size, as do the bronze-leafed, orange-flowered 'Wyoming' and vermilion 'King Humbert'. These are harshly brilliant flowers with great vigor. Even now they assert their supremacy over mass bedding displays of roadsides and public parks, often in combination with bold foliage plants such as yucca or pampas grass.

The popular Pfitzer and Grand Opera series are slightly shorter and come in a range of pastel shades more easily placed in gardens. The warm apricot 'Stadt Fellbach' is particularly fine. Another old Pfitzer introduction, 'Feuerzauber', is better known in the United States as 'Australia'; it boasts incredibly dark, glossy purple foliage in company with glowing red blooms. Also of value are large-flowered imports from India and Southeast Asia such as 'Cupid', a delicate porcelain-pink dwarf with lightly speckled, orange-throated blooms, and 'Pride of India' ('Taj Mahal'), reaching four to five feet and bearing rich, rose-pink blossoms.

Beyond these named varieties, nurseries sometimes offer strains that may be raised from seed. Seven Dwarfs series includes a mix of reds, roses, oranges, yellows, and salmons, all of which remain eighteen inches tall or less. 'Tropical Rose', one of a recently introduced series, grows so rapidly from seed that it may be used as a bedding annual. Its glowing, opalescent blossoms appear on lush green, two-and-one-half-foot plants.

When planting seeds of these or any cannas, it is best to file or break the hard coats first. Seeds may then be soaked in water and allowed to swell before planting in individual pots. With warm conditions, growth is amazingly rapid.

Fragrance

As successful as breeders have been with cannas, one characteristic they have neglected is fragrance. This is not an impossible wish, for the Venezuelan *Canna longiflora* produces long-tubed, creamy blossoms with the sweet scent associated with nocturnal flowers. Although rare, this tender species is presently in cultivation in the United States, and one may hope that it will someday become available for trial in the lower South. If crossed with present-day canna hybrids, what wonders it might produce. For the present, gardeners can content themselves with a few near-white, albeit scentless hybrids. Of these, the three-foot 'Ermine' and equally dwarf 'Milk Festival' are beauties with lush, green foliage and refreshingly pale, understated flowers compared to their raucously bright relations.

Gingers

Although built along common lines—creeping, tuberous rootstocks, sheathing leaves, and flowers contrived from modified stamens—gingers manage an air of grace few cannas can approach. These elegant perennials show a special affinity for the balmy, sometimes steamy climate of the South. Just as camellias command winter scenes with glittering leaves and silky blossoms, gingers take charge over summer plantings, affording luxuriant foliage and tantalizing, fragrant blooms. While climbing temperatures exhaust the wills of lesser plants, these robust exotics grow and blossom ever more profusely. For gardeners in the warm South, a summer without the opulent charms of gingers would be insufferable.

Approximately thirteen hundred species belong to the ginger family (Zingiberaceae), but many of these are full-fledged tropicals, adapted only to warm, frost-free conditions. The hardy gingers in Southern gardens hail from a broad zone of subtropical climate stretching from the foothills of the Himalayas in northern India and Nepal eastward through the warm-temperate forests of Myanmar, southern China, Japan, and Taiwan. Other gingers successful in the South derive from habitats in seasonally dry, monsoonal savannahs and jungles in peninsular India, Southeast Asia, Indonesia, Africa, and northern Australia. These naturally deciduous plants show a capacity to substitute Southern winters for their normal dry season of dormancy. Although the species of *Roscoea* and *Cautleya* are fully hardy, these alpine gingers dislike the summer warmth of the South and instead prefer temperate climates such as the Pacific Northwest. Montane gingers such as *Hedychium densiflorum*, *H. ellipticum*, *H. spicatum*, *H. yunnanense*, and *H. gracile* may also be expected to suffer in hot weather, requiring cool positions with shade and high humidity, as for rhododendrons.

In their homelands, gingers often grow as understory plants, thriving in warm, humid enclaves where they drip away the daily afternoon rains with the long, pointed tips of their foliage. In some varieties leaves are attractively mottled or striped with silver or bronze, and it seems that this coloration confers some metabolic efficiency or helps camouflage the plants from herbivores. Other gingers display leaves stained purple on their undersides, a common character of plants in tropical forests: botanists theorize this attribute may help collect light, modify temperatures, or otherwise provide some advantage in damp, shaded habitats. Charles Darwin noted the natural capacity of gingers to modify the effect of sunlight, observing that "in several species of *Hedychium* the lateral halves of the leaves when exposed to bright sunshine, bend downward so that the lateral margins meet."

Gingers set their roots into cool water along crashing mountain streams, seek tropical sun in seasonally damp meadows, choose rocky nooks along steep, mossy cliffsides, or nestle fleshy roots among tree limbs to grow as epiphytes. In gardens most adapt to any moist soil enriched with organic matter, so long as roots do not remain excessively damp during winter dormancy. Although a few gingers require positions in full sun for best flowering, the majority find open shade or part-day sun ideal.

More than any other tuberous plants, gingers are in the ascendancy. Large areas of Southeast Asia and Indonesia are only now being explored for their plant treasures, and these regions yield discoveries each year. As quickly as new varieties are found, dedicated plantsmen bring these often spectacular ornamentals into cultivation and begin hybridizing and testing their value for twenty-first-century horticulture. Modern techniques of tissue culture, or plant cloning, are being exploited by nurseries in the United States and Thailand, making it possible for ultra-rare novelties to enter commerce at a rapid pace. This is often before botanists give new species a proper christening and well before gardeners have had a chance to learn much about a plant's adaptability or landscape value. Interested gardeners in the South have a unique opportunity to participate in the discovery, selection, and breeding of new garden gingers.

Sweet Snow

In the forested warmth of Himalayan foothills, far below the eternal snows of the mountains, white-flowered butterfly gingers, *Hedychium coronarium*, colonize damp slopes and streamsides, scenting humid air with heavy perfume. These are the Indian *gandasuli* ("fragrance of the princess" in Sanskrit) and, for botanists, inspiration for the name of the genus (*Hedychium* is from the Greek *hedys chios*, "sweet snow"). Cherished in the South as ginger lilies, these nearly hardy, large-flowered perennials carry sweetly fragrant blossoms in exotic spikes borne at the tips of tremendously graceful, leafy stems.

The long-tubed flowers of *Hedychium* emerge from between greenish bracts that arrange themselves into a conelike or spike-shaped inflorescence. As the pointed flower buds expand, the slender petals open first, dangling like narrow ribbons as they release the often beautifully marked and lobed, furled upper segment, or labellum. This expands along with two petal-like staminodia and a slender, arching fertile stamen. In these irregularly modified blooms the sometimes colorful filament fuses with the style, which rests in a groove, so that the stigma just protrudes beyond the paired, pollen-bearing portions of the anther. This creates a unique flower with a delicate appearance suggestive of an exotic orchid or fanciful insect. The individual blooms last only a few days, but up to six flowers appear in succession from each bract so that the inflorescence can remain showy over several weeks.

Varying in height from species to species, from two to ten feet tall, the flowering canes of *Hedychium* (called pseudostems by botanists) shoot up from the perennial rhizomes in late spring. Elegant ranks of tapered leaves dispose themselves at angles along these upright or gently arching shoots, making members of this genus unusually beautiful as foliage plants. The exquisite flowers arrive by midsummer on most species, and several repeat bloom, with late shoots continuing to emerge until frost.

Most large-flowered hedychiums are naturally deciduous and hardy wherever ground does not freeze. In colder zones their cannalike rhizomes may be taken up in autumn. Storage is best accomplished in pots of barely moist soil, assuring that roots never dry completely. Flowering improves if clumps are lifted and thinned every three or four years. The branched, creeping rhizomes may be divided in spring before growth begins (be sure that each severed portion retains at least one pointed bud). The roots should be planted shallowly, with soil just covering the tubers. Where prolonged freezes can be expected, an autumn mulch of leaves, pine straw, or shredded bark may be applied, or the dried foliage of the previous summer may be left to help shield roots from penetrating frosts.

Butterflies

The two-inch, snowy blossoms of the white butterfly ginger (*Hedychium coronarium*) emit one of the most alluring fragrances of summer, sweet and intense, yet refreshing. In Hawaii these soft-petaled blooms are strung in leis and used to make perfume. Now widely naturalized in the moist tropics and subtropics, this popular ginger hails originally from the foothills of the Himalayas, ranging south to Indonesia and eastward through the mountains of southern China, where it grows at altitudes up to fifty-five hundred feet. The common form produces white flowers with shining green, heart-shaped eyes in the center of the labellum; its somewhat lax, six-foot stems carry lushly verdant leaves with soft, slightly felted undersides. In the South this favorite thrives in filtered shade or full sun and often naturalizes near streams or wetlands where it grows as a partial aquatic.

'Maximum', an impressively large-growing selection of *Hedychium coronarium*, is well worth growing for its oversized all-white blooms borne atop eight- to nine-foot stems. This is not the same, however, as *H. maximum*, a shade-loving species with ten-foot shoots and large, yellow, deeply lobed flowers with pinkish stamens and a distinctive scent.

In northern India a variant of the white butterfly ginger, with a yellow-orange, rather than greenish spot on the labellum, becomes common and is known as *Hedychium coronarium* var. *chrysoleucum*. Plants sold in North America under this name invariably prove to be 'Gold Spot', a wild-collected plant introduced by the nursery of Ganesh Mani Pradhan & Son in West Bengal, India. This lovely ginger displays creamy flowers with shining orange-gold eyes and complementary apricot filaments. Among the most fra-

Hedychium coronarium var. *chrysoleucum* 'Gold Spot'.

grant of the hedychiums, it bears clustered blooms late into the season on four- to six-foot canes ideal for close encounters in an evening garden.

Hedychium flavescens, an ally of the white butterfly ginger native to the same regions of India and southwestern China, produces blossoms entirely suffused with light yellow, bearing light orange-toned eyes. These blooms are especially fragrant and slightly larger than those of *H. coronarium*, expanding up to three inches across. The impressively tall plants are also more robust than *H. coronarium*, with broad foliage felted beneath and stout stems six to eight feet tall, but these handsome gingers are late to bloom, sometimes not coming into flower until August. Their lemony, jasminelike perfume is powerful.

Hedychium flavum, another yellow butterfly ginger, blooms earlier than *H. flavescens*, with smaller, darker, more uniformly yellow flowers; and its leaves lack the velvety undersurfaces common to *H. coronarium* and *H. flavescens*. As one might expect, these similar plants are commonly confused. Most yellow butterfly gingers labeled *H. flavum* in the South prove to be *H. flavescens*.

Bottlebrushes

Growing in the same Himalayan territories as these butterfly gingers are several hedychiums with smaller, more numerous blossoms arranged in upright spikes. These cylindrical inflorescences open blossoms from each bract simultaneously, with the long, stamens projecting from each bloom, suggesting a colorful bottlebrush. The showy display is highly attractive to butterflies, and in North American gardens also draws attention from hummingbirds.

The richest colors among these bottlebrush gingers belong to the brilliant orange-toned *Hedychium coccineum*. An upright, narrow-leafed species from India, Nepal, and Bangladesh, this well-known ginger bears six- to twelve-inch floral spikes with fifty or more slender, scarcely scented blossoms arranged in six neatly vertical rows. Four to six blooms emerge in succession from each bract, with the first spikes opening in midsummer. After the initial flowering, the plants rest for a few weeks before repeating, with newly emerged spikes coming into bloom in late summer and early autumn.

Botanists list several varieties of orange bottlebrush gingers, but these are difficult to distinguish and may represent natural hybrids, which are common among *Hedychium* species. Blooms vary in size and in color from pink and apricot to coral, with extending reddish stamens. Some of the best produce flower trusses of deep cinnabar, making a show against the distinctive, blue-green, ladderlike foliage of this species. The selection 'Disney' is especially popular, with spikes of vibrant orange flowers appearing from July to September on seven-foot canes of bluish foliage, tinted purple beneath. 'Flaming Torch', 'Woodlanders', and 'Peach' (a selection of *H. coccineum* var. *angustifolium*) send up shoots feathered with narrow, upright leaves, carrying oversized clusters of soft orange flowers.

With waxy, blue-green foliage and glowing tangerine blooms, 'Tara' and the very similar 'C. P. Raffill' are show plants that appear to be especially fine forms of *Hedychium coccineum*. The first is a clone raised from wild-collected seed

Hedychium 'C. P. Raffill'.   *Hedychium gardnerianum* (kahili ginger).

gathered in Nepal by British ginger enthusiast Tony Schilling, the second a purported hybrid developed by Charles Percival Raffill, assistant curator of Kew Gardens during the 1940s. These extraordinarily beautiful plants resemble *H. coccineum* at first glance, but produce only two flowers from each bract, with these appearing together and emitting a sweet, gardenialike fragrance. Together such mixed characters suggest hybrids of *H. coccineum* and the kahili ginger, *H. gardnerianum.*

Among the most beloved subtropical garden flowers, *Hedychium gardnerianum* has been carried throughout the warm parts of the world, spreading from its original Himalayan homeland. It has made itself perhaps too much at home in certain warm, moist places like New Zealand and Hawaii, where it is considered a pest in native forests. Nevertheless, Hawaiians revere these intoxicatingly fragrant flowers, conferring upon them the name *kahili* for their resemblance to the plumed standards carried in processions before native chiefs. Another name, garland flower, follows from Nepal, where this ginger provides traditional decorations for the festival of Indrajatra.

Wherever it is grown this giant of a plant attracts attention with broad, bluegreen foliage, forming stout canes to six feet In late summer lemony, precisely spaced flowers appear in foot-tall spikes, two blossoms emerging from each bract, with the bright red, two-inch stamens extending outward. These magisterial heads of bloom radiate a heavenly aroma that makes this ginger a favorite of all. The current epithet commemorates the Hon. Edward Gardner, representative for the East India Company at the court of Kathmandu. Reclassification of Hedychium is underway, however, and botanists will likely preserve the kahili ginger's older synonym, H. speciosum. Gardeners will be slow to accept this change.

Nurseries offer several desirable selections of *Hedychium gardnerianum* including the semi-dwarf, golden yellow four- to five-foot 'Compactum', and taller six- to eight-foot cultivars with light yellow flowers, such as 'Extendum' and 'Thai Kahili'. A variant from San Antonio ginger fancier Margaret Kane, 'Fiesta', offers red-throated, deep yellow blooms and lush, slightly drooping foliage.

Orange Delta

A unique hedychium native to Bhutan and a portion of eastern India, the redleaf ginger, or orange delta ginger (*Hedychium greenii*), occurs along jungle marshes, where its lush, three- to five-foot canes develop flourishing stands of polished foliage. The slender stems and undersides of the leaves reveal a dark, reddish coloring that complements five-inch floral spikes carrying crepe-textured, salmon-red flowers. These blooms are among the showiest in the genus, but unscented. They emerge from the green bracts a few at a time from midsummer through autumn. Botanists described the species from a plant growing in H. F. Green's Darjeeling garden in the early 1900s. Cultivated plants of *H. greenii* apparently stem from this original clone, a sterile selection that produces plantlets on the inflorescence after flowering and sometimes in lieu of flowers if it has been allowed to become too dry. These plantlets may be detached to start new clumps. The orange delta ginger thrives when planted as a marginal aquatic, its apparent habitat in nature.

Spiders

Oft-misspelled and -mispronounced, *Hedychium thyrsiforme* was named by William Roscoe for its large thyrse, or paniclelike cluster of flowers. This impressive inflorescence comprises a pale, rounded bottlebrush made up of slender, all-white flowers with long, exserted filaments, earning this ginger the nicknames white pincushion and frilly white. Although they are mostly unscented, the blooms, which appear at the end of summer and continue till frost, provide a graceful, spidery effect against the lush, gently corrugated foliage. Native to Nepal and eastern India, *H. thyrsiforme* makes a luxuriant specimen for moist soil under tall pines or at a woodland's edge, with broad leaves that gracefully bend the slender three- to four-foot pseudostems under their weight. A five- to six-foot hybrid introduced by Florida ginger specialist Tom Wood, 'Pink Sparks' provides a light rose version of *H. thyrsiforme* with a bonus of soft fragrance and rippled foliage tinted burgundy as it unfurls.

Although not much trialed in the South a few other spider-flowered hedychiums may be available from specialists and could prove successful. The huge *Hedychium stenopetalum* is the largest species in the genus, with ten- to twelve-foot pseudostems and feathery white blossoms assembled into foot-tall spikes, making a dramatic specimen for a sheltered site. A plant grown for many years as *H. forrestii* was originally introduced by famed plantsman Joseph Rock, presumably from Chinese collections. It has proven one of the hardiest gingers in British gardens, producing lush, seven-foot clumps of foliage topped by white, spidery blooms with a strong, sweet scent. The pink stamens of this plant suggest that it is actually a form of *H. spicatum*, a similarly spider-flowered Chinese ginger, as true *H. forrestii* has all-white flowers. This English garden clone, presently available from U.S. nurseries, may prove successful in the upper South, but will probably struggle in warmer areas. In these regions the true *H. forrestii*, native to lower elevations in China and Vietnam, might be a better choice.

Hybrid Ginger Lilies

Beyond these intriguing species, cultivars of *Hedychium* have become legion in recent decades. Southern gardeners may find themselves overwhelmed with this richness, but can hardly complain, as nearly all are beautiful. The Hawaiian introduction 'Anne Bishop' is a typically fine hybrid, combining the compact habit, broad foliage, intense fragrance, and reddish stamens of the kahili ginger with luscious apricot blooms of butterfly form. 'Palani' provides richly colored spikes suggestive of *H. coccineum*, but these are scented and show purplish overtones, as does the handsome foliage of this introduction. A beautiful wild-collected hedychium introduced as 'Thai Spirit' produces clear orange bottlebrush flowers with strong, sweet fragrance. A recent Tom Wood hybrid, 'Tarissima' promises sweet scent and enlarged, colorful blooms in the spirit of 'Tara'.

For lovers of pastels there are delectable choices, including several old cultivars such as 'Kewense', 'Samsheri', and 'Pradhani', probably derived from crosses between *Hedychium coccineum* and *H. coronarium* or near relatives. These carry lush, ladderlike, often blue-toned foliage, and bear wide clusters of fragrant, creamy blooms decorated with pinkish stamens and rose or peach-toned eyes. Modern hybrids like the floriferous 'Pink V', slender-caned 'Gold Flame', and tall-spiked Tai series also make long-blooming, fragrant garden subjects that display gently colored flowers. 'Daniel Weeks', a supposed cross of *H. gardnerianum* and *H. coronarium*, provides generous spikes of gold-centered, creamy-yellow blossoms that begin opening in June, continuing till frost. It is deliciously fragrant.

The rounded, apricot-suffused blooms of 'Orange Crush', 'Peach Delight', and 'Coronata Cream' resemble each other and an old favorite hybrid, 'Kinkaku', reportedly introduced from

Variegated *Hedychium* 'Dr. Moy' interplanted with parrot lily (*Alstroemeria psittacina*) and mother fern (*Woodwardia orientalis*) at Mercer Arboretum.

Hedychium 'Moy Giant' flowering at the San Antonio Botanical Garden.

Hawaii in the 1960s by a Mr. Koyama. These exquisite, six- to seven-foot plants crown the pastel theme. Their extra-wide segments, notched lips, and pinkish stamens create oversized, fragrant blossoms that appear in big clusters from late June till frost.

Vibrant colors, along with distinct form and fragrance, may be had from many other *Hedychium* hybrids. A true show plant, 'Elizabeth' sets large clusters of flamingo-pink blossoms with apricot buds and stamens on leafy, seven-foot stems; 'Tac Moto' gives fragrant flowers of deep, clear yellow; 'Lemon Sherbet' mixes soft yellow blooms with pink stamens and sweet aroma; 'White Starburst' presents icy, scented blossoms of butterfly form in a whorled inflorescence; 'Kai Yang' offers creamy flowers with the aroma of coconut. Although only lightly scented, the cream-colored 'Four-Way' (often sold as 'Rayna') and pale apricot 'Sherry Baby' make impressive specimens for gardens with arching, four-foot stems carrying rounded clusters of bloom over a long season.

'Dr. Moy', a four- to five-foot hedychium introduced in 1995 by the San Antonio Botanical Garden, graces gardens worldwide. This elegant plant displays spikes of attractive, peach-toned flowers in season, but its special value comes from an understated variegation of slender, creamy streaks dashed through the narrow, upright foliage. 'Moy Giant', another SABG introduction, sends up robust stems dressed in broad leaves and foot-tall trusses of sweet-scented, light yellow blooms. The creator of both, Ying Doon Moy, left a promising career as a plant breeder in China to escape to the United States with his family. He retired from the SABG in 1998, but his gingers, amaryllis, hardy mallow hibiscus, and papaya cultivars continue to enrich gardens in the South and elsewhere.

Epiphytes and Dwarfs

Surprisingly, a few of the tropical epiphytic hedychiums seem nearly hardy. The giant moth ginger (*Hedychium hasseltii*) typifies this group of tree-dwelling species, producing three-foot stems with elongated leaves and small spikes of long-tubed flowers. The yellowish buds open to reveal reddish stamens and creamy, sweet-scented blooms large for the plant. These slender flowers later ripen ornamental pods, displaying tangerine interiors and the bright red arils of the seeds. In their homeland in the highlands of Java the bright seeds attract birds and other animals, who carry them off, starting new plants in the branches of forest trees. *Hedychium hasseltii* makes a quietly attractive garden specimen and will survive in the lower South if given well-drained soil and protective mulching during hard freezes.

These unusual gingers have parented a series of usefully dwarf hybrids introduced by Tom Wood. 'Luna Moth', a beautiful, leafy, three- to four-foot selection, combines the elegant, winglike floral form of *Hedychium hasseltii* with the luscious fragrance and size of the white butterfly ginger. The magnificent blooms appear from July to November atop stout, upright pseudostems. The three- to four-foot 'Filigree' offers lush, arching foliage ideal for a foundation planting. Its small, sweetly fragrant flowers expand from golden buds in summer and fall, laxly displaying slender segments and a yellow throat. Although only four to five feet tall, 'Carnival' affords a show, with upright stems topped by long-blooming twelve-inch spikes in late summer. Its pale, peach-colored blossoms send out a lemony fragrance and show a birdlike form, suggesting a possible cross of *H. hasseltii* with *H. gardnerianum*. Another dwarf, 'Golden Glow', provides six-inch spikes of spicily fragrant blooms the color of orange soda. These translucent flowers, appearing in crops over the summer and fall, comple-

Hedychium 'Golden Glow' with needle palm (*Rhapidophyllum hystrix*), *Asparagus virgatus*, and *A. macowanii*, author's garden, Austin.

ment bright green, arching foliage. In our Austin garden, 'Golden Glow' has proven more forgiving of drought than other hedychiums, a capacity likely inherited from its epiphytic parent.

The extraordinarily showy hornbill ginger (*Hedychium longicornutum*) attaches roots to jungle trees in Malaya and southernmost Thailand, producing numerous heads of pointed, rust-colored buds, opening to coppery yellow flowers with curling petals and extra-long white stamens. The white, spidery-flowered sweet reed (*H. villosum* var. *tenuiflorum*) sets leathery roots to grow over damp, limestone ledges in the mountains of Yunnan. Although these species make worthwhile container subjects, their winter flowering cycles preclude garden use beyond frost-free areas. A four-foot hybrid of *H. longicornutum*, 'Lava Dome' flowers in summer and might be trialed in Southern gardens. At just two feet, 'Tropic Bird' is a compact specimen ideal for containers, and this drought-resistant, root-hardy cultivar might also succeed as a late-flowering subject for a protected courtyard, offering domed clusters of long-lasting blooms from September through February if not silenced by frost.

As flowers fade *Hedychium* 'Golden Glow' sends out new buds from the bracts of the old inflorescence.

An epiphyte usually sold as *H. muluense*, the dwarf Borneo ginger (*Hedychium philippinense*) carries sparse clusters of tiny blooms with long tubes and irregular, undulating segments. This and another small-flowered species from Indonesia, *H. horsfieldii*, are powerfully fragrant when in bloom, with handsome foliage and seed pods, but otherwise serve more as curiosities than ornamentals. A somewhat larger, free-blooming hybrid, 'Mutant', preserves the odd appeal of these species and adapts more readily to garden life.

Hedychium 'Lava Dome'.

Scitaminean Plants

William Roscoe, who had grown up in pre-industrial Liverpool, challenged the slave trade dominating his city with a poem, "The Wrongs of Africa": "Blush ye not, to boast your equal laws, your just restraints, your rights defin'd, your liberties secur'd, whilst with an iron hand ye crush to earth the helpless African." As a member of parliament, Roscoe sympathized with U.S. independence and later became a friend to Thomas Jefferson. Like Jefferson, Roscoe was a reformer and a gentleman gardener, importing plants from around the world to cultivate in his "stove," or heated greenhouse. In 1802 he founded the Liverpool Botanic Garden and in 1828, at his own expense, Roscoe published a sumptuously illustrated treatise on gingers and their relations, at that time known to botanists as *Monandrian Plants of the Order of Scitamineae*. Describing his favorite genus, Roscoe wrote:

> If *Hedychium* be the most splendid and *Alpinia* be the most elegant, *Curcuma* is undoubtedly the richest and most magnificent of the whole tribe of Scitaminean Plants; the lively and variegated colors of its singularly constructed flowers, the grandeur of its crimson and turbanlike coma or crown, and the luxuriance of its ample foliage, beautifully diversified with red in its stems, its petioles, and its leaves, all contributing to add to the Eastern-like magnificence of this stately genus.

As much as he extolled the beauty of *Curcuma*, Roscoe noted the greater value of these plants as foods, dyes, and medicines. The name of the genus derives from the Arabic *kurkum* for the yellowish color of Indian saffron, which is made from the roots of turmeric, *C. longa*. This treasured spice, of ancient cultivation in Asia and known in the West since Roman times, is a principal ingredient of curries and provides the rich orange dye that colors Buddhist robes. Turmeric figures in traditional ayurvedic medicine, and recent research confirms its antimicrobial and antioxidant qualities. Curcumin, turmeric's chief extract, demonstrates wound-healing, anti-fungal, anti-allergic, and anti-HIV properties as well as potency in suppressing cancers.

The soft, bananalike leaves and unique inflorescence of *Curcuma* give these heat-loving gingers a character different from *Hedychium*. Long-lasting, waxy scales form into a showy, conelike structure, in most species topped by a coma of colorful sterile bracts. The true flowers remain small, usually white or yellowish, with a prominent funnel-shaped lip, appearing a few at a time between the lower fertile bracts. In some species the inflorescence emerges at the tips of a leafy false stem during summer; in others it appears separately, directly from the ground, along with or prior to leaf emergence in spring. A few varieties flower in both spring and summer. Because gardeners discover blooms set down among the lush foliage, curcumas are commonly known as hidden gingers.

These deciduous plants grow naturally in monsoonal regions of India, Southeast Asia, and Indonesia, with one species ranging south to northern Australia. In order to survive the annual dry season, *Curcuma* species possess swollen rhizomes and wiry masses of thickened roots with clusters of aromatic tubers. The globular swellings contain food and moisture that help the plants endure dormancy, but, as with the similar roots of daylilies (*Hemerocallis* spp.), the secondary tubers do not have the capacity to form new stems on their own. When dividing curcumas for the garden it is essential to include a piece of the crown rhizome that carries buds from which new leaves and flowers may grow. Although this genus is native to essentially tropical climates, a surprising range of species have proven hardy in the South, so long as they are not kept unduly moist during winter dormancy.

Domestics

A number of curcumas in India, China, and Southeast Asia have been cultivated for millenia. One such is turmeric (*Curcuma longa*), formerly known and still sold as *C. domestica*. In the South this easy-growing three- to five-foot ginger produces modest, mostly green cones, blushed white with a bare tinge of lavender. The snow-capped inflorescence supports small yellow blooms that protrude from the bracts over several weeks. Flowering generally begins in midsummer, with cones set down among the broad, ribbed leaves, although some *C. longa* reportedly flower in spring, as well. Cultivars of turmeric appear to be sterile clones selected over the four thousand years this species has been in gardens. Their pungent, orange-colored tubers exude bright yellow juices, staining hands when cut, and can be dried in the sun and powdered to make the culinary spice. In the South this agricultural antique makes a quietly attractive subject for medium sun or bright shade.

Some ornamental gingers seem to be near relations of turmeric. The curcuma known as queen lily, or common hidden ginger, differs mainly in its longer-lasting, more rose-infused inflorescence and less pungent tubers. Generally sold as *Curcuma petiolata*, botanists suspect this variety represents an old selection of *C. longa*. The variegated 'Emperor' also appears to be a *C. longa* variant. Occasional creamy stripes stray inward from its whitened leaf edges, making handsome foliage patterns all season, with the pink cones joining the scene in midsummer. Another garden heirloom, 'Empress', is a selection of mango ginger (*C. amada*), which is widely cultivated in India for its edible tubers scented of green mango; this cultivar produces showy, felted cones in June along with luxuriant, sun-tolerant foliage. These heirloom hidden gingers are among the most successful and hardy curcumas, making fast-growing clumps of three- to five-foot, bright green, attractively pleated foliage. Gardeners willingly sacrifice some of this greenery, removing a few leaves to better reveal the rosy purple, pink, and green cones, which may also be enjoyed as cut flowers.

The most widely grown curcuma in the South, the giant plume of Burma (*Curcuma elata*), is a spring-blooming species introduced from the gardens of Myanmar. Before its foliage expands in May, apple-green cones sprout from the bare earth like fantastic mushrooms. Masses of rose-pink bracts create colorful comas at the tops of the inflorescences, distracting from small, pale yellow, true flowers. The garden effect can be spectacular and lasts for several weeks until leaves unfurl to obscure the fading blooms.

A hidden ginger sold as "*Curcuma petiolata*" nestles showy summer blooms among its leaves.

The giant plume of Burma (*Curcuma elata*) sends up its blooms in spring before the foliage.

The summer foliage of *Curcuma elata* resembles the leaves of bananas.

When well grown, the robust, pale green foliage of the giant plume ginger reaches four to eight feet. Wide, pleated blades rise directly from the ground, arranging into opposite ranks like gigantic oriental fans, with leaf stalks overlapping to give the plants a banana-like character. The broad foliage usually has a slight purplish feathering along the midrib, and, when touched on the underside, exhibits a surprising, silky texture. A few weeks before the arrival of killing frost this abundant greenery yellows and collapses, dying away until next summer.

Although not widely cultivated in the South, two hardy species native to the foothills of the Himalayas share the giant plume's spring-blooming habit and velvety underleaves. *Curcuma angustifolia* is a big plant, like *C. elata*. *Curcuma aromatica*, cultivated in southern China and Southeast Asia as a substitute for turmeric, provides wide, elliptical leaves terminating in long drip tips, an adaptation that helps shed water during annual monsoons.

Curcuma attenuata ranges from India into Thailand, producing distinctively narrow, silvery-green leaves that cup upward to reveal velvety undersurfaces. The slender, wine-topped cones appear before the leaves in spring and sometimes again in summer, assembling colorful, pointed bracts into tiered towers suggestive of fanciful pagodas. Thai nurseries offer varicolored selections originally collected from the wild, such as the wine-flushed 'Maroon Beauty' and darkest purple 'Black Thai'.

Zedoary and Other Burgundies

Another spring-flowering curcuma cultivated as a spice in the East, zedoary (*Curcuma zedoaria*) has proven easy as a garden plant in the lower South. Its wide, pleated leaves, smaller than those of *C. elata* at only three feet, display dark, purplish striping along the midribs, making a clump of these gingers ornamental even without bloom. In Malaysia the pungent foliage is used to wrap fish, imparting a pleasant gingerlike flavor when steamed. Zedoary thrives

Zedoary, *Curcuma zedoaria*.

Curcuma sp. 'Panama Purple'.

in filtered sun, sending up burgundy-tipped cones along with the new foliage in late spring. Plants offered in the trade as *Curcuma inodora*, *C. nilghierrensis*, and 'Panama Purple' are handsome, early bloomers that resemble zedoary.

With narrower, slightly taller foliage, pink and blue ginger (*Curcuma aeruginosa*) carries wine-colored featherings on its leaves, as well. This species gets its common name from its edible, pinkish tubers, which display blue-green stains when cut; these are valued as medicine and spice. Originally described from Myanmar, *C. aeruginosa* has, like other culinary gingers, a long history in gardens. Its rose- and wine-tipped inflorescences appear in spring along with the leaves, and sometimes again in summer. The tall-growing Chinese *C. yunnanensis* (Yunnan plume) also produces blue-staining tubers and rapidly forms clumps of broad, wine-streaked leaves. Appearing from July to October, hidden among the lush foliage, its plum-tipped cones have slender bracts.

With red featherings on the upper portions of its leaves and a ruddy flush on the base of its stems, 'Raspberry' is a long-blooming *Curcuma* that offers flowering cones of dark, purplish maroon bracts. These appear on separate stems in the spring, but in summer are set down in the midst of the smooth, spear-shaped leaves. Contrasting light yellow and gold flowers embraced by rose-flushed corolla lobes may be seen peeking out among the fertile bracts nearly to the top of the inflorescence. This strong-growing, showy ginger eventually reaches four feet along the Gulf, thriving in bright shade or part sun.

One of the most striking of the plume gingers, *Curcuma ferruginea* not only displays strong wine stripes on its foliage but also shows off rich burgundy-colored stems. The dark-toned shoots emerge along with mostly white cones in spring, complementing fertile coma bracts, tipped purple as if they had been dipped in bowls of wine. *Curcuma ornata* produces similar burgundy-brushed cones and has equally dark midribs and flowering stalks, but develops leaves with petioles flushed purple only at the base. *Curcuma* sp. 'Big Purple Thai' combines dark purplish stems with rosy, narrow-bracted cones like those of *C. yunnanensis*. These normally spring-blooming inflorescences also appear in summer on mature plants.

At present the most cold-resistant of the red-stemmed curcumas appears to be a selection of *Curcuma leucorhiza* introduced by North Carolina plantsman Frank Galloway as 'Summer Snow'. Its solid maroon leaf sheaths combine attractively with white flowering cones. These appear on two-foot stems at the end of summer, set among the lush, green, six-foot-high foliage. 'Summer Snow' endures near zero degree weather if not kept overly wet during dormancy.

Along the Gulf and in Florida the most remarkable red-stemmed curcuma is a plant originally imported from Thailand by Mike McCaffery of Gainesville, Florida. Now widely grown as 'Scarlet Fever' and offered by Thai nurseries as 'Big Red' or 'Red Giant', this spectacular cultivar combines beet-red stems with elegantly upright, gray-green leaves that display contrasting red midribs. The

Curcuma 'Raspberry'.   *Curcuma* sp. 'Scarlet Fever'.

pinkish spring cones, resembling those of zedoary, offer a bonus when they bloom, but hardly seem crucial given this plant's impressive foliage. 'Scarlet Fever' is more sun-tolerant than most curcumas and its handsome leaves are among the last to yellow in the fall.

Botanists have yet to weigh in on the exact identity of this ginger, but it is close to another striking, red-stemmed species, *Curcuma rubescens*. As a landscape specimen, *C. rubescens* produces wide, pleated, green foliage with a purplish overlay, along with remarkable waxy, deep red stems and midribs. Like 'Scarlet Fever', this sun-lover is safely hardy in the lower South and handsome enough to warrant bedding out or planting in containers beyond this range.

Summer Blooms

Not all summer-flowering curcumas are hidden gingers, as several species hardy along the Gulf produce stems that hold cones effectively above their foliage. One of these, the Aussie plume, or Cape York lily (*Curcuma australasica*), is a native of the sandstone country of northern Queensland, where it grows along freshwater streams and seasonally moist pockets in Cape York, Arnhem Land, and Thursday Island. The only curcuma native to Australia, *C. australasica* seems thoroughly at home in the South, swiftly forming impressive clumps to four feet. Aussie plume sometimes offers its warm rose flowering cones in spring, but

Aussie plume, or Cape York lily (*Curcuma australasica*).

Curcuma sumatrana 'Olena'. Photo by Lauren S. Ogden.

more typically produces them in summer along with the apple-green, elliptical foliage. The handsomely veined leaves arrange themselves neatly around the precise-looking cones, making a tidy flower display through the summer. A similar, magenta-bracted species from Indonesia, *C. sumatrana*, also makes a striking garden ginger, remaining compact at just two feet. It is available from nurseries as the cultivar 'Olena' (the Hawaiian word for turmeric). Both these attractive species thrive in bright shade, returning faithfully if sited on well-drained soil.

A recent hybrid (or possibly an unidentified *Curcuma* species from Thailand), 'Purple Prince' is another hidden ginger that offers a long-lasting summer display. Shortly after new shoots emerge in May, thick four- to five-inch cones develop in the heart of the plant, rising on stems held above rosettes of lance-shaped, silvery green leaves. Like the raucous, colorful blooms of tropical bromeliads, these compact cones grade upward from green through white to wine-infused coma bracts, making the two-foot plants festive choices for pots and plantings in filtered shade.

Jewels of Siam

Among the most beautiful summer-flowering curcumas is a plant with tall, mostly pink cones known as the layered lotus or jewel of Thailand. Nurseries list it as *Curcuma cordata*, but botanists note prominent petioles on the leaves and the close accord of this species with an illustration in Roscoe's treatise of *C. petiolata*. However designated, this treasure is a magnificent flower, with waxy bracts stacked into a precise tower and set amid, but not obscured by, handsomely rippled, medium green leaves. These flowering cones often exceed a foot in height, with the whole plant less than two feet, creating a dramatic impression over several weeks as the tiny yellow true flowers take turns protruding among the bracts. 'Alba' is a beautiful white form of this plant, and Thai nurseries are developing more selections for the cut flower trade. These aristocratic gingers should be afforded raised positions with rich, well-drained soil that will not be soggy during winter dormancy. They otherwise seem remarkably easy-growing, thriving in medium sun or high, filtered shade.

With emerald leaves and fiery, terra-cotta bracts coalesced into a glistening spire, the pride of Burma (*Curcuma roscoeana*) is even more fabulous, but it is also more finicky as a garden subject. This queenly native of the Irrawaddy River delta in Myanmar prefers light, sandy soils. The rhizomes are apt to rot away over winter if left in cold ground, but also resent entirely dry storage. Most gardeners succeed only by keeping *C. roscoeana* as a summer pot plant or bedding subject in a rich, loamy mix of peat, coarse sand, and compost. 'Alimanda' is a tissue-cultured selection of the species with fiery red-orange blooms ideal as cut flowers, and may prove more tractable in gardens. Hybrids between the jewel of Thailand (itself sometimes called pink roscoeana) and *C. roscoeana* may also prove easier to grow and promise magnificent colors; 'Sulee Rainbow' and 'Royal Scepter' offer fantastic multicolored cones with waxy bracts shading upward, sunset-style, from orange through pink.

The rainbow curcuma (*Curcuma aurantiaca*), from the borders of Thailand and Cambodia, duplicates some effects of these crosses, with graded bracts in shades of brown, red, orange, and pink. Some less highly colored, but no less attractive variants produce entirely lime-green cones. These, together with glossy, rippled foliage, complement unusually conspicuous true flowers, which in this species are bright golden orange. The fat, burnt-copper inflorescence of 'Khymer Orange' suggests that this Cambodian introduction is a selection of *C. aurantiaca*. These compact gingers make fine pot plants and seem adaptable to gardens.

Karst Tulips

North and east from the temple-filled city of Chiang Mai the landscape rises toward the infamous Golden Triangle. The hills in this part of Thailand, formed from karst limestones, support tropical savannahs with unique plants adapted to the shallow soils. These parch completely during the dry season, only to become waterlogged as moisture percolates through the lime rock during the monsoon. This unusual habitat provides a home to the beautiful Siam tulip, *Curcuma alismatifolia*—and also creates a challenge for gardeners who wish to cultivate these plants.

With slender, leathery, gray-green leaves, enlarged petal-like coma bracts, and compact cones on tall stems, *Curcuma alismatifolia* approximates a tulip in silhouette. Its pale, mauve-pink bloom also suggests the poppies formerly planted in this region for the opium trade. Now an important bulb and cut flower crop in Thailand, Siam tulips may be had in numerous cultivars, the most familiar of which are color forms such as 'Chiang Mai Pink', 'Chiang Mai Ruby', and 'Tropic Snow'. Newer selections, such as 'Kimono Pink', exhibit useful dwarf habits, remaining only eighteen inches tall, while others, like the magenta-bracted 'Thai Beauty', show attractive maroon striping on the leaves. All sprout from distinctively clustered masses of teardrop-shaped tubers, and all produce a succession of small, lavender-lipped true flowers, which are typical of this section of *Curcuma*. A position in full sun with unfailing summer moisture followed by dry conditions during dormancy are this plant's needs. This makes *C. alismatifolia* easy as a container subject, but challenging for more general garden use.

The very slender Cambodian varieties 'Siam Ruby' and 'Pink Pearls' seem more forgiving and successful in partial shade. These grassy-leafed miniatures make charming pot plants with small cones that carry colorful bracts tipped white or green. They must be planted en masse to have any effect in the garden. Sometimes identified as forms of *Curcuma sparganifolia*, they are known in Thailand as precious patumma.

A group of gingers imported from Laos and sold as *Curcuma gracillima* have similarly small cones marked with dark reddish striping. These graceful plants produce gray-green foliage, varying from narrowly grassy in the dark-flowered clone 'Violet' to broad spears in the white and maroon 'Candy Cane' ('Chocolate Zebra'). Botanists now identify these as selections of *C. rhabdota*. In the South they seem more adaptable than Siam tulips, blooming successfully in medium sun to part shade.

Another good performer, *Curcuma parviflora* produces elegant, white-topped cones held on twelve- to eighteen-inch stems above dark green, long-stemmed leaves. The spiraling green fertile bracts house a succession of impish, purple-lipped blossoms that take turns peeking from the inflorescence. *Curcuma thorelii* (Chiang Mai snow) offers similar white and green cones on tall plants with fewer leaves; it is popular as a florist's crop. Also good as a cut flower, the all-green *C. harmandii* captures rainwater in its upturned bracts, sporting small, orchidlike true flowers. It is a curiosity in the garden rather than a show-piece, thriving in half-day sun or bright shade.

'Ladawan' is a remarkable natural hybrid between *Curcuma alismatifola* and *C. cordata*. Its pearly, mauve-pink coma bracts resemble those of the Siam tulip, but the rest of its tall inflorescence has more of a jewel-of-Thailand character, with precisely sculpted, waxy green bracts grading upward to the pink top. The pointed tubers and rhizomes of 'Ladawan' are similar to those of *C. alismatifolia*, but it inherits the attractively pleated foliage of *C. cordata*. This elegant, easy-to-grow curcuma has long-lasting pink blooms, and, like its parents, makes a show for containers or borders.

Runners

One group of curcumas has specialized in life as colonial denizens of forest floors. Their wormlike, questing rootstocks periodically send up fans of attractive, pleated leaves, spacing the bright tufts of green a foot or so apart to make

Curcuma rubrobracteata edging a shaded path at Mercer Arboretum.

sparse but extensive patches of foliage. These rambling gingers produce flowering cones that lack a coma, bearing them in such a way that they seem to erupt from the ground, although they actually sprout, at or below the soil, from the bases of the leaves.

Looking like fantastic jungle toadstools, the summer-blooming cones of *Curcuma rubrobracteata* make balls of glossy, orange-red, all-fertile bracts with protruding bright yellow true flowers. This species quickly naturalizes along the Gulf, enlivening otherwise drab summer woodlands. It is commonly sold as "*Curcuma flaviflora*" or as 'Fire' ('Ruby', 'Red Fireball'). A similar, narrow-leaved species, sold as 'Ribbon', produces hot-pink cones with light yellow blooms.

Curcuma bicolor, nicknamed candy corn ginger for its loudly colored, orange and yellow inflorescence, is another leafy species that spreads rapidly through woodlands. 'Sri Pok', a Vietnamese cousin, is likewise festive, with red bracts, orange blooms, and maroon-blushed petioles. More subdued purplish cream cones bearing snowy blossoms striped with yellow appear from the sleeping princess or gold band ginger (*C. pierreana*). These novelties seem easy to grow in moist, shaded situations. For showing off their ground-level flowers, a raised bed would be an assist.

Minor Relations

A *Curcuma* ally with pagodalike, white cones and long-tubed, pale yellow flowers, is sometimes offered by importers as *Smithatris supraneenae* 'Siam Plati-

num'. A similar species with blue-toned foliage, greenish cones, and long, exserted white blossoms, may be had as *Hitchenia glauca* 'Rangoon Beauty'.
Although delicate and fragrant, these remain rare in gardens and have not been
widely tested for hardiness.

Another minor *Curcuma* relation, *Stahlianthus involucratus*, has shown itself to be a stalwart performer, thriving in the lower South and up through
coastal North Carolina. Native from south China to Thailand, this small ginger
makes an attractive, dwarf, foliage perennial with dense clusters of eight- to
twelve-inch, lance-shaped leaves suffused red on the undersides and striped red
along the midrib above. Tiny, white flowers, more curious than beautiful, appear one or two at a time in late spring as the new shoots emerge. *Stahlianthus
involucratus* prospers through hot weather and helps furnish shady gardens
with luxuriant greenery.

Also useful in this regard is *Boesenbergia rotunda*. Long cultivated in Asia
for its thick, aromatic roots, this spice plant (commonly known as *khao chae*,
"Chinese keys") makes clumps of mid-green, heart-shaped leaves on four- to
six-inch petioles. Small, rose-purple flowers appear singly along the leaf stems
in summer, but it is the lush, hostalike foliage that provides the principal ornament, particularly in the selection 'Maroon Keys', which is suffused burgundy
on the leaf undersides.

Cornukaempferia aurantiflora (upper right)
with a collection of dwarf *Kaempferia*
species and *Iris japonica* 'Eco Easter',
author's garden, Austin.

Velvet Butterflies

Such foliage utterly pales, however,
when compared to leaves of the genus
Cornukaempferia. First described in
1997 from plants collected in northern
Thailand, these remarkable gingers
produce broad, oval foliage not only
tinted purple below but also decorated
above with reflective, silvery spots set
against a satiny, black-green background. Glowing orange-yellow flowers appear sporadically in summer,
providing interest, although they
hardly surpass the stunning effect of
the clustered, prostrate leaves. Although only recently brought into cultivation, *C. aurantiflora* 'Jungle Gold'

has been widely introduced from tissue culture. This selection is proving to be an easy-growing, deciduous ginger for shaded gardens in the lower South, far tougher than its exotic-looking foliage might suggest. Another species, *C. longipetiolata*, produces taller, less spotted leaves along with slightly larger blooms; it may also prove hardy along the Gulf.

Peacocks

Throughout Southeast Asia one genus of small, deciduous gingers has specialized in exploiting root-filled soils beneath jungle trees and crevices among limestone rocks, places that remain dry much of the year, but become moistened during the annual monsoon. With attractive white, pink, or lavender blossoms, and stemless, often magnificently patterned leaves, these peacock gingers (*Kaempferia* spp.) have few rivals as hot-weather ornamentals. In the lower South they have become popular as basic summer furnishings for shaded gardens.

Although generally easy-growing, *Kaempferia* species can try a gardener's patience, sometimes waiting as late as mid-June before breaking dormancy. This tardy appearance mimics the natural cycle of the Asian monsoon, which is preceded by an extended dry period with hot, sweltering weather. *Kaempferia* and other gingers attuned to this rhythm require several weeks of truly warm soil temperatures before coming into growth. This makes them the very last perennials to waken from winter sleep and may be a cause for surprise to gardeners who have given up on their return. Like curcumas, these small gingers sprout from thickened rhizomes that also carry storage tubers; the fast-multiplying rootstocks offer a ready means for increase and may be divided in spring as they break from dormancy.

With paired, long-stemmed leaves up to two feet, the resurrection lily, or tropical crocus (*Kaempferia rotunda*), is among the tallest of the peacock gingers. The oblong foliage arranges into upright fans that provide an attraction all summer, showing dark purple undersides and silver-flecked variegations on their upper surfaces. Several weeks before the leaves appear, *K. rotunda* carpets the ground with white and lavender flowers. These seem to sprout directly from the earth, often blooming crocus-style with fallen leaves as their only foils. Three elongated corolla lobes (the petals) frame a lavender lip and two white, petal-like segments, fashioning blooms with the overall look of an orchid. The three-inch blossoms possess a sparkling, succulent quality reminiscent of African violets and have a pleasant fragrance. They last only a day, but new ones pop up each morning for a fortnight. Established clumps make a striking statement in the foreground of a shady border.

Kaempferia rotunda stands a good deal of cold if mulched during winter and is fully hardy south of a line from Austin to Charleston. Native from southern China through Thailand and the Himalayan foothills, it is also widely cultivated in Asia for its young leaves, shoots, and rhizomes. The common culinary form of the species sends up olive-green foliage decorated with silver markings and red-feathered undersides. A selection discovered near the border of Thailand and Laos, 'Raven' offers an improvement on this with narrowly upright leaves infused with purple and brushed silvery-gray above.

Spring blooms of *Kaempferia rotunda* 'Silver Diamonds'.

Most striking of all, 'Silver Diamonds' displays leaves that combine saturated, ruby-toned undersides with upper surfaces painted in large, platinum swatches against a dark green background. Although the spring flowers of 'Silver Diamonds' appear typical for *Kaempferia rotunda*, its distinctive foliage appears on short, obliquely held petioles. This makes this variety especially showy in the garden and also suggests it might deserve separate taxonomic recognition.

A number of novel gingers have made their way into gardens via Bangkok's immense Chatuchak weekend market, having been brought in from the wilds of Southeast Asia to some of its nine thousand vendor stalls. Others have been discovered by plant explorers like John Banta of Alva, Florida, who had one of the best days of his career when he walked up on a giant-leafed, spotted kaempferia growing in the darkened understory of a bamboo forest. Although the beautifully patterned ginger looked a good deal like *Kaempferia rotunda*, everything about it was bigger, with wide, ruby-backed leaves just shy of two feet long. When the rosy purple blossoms arrived (pre-

Summer foliage of *Kaempferia rotunda* 'Silver Diamonds' with *Ajuga reptans* 'Valfredda'.

cociously, as in *K. rotunda*), they proved the largest in the genus, over three inches across with distinctive yellow throats. Not yet described by botanists, this robust species has already become a popular garden plant in the South, making its way as 'Grande'. In some instances the showy blooms recur in summer; its remarkable leaves flaunt multiple ranks of silvery blotches, rivaling the most exotic tropical foliage.

Several other kaempferias remain quietly green. The fingeroot or lesser galangale, *Kaempferia galanga*, is one of these, native from India through Thailand, subtropical China, and Taiwan. Its wide, oval leaves hug the ground in flattened pairs up to a foot and a half across. Such shy habits are typical of *Kaempferia* species adapted to rocky places, where their spreading, stemless foliage helps plants cling to steep embankments and barren slopes. *Kaempferia galanga* makes an attractive garden ginger, bearing one-inch white blooms with purple-blotched lips; these nest attractively in the midst of the smooth, green foliage in summer. Its fleshy roots are cultivated for medicine and spice and are the inspiration for its botanical name, a distortion of the Chinese *liang jiang* ("mild ginger").

Also green, but with much narrower leaves and fast-multiplying roots, *Kaempferia angustifolia* is another dwarf variety native to rocky embankments, where it makes a versatile summer groundcover. The lush, undulating foliage develops into thick clumps, preceded and sometimes accompanied by small, white blossoms. These have lavender lips with purple blotches and are delicately attractive. 'Gilbert' (*K. gilbertii*), a selection with a creamy marginal variegation, and '3-D', a sport introduced by Tom Wood with a mixture of white, lime, and dark green foliage, add interest to this species, but are slower to multiply.

Another kaempferia with simple green foliage, *Kaempferia parviflora* has long petioles, making leafy clumps flushed red beneath. It looks like *Boesenbergia*, save for its white and purple flowers. Thais consider this modest-looking ginger to be an aphrodisiac, placing it in high demand as an herbal treatment for impotence.

For gardeners, however, it is the heavily patterned, ground-hugging kaempferias that deserve pride of place. Among the most beautiful, the jewel-like *Kaempferia atrovirens* displays repeated designs of silver and chocolate paralleling the leaf margins, with pale, reflective undersurfaces. White, pur-

Spring flowers of *Kaempferia* sp. 'Grande'.

ple-lipped blooms appear before the foliage, as with *K. angustifolia*. Although described originally as a native of tropical Borneo, this species endures in gardens along the Gulf, so long as it is offered shade and fast-draining soil. It makes attractive clumps in time.

Faster and altogether easier, however, are several varieties of *Kaempferia pulchra*, the thriftiest of which is 'Manson'. This fast-multiplying selection emerges in early summer with bronze-toned foliage vaguely marked by darker peacock patterns. These leaf colorings fade to near green by midsummer, but 'Manson' is especially floriferous, offering a daily succession of lavender-pink blossoms. Flowers of this and other *K. pulchra* forms display lobed lips along with pairs of oval segments, so that the blooms appear to have four equally rounded petals.

The common bronze-leafed *Kaempferia pulchra* is less inclined to multiply than 'Manson'. Its wide leaves unfurl to show a translucent copper tone that matures to ruddy purple. Sparkling lavender blooms complement the velvety, nonfading foliage, which also bears subtle patterning and several chevronlike flecks of silver.

If gardeners had to choose only one variety of this species, however, it might be 'Silverspot'. The oblong foliage of this remarkable selection shows a pale, silvery-turquoise heart surrounded by serrated bands of chocolate-green and silver. These gingers form lusty, fast-multiplying clumps that soon become crowded, turning an occasional leaf to expose the pale undersurface and showing off frosted lavender blooms. Uniquely, the thick-textured leaves of 'Silverspot' remain in good condition until cut down by frost, making this the last peacock ginger to enter winter dormancy.

Kaempferia pulchra 'Manson' with *Dianella tasmanica* 'Variegata'.

With a similarly dramatic banded pattern and large, nearly circular leaves, *Kaempferia pulchra* 'Roscoe' is another especially beautiful selection, available in both purple- and white-flowered forms. John Banta used the white-flowered 'Roscoe' to create 'Alva', an impressive hybrid with rounded leaves nearly twelve inches across. Light mauve-pink blooms with white eyes are set off by thick foliage attractively brushed with rippled bands of chocolate. As with many hybrids, 'Alva' shows improved vigor; in Austin it has proven one of the most reliable peacock gingers.

Although casually similar to the white-flowered parent of 'Alva', the true *Kaempferia roscoeana* differs by producing just two circular leaves decorated with black feathering and banding. These entirely flatten against the ground, and if plants are dug up, will close around the roots. Such soil-grabbing foliage seems to help these small gingers cling to crevices and cliffs in their native homes.

Several peacock gingers formerly listed as forms of *Kaempferia laotica* are now included as variants of *K. elegans*, a widespread species native from India through Southeast Asia, Sichuan, and the Philippines. Taxonomically inclined gardeners may distinguish these from *K. pulchra* by an enlarged anther crest and slightly longer floral tubes, although the effects of their patterned leaves seem much the same.

An especially striking peacock ginger, *Kaempferia pulchra* 'Silverspot' with *Stahlianthus involucratus*.

The small-growing 'Green Ripple' is the least dramatic selection of *Kaempferia elegans*, with wavy-edged, medium green leaves and iridescent, soft purple blossoms. It is slow to spread. In contrast, 'Satin Checks' prospers, soon making an effective groundcover of satiny green leaves boldly splashed with arched ranks of black swatches. 'Brush Strokes' offers a similarly low, spreading habit, but displays a less obvious, blurred patterning. These patterned selections are good doers, making many small tubers that may be split off to start new plants.

Discovered by John Banta in the same bamboo forest with 'Grande', the stunning 'Shazam' displays six-inch platinum leaves boldly patterned with jagged rows of purplish maroon checks. As with all *Kaempferia elegans* forms, glistening four-"petaled" purple flowers appear among its foliage through sum-

Kaempferia 'Alva'.

Kaempferia elegans 'Shazam'.

Kaempferia sp. 'Hieroglyphics'.

mer. This remarkably decorative ginger affords leafy cover under live oaks, succeeding with competitive roots and considerable drought. Perhaps this is not a surprising feat for 'Shazam', given its challenging native habitat.

More novel kaempferias continue to find their way into gardens. An undescribed, narrow-leafed species from Laos bears paired leaves, striped lengthwise with silver; the even more remarkable 'Hieroglyphics' shows transverse patterns of delicate netting against wide green midribs. Both carry oblong leaves something like those of *Kaempferia angustifolia*, but hold them close to the ground. Other ground-huggers include an unusual maroon-leafed species, as yet unnamed, and the recently described *K. grandifolia* ('Rex'), an enormous, green-foliaged species with two- to three-foot circular leaves. A new John Banta hybrid, 'Titan', combines this foliar giant with 'Grande'. A night-blooming species dubbed 'Red Knight'; the aptly named, thread-leafed *K. filifolia*; a unique species with camouflagelike mottling known as 'Leopard Spot'; and *K. candida*, a white-flowered relation of *K. rotunda*, suggest the further promise of this genus. For shaded beds in the lower South it is hard to imagine more rewarding summer subjects.

Pinecones

Although few members of the genus *Zingiber* are as obviously showy as peacock gingers, some of the most architecturally satisfying gingers belong here, with sheltering, leafy stems that arch gracefully upward in the habit of butterfly gingers. In most species, densely bracted, oval cones appear on separate leafless shoots. Often, these basal inflorescences resemble pinecones.

This genus includes the culinary gingerroot, *Zingiber officinale*, namesake of the ginger family, Zingiberaceae. Both the generic and common name derive from the Sanskrit *shringavera* ("shaped like a deer horn"), an apt description of the branching rhizomes of *Z. officinale*. Although adapted to garden culture in the warm South, the culinary ginger is not especially ornamental.

The Japanese woodland ginger (*Zingiber mioga*), a surprisingly hardy member of this group, bears lance-shaped, aromatic leaves and pungent, edible rhizomes. In Hawaii the bracts of its cone are sliced as relish and in its native Japan the orchidlike flowers are eaten in tempura. In late summer these translucent blooms appear at ground level around established clumps, creating an effect like hundreds of creamy yellow crocuses. This handsome, temperate ginger thrives from the coastal Carolinas into the upper South, but may sulk in hotter areas unless heavily watered. 'Dancing Crane', an attractive variegated selection introduced by Japanese horticulturist Dr. Masato Yokoi, makes

Zingiber mioga 'Dancing Crane' with *Farfugium japonicum, Helleborus foetidus,* and hostas in Alan Galloway's garden, Raleigh, N.C.

a showy subject for positions in bright shade; its two-foot shoots carry dark green leaves with white flares streaming from the midribs.

In the lower South *Zingiber zerumbet* is popularly known as shampoo ginger or red pinecone ginger. Its leafy pseudostems sprout with the advent of hot weather, and in midsummer this splendid subtropical sends up numerous foot-high stems bearing four- to six-inch, greenish flowering cones. When squeezed these emit sudsy, aromatic juices used as shampoo in Hawaii, where this ginger, known as *awapuhi*, has long been naturalized. After the small white flowers finish peeking from between the scales, the long-lasting cones slowly turn a vibrant red.

Zingiber zerumbet revels in damp, shaded positions where its creeping roots may be allowed to ramble among ferns or other loose groundcovers. Although the pseudostems become several feet long, they usually bow back toward the

Shampoo ginger (*Zingiber zerumbet*)
with *Iris japonica*, Chinese star anise
(*Illicium henryi*), and yellowing foliage
of red buckeye (*Aesculus pavia*).

earth so that the overall height of the plants remains less than four feet. Over time a graceful sea of arching stems fills the background of a shady garden. As frost approaches these bright green pseudostems turn yellow, collapsing over the spent, reddish cones.

'Darcey', a very beautiful variegated form of *Zingiber zerumbet*, bears glossy leaves edged and marked with creamy striping. Other selections of the species include 'Hainan Pink', from south China, with pyramidal, rose-colored cones, and an unusual selection from Tim Chapman, 'Twice as Nice', that bears small cones on the ends of the leafy pseudostems as well as on separate basal shoots. A similar species from Thailand, *Z. ottensii*, offers purplish stems and prolific flowering cones. These emerge with a ruddy, purple-red tone from the start, bearing small orange flowers.

Although many *Zingiber* species are naturally deciduous and hardy in the South, the very beautiful *Z. spectabile* is by nature evergreen, requiring a sheltered position protected from hard freezes if it is to offer its magnificent waxy cones. These water-storing inflorescences reach a foot in height with overlapping bracts bearing rolled lips, darkening from green to red as they mature. 'Singapore Gold' and 'Pink Maraca' are color selections of the species. As with the common red form, they flower reliably only where freezes are rare, although the plants themselves recover from such setbacks.

The deciduous jewel pagoda (*Zingiber neglectum*) is more forgiving of cold snaps. Like *Z. spectabile*, this Indonesian ginger is blessed with spectacularly large flowering cones with waxy, pouchlike bracts. The tapered inflorescences appear among upright, six-foot pseudostems in late summer, blushing red from the bottom as small, white and lavender flowers peer from the bracts. A spectacular cut flower, this species is not yet widely grown in the South. A ginger sold as 'Burmese Ruby' appears similarly worthwhile.

Also exceptional, *Zingiber collinsii* produces arching purplish pseudostems with dark-toned leaves handsomely barred in silver chevrons. Such foliage is reason enough to have this dwarf ginger in a shaded garden, but the species also offers late summer clusters of pointed cones, which turn a brilliant orange-red as they mature. This showy, easy-growing Vietnamese ginger has proven hardy wherever *Z. zerumbet* succeeds.

Other deciduous *Zingiber* species, such as the ivory-coned *Z. niveum*, popularly sold as 'Milky Way', and the pale yellow *Z. parishii* ('Ivory Ice', 'Lemon Lights') also succeed in the lower South. These delightful plants produce narrow, pale green foliage to three feet, thriving with abundant summer moisture. A four- to six-foot Thai species available from tissue culture as *Z. citriodorum*, Chiang Mai princess appears more challenging to grow, but holds out a reward of gray-green foliage and angular cones composed of brilliant red pointed bracts. The chocolate pinecone ginger (*Zingiber montanum*) lives up to its common name by producing unusual brown floral cones among slender, upright pseudostems. This six-foot species (formerly *Z. cassumunar*) is widely cultivated as a medicinal plant in Asia.

The squat red cones of *Zingiber rubens* project just far enough above the soil to allow its rose-blushed, red-flecked blooms to emerge. Such ground level displays are usually more intriguing than showy, but this prodigious Indian ginger also offers handsome, tropical-looking foliage. Another species worthwhile as a foliage plant, the palm-leaf ginger (*Z. gramineum*) sends up arching pseudostems that look like the feathered fronds of a cycad.

Dancing Girls

The fancifully named dancing girls (*Globba* spp.) are so called for their original-looking flowers, each of which bears a small, irregular lip clustered with two petal-like segments, three narrow lobes, and a long, arching filament tipped, cometlike, by an enlarged, winged anther. These odd, fairy-sized blooms combine in racemes with several loosely arranged bracts, sometimes of different colors, to create a unique inflorescence held at the tips of the short pseudostems. *Globba* enjoys the same growing conditions as other dwarf ginger genera native to Southeast Asian understories, developing gracefully arching foliage like miniature versions of *Zingiber* or *Hedychium*. Plants are hardy in the lower South and in Florida.

The yellow dancing girl (*Globba schomburgkii*) is among the most prolific, due largely to numerous small bulbils that develop on its pendulous inflorescence. These may be gathered and planted, or left to fall naturally in the garden,

The patterned leaves of variegated shell ginger provide an elegant resting place for a green tree frog.

and will grow to flowering size in a year or less, quickly increasing a colony of these small gingers to impressive dimensions. The long-lasting sprays of tiny, golden blooms carry through most of the summer, appearing at the tips of twelve- to eighteen-inch stalks furnished with dusty, blue-green leaves. A small colony of this gracefully arching species makes a satisfying treatment for a shady slope.

The mauve dancing girl, *Globba winitii*, sports a vibrant combination of purplish bracts and cascading yellow flowers on a small plant dressed with pendant leaves that have distinctive, overlapping, heart-shaped bases. This elegant species rarely produces bulbils, but its rhizomes multiply steadily and may be divided at any time. A species with similar habits and foliage is *G. magnifica*; its selection 'White Dragon' dangles long-lasting white bracts as foils for its small yellow blooms.

Usually sold as forms of *Globba winitii* are several selections of a species with purplish leaf undersides and small, mauve-pink flowers. At less than a foot in height the mauve-toned 'Lavender Dragon', maroon 'Ruby Queen', rosy 'Pristina Pink', white-bracted 'Purest Angel', and pink and white bicolor 'Blushing Maiden' make decorative pot plants. Marketed as the Jungle Jewels series, all possess extraordinarily persistent blooms, staying in good condition for up to a month, a character they share with 'Elegant Lace', a white-bracted variety without the maroon-backed foliage of the Jungle Jewels.

Purple globe ginger (*Globba globulifera*) is another prolific species that naturally reproduces by bulbils, bearing a rounded, purple inflorescence with tightly clustered bracts and flowers. 'Silver Comet' (usually listed as a form of *Globba pendula*) is one of several species with attractively marked foliage; in this instance, burgundy-backed leaves with silvery striped midribs and margins. As with *Globba colpicola*, usually sold as 'Golden Dragon', this robust species develops a compound inflorescence with many golden yellow blooms and pale, inconspicuous bracts.

The porcelain, grapelike flower clusters of variegated shell ginger, *Alpinia zerumbet* 'Variegata'.

The mauve dancing girl (*Globba winitii*).

Shells

The grand, evergreen gingers of the genus *Alpinia* manifest an almost military bearing, with bamboolike stems up to nine feet. These are furnished with alternate ranks of broad, spear-shaped leaves, often smelling of cinnamon when crushed or bruised. In warmer regions these mostly tropical gingers are highly regarded for both foliage and flower. Even relatively hardy varieties suffer if frozen, however, as their blooms appear only from the tips of second year stems. These evergreens also resent extended dry storage; their creeping rhizomes may be divided in spring or fall, but should be immediately replanted.

Native to Taiwan, *Alpinia zerumbet* is the common shell ginger of gardens, bearing dense clumps of long-bladed, leathery leaves on gently arching, outward-leaning canes to twelve feet. This majestic plant shows tremendous vigor and tolerates drought and sun better than many gingers. If given a mild winter or frost-sheltered position, abundant flower buds will appear in spring, hanging from the tips of the outstretched stems like bunches of porcelain grapes. These open one at a time over several weeks, expanding bell-shaped, waxy lips, striped with delicate red and yellow markings. The pendulous clusters of iridescent bloom underscore the romantic qualities of the shell ginger, a subject of countless photographs in books on tropical horticulture.

A slightly shorter, yellow-striped form of *Alpinia zerumbet* possesses one of the most satisfying variegations of subtropical perennials. Once a high-priced rarity, *A. zerumbet* 'Variegata' has become common through micropropagation and is now a standard landscape plant in the coastal South. This showy variety withstands more sun than many variegated plants and is popular for containers. 'Yu Hwa' ('Chinese Beauty') is an *A. zerumbet* cultivar with mostly dark green leaves gently striated lighter green.

'Sun Spice', a brightly variegated selection of the even hardier Chinese species *Alpinia intermedia*, offers gold-brushed foliage on compact stems to three feet. This recent introduction recovers quickly from hard freezes and promises to become popular in much of the South, as it can remain evergreen through temperatures in the low twenties. The extraordinary *A. formosana*, an apparent hybrid between *A. zerumbet* and *A. intermedia*, has also proven fairly cold resistant, offering a unique pinstripe variegation. Although not commonly cultivated, the green-foliaged form of *A. intermedia* is attractive and worthwhile in the lower South; it is known as white blizzard for its upright clusters of small, white flowers.

After a mild winter *Alpinia formosana* produces showy blooms from the tips of the previous year's stems.

The unique pinstripe variegation of *Alpinia formosana*.

These massed blooms resemble the inflorescence of the culinary galangale, *Alpinia galanga*, treasured in Thai cooking (its aromatic roots give tom yum soup its distinctive pinelike scent). Although not especially ornamental, *A. galanga* blooms reliably even after hard frosts, producing buds from the current season's growth. Nevertheless, this and other spice-yielding alpinias such as *A. conchigera* are uncommonly planted in the South.

Resisting frost to 20°F, *Alpinia japonica* is, perhaps, the most cold-hardy alpinia in Southern gardens, making two-foot mounds of dense, green foliage, felted beneath. Upright clusters of pink and white blooms appear at the tips of its stems in spring. Long naturalized in warm parts of Japan, *A. japonica* is originally native to southern China and Taiwan. 'Strawberries and Cream', a Tom Wood hybrid of this species, offers larger, showier blooms. 'Extra Spicy' is an attractively variegated *A. japonica* selection. The pink- and white-flowered ginger sold as *A. japonica* 'Peppermint Stick' seems to be a hybrid cross of *A. japonica* with *A. intermedia*.

Other Chinese *Alpinia* species, such as the undulate-leaved *A. hainanensis* (usually sold as *A. henryi* or *A. katsumadae*), also seem well adapted in the South. Although *A. hainanensis* can become nearly as large as *A. zerumbet*, it commonly remains under four feet in gardens, making attractive mounds of smooth, dark green leaves. Following a mild winter, jonquil-scented blooms appear in upright clusters at the tips of the stems, opening from creamy buds to display yellow interiors gently brushed with red.

A pink-flowered ginger recently introduced from China and sometimes sold as *Alpinia henryi* 'Pink Perfection' may also be listed as a variety of the related *A. oxyphylla* as 'Pink Sensation'. By either name this ginger appears to be an exciting prospect for Southern gardeners, offering relatively hardy, wavy foliage with velvety undersides and showy, pink, honey-scented blooms. A white-budded selection listed as *A. oxyphylla* 'China White' also seems promising.

Alpinia rugosa, a four-foot species recently described from Yunnan, offers remarkable olive-green leaves wrinkled and folded like miniature relief maps. Although this species has attractive white and red blooms, its uniquely sculptural foliage is the main draw. The dwarf, creeping *A. pumila* is another Chinese species with interesting foliage, offering velvety, green blades barred with silver, much like those of *Zingiber collinsii*. These wide leaves withstand hard frost and are held just six inches above the soil, rising periodically from branching rhizomes that ramble through shaded forest understories. In spring, these shy plants bear small, white flowers striped with pink.

Often sold incorrectly as dwarf cardamom, *Alpinia nutans* makes a dense mound of dark green, cinnamon-scented leaves. These slender-stemmed plants reach four feet in height, giving a cool, green look to shady summer borders, although they rarely flower in cultivation. A similar aromatic species with reedy stems and narrow leaves, *A. calcarata* is more regular in bloom, but only if given rich soil and a nearly frost-free situation.

Africans

As with blooms of *Alpinia* species, the showy, pansylike flowers of *Siphonochilus* are composed mostly of enlarged lips, although these can be lobed in such a way as to resemble the four-parted blooms of certain *Kaempferia* species. Native to seasonally dry parts of tropical Africa, these stemless gingers succeed along the Gulf if given ideally drained positions in raised beds of sandy soil. Their pleated foliage resembles a small, green curcuma, with the blooms opening on separate shoots usually produced before the leaves. The extremely showy blossoms are usually borne with male and female flowers on separate plants.

When in flower, the South African *Siphonochilus aethiopicus* (Natal ginger) is especially beautiful, with four-inch, lavender-pink blossoms marked with lighter yellowish and white throats. The east African *S. kirkii* is similarly large and showy. *Siphonochilus carsonii* adds two dark purplish spots beside its yellow throat in a bright pink bloom. *Siphonochilus decorus* offers all-yellow flowers after its leaves emerge and may repeat bloom later in the summer. This is the easiest doer in the genus, but, like its cousins, must be given a nearly dry winter rest in a position with well-drained soil.

Spirals

Botanists now place the spiral gingers (*Costus* spp.) in their own family, Costaceae, based on unique characters including their distinctive chemistry. The remarkable, helically disposed stems of the spiral gingers carry aloft their terminal, sometime colorful floral cones. From these emerge conspicuous, textured blossoms. As with *Siphonochilus*, these flowers seem to be all lip.

Innumerable *Costus* species occur in Latin America, with more in tropical Africa and a few in Southeast Asia and Indonesia. Although most are tropical and naturally evergreen, a handful are naturally deciduous. Several species sprout lustily even when cut back by hard frost, and these are the types that make successful perennials in the South. Most propagate quickly from seed or division; stem cuttings may be taken in summer, rooting easily in ordinary potting soil.

A widespread native of Asia and Indonesia, crepe ginger (*Costus speciosus*) reaches nearly ten feet when well grown, bearing rich green, downy foliage and five-inch flower heads formed by masses of wine-purple bracts. Through several weeks of summer, crumpled, white, funnel-shaped blooms protrude from the cones, displaying delicate, crepe-textured lips. According to the *Kama Sutra* a fire-blackened powder made from blooms of this crepe ginger and other flowers could "be used as an unguent of adornment" and when applied to the eyelashes had "the effect of making a person look lovely."

Crepe ginger (*Costus speciosus*).

Gardeners often confuse crepe ginger with a nearly related species from southern China and Vietnam, *Costus lacerus*, a variety with waxy green leaves that are velvety beneath and bracts feathered into multiple, fibrous segments. Such details hardly matter in garden plantings, and both species thrive in full sun along the Gulf. A cream-striped form of *C. speciosus*, 'Variegatus', is less vigorous but tolerates sun (unusual for such a strong variegation). It makes a striking specimen with gently curving purplish stems to contrast with its white-splashed leaves. A superficially similar white-striped ginger, *C. arabicus* 'Variegatus', lacks the attractive reddish stems, cold hardiness, or sun tolerance of *C. speciosus*. It is often sold as *C. amazonicus*.

'Tetraploid' and 'Nova' are heavy-blooming, compact selections of *Costus speciosus*, usually remaining under three feet; Indonesian selections, such as the

Costus speciosus 'Variegatus'. Photo by Lauren S. Ogden.

tender, rose-flowered 'Java Pink', seem best suited to frost-free regions. Introduced from Brazil, where it is grown as a medicinal plant, 'Tropicais' is an apparently spontaneous hybrid of *C. speciosus* with the native South American *C. spiralis*. Its trumpet-shaped, blushing pink flowers have yellow-striped lips and emerge from tight, ruby-colored cones.

Formerly called *Costus igneus* for its broad-lipped, flaming orange flowers, *C. cuspidatus* hails from mountainous regions of southeastern Brazil. It is hardier than most *Costus* species, although its rhizomes may rot during winter dormancy if kept overly wet. This species lacks the prominent, bracted cones typical of the genus, but provides dense, eighteen-inch mounds of greenery as foils for its oversized, vibrant flowers, making a beautiful summer groundcover for positions shaded from hot afternoon sun. The dwarf, yellow-flowered *C. subsessilis* is a similar species from Bolivia that becomes naturally deciduous during the dry season. Also naturally dormant and a relation of these South American species, the African *C. spectabilis* makes low mounds of succulent foliage, carrying large, bright yellow flowers in summer. Although not widely tested for hardiness, it has a promising colonial habit, spreading by long, slender rhizomes.

Native to the highlands of southern Mexico and Belize, *Costus pictus* is one of a handful of *Costus* species hardy in Gulf Coast gardens, growing well in partial shade to full sun. Its strong-growing stems, reaching five to seven feet, carry glossy, dark green, rippled foliage. Tubular, pale yellow flowers, stippled

Handsome leaves of *Costus barbatus* fill a shaded bed at Mercer Arboretum, with help from curcumas. Photo by Lauren S. Ogden.

with red along the edges of the lip, appear one or two at a time from small, greenish cones. Sometimes sold as *Costus* sp. 'Hieroglyphics' in reference to the gray and brownish red bandings on its stems, *C. pictus* also occurs in a solid red-stemmed form.

Although thoroughly hardy as a foliage plant, *Costus barbatus* needs shelter from hard frosts in order to produce its bright red cones and warm yellow flowers. Its lush, spiraled leaves are handsome in themselves, with remarkably soft, felted undersides. The Indian head ginger, *C. scaber*, often sold as *C. spicatus*, produces reddish orange flowers from tight, pointed cones made up of similarly colored bracts. Native from Mexico to South America, this species grows readily in the lower South. The similar *C. pulverulentus* bears scarlet to bright pink blossoms, opening to show a protruding red stamen and a yellow lip. Usually sold by nurseries as *C. curvibracteatus*, *C. productus* produces the lush, medium green, spiraling foliage typical of its genus, with densely clustered stems tipped by bright red (in some forms, orange-red) cones. From these the tubular, apricot-yellow flowers appear one or two at a time, making a late summer show in Gulf Coast gardens, even if cut back by hard frost in winter.

Less hardy spiral gingers popular in Florida gardens include *Costus erythrophyllus* (blood spiral), one of several species with yellow, red-edged blossoms, and *C. spiralis*, a stout, West Indian species with large, shiny foliage, red cones, and rose-pink flowers. *Monocostus uniflorus* is a tender *Costus* relation with delicate, short spirals and large, clear yellow blossoms.

Aroids

The arum family (Araceae) offers gardeners a sort of herbaceous analog of the palms. Although soft and succulent in leaf and stem, many aroids develop lush fountains of growth and large blades of foliage. In the mildest parts of the South a few approach tree proportions.

The typical aroid "flower," formed by a leafy bract, or spathe, that may be brightly colored, enfolds a slender spike, or spadix. The spadix is closely packed, forming a compound bloom made up of inconspicuous true flowers. In some species all the blossoms on the spike produce stamens and styles. In others, the spadix divides into male and female sections. Often these strangely built flowers function as insect traps, attracting flies or midges with the scent of fungus or carrion. After pollination, they ripen compact clusters of fleshy berries. Generally a showy red, these appear in autumn like scarlet cobs of corn.

The arum family harbors both classically tropical genera, such as *Philodendron*, and hardy flowers, such as the jack-in-the-pulpit (*Arisaema triphyllum*).

Several tuberous aroids, including the genus *Arum*, favor cool Mediterranean climates. Nearly all enjoy rich, boggy conditions during their growing season.

Tree Philodendrons

Philodendrons are not really tuberous plants, but at least one species, the Brazilian tree philodendron (*Philodendron selloum*), produces such a heavy, swollen stem that it functions, in effect, as a tuber. This enables this erstwhile tropical vine to recover from periodic bouts of frost. In the lower South *P. selloum* is popular as a foliage plant for shady courtyards. The big, glossy green, scalloped leaves have a luxuriant appearance and illustrate the palmlike character of tropical arums.

'Ape

More honestly tuberous, yet still treelike in near tropical climates, is the Asian 'ape, *Alocasia macrorrhiza*. This is one of several aroids with large, spade-shaped leaves and edible, tuberous roots. The small, greenish flowers are of little importance in the landscape. It's the bold greenery which gardeners enjoy. With its oversized leaves, the 'ape is one of many plants affectionately known as elephant ears. The starchy corms provide an important subsistence food throughout tropical Asia. In legends of the south Pacific island Rarotonga, the hero Ru used 'ape to hoist the heavens above the earth.

The shiny green blades of this alocasia spring from a thick stem, which may remain below ground or extend a few feet upward as a ringed trunk. Bold, succulent leaves on long stalks point upward, adding several feet of height. Small strains of *Alocasia macrorrhiza* remain only two to three feet high, but large forms reach four to five feet or more before they begin to form a trunk, eventually ascending to ten feet if not halted by frost.

The common 'ape is hardy in the middle and lower South. With its arrow-shaped leaves pointed to the heavens, it offers one of the most striking summer foliage plants. Ordinary garden conditions produce grand success, and either sun or part shade is satisfactory. A favorite use is in or near ponds. Aquatic culture yields prodigious growth from these and most other elephant ears.

Collectors also cultivate several exotic selections of 'ape, although only some of these are hardy north of the Gulf Coast. Among cultivars adapted to the middle South, 'Blackstem' is a fast-multiplying form with stunning ebony petioles. These carry dark green, arrow-shaped leaves, bearing netted patterns above, and appearing pale and whitened, with black veins on the undersides.

'Storm Warning' is similar in appearance but has not yet been tested for hardiness.

Alocasia macrorrhiza selections suited to the lower South include 'Borneo Giant', an exceptionally large form of the species with boldly upright leaves up to six feet across and twelve feet long. 'Lutea' displays creamy yellow petioles that make the plants look like gigantic, bright-colored chards. Originally native to Papua New Guinea, this cold-sensitive variety has undulating leaves and flowers cupped by bright yellow spathes. 'Seven Colors', with stems tinted red, purple, peach, or pink, is a variation of 'Lutea'. The similar 'New Guinea Gold' shows prominent yellow leaf veins, and, in late summer and autumn, also produces leaves flecked and marbled with yellow. 'Variegata' offers a mixture of rich green, celery, gray, and cream marbled over each leaf. 'Violacea' produces dark green blades with blackish purple stems and veins.

Of several related species, the night-scented lily (*Alocasia odora*) is among the most cold hardy and reliable in the South. Native to the Philippines and Taiwan, this species produces bright green, heart-shaped leaves that undulate neatly along the margins. Held stiffly upright as in *A. macrorrhiza*, this lush, glossy foliage may be up to three feet tall. Numerous tiny, sweet-scented flowers comprise the cream-colored spadix.

Alocasia macrorrhiza 'New Guinea Gold' with *Curcuma elata* and *Perilla* 'Magilla' at Mercer Arboretum.

LariAnn Garner of Aroidia Research in Florida has used this robust species to breed new elephant ears, several of which have proven hardy in the middle South. 'Portodora', a selection by Ron Weeks from her cross of *Alocasia odora* with *A. portei*, makes clumps of giant, gently undulated, dark green leaves. These are held on strong, purple leaf stems, offering imposing architecture for shaded positions with rich, moist soil. 'Calidora', from a cross of *A. odora* with *A. gageana*, makes an easy-growing, tropical-looking elephant ear with three-foot-wide, serrated leaves on plants to seven feet or more in height.

With heart-shaped blades only about a foot long, *Alocasia cucullata* is one of the smallest elephant ears adapted to the South. Originally native to India and Myanmar, this dwarf alocasia is common in older plantings along the Gulf, where it builds into lush, three-foot clumps. The thick, smooth foliage ends in protracted, curled tips that help give these plants an impish character. Their hooded (cucullate) flower spathes only add to this impression.

Although not quite as cold hardy as *Alocasia cucullata*, the exotic-looking green shield (*A. clypeolata*) is another intriguing dwarf alocasia suited to gardens in the lower South. Like fanciful maps in relief, these beauties display elliptical, lime-green leaves with sunken veins darkening to near black. The lower leaf surfaces are pale green. Long confused with the more frost-tender, coppery *A. cuprea* from Borneo, *A. clypeolata* was described as a new species from the Philippines in 1999.

Reversing the color patterns of green shield, *Alocasia wentii* displays green veins against dark-toned leaves backed with bronze. When sunlight passes through the foliage, the contrasting chartreuse veins and translucent, coppery blades fluoresce together. Despite tropical origins in the mountains of New Guinea, *A. wentii* seems as hardy as any elephant ear in the South, forming clumps similar in size to *A. cucullata*.

Some gardeners believe 'Sarian' to be a huge hybrid of *Alocasia zebrina* and *A. micholitziana*, although no one has taken credit for this cross. In any case, this is a distinctive and beautiful alocasia with striped leaf stems and robust, wavy-edged, dark green leaves displaying contrasting, snow-white veins. This show plant can grow up to twelve feet and seems perfectly hardy along the Gulf, in spite of its very tropical appearance.

Alocasia cuprea.

Also worthwhile along the Gulf, *Alocasia plumbea* 'Nigra' raises large, upright, dark olive-green leaves with a blue-gray, metallic sheen. These have the wine-colored lower surfaces typical of many tropical understory plants and are held on dark purplish brown petioles, reaching up to eight feet when well grown. Long cultivated in Southeast Asia, this species has never been found in the wild and may be an old garden form of *A. macrorrhiza*. When backlit, its slightly quilted, purplish leaves display a watery pattern between the veins. *Alocasia plumbea* 'White' is a beautiful, pale-stemmed version of this plant.

The kris plant (*Alocasia sanderiana*) and its hybrids (*A. ×amazonica*, for example) possess gorgeous, blackish green leaves highlighted with silvery veins and margins. Another highly decorative plant, 'Hilo Beauty', is usually listed as an alocasia but appears more like a large *Caladium* species, with papery, cream-spotted foliage marked by irregular areas of pale chartreuse. These heart-shaped leaves appear on bluish black stems, displaying camouflagelike patterns of dark and light greens. Although these and several other tropical alocasias are not difficult to grow in shady summer gardens, their tubers usually rot if left in the ground over winter. North of Florida, such exotics may be used as arresting items for pots or for summer bedding.

Taro

The 'ape and its varieties are often confused with the equally robust and leafy taro, or dasheen (*Colocasia esculenta*). The plant known to many American gardeners as elephant ear is a large-growing strain of taro. In the tropics this staple has been cultivated for its edible roots since ancient times. The potatolike tubers are boiled and eaten, and the tender leaves cooked to provide nutritious greens. During the era of slavery, these easy-growing plants comprised much of the diet of African-Americans. Taro is still a popular food in the Caribbean.

Although casually similar to 'ape, taro holds its leaves perpendicular to its stems, so that the blades face outward and point to the ground. The stalks attach within the blade, rather than at the margin of the leaf, a shieldlike arrangement that botanists call peltate. It's worth a gardener's time to learn this term, for the contrasting leaf designs offer a simple method for distinguishing the various elephant ears. The leaves of *C. esculenta* also differ from 'ape in their color, being a soft, velvety green.

Ordinary taro roots found in grocery stores may be planted for ornament, but the edible strain, dasheen, is usually fairly small. Many gardeners want to grow the biggest, grandest elephant ears possible, so large-leafed horticultural forms are preferred. Florida growers send out heavy, brown, globular tubers in

Colocasia esculenta 'Black Runner' with pindo palm (*Butia capitata*) and chartreuse sweet potato vine (*Ipomoea batatas* 'Margarita').

The imperial taro, *Colocasia esculenta* var. *antiquorum* 'Illustris'.

spring, and these are widely available at nurseries and garden centers. The most massive roots give the grandest results.

Elephant ears should be sited out of strong wind or hot sun, in deep, rich soil, and given plenty of moisture. A single tuber will grow up to six feet in height, with leaves four feet long and three feet wide. To develop such a specimen, the plant should receive a thorough watering every day it does not receive rain. In the South *Colocasia esculenta* is completely hardy if mulched to preserve the fleshy roots from frost.

Among several ornamental selections, 'Ruffles' is an attractive clumping form with wavy-edged leaves. 'Chicago Harlequin' spreads by runners and is variously blotched with green and yellow. 'Black Magic' is entirely black-purple, as is the similar 'Black Runner', but with more ruffled foliage and fast-spreading stolons. With green leaves that gradually blush cream around the base of the petioles, 'Nancy's Revenge' makes striking clumps of variegated foliage. 'Rhubarb' offers brilliant cranberry-red petioles. 'Burgundy Stem' produces huge green leaves with rosy-purple petioles and bears creamy yellow blooms with a fruity fragrance. 'Fontanesii' has similar blossoms, combining with spectacularly large masses of foliage held on blackish petioles to seven feet long. Several of these may be selections of the water taro, *Colocasia esculenta* var. *aquatilis*, a purple-stemmed variety that has run wild along the banks of Southern streams. A popular water garden subject, it spreads rapidly by stolons. Valued for apple-green foliage marked purplish black between the veins, the imperial taro ('Illustris') is a stoloniferous selection often listed as a cultivar of the Himalayan *C. esculenta* var. *antiquorum.*

One of the most beautiful *Colocasia* species, *C. affinis* 'Jenningsii' makes a charming dwarf with velvety, blackish, shield-shaped leaves that show radiating patterns of pale veins around a bright central blotch. Small yellow flowers appear among the leaves during summer. As with gingers native to the same regions, this Himalayan elephant ear adheres to a monsoonal schedule, becoming dormant in fall, with or without frost, and returning in early summer well after most perennials. *Colocasia fallax*, a related species from Thailand and Vietnam, displays matte green foliage with pale veins and blotching similar to *C. affinis.*

Also from Southeast Asia, the extra-large *Colocasia gigantea* carries wavy-edged, glaucous-green foliage on stout petioles arranged in a partially upright stance. Large forms of the species, such as the Thai Giant strain, can produce heart-shaped blades up to five feet long and four feet across. Fragrant white flowers accompany the immense summer foliage.

Remusatia vivipara and *R. pumila* are small-growing, half-hardy elephant ears related and casually similar to *Colocasia*, but with more glossy foliage and odd, prickly-looking bulbils forming late in the year.

Yautia

The Latin American elephant ear or yautia, *Xanthosoma sagittifolium*, is close in appearance to taro but has triangular leaves dulled by a white powder when young. Close inspection also reveals prominent veins running along the margin of the blades, milky sap, and leaves that are not peltate, yet for garden purposes the yautia is simply another in the herd of elephant ears. The edible tubers, once known in the South as tanyah, sometimes elongate to form short trunks as in *Alocasia.*

The Mexican *Xanthosoma robustum* is an even larger species that spreads rapidly by stolons. Its gigantic gray-green leaves are big enough to be used as impromptu umbrellas by residents of the Chiapas highlands, where this species is native. Its flowering stems, appearing through much of the summer, expand to purplish swellings topped by cream-colored spathes.

The blue elephant ear (*Xanthosoma violaceum*) is an especially vigorous relative of yautia with purplish stems and leaves covered in a waxy, bluish powder. The golden elephant ears, 'Aurea' and 'Lime Zinger', are selections of the Latin American root crop malanga, *X. mafaffa*. These produce fast-growing chartreuse leaves, thriving in the lower South if supplied with abundant, mineral-free water.

An odd form of the Ecuadorian *Xanthosoma atrovirens* is sometimes grown in the South. Known as 'Variegata Monstrosa', this weird elephant ear has leaves with cream-variegated margins coalesced into distorted, pouchlike structures at the downward-pointing tips of the leaves. Such curiosities intrigue gardeners even when they have little obvious beauty or purpose.

Caladiums

It is the fancy-leafed caladium that offers the bedding plant par excellence. The flattened, knobby tubers handle with ease and swiftly grow into the most splendid of summer foliage plants. Although not hardy north of the Gulf, these dwarf allies of *Xanthosoma* are particularly fine in the South. Reveling in warmth and humidity, they give a long season of beauty in return for a minimal investment of the gardener's effort.

The green- and red-spotted heart of Jesus (*Caladium bicolor*) was the first *Caladium* species introduced to horticulture, appearing as early as 1769. This native of the Para state in Brazil is the principal ancestor of the many heart-leafed hybrids now grouped under the name *C. ×hortulanum*.

Although *Caladium bicolor* itself has long been neglected as a garden plant, nurseries have propagated its Ecuadorian variant, var. *rubicundum*, through tissue culture. The beautiful leaves reach up to three feet, displaying scattered pink spots against a deep reddish green background. New leaves emerge a glowing dusty-rose. Formerly included in *Xanthosoma*, *C. lindenii* 'Magnificum' is another intriguing plant with bold, fish-bone patterns of creamy veins against rich green foliage. The vibrant *Caladium* hybrid 'Thai Beauty' is another large-growing variety, showing off translucent rose-pink foliage with netted green and white veins. All of these make favored pot plants that have the advantage of not going fully dormant in the winter in warm climates.

In contrast, most *Caladium* hybrids are naturally deciduous. Breeding of the modern, fancy-leafed varieties began in the mid-nineteenth century with the introduction of species from the Amazon

Caladium 'Thai Beauty'.

region. Louis van Houtte and Alfred Bleu in France, and several breeders of German descent—C. J. Bause, J. Luther, Adolphe Jaenicke, Adolph Litze—were active during the Victorian era. In the early twentieth century Henry Nehrling and Theodore Mead made important contributions. Several of their hybrids remain in cultivation.

Although wild *Caladium* species are rarely planted in present-day gardens, the jewel-like *C. humboldtii* is one that is still worth growing. Its six-inch, heart-shaped leaves are boldly splashed with white, contrasted against dark green veins. This Venezuelan miniature was once known as *C. argyrites* ("silver caladium"). 'Mini White' and 'Marcel' are especially choice dwarf selections of *C. humboldtii* available from tissue culture.

The color patterns of *Caladium humboldtii* are preserved in the well-known 'Candidum'. This hybrid from 1868 juxtaposes rich green, netted veins against its large, silvery-white leaves. It is still the most popular of caladiums, the cool whiteness of its foliage refreshing numerous summer-bedding schemes. 'Candidum' is especially strong growing and stands direct sun better than many of its colorful brethren. 'Carolyn Wharton', 'Pink Beauty', and 'Red Flash' exhibit patterns more like *C. bicolor*, with vivid splashes of pink, red, and green together. 'Blaze' ('T. L. Mead'), 'John Peed', 'Frieda Hemple', and 'Postman Joyner' produce wine-red leaves edged in green. All are vigorous, reaching twelve to eighteen inches in height. They make striking beds nestled among the feathered greenery of Southern shield ferns (*Thelypteris kunthii*).

Breeding programs sponsored by the University of Florida have introduced several handsome, vigorous cultivars. 'Florida Beauty' is particularly striking, with thick-textured, medium green foliage mottled in chartreuse, deep rose, and vibrant pink. 'Florida Roselight',

Caladium 'Candidum' with rose-red *C.* 'Postman Joyner'. Photo by Lauren S. Ogden.

Caladium 'Red Flash'.

'Florida Elise', and 'Florida Calypso' are similar pink-mottled types, all bred for improved sun tolerance over traditional caladiums. Another good performer in full or part sun, 'Galaxy' offers white-centered leaves with green borders and a celestial overlay of pale pink flecks.

With the first cool breezes of autumn, caladium leaves begin to flop or wilt, and at this time the tubers may be taken up for winter storage. The tender roots should be kept dry and warm over winter, placed in boxes of sphagnum moss or rice hulls to absorb excess humidity. Although the effort required to conserve them is small, many gardeners choose to purchase fresh tubers each season. Roots may be started into growth in early spring if potted and kept near warm, bright windows.

It is tempting to set caladiums out when the first sunny days of spring arrive, but if the ground has not warmed completely, tubers will rot in short order. A single breath of cool air from an April norther is all that is needed to check the growth of a young plant, and it will not develop properly thereafter. Caladiums should be given rich soil, unfailing warmth, abundant moisture, and bright, filtered light.

The large-growing "eyes" visible on the tops of the dormant roots contain buds of flower spikes for the coming summer. Most gardeners plant caladiums for their showy, variegated foliage, removing the greenish flowers as they appear. Knowledgeable planters sometimes use a sharp knife to carve out the larger growing points from the tubers. Done several days or weeks before the roots are to be planted, this stimulates side branching, developing a lush, leafy appearance. Roots sprout from the tops of the tubers, so they should be covered by at least an inch of soil when planted.

Lance-leafed Caladiums

Among the novelties developed by Theodore Mead is a race of lance- or strap-leafed caladiums. Descended from crosses of the narrow-foliaged *Caladium albanense* among the larger hybrids, these inherit tougher constitutions than ordinary heart-leafed varieties. As a group, the strap-leafed caladiums are more tolerant of direct sun and are less likely to flag in drought. These hybrids rarely bother to flower, so they do not need to be disbudded.

'White Wing' is a choice white "strap" with green-edged, ruffled leaves. 'Gingerland', an amazing greenish cream, is flecked all over with purplish pink. 'Rosalie' and 'Red Frill' are deep wine. All are easy, low-growing plants, with interesting mounds of slender foliage. They are ideal to bed among boulders or mix with dwarf ferns such as the Venus' maidenhair (*Adiantum capillus-veneris*).

Among newer, lance-leafed caladiums, 'Florida Sweetheart' offers bright pink leaves with deep rose veins and netted, green margins. 'Florida Whitewater' makes compact mounds of long, white, gently undulating foliage, thriving in shade or full sun. 'Florida Irish Lace' produces mounds of unique, heavily ruffled, olive-green foliage. 'Florida Red Ruffles' seems more cold tolerant than older red-leafed cultivars.

Snake Palms

One of the truly bizarre tuberous plants of the subtropics is the snake palm, or devil's tongue (*Amorphophallus konjac*). The globular corms send up only a single leaf, but this is so marvelously built and branched as to suggest a small palm tree. If the tubers are large, the foliage may reach as much as four feet in height. The rounded, fleshy leaf stem is mottled all over with olive and purple. At its top it divides again and again to form a broad, leafy umbrella of dark green. In a sheltered spot in the shade, this novel foliage remains in good condition all summer, yellowing and dying down in autumn.

If the tubers are kept dry over winter and are of sufficient size, a flower spike will appear in spring before the next season's leaf emerges. The bloom is constructed on the typical arum plan, with a large central spadix surrounded by a fleshy bract. In this strange genus the flowers are so enormous that they always provoke com-

The snake palm or devil's tongue, *Amorphophallus konjac* in fruit.

Amorphophallus bulbifer in the author's Austin garden with *Stahlianthus involucratus, Ajuga reptans,* and *Zamia pumila* (Caribbean coontie cycad).

ment. Blackish red goblets up to three feet tall rise from the bare earth and emit a foul stench.

Although the snake palm is usually kept as a collector's curio, it is fairly cold hardy if planted in well-drained soil. In Southeast Asia and Japan the cormous roots are grown as an edible. Usual garden strains of *Amorphophallus konjac* bear mottled stems, but there is also an interesting all-black cultivar.

In the present era fans of *Amorphophallus* can obtain several species, including the gigantic *A. titanum*, famed for producing the plant kingdom's largest inflorescence. Although *A. titanum* and many other varieties are tender, several species are surprisingly cold hardy. *Amorphophallus bulbifer* succeeds in the middle South, sending up olive-streaked leaf stems with lush, divided foliage. These develop small tubers in the fall as the leaves wither, offering a ready means for increase. Safely hardy along the Gulf Coast, *A. paeoniifolius* produces huge tubers and large, irregular, flesh-colored blossoms. Although the enormous flowers have the unpleasant aroma typical of this genus, they are thankfully short-lived. The peonylike, divided leaves are a pleasant green, borne on pinkish, mottled leaf stems. A select form of *A. paeoniifolius*, 'Gajendra', is cultivated for edible tubers known as elephant foot yams.

Monarch of the East

Another equally sinister-looking aroid, also hardy in the South, is known variously as red calla, monarch of the East, or voodoo lily. Although the leaves of this Indian perennial, *Sauromatum venosum*, are not so spectacularly divided as those of the snake palm, they are still substantial and exotically lush. The compound leaves radiate in a distinctive pattern, as if the lobes were attached to the back of a horseshoe. The large, central segment extends up to eighteen inches from the middle of the blade, with six to ten smaller lobes distributed on either side, grading down to the tips. In the common horticultural variety, the leaflets bear prominent veins. The husky, three-foot leaf stalks are marked with dark purple spots.

One of the weird attributes of monarch of the East is its capacity to flower as an unplanted tuber, and this is the primary reason why nurseries bother to sell this oddity. The evil-smelling blooms produce bracts that are green outside, yellow and reddish purple on the interior. These surround long, blackish purple central spikes. Well-grown tubers reach five inches in diameter and will throw up twelve- to twenty-four-inch flowers.

Although these plants are entirely perennial in the South and enjoy moist, shady conditions, they need a well-defined, dry rest period to induce bloom. If, for curiosity's sake, the malevolent-looking flowers are desired, it is best to take up the tubers in autumn. They may be replanted in spring and will flower before the leaves emerge.

Garden Dragons

The temperate relations of *Sauromatum* belong to the large genus *Arisaema*, embracing a tremendous variety of forms, both strange and beautiful. Most species are modest in foliage compared to their tropical allies, but many retain the horseshoe pattern of the leaves. With their smaller stature, this radial foliage looks remarkably like that of another woodlander, the Lenten rose (*Helleborus orientalis*). All arisaemas gradually form clumps of offsets, which may be divided. Their red berries, containing a single, stonelike seed, will grow to flowering size in three seasons.

The most widespread of the South's native *Arisaema* species is also the easiest to grow. It has the alluring common name of green dragon, and this reptilian title is codified in its botanical name, *A. dracontium*. In the wild, green dragon occurs in damp woods along streams, but the tubers endure ordinary garden conditions in bright shade. They will accept summer drought, so long as they are watered during the spring growing season. The leafy, green, many-parted foliage comes up in mid-spring, with the flowers following in May or June.

The modest blooms are dominated by pale green, tubular spathes, which fold forward at the top, as if to cover the spadix and shield it from rain. The wayward spike will have none of this and escapes upward as a prolonged, tapering "dragon's tongue," five to six inches long. Although these blooms are hardly showy, they are intriguing and often ripen attractive, scarlet fruit in the fall. A cousin of the green dragon from Mexico, *Arisaema macrospathum*, has slightly larger, greenish blooms, which appear before the foliage.

The better-known jack-in-the-pulpit, *Arisaema triphyllum*, is a more beautiful flower, with an equally hooded spathe, striped vertically with purple and green, and surrounding a thick, purple spike. It occurs naturally in rich, damp woods southward to central Florida. In garden culture the roots must never suffer drought. The three-parted leaves, making handsome accents for a shady bed of ferns, are not so exotic as the green dragon's. With luck, attractive red fruits appear in autumn. The five-leafed Jack-in-the-pulpit, subsp. *quinatum*, is a similar Southern native with greenish white spathes and five-parted foliage.

Most of the beautiful Asiatic *Arisaema* species enjoy the same retentive soils and cool, shady positions as the jack-in-the-pulpit. *Arisaema candidissimum*, however, is a mountain species that sometimes grows out in the sun among dry, scrubby vegetation. The hooded, white spathes of this Sichuan native are delicately striped pink inside, with pale green markings outside. They appear in late spring before the three-parted leaves expand. *Arisaema flavum* also does well in sun and produces greenish yellow spathes, marked inside with yellow and purple. Another Chinese species from the same general region, *A. fargesii*, displays purplish striped pitcherlike spathes.

Arisaema consanguineum offers blooms similar to the green dragon's, but often striped with olive or purple. Its robust, divided, radial leaves and elongated spathe bear exaggerated drip tips. Native to Japan and Korea, as well as China, *A. ringens* is an easy-growing species whose hooded, purple-throated blooms have earned it the common name cobra lily.

Such close cousins of *Arisaema* as the Asiatic *Pinellia pedatisecta* multiply more rapidly, running underground on short stolons. The foliage is trilobed, making a short, exotically leafy groundcover for a shady bank. The interesting, greenish blooms are like small versions of the green dragon and appear sporadically through the summer. If not picked, they often set seed and will volunteer in moist, shady nooks. *Pinellia tripartita* is similar, with broad foliage and waxy, green blooms. *Pinellia ternata* has interesting purplish blossoms, but may become a dangerous weed in gardens that are to its liking.

Perhaps the most dragonlike of all the arums is *Dracunculus vulgaris*, which differs from these forest flowers in its preference for sunny, Mediterranean slopes. It certainly looks menacing, with its monstrous, deeply divided foliage and velvety, blackish purple spathes. The whole curious plant may reach three feet in height, with the blooms achieving half this stature.

Like other Mediterranean natives, *Dracunculus vulgaris* grows in winter, with flowers following in mid-spring. The foliage is handsome and seems proof against ordinary frosts. The odor of the dark, plum-colored blooms, and of the plant as a whole, is fetid, but the stems may ripen weighty heads of attractive berries. These change gradually through the summer from green to shades of red.

This coarse perennial increases swiftly from offsets formed at the base. In the South the dormant tubers may be protected from excess summer moisture by planting in raised beds of gritty soil. Several seasons are usually required for the young tubers to gather strength before flowering, but the attractive leaves may be enjoyed while awaiting the dragon's emergence from his cave.

True Arums

Of the true arums only *Arum italicum* is much planted in the South, but it is such an unqualified success, gardeners should be stirred to explore the genus

Winter foliage of *Arum italicum* 'Marmoratum'.   The mottled blooms of *Arum dioscoridis*.

further. The Italian arum is a plant of quiet beauty, appearing when it is of the greatest value, during fall and winter. The arrow-shaped leaves unfurl in November, rising from the small, rounded tubers. In the popular garden form 'Marmoratum', the shiny green surface is marbled with gray and cream veins.

The groups of leaves form lush, eight- to ten-inch clumps, which are suited to positions under trees or almost anywhere else they might be desired for winter interest. The flowers follow in mid-spring, just before the leaves die away for summer. Greenish white, with a creamy spadix, they are not particularly showy, but seem very ready to set fruit. When the berries turn to waxy scarlet in autumn, they are often the brightest stars in the garden.

More unusual arums might also succeed in the South, but are seldom tried. Green-leafed lords and ladies (*Arum maculatum* var. *immaculatum*) is one which is very similar to *A. italicum*, but with plain, unspotted foliage. With gray-green spear-shaped foliage, *A. dioscoridis* is a smart-looking species from Greece. Its green spathes, marked inside with black, dark purple, and cream, make intriguing floral displays for late spring. The Mediterranean black callas, *A. palestinum* and *A. pictum*, have shiny, green, arrow-shaped leaves like *A. italicum* and chocolate-colored flowers like *Dracunculus vulgaris*. Uniquely, *A. pictum* produces its deep purplish black blooms in the fall along with its newly emerging leaves. *Arum creticum* sends up a striking, creamy yellow spathe around a golden spadix—a truly beautiful flower with a sweet fragrance uncommon in this family. All are suited to the South if sheltered from excess summer rain.

Some older gardens harbor a small cousin of the arums. Known as the mouse plant, *Arisarum proboscideum* is a curious little aroid with purplish spring blooms bearing long, white tails on each spathe, suggesting a group of tiny mice. A Mediterranean native, the mouse plant makes attractive, low mounds of dark green foliage during the winter, becoming dormant when summer heat arrives. This heirloom thrives in moist, shaded situations.

Callas

White calla lilies (*Zantedeschia aethiopica*) are beautiful, easy, winter growers, but are not so hardy as arums. The common strains tolerate modest frosts, but are sufficiently hardy only for the lower South. Their semi-aquatic tubers revel in the black muck of ponds, and it is customary to set these plants in, or near, water, when possible, as this helps to ward off unusually hard freezes. Either sun or partial shade is satisfactory.

The glossy, arrow-headed foliage remains in growth through winter, or all year if the tubers are planted aquatically, forming lush clumps one-and-a-half feet tall. In the spring, these are joined by a succession of three-foot flowering stems, each with a showy white spathe surrounding the thick, creamy spadix. These make magnificent cut flowers, lasting a week or two in a vase.

Zantedeschia aethiopica 'Green Goddess'.

Florists in the lower South have long grown the semi-dwarf white calla 'Godfrey', a selection that will sometimes also be met in gardens. Sir Cedric Morris' introduction 'Green Goddess' is an especially robust clone, withstanding more cold than many others. Its spathes are almost entirely green, with patches of white appearing only in the throat. The strong-growing 'Pink Mist' shows pale porcelain-rose blossoms with deeper pink throats. With ruffled, four-foot leaves flecked in silver, 'White Giant' makes an attractive garden plant even without its creamy blooms, which, when they come in spring, arrive on seven-foot stems.

In their native South Africa, white callas grow in both winter- and summer-rainfall regions, although only the winter-growing Cape forms appear to have been introduced to garden culture. *Zantedeschia aethiopica* populations from the Northern Province and the KwaZulu-Natal coast extend their flowering into midsummer, tending to die down during the coldest parts of the year. These types might prove more adaptable to Southern conditions than current garden strains. Except for *Z. aethiopica*, all other *Zantedeschia* species grow and flower in summer. These may be counted entirely hardy in the South.

The white-spotted calla (*Zantedeschia albo-maculata*) looks like a smaller version of *Z. aethiopica*, but its tubers produce only one blossom each, making these callas valuable for only a short season. Flower stems appear in early summer, usually reaching eighteen inches. They carry milky blossoms with purplish blotches inside at the base. The arrow-shaped foliage has curious transparent zones, which give the enjoyable effect of white spots. The plants are not particular as to soil or exposure.

The golden calla (*Zantedeschia elliotiana*) and its hybrids are the best callas for hot, sunny positions, but also grow well in partial shade. The original yellow type appears in May, sending up deep, golden blooms accompanied by spotted leaves like those of *Z. albo-maculata*. This species has been widely crossed with the white-spotted calla, the strap-leafed pink calla (*Z. rehmanii*), and the golden, black-centered *Z. pentlandii*. Available hybrids come in an array of warm colors and deserve wider appreciation than they presently enjoy.

'Mango' is a gorgeous apricot-orange, shading yellow and green at the throat; 'Pink Persuasion' is a deep rose. 'Treasure' is rich cinnabar, with golden shadowing, 'Lavender Gem' a dusty shade of rose. 'Cameo' is creamy apricot, highlighted with flashes of yellow and red. 'Edge of Night' offers dark, near-black blossoms combined with dramatic, purple-edged foliage. The heavy-textured blooms appear for several weeks in early summer. As with all these hybrids, it also shows attractive white flecks on the leaves for contrast.

Chapter 10
⬥ Designing with Southern Bulbs

THE BULBS of Southern gardens first caught my attention during high school days, when I noticed several types persisting around cemeteries and vacant lots near our home in north Texas. Dozens of narcissi, white French-Roman hyacinths, Madonna lilies, *Leucojum*, *Muscari*, *Ornithogalum*, *Lycoris*, *Sternbergia*, irises, rain lilies, Byzantine gladiolus, crinums, and oxblood lilies thrived on the heavy clay soils, multiplying and returning happily, often without an assisting gardener's hand. I was awed by the tenacious beauty of these plants and intrigued by their exotic, sometimes antique origins. What compelled my interest further was their largely untapped potential for Southern gardens.

What Bulbs Do for Gardens

Here were plants that conveyed a sense of spontaneity, that were in syncopation with the erratic rhythms of rainfall and regional climate in the South. In contrast to the perpetually glittering shrubs and massed bedding flowers common in suburban yards, these thrifty flowers had the flavor of real garden perennials: lavish, abundant, and persistent. They came and went at their various seasons, responding to stimuli of cold, heat, dampness, and drought, offering lively performances to celebrate the moments of the year. Bulbs provided spirited growth and bloom to draw people out into their gardens.

As they grew, these naturalizing bulbs also increased in size and quantity, embodying a vision of nature as a benign partner to the garden. This romantic notion of abundance lies close to the hearts of gardeners, who understand that well-attuned bulbs assure full, expanding borders, blooms in season, and plants to share and trade with others. The allure of these self-reliant, responsive flowers was undeniable. Including them in gardens promised to redeem plantings from the ordinary, while at the same time tying the garden to the cadences of its region.

Foils, Alternates, and Guilds

To make the most of such seasonal performers requires some planning. Unlike annual bedding tulips or caladiums, which may be simply orchestrated in temporary schemes all to themselves, perennial bulbs need more permanent placements that can show off flowers and foliage in season, yet allow for natural senescence and dormancy. For most varieties this means including several partner plants over the year, one or more to act as foils or companions for the bulbs while they are in growth and bloom, and others to fill in blank spaces during times of the year when they are fading or dormant. Creating a guild of flowering and foliage plants around the bulbs provides a means to show off attractions in season while minimizing a particular bulb's less desirable characters or off-season lapses.

For example, one successful combination in our Austin garden began with a group of *Crinum* 'Mrs. James Hendry'. These make an attractive planting near a path in partial shade, with lush rosettes of green, fountainlike foliage in summer, joined periodically by stems bearing fragrant, blush-colored blossoms. The strong form of the crinum leaves benefits by interspersing a summer foliage companion with contrasting feathery texture, in this case the dwarf shield fern,

White heirloom amaryllises (*Hippeastrum* Mead strain) flowering in spring with *Trillium ludovicianum* and *Ajuga reptans* amid the foliage of cycads, palms, crinums, giant groundsel (*Farfugium japonicum*), twist-leaf yucca (*Yucca rupicola*), and *Lycoris radiata*, author's garden, Austin.

Hippeastrum ×*johnsonii* (St. Joseph lily) combines in a spring border with ox-eye daisies, *Iris pallida* 'Dalmatica', peach-colored musk roses, and the foliage of daylilies, Tyler Municipal Rose Garden, Texas.

Winter-growing *Freesia laxa* blooming in early spring through the new green of *Crinum* 'Mrs. James Hendry' and *Thelypteris normalis* var. *lindheimeri*, author's garden, Austin.

Thelypteris normalis var. *lindheimeri*. In the winter, however, both the crinum and the fern die away, leaving bare earth. During this cool-season interregnum an overplanting of *Freesia laxa* fills in with grassy winter greenery. The coral-colored blooms of the freesia arrive in April, just as the new fiddleheads of the thelypteris and fresh shoots of 'Mrs. James Hendry' sprout. The foliage of the ferns and the crinums expands to hide the freesia as it goes dormant for summer, so that the whole alternating guild of plants works together to create complementary scenes through the year.

Another crinum, 'Ellen Bosanquet', offers its glowing, wine-red blossoms in early summer. Although these beautiful flowers appear on sturdy stems, providing a tremendous show while in bloom, the massive, undulating foliage of this clone often appears untidy. In this instance, a foreground planting of similar-sized companion plants, such as Caribbean coontie cycad (*Zamia pumila*) and giant groundsel (*Farfugium japonicum*), remediate the planting by blocking the crinum foliage from view. This helps bring order to an otherwise unruly scene, offering prettier foils for the deserving blossoms. Since the cycads and giant groundsel are evergreens, they also help hold interest during winter when the crinum leaves freeze back.

The dark green foliage and pearly blossoms of *Narcissus tazetta* 'Grand Primo' are at their best in late winter, enjoying the cool, sunny weather while other plants remain dormant. To enhance the beauty of these fragrant, early flowers, several groups of blue *Ipheion* sp. 'Rolf Fiedler' carpet the ground around the narcissus, blooming at the same time. Mounding, ever-gray foliage companions, such as *Artemisia* 'Powis Castle', *A.* 'Huntington', and curry plant (*Helichrysum thianschanicum* 'Icicles'), offer silvery foils for these early flowers, remaining attractive thereafter through months when the bulbs are yellowing or dormant. A few corms of *Gladiolus byzan-*

Pearly blooms of *Narcissus tazetta* 'Grand Primo' mingle with silvery filigrees of *Artemisia* 'Huntington'.

Caribbean coontie cycad (*Zamia pumila*) provides a lush foil for June blooms of *Crinum* 'Ellen Bosanquet', author's garden, Austin.

Spring blooms of *Alstroemeria psittacina* thread through the leaves of *Malvaviscus drummondii*, while shoots of *Iris domestica* and *Lilium formosanum* hint at summer flowers to come, Stephen F. Austin State University Mast Arboretum, Nacogdoches, Texas. Photo by Lauren S. Ogden.

tinus join this scene to flower as the narcissi fade. Garden interest carries through the remainder of the year by layering over with alternate summer-growing bulbs, such as Philippine lily (*Lilium formosanum*) and candelabrum lily (*Albuca nelsonii*), whose white chalices and robust, architectural foliage complement the silvery froth of the artemisia and helichrysum. Groupings of small-scale summer and fall bulbs, such as creamy-white *Zephyranthes* 'Cookie Cutter Moon' and deep crimson *Rhodophiala bifida*, finesse the planting, along with low, gray-toned groundcovers of *Dichondra sericea* 'Silver Falls' and clover fern (*Marsilea macropoda*).

Bulbs in Grass

A drive through the Southern countryside in late February invariably brings travelers face to face with an array of cluster-flowered narcissi, trumpeting daffodils, and sweet-scented jonquils set against the green winter grasses of lawns and meadows. This simple foil is one of the most effective for these early bulbs and such others as *Muscari*, *Ipheion*, *Crocus tommasinianus*, or *Allium neapolitanum*, but it requires cool-season grasses—brome, rye, or fescue—rather than the warm-season grasses typically planted in the South. It also demands restraint of the mower until late May, something few gardeners can manage in an

A grassy meadow of *Zephyranthes drummondii* opening fragrant flowers in early evening.

actual lawn. Although buffalograss makes a ready companion for early bulbs such as *A. drummondi* and *Tulipa saxatilis* 'Lilac Wonder', it provides a very different, Mediterranean-style aesthetic, remaining brown and dormant when early blossoms appear.

Stipa avenacea (black-seeded needlegrass) is a Southern meadow grass gardeners might employ as a foil for early bulbs like Lent lilies or campernelles, although it is rarely seen in gardens. This well-behaved native makes shining, evergreen mounds of fine-textured blades ideal as groundcover over most of the year. Naturally growing under longleaf pines, *S. avenacea* succeeds in partial shade as well as sun. Silky, reflective blooms appear on slender, eighteen-inch stems at the end of April, offering glistening, smoky adjuncts for late spring bulbs like *Gladiolus dalenii* and early leaves of cannas or crinums.

Another valuable native, Scribner's rosette grass (*Dichanthelium oligosanthes* var. *scribnerianum*) is one of several low-growing grasses in the South sometimes listed among the panic grasses (*Panicum* spp.). These delightful evergreens display wide, apple-green blades clustered in tufts during the winter months. The short stems elongate slightly in summer so as to resemble pygmy bamboos, carrying small clusters of branched, feathery seeds at the tips. All year they provide fresh greenery ideal as a foil for blooming bulbs, thriving in part shade as well as sun.

Several evergreen sedges of the genus *Carex* also make useful, meadow-style companions for bulbs. These grass relations have soft, feathery textures that

Red spiderlilies (*Lycoris radiata*) warm up the cool silvery rosette of *Agave striata* 'Espadina Form', author's garden, Austin.

belie their rugged constitutions, making long-lived groundcovers or lawn substitutes that seldom require mowing. Their tousled leaves provide a more natural-looking background for flowers than most *Ophiopogon* or *Liriope* varieties, and their feathered roots create less competition.

Carex perdentata (meadow sedge) and *C. retroflexa* (Texas sedge) are two generally adapted species with bright green clumps of foliage and short, feathery spikes of spring blooms. Massed in our Austin garden, these have made a lawnlike matrix to show off the periodic blooms of rain lilies, effectively disguising the grassy leaves of the zephyranthes so that the effect created is of an evergreen meadow dotted with colorful flowers.

The extraordinarily fine-textured *Carex appalachica* is an excellent light green, shade-loving companion for cyclamen in the upper South. This slowly creeping sedge beautifully contrasts with the texture and color of cyclamen foliage in winter, and helps distract from the fading or absent cyclamen leaves during the summer. Adapted all through the South, *C. flaccosperma* prospers in shade, offering tufts of wide-bladed, blue-toned leaves as a contrasting backdrop for *Kaempferia* varieties while in summer growth, remaining usefully evergreen when these small gingers go dormant. This silvery-gray sedge also makes a beautiful foil for the warm-toned flowers of *Lycoris* or *Rhodophiala*, prospering in the same dry, shaded positions enjoyed by these bulbs.

Other Companions

Low, bronze-leafed, shade-loving groundcovers such as the dwarf chocolate chip ajuga, (*Ajuga reptans* 'Valfredda') offer valuable contrast for pale spring flowers that bloom near the ground, such as those of *Kaempferia rotunda* or *K.* sp. 'Grande', and also complement their purple-toned summer foliage. The shade-tolerant, summer-deciduous *Zephyranthes* sp. 'Labuffarosa' combines happily with dwarf, green-leafed *Ajuga reptans* 'Hill Country Form'. Large-growing gingers such as *Hedychium* or *Alpinia*, and robust, shade-tolerant amaryllids such as *Hymenocallis* 'Tropical Giant' or *Lycoris squamigera* can endure the heavy competition of English ivy or Asiatic jasmine. For more slender, rambling gingers such as *Zingiber* or *Curcuma*, low-growing, dwarf *Liriope minor*, *Ophiopogon chingii*, or any of the numerous dwarf forms of *O. japonicus* provide lush summer greenery and make good place-keepers during winter. *Liriope spicata* 'Silver Dragon', *L. muscari* 'Okina', and *L. muscari* 'Peedee Ingot' offer tufts of white and gold-variegated leaves to intersperse among lycoris, oxblood lilies, Spanish bluebells, or small spiderlilies such as *Hymenocallis maximiliani*.

Shrubby companions such as boxwood, holly, viburnum, and other evergreens make popular backdrops for many spring-blooming bulbs. These woody plants maintain a strong form through summer, helping to set off the lax-looking foliage of subtropical bulbs such as *Hippeastrum* ×*johnsonii*. Other plants with strong forms, such as needle palm (*Rhapidophyllum hystrix*), yucca, *Dasylirion*, *Agave*, or cycads, offer novel companions for bulbs, playing off the equally architectural qualities of plants such as gingers, aroids, crinums, and lycoris. A few bulbs, such as the boldly upright *Alocasia macrorrhiza* or those with especially striking, leafy rosettes, such as the fountainlike *Crinum macowanii*, pewter-gray *C. bulbispermum*, or agavelike *C. asiaticum*, are themselves strong design elements.

Ajuga reptans is a subtle groundcover partner to spring-blooming *Trillium ludovicianum*, early shoots of *Hippeastrum* Mead strain, and grassy winter-growing foliage of *Lycoris radiata*, author's garden, Austin.

Useful foils for sun-loving crocuses, rain lilies, alliums, and *Ipheion* include low-growing, nonaggressive groundcover companions such as sedums. These have shallow roots that won't compete with the bulbs for food or water, and they look at home on rockeries, which are often the best places to show off these small bulbs. Little gray sedum (*Sedum diffusum* 'Potosinum'), blue spruce sedum (*S. rupestre* 'Reflexum'), Mexican sedum (*S. mexicanum*), Turkish sedum (*S. hispanicum* var. *bithynicum*), Texas sedum (*S. texanum*), Palmer's sedum (*S. palmeri*), Hidalgo sedum (*S. confusum*), Chinese sedum (*S. tetractinum*), and Mexican creeping sedum (*S. reptans*) are some of the most adaptable to Southern conditions.

Bulbs in Gravel

Many bulbs prosper with gravel mulches, and this can be an effective way to show off varieties with especially good rosette forms, such as *Manfreda*, *Scilla*, or *Hypoxis*. Rain lilies, freesias, moraeas, alliums, and cyclamen will often seed out and naturalize in gravel or grit. These and other bulbs can be combined with tidy perennials such as *Scutellaria suffrutescens* or *Phlox subulata* to create attractive garden scenes, partially disguising the gravel surface. In the steamy climate of the South, however, hard surfacings should receive careful consideration, as they may become very warm in summer if not shaded. Very light-colored materials like white crushed shell or exceptionally dark gravels should be avoided if the bed will be in full sun. For these areas, a mulch of small pebbles in mixed earth tones would be preferable.

How Many? What Style?

Large or clumping bulbs with architectural foliage such as irises, crinums, or gingers make effective specimens and may be set as individuals or in small groups to anchor garden beds in the same way as many large perennials or shrubs. Other bulb varieties often bear scant foliage and provide strictly seasonal blossoms. Such ephemeral performers as narcissi, rain lilies, alliums, crocuses, and lycoris give their most telling effects when used in masses. Although a dozen blooming *Narcissus* 'Trevithian' might provide a fragrant floral accent, this will soon be lost in the rush of spring blooms. A thousand of the same variety creates a spectacle to be remembered all year and to be anticipated for springs to come. As a rule, the more fleeting the floral display, the more generosity is called for. From a practical standpoint, ordering seasonal bulbs by the hundred offers a useful minimum.

Deciding how many bulbs to include in plantings may also depend on the general style of the garden. Gardens of formal style often have linear features such as long beds, boxwood hedges, or lawns set on an axis. In these instances enough bulbs will be desired to repeat their appearances up and down the axis, drawing the eye along the perspective. In a formal planting in Austin I used repeated groups of the cyclamineus narcissus 'Surfside' along either side of a central rill of water. The nodding, long-cupped blossoms echoed the arching forms of the alternating water jets dribbling into the pond, leading the eye in the same

The bold, bronze leaves of *Crinum procerum* 'Splendens' and chocolate-stained foliage of *Colocasia esculenta* var. *antiquorum* 'Illustris' provide instant garden architecture.

The delicate, pale yellow *Narcissus* 'Hawera' interspersed among ivory-striped fans of *Acorus calamus* 'Variegatus' (variegated sweet flag)—a striking combination for thoroughly moist, sandy or loamy soil.

way as these architectural adornments. Bulbs with strong foliage forms, such as *Curcuma* sp. 'Scarlet Fever' or *Crinum asiaticum*, also lend themselves to repetition in formal designs, making excellent choices for summer pots.

Informal plantings also benefit from repetition and from massing in groups, as this can serve to unify otherwise random plantings. Bulbs may be clustered in borders and also feathered out to mix with adjacent perennials or intermingled among shrubs. The choice of varieties for informal-style gardens tends toward more natural-looking colors and wildflowery forms, for example, opting for pale yellow or white, small-flowered narcissi in the jonquilla, triandrus, cyclamineus, or tazetta sections rather than overbred, large-cupped daffodils with brilliant orange and gold blossoms.

In certain situations the character of the bulb itself suggests an appropriate planting style and quantity. For instance, many crinums and hymenocallis enjoy semi-aquatic conditions; an impressive grouping of these large bulbs might be planted together to bloom in a good-sized swale or depression, along with moisture-loving companions such as *Narcissus* 'Sailboat', *Leucojum aestivum*, *Crocosmia* ×*crocosmiiflora*, *Zephyranthes candida*, and Louisiana iris.

Color, Texture, and Light

The volatile qualities of natural light influence how colors and textures combine in any garden. Along with the fickle nature of the plants, this makes creating a garden composition uniquely challenging and quite unlike static arts such as painting or sculpture. At Southern latitudes sunlight can be strong (even sunny

Tuscany lies well to the north of the South, on a line roughly equivalent to Albany, New York). This strong light, combined with the rapid pace of plant growth in this climate, makes gently graded color schemes, such as those advocated by famed English gardener and painter Gertrude Jekyll, difficult to achieve here. Fortunately, working with strong light is one of the design challenges bulbs can help us meet.

One remarkable quality many bulbs possess is translucence, evident both in the succulent petals of flowers and in foliage. Viewed with sunlight coming from behind, daffodils, tulips, irises, and rain lilies seem to fluoresce, playing with the early season sunrays. The succulent, textural leaves of cannas, alocasias, gingers, and amaryllids such as crinums or hymenocallis can be just as stunning when lit from behind. To make the most of these luminaries, plantings should be laid out with an east-west orientation, so that plants may be viewed with morning and/or evening sunlight behind them.

Other bulbs offer foliage that glistens in direct sunlight, and this can be

Summer sun shines through the translucent petals of *Zephyranthes* 'Grandjax'.

Backlighting shows off the luminous, fragrant blooms and handsome leaves of *Hedychium* 'Golden Glow'.

used in designs, as well. Cool-season growers such as Spanish bluebells or *Oncostema* (*Scilla*) *peruviana* provide glossy leaves to catch the winter sun. *Hymenocallis* 'Tropical Giant', *Agapanthus* 'Ellamae', and red-leafed forms of *Crinum procerum* shine while in active summer growth, making effective contrast to the light-trapping, feathery foliage of asparagus ferns or grasses. Dutch iris hybrids descended from the Moroccan *Iris tingitana*, such as 'Blue Magic', offer uniquely silvered, reflective leaves for several months in winter and early spring.

In the South, many early bulbs come into bloom while the sun's rays are at low angles. This influences the direction of growth for flowers such as daffodils, whose blooms invariably turn toward the south or southeast. Ideally, these light-sensitive bulbs should be placed to the north of positions from which they will be observed, so that the trumpets of the blooms face forward.

Fragrance

The humid climate of the South makes it especially rewarding to grow fragrant plants, and many bulbs are especially sweet-scented. Whenever possible, it is desirable to place these varieties near paths, patios, or in other places where they can be appreciated up close. The narrow beds surrounding courtyards in many older gardens of Charleston and New Orleans are often charmingly overgrown with fragrant butterfly gingers such as *Hedychium coronarium* var. *chrysoleucum* 'Gold Spot', ambrosial spiderlilies like *Hymenocallis latifolia*, or oversized crinums like the spicily scented, wine-striped *Crinum augustum* and redolent, rose-pink 'Emma Jones'. In these close quarters the blooming stems of the gingers and flopping stalks of the crinums can be tied to walls for support or allowed to grow up through adjacent gardenias, sweet olives, or roses, to hold their clustering blooms at nose level.

Although the sweet, musky scent of paperwhite narcissus often carries for several feet on winter air, the fragrances of other daffodils, jonquils, hyacinths, irises, cyclamen, and schoenocaulon are often best appreciated when gardeners get down on their knees. These varieties may be planted in raised beds to encourage close encounters. Night-flowering bulbs such as tuberoses, spiderlilies, crinums, and nocturnal rain lilies should be placed near pale-colored stones, or along paths, walls, or other places where they can be readily found and visited after nightfall to enjoy their sweet scents.

Cultivation and Irrigation

Semi-wild areas of the garden, such as seldom-mowed lawns, meadows, or woodland, offer opportunities for naturalizing bulbs. Many heirloom varieties common to the South prosper from benign neglect, often performing better in these areas than in more carefully tended spaces. In many instances this preference reflects the absence of artificial irrigation.

Few things prove more destructive to cool-season bulbs than an automated sprinkler system. When these devices are used to keep gardens lush and green through the summer, they interfere with the natural dormancies of the bulbs, promoting fungal growth and rot. Moreover, water taken from municipal supplies is rarely pure and will slowly add minerals to the soil. In many areas this causes the leaves of susceptible plants to yellow (chlorosis). Although warm-season bulbs are less directly threatened by irrigation systems than winter growers like narcissi or lycoris, they are susceptible to these mineral imbalances. For any serious bulb gardener, an in-ground irrigation system is a nuisance, invariably suffering breaks in the lines when bulbs are divided and replanted. Manual irrigation, only when absolutely needed, is the preferred treatment for any bulb and for most other garden perennials, as well.

When it comes to fertilizing bulbs, the essential rules for Southern gardeners are that most summer-growing varieties enjoy added fertilizers, manures, or composts, but winter-growing bulbs usually get along best without them. If cool-season bulbs are to be fed at all, it is important to abstain from rich nitrogen fertilizers or manures, and to avoid feeding in spring or summer when soil temperatures are warm and fungi are active. The principal subjects of this book, naturalizing bulbs, are plants that, by definition, require no supplemental fertilization. Adding rock phosphate or bone meal is of questionable worth if soils are alkaline.

Mediterranean Beds

Bulbs from southern Europe, Asia Minor, the Cape Province of South Africa, or California usually accomplish their growth during winter and spring months when moisture is readily available. They receive little rainfall during their long summer dormancy. These plants sometimes succumb to soil fungi or bacteria if kept moist through summer. A raised bed of gravelly earth simulates the dry-summer habitat of these winter-rainfall plants and affords them congenial homes in the humid South.

Where heavy clay soils prevail it is a simple matter to construct raised beds of rubble, sand, or decomposed granite to accommodate these drought-loving varieties. Once built and planted, these Mediterranean beds require only minimum maintenance. They greatly extend the variety of bulbs that may be cultivated.

A bed eighteen to twenty-four inches tall is sufficient to accommodate a wide range of bulbs. Edgings of stone flags or boulders can help consolidate the mounded plantings, and will offer valuable niches and crevices in which to nestle dwarf corms and tubers like crocuses or oxalis. A thin mulch of composted leaves or stony gravel should be spread over this well-drained substrate to dress up the bed and get the plantings off to a good start. Since the purpose of these beds is discouragement of summer rots, nitrogen fertilizers and manures should be avoided.

Many bulbs enjoy these types of raised beds. Spring starflowers (*Ipheion uniflorum*) are easy and permanent on raised mounds of sand. These low-growing clumpers bear light blue flowers from late winter through spring, and make good plants for an informal edging. Daffodils of the *Narcissus cyclamineus* section such as 'February Gold' or 'March Sunshine' enjoy deep beds of sand or crushed granite. The tiny fragrant *N. jonquilla* is easy and permanent on sand, if well watered during its growing season. Sand-loving subtropical bulbs also enjoy these Mediterranean beds, and ×*Amarcrinum*, *Lycoris aurea*, and *Pancratium maritimum* all benefit from this type of culture.

Bulbs for Heavy Soils

It's a widely accepted and repeated horticultural myth that all bulbs require good drainage. Fortunately for Southerners who contend with tight clays, no claim could be more exaggerated. Many bulbs receive summer rains in their native habitats and seem to thrive on rich, mucky soils. The seasonal buffalo wallows of American prairies and the temporary pans (*vleis*) of the South African veld are examples of such environments. These habitats offer distinctively adapted bulbs geared to grow in concert with alternating surfeits and deficits of moisture.

Many spring-blooming bulbs come from soggy homes and have the capacity to grow in waterlogged soils during the cool spring months. Such flowers as summer snowflake (*Leucojum aestivum*), Dutch iris (*Iris* ×*hollandica*), Naples onion (*Allium neapolitanum*), large-flowered buttercup (*Ranunculus macranthus*), and jonquil hybrids such as 'Trevithian' will bloom happily even in standing water. The strong-growing, old-fashioned campernelle narcissus, the tazetta variety 'Grand Primo', white French-Roman hyacinths, Byzantine gladiolus, and virgin's spray (*Ornithogalum narbonense*) are also good on heavy ground.

Summer bulbs from such genera as *Colocasia*, *Zephyranthes*, *Crinum*, *Hymenocallis*, and *Canna* develop fleshy roots especially adapted to waterlogged conditions. Many plants in the ginger and iris families also thrive on swampy ground. All of these may be freely fed with rich manures and composts.

Bulbs for Shade

Given that shade is a common condition for gardeners in the South, it is fortunate that many bulb varieties thrive with full to part shade. Valuable shade-loving bulbs for spring include Spanish bluebells, Naples onions, summer snowflakes, *Freesia laxa*, *Hippeastrum* ×*johnsonii*, *Oxalis crassipes* 'Alba', *Arisaema*, *Iris japonica*, and *I.* 'Nada'. Summer garden designs can make use of gingers and crinums, *Oxalis regnelli* 'Triangularis', *Agapanthus* 'Ellamae', alocasias, and

A guild of spring flowers, including *Hippeastrum* 'Giraffe', *Freesia laxa*, *Anemone coronaria*, violas, nemesias, anagalis, and *Ajuga reptans* 'Valfredda', on heavy clay soil, Tom Peace's garden, Lockhart, Texas.

A mixed planting of *Crinum* 'J. C. Harvey' and *Thelypteris kunthii* (Southern shield fern) in the shade of a live oak.

Amorphophallus. Lycoris, oxblood lilies, and *Zephyranthes* sp. 'Labuffarosa' provide flowers in late summer and autumn, and their winter foliage contributes lushness to shaded gardens during the cool season. *Arum italicum* 'Marmoratum', *Cyclamen hederifolium,* and *Trillium ludovicianum* also provide verdant winter foliage. For the very dry shade sometimes found under live oaks, Mediterranean subjects such as *Iris unguicularis, Sternbergia lutea,* and cyclamen are tough and long-lived.

⟳ Bibliography

Allen, C. L. *Bulbs and Tuberous Rooted Plants*. New York: Orange Judd, 1915.

Bailey, Liberty Hyde, and Ethel Joe Bailey. *Hortus Third*. New York: Macmillan, 1976.

Bowles, E. A. *A Handbook of Narcissus*. London: Waterstone, 1934. Reprint London: Thames & Hudson, 1985.

Baron, Robert C., ed. *The Garden and Farm Books of Thomas Jefferson*. Golden, Colorado: Fulcrum, 1987.

Barre, Peter. *Ye Narcissus or Daffodil Flowre, and hys Roots*. London, 1884. Reprint American Daffodil Society, Washington, D.C., 1968.

Bown, Demi. *Aroids: Plants of the Arum Family*. Portland, Oregon: Timber Press, 2000.

Branney, T. M. E. *Hardy Gingers*. Portland, Oregon: Timber Press, 2005.

Caillet, Marie, and Joseph K. Mertzweiller. *The Louisiana Iris*. Waco, Texas: Texas Gardener Press, 1988.

Chapman, Tim. *Ornamental Gingers: A Guide to Cultivation and Selection*. St. Gabriel, Louisiana, 1995.

Correl, Donovan Stewart, and Marshall Conring Johnston. *Manual of the Vascular Plants of Texas*. Richardson: University of Texas at Dallas, 1979.

Eliovson, Sima. *South African Flowers for the Garden*. Cape Town: Howard Timmins, 1957.

Goldblatt, Peter, and John Manning. *Gladiolus in Southern Africa*. Vlaeberg: Fernwood Press, 1998.

Gorer, Richard. *The Development of Garden Flowers*. London: Eyre and Spottiswoode, Ltd., 1970.

Hannibal, L. S. "Garden Crinum." *Bulletin of the Louisiana Society for Horticultural Research*, Vol. 3, No. 5, 1970–71.

Heath, Brent, and Becky Heath. *Daffodils for American Gardens*. Bright Sky Press, 2002.

Howard, Thad M. *Bulbs for Warm Climates*. Austin: University of Texas Press, 2001.

Johnson, Hugh. *The Principles of Gardening*. New York: Simon and Schuster, 1979.

Killingback, Stanley. *Tulips*. Secaucus, New Jersey: Chartwell Books, 1990.

Kohlein, Fritz. *Iris*. Portland, Oregon: Timber Press, 1987.

Larsen, Kai, with H. Ibrahim, S. H. Khaw, and L. G. Saw. *Gingers of Peninsular Malaysia and Singapore*. Borneo: Natural History Publications, 1999.

Lawrence, Elizabeth. *The Little Bulbs*. New York: Criterion Books, 1957.

———. *A Southern Garden*. Chapel Hill: University of North Carolina Press, 1991.

Lee, George S. "Daffodil Handbook." *The American Horticultural Magazine*, Vol. 45, No. 1, January 1966.

Linnegar, Sidney, and Jennifer Hewitt. *Irises*. London: Cassel/The Royal Horticultural Society, 1990.

Mallary, Peter, and Frances Mallary, with Joan Waltermire and Linney Levin. *A Redouté Treasury*. New York: The Vendome Press, 1986.

Manning, John, Peter Goldblatt, and Deirdré Snijman. *The Color Encyclopedia of Cape Bulbs*. Portland, Oregon: Timber Press, 2002.

Mathew, Brian. *The Smaller Bulbs*. London: Batsford, 1987.

McFarland, J. Horace, with R. Marion Hatton and Daniel J. Foley. *Garden Bulbs in Color*. New York: Macmillan, 1941.

Miles, Bebe. *Bulbs for the Home Gardener*. New York: Grosset & Dunlap, 1976.

Mitchell, Sydney B. *Gardening in California*. New York: Doubleday, Page & Co., 1924.

Parkinson, John. *Paradisi in Sole, Paradisus Terrestris*. 1629. Reprint 1976.

Phillips, Roger, and Martyn Rix. *The Bulb Book*. London: Pan Books, 1981.

Pooley, Elsa. *A Field Guide to Wild Flowers KwaZulu-Natal and the Eastern Region*. Durban, Republic of South Africa: Natal Flora Publication Trust, 1998.

Rix, Martyn. *Growing Bulbs*. Portland, Oregon: Timber Press, 1983.

Robinson, Benjamin Lincoln, and Merrit Lyndon Fernald. *Gray's New Manual of Botany*. New York: American Book Company, 1908.

Roscoe, William. *Monandrian Plants of the Order of Scitamineae*. Liverpool, 1828.

Royal Horticultural Society. *Manual of Bulbs*. John Bryan and Mark Griffiths, eds. Portland, Oregon: Timber Press, 1995.

Scott, George Harmon. *Bulbs*. Tucson, Arizona: HP Books, 1982.

Scruggs, Mrs. Gross R., and Margaret Ann Scruggs. *Gardening in the Southwest*. Dallas: Southwest Press, 1932.

Stearn, William T. *Stearn's Dictionary of Plant Names for Gardeners*. London: Cassel Publishers, Ltd., 1992.

Stern, Sir Frederick C. *A Chalk Garden*. London: Thomas Nelson and Sons, Ltd., 1960.

Sunset Western Garden Book. Menlo Park: Lane Publishing Co., 1988.

Thomas, Graham Stuart. *Perennial Garden Plants*. London: J. M. Dent and Sons, Ltd., 1982.

Van Beck, Linda M., and Sara L. Van Beck. *Daffodils in Florida: A Field Guide to the Coastal South*. Tallahassee, 2005.

Verdoorn, I. C. "The Genus Crinum in Southern Africa." *Bothalia*, Vol. 11, Nos. 1 and 2, 27–52, 1973.

Warburton, Bee. *The World of Irises*. Wichita, Kansas: American Iris Society, 1978.

Welch, William C. *Perennial Garden Color*. Dallas: Taylor Publishing Co., 1989.

Wilder, Louise Beebe. *Adventures with Hardy Bulbs*. New York: Macmillan, 1990.

———. *Adventures in a Suburban Garden*. New York: Macmillan, 1931.

Wills, Mary Motz, and Howard S. Irwin. *Roadside Wildflowers of Texas*. Austin: University of Texas Press, 1969.

Woodward, Marcus. *Leaves from Gerard's Herball*. New York: Dover, 1969.

 # Sources

U.S. Sources of Bulbs

All Things Iris
33450 Little Valley Rd.
Fort Bragg, CA 95437
tel: (888) 833-4747
fax: (707) 473-9771
e-mail: support@allthingsiris.com
Web: www.allthingsiris.com

Aloha Tropicals
P.O. Box 6042
Oceanside, CA 92052
tel: (760) 631-2880
fax: (760) 631-2880
e-mail: alohatrop@aol.com
Web: www.alohatropicals.com/
Gingers

Amaryllis Plus Bulb Company
   (Kevin D. Preuss)
1932 20th Ave. N
St. Petersburg, FL 33713
tel: (727) 820-0852
e-mail: hyline@tampabay.rr.com
Web: www.amaryllis-plus.com
Hippeastrum, Hymenocallis

Argyle Acres Iris Gardens
   (Joe and Donna Spears)
910 Pioneer Circle East
Argyle, TX 76226
tel: (940) 464-3680
fax: (866) 320-4747
Web: www.argyleacres.com

Arrowhead Alpines
P.O. Box 857
Fowlerville, MI 48836
tel: (517) 223-3581
fax: (517) 223-8750
Web: www.arrowhead-alpines.com
*Arisaema, Anemone, Crocus, Narcissus,
Cyclamen, Iris species*

Asiatica Rare Plant Resource
   (Barry Yinger and Andrew Wong)
P.O. Box 270
Lewisberry, PA 17339
tel: (717) 938-8677
e-mail: asiatica@nni.com
Web: www.asiaticanursery.com
*Arisaema, Arisarum, Alpinia, Zingiber, other
shade plants from Asia*

Brent and Becky's Bulbs
7463 Heath Trail
Gloucester, VA 23061
tel: (877) 661-2852 (toll-free)
fax: (804) 693-9436
e-mail: bbheath@aol.com
Web: www.bbbulbs.com
*Wide range of hardy bulbs, many varieties
of Narcissus*

Bulbmeister.com (Kelly M. Irvin)
4407 Town Vu Rd.
Bentonville, AR 72712
e-mail: bulbmeister@bulbmeister.com
Web: www.bulbmeister.com
*Specializing in Lycoris "in the green," also
spring and fall bulbs*

Bill the Bulb Baron of Carmel Valley
(William R. P. Welch)
P.O. Box 1736
264 West Carmel Valley Rd.
Carmel Valley, CA 93924
tel: (831) 659-3830
e-mail: billthebulbbaron@aol.com
Web: www.billthebulbbaron.com
Narcissus tazetta

Bulbmania (M and C Willetts)
P.O. Box 446
Moss Landing, CA 95039-0446
tel: (831) 728-BULB
e-mail: sales@bulbmania.com
Web: http://www.bulbmania.com/
Crinum, ×Amarcrinum, Zantedeschia

Buried Treasures (Chris Moore)
4613 Harder Ave.
Sebring, FL 33875
e-mail: chris@buried-treasure.net
Web: http://www.buried-treasure.net
Subtropical to tropical bulbs

Comanche Acres Iris and Water Gardens
12421 SE State Hwy 116
Gower, MO 64454
tel: (800) 382- 4747, (816) 424-6436
fax: 1-816-424-3836
e-mail: comanche@ccp.com
Web: www.comancheacres.com

Jim Duggan Flower Nursery
1452 Santa Fe Dr.
Encinitas, CA 92024
e-mail: jimsflowers@thebulbman.com
Web: www.thebulbman.com
South African bulbs

eBay
Web: www.ebay.com

Fancy Plants Farms
88-5 Knox Ln.
Lake Placid, FL 33852
tel: (800) 869-0953
fax: (863) 699-0173
Web: www.caladiums.com
Caladiums

Florida Market Bulletin
Mayo Building
407 S. Calhoun St.
Tallahassee, FL 32304
Web: www.florida-agriculture.com/fmb

Flowers & Greens (Roy Sachs)
35717 Lasiandra Ln.
Davis, CA 95616
tel: (530) 756-9238
fax: (530) 756-7798
e-mail: roysachs@yahoo.com, rmsachs@
ucdavis.edu
Web: www.buy-alstroemeria.com
Alstroemeria, Crocosmia, Acidanthera

Gingerwood Nursery (Tim Chapman)
St. Gabriel, LA
Web: www.gingerwoodnursery.com
Gingers

Happiness Farms, Inc.
704 County Road 621 E.
Lake Placid, FL 33852
tel: (866) 892-0396 (toll-free)
e-mail: info@happinessfarms.com
Web: www.happinessfarms.com
Caladiums

Iris City Gardens (Macey and Greg McCullough)
7675 Younger Creek Rd.
Primm Springs, TN 38476
tel: (800) 934-4747, (615) 799-2179
fax: (615) 523-8399
e-mail: icity@e-mail.msn.com
Web: www.iriscitygardens.com

Jacques Amand
P.O. Box 2448
Westport, CT 06880
tel: (800) 452-5414
fax: (203) 845-0830
e-mail: info@jacquesamand.com
Web: www.jacquesamand.com
Diverse selection of bulbs, many novelties, especially Hippeastrum

Kelly's Plant World (Herb Kelly Jr.)
10266 E. Princeton
Sanger, CA 93657
tel: (559) 294-7676
fax: (559) 294-7626
e-mail: Hkellyjr76@aol.com
Crinum, Canna, Hippeastrum, Hymeno-
callis, Lycoris, Zephyranthes

Louisiana Market Bulletin
P.O. Box 3534
Baton Rouge, LA 70821-3534
tel: (225)922-1284
fax: (225)922-1253
e-mail: marketbulletin@ldaf.state.la.us
Web: www.ldaf.state.la.us/divisions/
    marketing/marketbulletin/default.asp

Louisiana Nursery (Ken Durio)
1908 Parkview Dr.
Opelousas, LA 70570
e-mail: dedurio@yahoo.com
Web: http://www.durionursery.com/
Louisiana iris, Crinum

Marcelle's Crinums (Marcelle Sheppard)
440 Oak Ln.
Vidor, TX 77662
tel: (409)769-3585
e-mail: Margie1685@aol.com
Web: marcellescrinums.com/index.html

McClure & Zimmerman
108 W. Winnebago
P.O. Box 368
Friesland, WI 53935-0368
tel: (800) 883-6998
fax: (800) 374-6120
e-mail: info@mzbulb.com
Web: www.mzbulb.com/

Grant Mitsch Novelty Daffodils
    (Richard and Elise Havens)
P.O. Box 218
Hubbard, OR 97032
tel: (503) 651-2742
fax: (503) 651-2792
e-mail: havensr@web-ster.com
Web: www.web-ster.com/havensr/mitsch/

Mississippi Market Bulletin
Claude Nash, Editor
P.O. Box 1118
Jackson, MS 39215
tel: (601) 359-1123
fax: (601) 359-1260
e-mail: Claude@mdac.state.ms.us
Web: www.mdac.state.ms.us/n_library/
    pub_form/mkt_bulletin/
    index_marketbulletin.asp

Nurseries Caroliniana (Ted Stephens)
22 Stephens Estate
North Augusta, SC 29860
tel: (803) 279-2707
Web: www.nurcar.com
Canna, Iris, gingers

Odyssey Bulbs (Russell Stafford)
604 Boothbay Rd.
Edgecomb, ME 04556
tel: (877) 220-1651 (toll-free, security code
    4642)
e-mail: mail@odysseybulbs.com
Web: www.odysseybulbs.com
Diverse bulbs including Mediterranean and
subtropical genera

Old House Gardens (Scott Kunst)
536 Third St.
Ann Arbor, MI 48103-4957
tel: (734) 995-1486
fax: (734) 995-1687
e-mail: OHGBulbs@aol.com
Web: www.oldhousegardens.com
Heirloom bulbs

Geo. W. Park Seed Co. Inc.
1 Parkton Ave.
Greenwood, SC 29647-0001
tel: (800) 845-3369
fax: (800) 275-9941
e-mail: info@parkseed.com
Web: www.parkseed.com

Plant Delights Nursery, Inc.

(Tony Avent)
9241 Sauls Rd.
Raleigh, NC 27603
Web: www.plantdelights.com
Alocasia, Alstroemeria, Amorphophallus,
Arisaema, Arisarum, Arum, Asparagus,
Belamcanda, Bletilla, Canna, Colocasia,
Crinum, Crocosmia, Curcuma, Cypella,
Eucomis, Gelasine, Gladiolus, Habranthus,
Hedychium, Hippeastrum, Hymenocallis,
Iris, Ledebouria, Lilium, Lycoris, Nerine,
Oxalis, Pinellia, Polygonatum, Remusatia,
Rhodophiala, Sauromatum, Sisyrinchium,
Sprekelia, Trillium, Zantedeschia,
Zephyranthes

Plumeria People (Milton L. Pierson)

P.O. Box 31668
Houston, TX 77231-1668
e-mail: miltonp@botanictreasures.com
Web: botanictreasures.com
Canna, Crinum

Seneca Hill Perennials (Ellen Hornig)

3712 County Route 57
Oswego, NY 13126
tel: (315) 342-5915
fax: (315) 342-5573
Web: http://www.senecahill.com/
Cyclamen, Gladiolus, Iris, Arisaema, Arum,
Moraea

Shields Gardens Ltd. (Jim Shields)

P.O. Box 92
Westfield, IN 46074
tel: (317) 867-3344
fax: (317) 896-5126
e-mail: jim@shieldsgardens.com
Web: www.shieldsgardens.com
Hippeastrum, Hymenocallis, Nerine,
Crinum, Scadoxus, Sprekelia, Gladiolus,
Haemanthus, Cyrtanthus, Zantedeschia

Southwestern Native Seeds Inc.

(Sally Parker)
P.O. Box 50503
Tucson, AZ 85703

Sister's Bulb Farm

Rt. 2, Box 170
Gibsland, LA 71028
Heirloom daffodils

Stokes Tropicals

4806 E Old Spanish Trail
Jeanerette, LA 70544
tel: (800) 624-9706, (337) 365-6998
fax: (337) 365-6991
e-mail: info@stokestropicals.com
Web: http://www.stokestropicals.com/
Gingers and other tropical bulbs

Tejas Native Bulbs

PMB162
6705 Hwy 290 West #502
Austin, TX 78735
e-mail: support@tejasnativebulbs.com
Web: www.tejasnativebulbs.com

Telos Rare Bulbs (Diana Chapman)

P.O. Box 4147
Arcata, CA 95518
e-mail: rarebulbs@earthlink.net
Web: www.telosrarebulbs.com
South African, South American, Californian,
and Mediterranean bulbs

Van Bourgondien

P.O. Box 1000
Babylon, NY 11702
tel: (800) 622-9997
e-mail: blooms@dutchbulbs.com
Web: www.dutchbulbs.com

Van Engelen, Inc.

23 Tulip Dr.
Bantam, CT 06750
tel: (860) 567-8734
fax: (860) 567-5323
e-mail: Customerservice@vanengelen.com
Web: www.vanengelen.com

Nancy R. Wilson Daffodils

6525 Briceland-Thorn Rd.
Garberville, CA 95542
fax: (707)923-2407
e-mail: nwilson@red.asis.com
Web: www.asis.com/~nwilson/
  nancynote.html
Species and miniature narcissi

Woodlanders Inc.

1128 Colleton Ave.
Aiken, SC 29801
tel: (803) 648-7522
e-mail: woodland@scbn.net
Web: www.woodlanders.net/

Guy Wrinkle Exotic Plants

11610 Addison St.
North Hollywood, CA 91601
tel: (310) 670-8637
fax: (310) 670-1427
e-mail: GuyWrinkle@rareexotics.com
Web: www.rareexotics.com
South African bulbs

Tom Wood, Nurseryman

P.O. Box 100
Archer, FL 32618
tel: (352) 495-9168
fax: (352) 495-3185
e-mail: gingers@gator.net
Web: www.oldcity.com/sites/gingers
Gingers

Yucca Do Nursery, Inc.

  (Carl Schoenfeld)
P.O. Box 907
Hempstead, TX 77445
e-mail: info@yuccado.com
Web: www.yuccado.com
*Achimenes, Albuca, Aristea, Asparagus,
Canna, Cypella, Crinum, Curcuma, Eucomis,
Freesia, Drimiopsis, Habranthus, Hippeas-
trum, Hymenocallis, Hypoxis, Kaempferia,
Ledebouria, Lilium, Manfreda, Oxalis, Poli-
anthes, Rhodophiala, Sinningia, Tigridia,
Zephyranthes*

International Sources of Bulbs

African Bulbs (Cameron and Rhoda McMaster) (formerly The Croft Wild Bulb Nursery)

P.O. Box 26
Napier 7270
Republic of South Africa
tel/fax: 27 (0) 28 423 3651
mobile: 27 (0) 82 774 2075
e-mail: africanbulbs@haznet.co.za
Web: www.africanbulbs.com/
Bulbs and seeds of South Africa

B & T World Seeds

Paguignan
34210 Aigues-Vives
France
tel: 33-(0)4-68 91 29 63
fax: 33-(0)4-68 91 30 39
e-mail: me@b-and-t-world-seeds.com
Web: www.b-and-t-world-seeds.com

Border Gateway Bulbs (Dirk Wallace)

4/1 Skipton Court
Wodonga, Victoria, 3690
Australia
tel/fax: 61-(0)2-6056 1430
e-mail: dirkwallace@bigpond.com
Web: www.bgbulbs.com

Bulb'Argence (Lauw de Jager)

Mas D'Argence
30300 Fourques
France
tel: 33-466-016-519
fax: 33-466-011-245
e-mail: DEJAGER@BULBARGENCE.COM
Web: www.bulbargence.com
*Mediterranean bulbs from South Africa,
Chile, California, and the Far East*

Chen Yi Nursery (Mrs. Chen Yi)

TuanLi CongLinZhuang Villa 75
Tong Zhou SongZhuang
Beijing 101118
Peoples Republic of China
fax: (86) 10-8955-7052
e-mail: chenyi@public.netchina.com.cn
Web: home.no.net/chenyi/index.html

Ganesh Mani Pradhan & Son, The Nursery

Ganesh Villa
Kalimpong 734301
West Bengal
India
tel: 91-3552-74517, 91-3552-74275
fax: 91-3552-74489
e-mail: thakro@vsnl.com
nagdhara@satyam.net.in
palms@dte.vsnl.net.in
Web: www.ganeshvilla.com
Aroids, gingers

Golden Lotus (Ruud Meeldijk)

186/98 Moo 7 World Club
Tambon Nong Kwai
Amphur Hangdong
Chiangmai 50230
Thailand
tel: 66-(0)53431398
fax: 66-(0)53431398
e-mail: goldenlt@loxinfo.co.th
Web: chmai.loxinfo.co.th/~goldenlt

Komoriya Nursery Ltd.

1196 Ohkido-cho
Chiba-city Chiba 267-0057
Japan
tel: 81-43-294-4387
fax: 81-43-294-8504
e-mail: bulb@komoriya.co.jp
Web: http://www.komoriya.co.jp/
    index-e.html

Mainly Amaryllids Garden

(Daryl and Maree Geoghegan)
P.O. Box 173
Barnawartha, Victoria, 3688
Australia
tel: 61 (0)2 6026 7377
e-mail: plants_man@bigpond.com
Web: www.mainlyamaryllidsgarden.com

Mauro Peixoto

Estr. Miguel Martins, 50
Caixa Postal 383
08710-971 Mogi das Cruzes SP
Brazil
e-mail: mpeixoto@uol.com.br
Web: brazilplants.cjb.net/
Seeds of indigenous Brazilian plants

Pacific Rim Native Plant Nursery

(Paige Woodward)
44305 Old Orchard Rd.
Chilliwack, BC V2R 1A9
Canada
tel: (604) 792 9279
fax: (604) 792 1891
e-mail: paige@hillkeep.ca
Web: www.hillkeep.ca
*North American source for rarer bulbs
grown by Antoine Hoog, formerly of Hoog
& Dix, now Antoine Hoog Authentic Plants*

Plant Group Co., Ltd

Suite 1106, Two Pacific Place
142, Sukhumvit Rd., Bangkok 10110
Thailand
tel: (66-1) 724-0771, (66-1) 867-1217
fax: (66-2) 653-2163, (66-53) 404-377
Web: www.plant-group.com
Gingers, aroids

Rare Plants (Paul Christian)

P.O. Box 468
Wrexham
LL13 9XR
U.K.
tel: 44 1978 366399
fax: 44 1978 266466
Web: rareplants.co.uk
Rare bulbs

Silverhill Seeds (Rachel and Rod Saunders)

P.O. Box 53108
Kenilworth, Cape Town 7745
Republic of South Africa
tel: 27-21-762-4245
fax: 27-21-797-6609
e-mail: silverhill@yebo.co.za
Web: www.silverhillseeds.co.za
*Seeds of South African plants including
many bulbs*

Societies and Publications

American Daffodil Society

Naomi Liggett
4126 Winfield Rd.
Columbus, OH 43220
tel: (614) 451-4747
fax: (614) 451-2177
e-mail: NLiggett@compuserve.com
Web: http://www.daffodilusa.org

American Iris Society

Web: www.irises.org/

Australian Bulb Association

P.O. Box 44
Wadonga, VIC 3689
Australia
Web: www.ausbulbs.org

Botanical Society of South Africa

Private Bag X10
Claremont 7735
Republic of South Africa
tel: 27-(0)21-797-2090
fax: 27-(0)21-797-2376
e-mail: info@botanicalsociety.org.za
Web: www.botanicalsociety.org.za

International Aroid Society

P.O. Box 43-1853
South Miami, FL 33143
e-mail: tricia_frank@hotmail.com.
Web: www.aroid.org

International Bulb Society, Inc.

P.O. Box 336
Sanger, CA 93657-0336
Web: www.bulbsociety.org

North American Lily Society

Robert Gilman
P.O. Box 272
Owatonna, MN 55060
Web: www.lilies.org

North American Rock Garden Society

P.O. Box 67
Millwood, NY 10546
Web: www.nargs.org

Pacific Bulb Society

Mary Sue Ittner, e-mail list administrator
e-mail: pbs-request@lists.ibiblio.org
Web: www.pacificbulbsociety.org

Society for Louisiana Irises

Web: www.louisianas.org

Southern Garden History Society

Old Salem, Inc.
Drawer F, Salem Station
Winston-Salem, NC 27108
Web: www.southerngardenhistory.org

Species Iris Group of North America (SIGNA)

Web: www.signa.org/
Spuria Iris Society
Web: www.spuria.org

Labels

Paw-Paw Everlast Label Co.

P.O. Box 93-C
Paw Paw, MI 49079-0093
Web: www.everlastlabel.com

Yucca DooHickeys

Yucca Do Nursery, Inc. (Carl Schoenfeld)
P.O. Box 907
Hempstead, TX 77445
e-mail: info@yuccado.com
Web: www.yuccado.com

Index